Language, Psychology, and Culture

Language, Psychology, and Culture

Essays by Wallace E. Lambert

Selected and Introduced
by Anwar S. Dil

Stanford University Press, Stanford, California 1972

Language Science and National Development

A Series Sponsored by the
Linguistic Research Group of Pakistan

General Editor: Anwar S. Dil

Stanford University Press
Stanford, California

Printed in the United States of America
ISBN 0-8047-0803-7
LC 71-183890

Contents

	Acknowledgments	vii
	Introduction by Anwar S. Dil	xi
1.	Measurement of the Linguistic Dominance of Bilinguals (1955)	1
2.	Developmental Aspects of Second Language Acquisition (1956)	9
3.	The Influence of Noun-Adjective Order on Learning (1956)	32
4.	The Use of Pareto's Residue-Derivation Classification as a Method of Content Analysis (1956)	38
5.	The Influence of Language-Acquisition Contexts on Bilingualism (1958)	51
6.	Linguistic Manifestations of Bilingualism (1959)	63
7.	A Pilot Study of Aphasia among Bilinguals (1959)	72
8.	Evaluational Reactions to Spoken Languages (1960)	80
9.	Verbal Satiation and Changes in the Intensity of Meaning (1960)	97
10.	The Relation of Bilingualism to Intelligence (1962)	111

11. Psychological Approaches to the Study of Language (1963) 160

12. Word-Association Responses: Comparisons of American and French Monolinguals with Canadian Monolinguals and Bilinguals (1966) 197

13. A Social Psychology of Bilingualism (1967) 212

14. The Use of Tu and Vous as Forms of Address in French Canada: A Pilot Study (1967) 236

15. A Psychological Investigation of French Speakers' Skill with Grammatical Gender (1968) 243

16. Bilingual Organization in Free Recall (1968) 252

17. Ethnic Identification and Personality Adjustments of Canadian Adolescents of Mixed English-French Parentage (1969) 266

18. Psychological Aspects of Motivation in Language Learning (1969) 290

19. Psychological Studies of the Interdependencies of the Bilingual's Two Languages (1969) 300

20. Measuring the Cognitive Consequences of Attending Elementary School in a Second Language (1971) 331

21. The Effects of Speech Style and Other Attributes on Teachers' Attitudes Toward Pupils (1971) 338

Author's Postscript (1971) 351

Bibliography of Wallace E. Lambert's Works Compiled by Anwar S. Dil 354

Acknowledgments

The Linguistic Research Group of Pakistan and the Editor of the Language Science and National Development Series are deeply grateful to Professor Wallace E. Lambert, Associate Member of the Group, for giving us the privilege of presenting his selected writings as the fifth volume in our series established in 1970 to commemorate the International Education Year.

We are indebted to the editors and publishers of the following publications. The ready permission on the part of the holders of the copyrights, acknowledged in each case, is a proof of the existing international cooperation and goodwill that gives hope for better collaboration among scholars of all nations for international exchange of knowledge.

Measurement of the Linguistic Dominance of Bilinguals. Journal of Abnormal and Social Psychology 50. 197-200 (1955). Copyright 1955 by the American Psychological Association and reprinted by permission.

Developmental Aspects of Second-Language Acquisition, Parts I, II, and III. Journal of Social Psychology 43. 83-104 (1956), with permission of the Journal Press.

The Influence of Noun-Adjective Order on Learning; with A. Paivio. Canadian Journal of Psychology 10. 9-12 (1956), with permission of the Editor.

The Use of Pareto's Residue-Derivation Classification as a Method of Content Analysis. Contributions à l'Etude des Sciences de l'Homme 3. 183-191 (1956), with permission of the Editor.

The Influence of Language-Acquisition Contexts on Bilingualism; with J. Havelka and C. Crosby. Journal of Abnormal and Social Psychology 56,2. 239-244 (1958). Copyright 1958 by the American Psychological Association and reprinted by permission.

Linguistic Manifestations of Bilingualism; with J. Havelka and R. C. Gardner. American Journal of Psychology 72,1. 77-82 (1959), with permission of the University of Illinois Press.

A Pilot Study of Aphasia Among Bilinguals; with S. Fillenbaum. Canadian Journal of Psychology 13(1). 28-34 (1959), with permission of the Editor.

Evaluational Reactions to Spoken Languages; with R. C. Hodgson, R. C. Gardner, and S. Fillenbaum. Journal of Abnormal and Social Psychology 60,1. 44-51 (1960). Copyright 1960 by the American Psychological Association and reprinted by permission.

Verbal Satiation and Changes in the Intensity of Meaning; with L. A. Jakobovits. Journal of Experimental Psychology 60,6. 376-383 (1960). Copyright 1960 by the American Psychological Association and reprinted by permission.

The Relation of Bilingualism to Intelligence; with Elizabeth Peal. Psychological Monographs 76,27. 1-23 (1962). Copyright 1962 by the American Psychological Association and reprinted by permission.

Psychological Approaches to the Study of Language, Parts I and II. The Modern Language Journal 47,3. 51-62, 114-121 (1963), with permission of the Editor.

Word-Association Responses: Comparisons of American and French Monolinguals with Canadian Monolinguals and Bilinguals; with Nancy Moore. Journal of Personality and Social Psychology 3, 3. 313-320 (1966). Copyright 1966 by the American Psychological Association and reprinted by permission.

A Social Psychology of Bilingualism. The Journal of Social Issues 23,2. 91-109 (1967), with permission of the Society for the Psychological Study of Social Issues.

The Use of _Tu_ and _Vous_ as Forms of Address in French Canada: A Pilot Study. _Journal of Verbal Learning and Verbal Behavior_ 6,4. 614-617 (1967), with permission of Academic Press, Inc.

A Psychological Investigation of French Speakers' Skill With Grammatical Gender; with G. R. Tucker, A. Rigault, and N. Segalowitz. _Journal of Verbal Learning and Verbal Behavior_ 7. 312-316 (1968), with permission of Academic Press, Inc.

Bilingual Organization in Free Recall; with M. Ignatow and M. Krauthamer. _Journal of Verbal Learning and Verbal Behavior_ 7. 207-214 (1968), with permission of Academic Press, Inc.

Ethnic Identification and Personality Adjustments of Canadian Adolescents of Mixed English-French Parentage; with C. Aellen. _Canadian Journal of Behavioural Science_ 1(2). 69-86 (1969), with permission of the Editor.

Psychological Aspects of Motivation in Language Learning. The _Bulletin_ of the Illinois Foreign Language Teachers Association, May 1969, pp. 5-11, with permission of the Association.

Psychologcial Studies of the Interdependencies of the Bilingual's Two Languages. _Substance and Structure of Language_, ed. by Jaan Puhvel (Berkeley and Los Angeles: University of California Press, 1969), pp. 99-126; reprinted by permission of the Regents of the University of California.

The Editor completed work on this volume during 1969-72, while he was in residence as Visiting Scholar at Stanford University. The financial assistance from the Principal's Special Fund of McGill University to cover typing expenses of the manuscript is gratefully acknowledged. He is personally grateful to the Committee on Linguistics of Stanford University for providing him with office accomodation.

The Editor also wishes to record his thanks to, the language scholars who have sent materials for the forthcoming volumes and others who are working with him in the preparation of further volumes in the Series. Clara N. Bush, Elizabeth Closs Traugott, and Afia Dil of the Committee on Linguistics, Stanford University, G. R.

Tucker and Gretchen S. Martin of McGill University, and Wes Pevrerieri of Stanford University Press deserve our gratitude for help in many ways. Saeqa Dil of the Massachusetts Institute of Technology has done most of the typing of camera-ready manuscript and she certainly deserves a word of appreciation.

This volume is affectionately dedicated to Janine Lambert who introduced the author to culture contrast and bilingualism.

EDITOR'S NOTE

These essays have been reprinted from the originals with only minor changes made in the interest of uniformity of style and appearance. A few changes in wording have been made in consultation with the author. In some cases bibliographical entries and notes have been updated. Footnotes marked by asterisks have been added by the Editor.

Introduction

Wallace E. Lambert was born in Amherst, Nova Scotia, on December 31, 1922. After receiving his bachelor's degree from Brown University in 1947, where his education was interrupted for three years by army service, he joined Colgate University and received his M. A. degree in psychology in 1950. During his army service he spent part of 1945 at Cambridge University, where he studied economics, philosophy, and psychology. He worked his way through his graduate program by serving as laboratory assistant at Brown University, as instructor at Hollins College (Virginia), Colgate University, and the University of North Carolina, where he went for his doctoral studies. During this period he spent two summers at the Université de Paris and the Université d'Aix-en-Provence and carried on a diversified program in psychology, anthropology, and sociology leading up to his Ph. D. degree in 1953. Soon after he went to McGill University, where he has been a Professor of Psychology since 1964.

Lambert has had a rich and varied experience ranging from psychiatric social work at the Rhode Island State Hospital during his undergraduate years, to research on the problem of morale in bomber squadrons, to studies on the attitudes of Canadians toward immigrants conducted for the Department of Citizenship and Immigration in Ottawa. He has also served since 1960 as a consultant to the Language Development Section of the U. S. Office of Education, and since 1964 as a member of the Advisory Board of the Center for Applied Linguistics in Washington, D. C. He has been a member of the International Advisory Council of the Centre for International Research in Bilingualism at Université Laval since its establishment, and served on the editorial boards of a number of professional journals. He has been a Visiting Professor at Cornell University (1958), Columbia

University (1963), the University of Michigan (1967), and Stanford University for three summers in recent years. He spent 1964-65 as a Fellow at the Center for Advanced Studies in Behavioral Sciences at Palo Alto working on problems in the psychology of language and the origins of prejudiced thinking in children. He was President of the Canadian Psychological Association for 1969-70. Recently he was elected a Fellow of the Royal Society of Canada.

Since he published his first paper in 1952, Lambert has had a remarkably productive career as a researcher. His first book, _Social Psychology_ (1964), an introductory text noted for its integrated overview of the field, was written in collaboration with his brother William W. Lambert of Cornell University. It is widely used in some half a dozen languages. An updated edition will be published in 1972. In _Children's Views of Foreign Peoples_ (1967), written with Otto Klineberg of the Université de Paris, a pioneering cross-national attempt was made to investigate the nature of children's stereotype thinking in ten different nations. _Attitudes and Motivation in Second-Language Learning_ (with Robert C. Gardner), and three other monographs completed in collaboration with G. Richard Tucker of McGill University, are awaiting publication. The first of these, _Bilingualism sans Larmes_, presents an analytical description of an innovative experiment in which English-speaking children proceed through schooling conducted mainly with French as medium of instruction; the results of this experiment suggest a challenging approach to education via a home-to-school-language switch. _Tu, Vous, and Usted_ is a cross-language empirical study of the relationship between address forms and social behavior. _French Speakers' Skill with Grammatical Gender_ probes the process of complex rule learning of French gender when no formal instruction is involved and raises basic questions about the notion that linguistic and grammatical systems are innate rather than acquired.

Perhaps a major turning point in Lambert's life was his army experience, which sensitized him to human relationships in situations of prejudice and aggression resulting from exaggeration of sociocultural differences among human beings along linguistic and national lines. His love for a French girl who had grown up during the war years involved him in problems of bilingualism and biculturalism in his own life. Later, observation of the growth of his bicultural children and the ease with which they moved from one language and culture to another made him question the notion of language barriers. Since then he has used Montreal, with its English- and French-speaking populations, as a research station where two groups of people living side by side are separated by language barriers that have been intensified and complicated by a number of factors.

Lambert's researches touch a sensitive area of national life, but his high degree of professional objectivity and his research-oriented approach have kept his experiments uncontroversial. His effective functioning in a climate charged with conflict should be encouraging to scholars who find themselves handicapped in similar research settings. Another impressive thing about Lambert is his remarkable ability to work with his undergraduate and graduate students in a mutually inspiring relationship of personal interaction and collaboration on significant research problems. Of special interest to sociolinguists is his battery of research methodology, which uses language and dialect variation in the speech behavior of individuals to elicit the sociocultural norms of contrasting groups.

The overall meaning of Lambert's work can perhaps be grasped best in terms of his aspiration to help create a climate of human life in which people are no longer restricted and bound by barriers of language and culture. In particular, he has sought to bring the benefits of bilingual and bicultural life within easy reach of common people and large sectors of populations rather than letting them remain the exclusive monopoly of the privileged few. In this sense Lambert is a crusader for the greater freedom of human beings to move freely and without discrimination across language and culture boundaries. Among the major theoretical generalizations that have emerged from his psycholinguistic experiments to date, the following can be identified as the broad outlines of his credo: that language barriers are not difficult to circumvent; that bilingualism does not imply various types of handicaps, but rather offers assets and enrichments of all sorts; that a person can comfortably become bilingual and bicultural; that one's attitudes toward the other group whose language is being learnt play an important role in language acquisition and that such attitudes both affect and are affected by one's motivation to learn the other language; that the study of language through an analysis of bilingualism is one of the most instructive ways of determining the cybernetic and neurophysiological functions of the human brain; that since styles of using language often engender social prejudice and unfair discrimination, safeguards against such discrimination must be built into educational, social, and political systems; and that the study of bilingualism as a personal and societal phenomenon, especially in situations of conflict, is a critical area of psycholinguistic and sociolinguistic inquiry.

Anwar S. Dil

Committee on Linguistics
Stanford University
May 1972

Language, Psychology, and Culture

1 Measurement of the Linguistic Dominance of Bilinguals

Educators and clinicians working with bilinguals have long sought for appropriate measures of various aspects of bilingualism (1, 2, 9, 10, 13). One of these aspects is linguistic dominance. This paper reports a method of measuring linguistic dominance and relates this measure to cultural and personality characteristics.

Warshaw (14) and Dunkel (4) have used the term automatic to differentiate the linguistic behavior of those using their native language and the stumbling efforts of the neophyte beginning the study of a new language. Head (6) has also referred to this phenomenon of automaticity, in both psychological and physiological terms. It occurred to the writer that automatic behavior is characterized chiefly by its speed. This is in line with the use of latency measures of the strength of a habit. Moreover, as early as 1877 Cattell (3) measured the time required for an English stimulus word to elicit the equivalent word in German, and found association time surprisingly long for English-speaking subjects familiar with German. This finding suggested to Cattell a means of "testing the difficulties of a polyglot life." In 1931, Saer (13) measured familiarity with languages in terms of speed of response. Preston (11), analyzing the speed of word perception, established relationships between perception speed and word familiarity, speed of reading, and vocabulary knowledge. Speed of reaction has recently been used as the dependent variable in two studies of language behavior by Pronko (12) and Herman (8, 9).

The subjects (*S*s) in the present research were given simple directions, such as "Push the key painted blue," in two languages, and speed of response was analyzed with reference to the different levels of *S*s' linguistic experience.

METHOD

Subjects. Three groups of 14 *S*s each are called undergraduate (Group U), graduate (Group G), and native French (Group F) to indicate their degree of experience with the French language. The undergraduates were college majors in French with at least a B grade average in general course work. The graduates were post-M. A. students all with French as a major. The native French came from Europe, where their daily and school language had been French. On the average they had been in an English-speaking country for about seven years and all had at least completed the French baccalauréat. Table 1 summarizes other comparisons of the groups.

TABLE 1
Comparison of Experimental Groups

Group	Average Age	Average Years in France or Quebec	Average Quarter Hours of Course Work in French	Sex	
				M	F
U	20.07	None	37.71	9	5
G	29.14	1.19	83.64	.8	6
F	30.21	23.21		6	8

Apparatus. The experimenter (E) controlled a key which simultaneously activated a reaction-time clock and a Ranschburg exposure apparatus. Directions were typed on a circular card and placed in the Ranschburg so that each time E touched his key a new direction would appear and the clock would start. The directions told *S* to push a certain one of his eight keys, the activation of any one of which would stop the clock.

Instructions. The following instructions were read: "You will place your hands on the eight keys as though they were on a typewriter. The directions will be of the order: 'Push the first key of the left hand,' but this will be condensed to 'Left, one.' The fingers are arbitrarily numbered from the index as number 1 to the little finger as number 4. We will have about a dozen practice runs."

Procedure. After the 12 practice trials, the following modification was introduced. "Now we will make one simple change in directions. In the place of numbers we shall use the name for colors. Note that the stem leading to each key is painted a different color. Directions might now be, 'Left, red' or 'Gauche, rouge.' Think about this for a minute and we shall start recording your time." Time, in hundredths of a second, was recorded for each trial. Thirty-two directions, 16 in each language, were presented in a random series. The English directions were: left, red; left, green; left, yellow; left, black, and the same color references for the right hand. The keys were colored green, red, yellow, and black for the left-hand fingers, and red, green, black, and yellow, for the right-hand fingers. In French the directions were: Gauche, rouge; gauche, vert; gauche, jaune; gauche, noir, and the same color references for the right hand (droite).

RESULTS AND DISCUSSION

The speed of response in a language was made relative to speed in *S*'s faster language, i.e., the language which elicits the faster speed of response. A given *S*'s score was computed by finding the difference between the total English reaction time and the French, and dividing this difference by the total time for the faster language. The general formula used is: French R.T. minus English R.T./ Faster R.T. This calculation of a percentage difference score corrects for individual differences in absolute reaction times. An *S* who is 10 per cent slower in reacting to French directions than English would receive a score of + 10, indicating that English was dominant in that degree; should he be faster in French by 10 per cent, he would receive a score of - 10, indicating that French was dominant. Table 2 lists the different scores (D) and the percentage difference scores (P).

The average percentage difference score for Group U is +12.21; for Group G, +5.07; and for Group F, -3.36. Each mean is reliably different from the others. The Group U mean is significantly larger than the Group G mean, which is significantly larger than the Group F mean (*t* tests reliable at the .01 level). The progression of means is consistent with experience in the two languages, i.e., Group U has had much less experience with French

TABLE 2

Reaction-Time Analysis

Entries in column D are the absolute difference in time (hundredths of a second) taken to respond to 16 French and 16 English directions. A minus sign indicates that the responses to French directions were faster. Entries in column P are the absolute differences divided by the total response time of the faster language. Entries in column *t* give the *t*-test score indicating the significance of the differences between the language speeds.

Undergraduates				Graduates				French			
Subject	D	P	*t**	Subject	D	P	*t*	Subject	D	P	*t*
U1	273	16	3.39	G1	-196	-11	2.08	F1	50	3	1.02
U2	172	8	2.33	G2	-86	-5	1.10	F2	-17	-1	.31
U3	235	10	1.73	G3	132	7	2.42	F3	-213	-9	1.84
U4	288	17	4.15	G4	207	8	1.95	F4	85	4	.97
U5	261	11	1.67	G5	212	10	3.14	F5	-335	-13	3.60
U6	129	7	2.61	G6	209	10	2.35	F6	-97	-5	1.19
U7	79	4	1.22	G7	178	9	2.37	F7	11	1	.21
U8	372	15	2.21	G8	93	6	1.49	F8	12	1	.16
U9	217	11	2.52	G9	39	2	.48	F9	-32	-2	.53
U10	169	10	1.72	G10	74	5	.94	F10	28	2	.35
U11	214	12	3.02	G11	250	14	3.12	F11	-204	-12	2.36
U12	282	15	3.28	G12	149	9	1.81	F12	-111	-4	.73
U13	354	20	3.86	G13	131	6	1.59	F13	-192	-9	3.02
U14	277	15	2.28	G14	19	1	.24	F14	-58	-3	.77

*Significance levels of *t* scores, one-tailed test, with 15 *df*: 1.75 at the .05 level of confidence, 2.60 at the .01 level of confidence.

than with English and Group F has had more experience with French than with English. If the three groups are ranked in terms of experience with a second language, Group U has least experience, Group G next, and Group F the most. The findings indicate that the differences between speeds of reaction in the two languages decrease as experience with a second language increases.

Individual differences in relative speed of response. It is possible to test statistically the degree to which each *S* responded consistently faster in one language than in the other. If one were a perfect bilingual—equally facile in both languages—there should be no difference between the speeds of response in the two languages; one could not reject the null hypothesis and indicate one language as dominant. Conversely, those who have a dominant language should give reaction-time scores such that the null hypothesis can be rejected.

Each *S*'s 16 reaction-time scores in French were compared to his scores in English and the extent to which he was consistently slower in one language was measured. Each *S* was assigned a *t* score indicating whether he was dominant in one language (*t* score significant above the .05 level), or whether he was a balanced bilingual (*t* score significant below the .05 level). (See Table 2.) The one-tailed test was used. The two-tailed test would be appropriate if no biographical material were available to suggest a dominant language.

Ten *S*s in Group U were found to be dominant in English and four were balanced bilinguals. Seven *S*s of Group G were dominant in English, six were balanced bilinguals, and one was dominant in French, which is not his native language. Only four *S*s in Group F were dominant in French, none was dominant in English, and ten were balanced. Group F therefore had the largest number of balanced bilinguals.

It was puzzling to find that two American graduate students measured dominant in French, but interviews with these *S*s and their friends supported this finding. G1 gave a biographical picture of cultural malcontent which was consistent with his linguistic reaction-time score of −11 for dominance in French over his native language. He was certain that he did "more thinking in French," had recently spent a year in France, and was planning to return as soon as possible. A friend volunteered the information that G1 "reacted against" anything which was non-European, and "only read" French materials. G2 had a score of –5. She was 35 years old and single, had taught French in a high school for about ten years, and studied French toward a higher degree during most of her summers. Her career demanded that she work and think in French.

Further research should be directed toward the personality variables involved in bilingualism. For example, some individuals may choose to study a foreign language as a means of social acceptance in another culture which is relatively more compatible with their social and individual needs. An interesting study by Child (4) using Italian-English bilinguals from New England points out that some subjects actively repressed all non-American aspects of their customs and speech. Others, however, made themselves "as Italian as possible" and were hostile to Americans and symbols of America. The reaction-time measure developed here would be valuable as a means of testing the effects of social influences on language behavior in studies such as Child's.

The relation between speed of response and verbal output. Another phase of this investigation involved the elicitation of continuous verbal associations in the two languages. Sixteen words were chosen as stimuli from the first-thousand category (most commonly used) of word-count tabulations in both English and French. The *S*s were asked to give "all single words which come to mind when you think about the stimulus word," and were required to respond in the language of the stimulus word. Responses were recorded on tape for 45 seconds following the presentation of the stimulus word.

Each *S*'s associational responses in both languages were counted and the difference between French and English totals was divided by the total number of responses given in the language that elicited the larger number of responses. Thus an index of verbosity difference between English and French was obtained, similar to the index of reaction-time difference. The prediction seems reasonable that one who is dominant in English will have a plus verbosity rating, indicating that he is able to give more associational responses to English than to French stimuli. A correlation between the percentage of verbosity difference and percentage of response-time difference was calculated for the 42 *S*s. Rho is .82, indicating a high relation between the performance on the reaction-time keys and active verbal output in associating to stimulus words.

SUMMARY

A reaction-time method for measuring the extent of bilingualism was tested using three groups of bilinguals, an undergraduate French major group, a graduate French major group, and a group of French natives whose second language is English. The groups differed reliably in speed of response to directions given in both languages and in the direction predicted from their language experiences. (a) This method permits statistical analysis and scoring of language dominance or language balance. (b) The reaction-time measure was related to *S*s' active verbal output (rho = .82). (c) Language dominance was related to cultural and personality characteristics.

NOTE

The author expresses appreciation to Professor H.G. McCurdy for advice and assistance.

REFERENCES

1. Arsenian, S. Bilingualism in the postwar world. Psychol. Bull., 1945, 44, 65-86.
2. Bovet, P. Bilinguisme et éducation. Report made for the Commission du Bilinguisme, Geneva, 1932.
3. Cattell, J. Experiments on the association of ideas. Mind, 1887, 12, 68-74.
4. Child, I. L. Italian or American? The second generation in conflict. New Haven: Yale Univer. Press, 1948.
5. Dunkel, H.B. Second-language learning. New York: Ginn and Co., 1948.
6. Head, H. Aphasia and kindred disorders of speech. London: Cambridge Univer. Press, 1926.
7. Herman, D.T. Linguistic behaviors: I. Some differentiations in hearer responses to verbal stimulation. J. gen. Psychol., 1951, 44, 199-214.

8. Herman, D.T. Linguistic behaviors: II. The development of hearer interaction with holophrastic stimuli. J. gen. Psychol., 1951, 44, 273-292.
9. Hoffman, M.N.H. The measurement of bilingual background. New York: Bureau of Publications, Teachers Coll., Columbia Univer., 1934.
10. Lambert, W.E. Developmental aspects of second-language acquisition. Unpublished doctor's dissertation, Univer. of North Carolina, 1953.
11. Preston, K.A. The speed of word perception and its relation to reading ability. J. gen. Psychol., 1935, 13, 199-203.
12. Pronko, N.H. An exploratory investigation of language by means of oscillographic and reaction time techniques. J. exp. Psychol., 1945, 35, 433-459.
13. Saer, H. Experimental inquiry into the education of bilingual peoples. In Education in a changing commonwealth. London: New Education Fellowship, 1931.
14. Warshaw, J. Automatic reactions in practical foreign language work. Mod. Language J., 1934, 9, 151-158.

2 Developmental Aspects of Second Language Acquisition

I. ASSOCIATIONAL FLUENCY, STIMULUS PROVOCATIVENESS, AND WORD-ORDER INFLUENCE

A. THE PROBLEM

The purpose of this research is to isolate some of the differentiating variables in the linguistic behavior of those who are at different stages of development in a language, where that language is not the only one known. The language under prime consideration is French. The subjects selected were American undergraduate students majoring in French, American graduate students majoring in French, and mature French natives living in this country who know and daily use English. Attention is directed to the associational responses to stimulus words given in the two languages. This method was chosen because it would entail the more spontaneous and active aspects of language. Other means of obtaining brief verbal responses were considered, and rejected because experimental control would be reduced and measurement be less objective.

The three groups of *S*s were chosen to differ with respect to experience in French. Note, however, that they had complicated a single language with a second and were consequently caught in the web of bilinguality. These *S*s, therefore, though at different developmental stages of language acquisition, can be compared to children advancing in their native language only hypothetically. Nevertheless, it is an interesting question, adding coherence to the investigation, whether, when one acquires a second language, there are involved the same or similar processes as when a child learns its first.

The importance of this investigation lies in its focus on the general problem of language acquisition which, with this experimental design, may be viewed in slower motion; its direct relation to the process of learning a second language; and its introduction of a series of original measures of psycholinguistic behavior.

B. METHOD

1. Subjects

Three groups of 14 *S*s each were used. The groups are labeled undergraduate (*U*), graduate (*G*), and native French (*F*) to indicate their degree of experience with the French language. All of the *U* group were academic majors in French at the college level with a *B* grade-average or better in general course work. The *G* group is made up of graduate students all of whom have French as a major academic interest. The *F* group comprises native French speakers who originated from Europe where their daily language and school language was French; they have been in an English speaking country for approximately seven years on the average and all had at least two years of college education in France. A more detailed description of the sample is given in (9).

2. Procedure

The investigation was introduced with these directions:

> In this part of our study, we are interested in the words which come to mind when you are presented with a French or English stimulus word. This is not a psychological examination in the popular sense; we are not going to analyze you with reference to the words you give. We are primarily interested in the words you have available to use when a stimulus word orients your thinking. For the first few trials, you will be given as many individual words in either French or English. You are to give as many individual words as come to mind, one after the other, for a period of 45 seconds. Don't give a sentence or phrase, but single words, and as many of them

> as come to mind. For the first four words, no matter what language they may be in, you are free to give your associations in either French or English; you have a choice of languages in which to associate.

The "choice" stimuli were: school, pays, chaise, and narrow.

After the choice situation, the *S*s were told: "From now on, you are asked to give your associations only in the same language as the stimulus word. We shall start with a set of French words and I will let you know when we will switch to English." The stimuli were given in the series 8 French followed by 16 English and finally 8 French words. This is the familiar a-b-b-a order used to control for the effects of practice and fatigue as a function of time in the experimental session. Responses were recorded on tape.

The French stimulus words, in the order of presentation, were: maison, libre, pauvre, esprit, grand, idée, jour, ami, petit, triste, jeune, rouge, temps, argent, main, juste. The English stimuli were: large, garden, happy, idea, food, little, sad, dear, honor, child, house, peace, rich, thought, strong, bad. For each language one-half of the stimuli were nouns and one-half adjectives. The words were selected from among the most frequently used, as determined by frequency counts, in English and French, according to Thorndike and Lorge (15), Vander Beke (16), and Eaton (4). The nouns were chosen to fit a category of "concrete" or "abstract." If the referent of the noun was a touchable or manipulatable thing it was concrete; if not, it was abstract. Thus, the French and English stimuli were equated for part of speech, word-frequency, and abstractness-concreteness.

C. RESULTS AND DISCUSSION

The data obtained were subjected to a series of different analyses, each following from an hypothesis.

Hypothesis A: As bilinguals progress in experience with a particular language, they will give more associational responses to stimulus words in that language.

The mean number of responses for each group in both languages was determined. It is reasonable that as experience in a second language increases so should the total number of associational responses in that language. Noble (14) defines "meaningfulness" in terms of the richness of association; a stimulus word which calls forth a greater average number of associations is more meaningful than another which elicits fewer associations. Accordingly, the hypothesis might be stated thus: As one progresses in experience with a language, the words in that language become more meaningful to him.

The average number of associational responses for the U group in French was 132.36, for the G group 166.21, and for the F group 221.86. Because of large within group variability, the nonparametric H-test (7) was used to test for reliability of group differences. The H among the three groups in French was 5.20, significant at better than the 5 per cent level of confidence. The U and G groups were reliably different, H = 3.21, significant at the 3 per cent level. The G and F groups were not reliably different, H = 2.02 where 2.71 is needed at the 5 per cent level. Thus the means are in the direction predicted with the U group mean reliably smaller than both G and F. The G group mean number of responses to French stimuli was not reliably different from that of the F group. In English, there was no reliable difference among the mean number of response emitted. Hypothesis A is confirmed.

Hypothesis B: As bilinguals progress in experience with a particular language, they will give more associational responses in that language when given a choice of languages to use.

*S*s were given four stimulus words, two in English and two in French, with the understanding that they could respond to the stimuli in either language. The experimental plan was to test whether those at different stages of acquisition of the French language would respond with different proportions of French associations when given a choice of languages to use. It was predicted that the U group would give fewer French associations than the G group who in turn would give fewer than the F group.

If an *S* gave 28 associational responses to all four stimulus words, for example, and 7 of these were in French and 21 in English, his scores here would be the percentages 25 and 75. The over-all

H-test of the difference among groups was 11.09 where only 9.21 is needed at the 1 per cent level. The *U* group gave reliably fewer responses in the French language than the *G* group, *H* = 5.83, significant at the 1 per cent level. The *G* group was not reliably different from the *F* group, however, *H* = 2.44 where 2.71 is needed at the 5 per cent level.

When each group was tested to determine if more French or English responses were given to all four stimulus words, it was clear that the *U* group gave reliably more English responses, *H* = 12.04, where only 6.64 is needed at the 1 per cent level; the *G* group gave about an equal amount of responses in both languages (*H* is not significant); while the *F* group gave more responses in French, but not a reliable amount (*H* = −3.00). Thus one who is at a comparatively elementary stage of language acquisition will associate more in his "own" or native language, but as the second language becomes more of a competitor with the native, his associations will be as plentiful in either when he is given a choice of languages to use. Hypothesis *B* is confirmed.

Hypothesis C: As bilinguals progress in experience with a particular language, they will approach the pattern of provocativeness of stimulus words shown by native users of that language.

A stimulus word which elicits more associational responses than another is the more provocative. The stimulus words in the two languages were ranked from high to low provocativeness for each group of *S*s. The similarity of ranking patterns were then tested with a correlation technique where a high correlation would indicate a similar ranking pattern for two groups. It is assumed that there is a characteristic provocativeness pattern for native users of a language which is determined by historical and cultural influences. For example, "reason" might be particularly provocative for French *S*s and yet have a low provocative rank for *S*s from another culture.

It was predicted that the *G* rather than the *U* group would approach more closely the ranking pattern of the *F* group. For the ranking in the French language, rho's between Groups *U* and *G*, *U* and *F*, and *G* and *F* are, respectively, .95, .55, .76. The correlations are in the direction predicted—the *G* group has a ranking pattern more similar to the *F* group than does the *U* group. However, when the rho's are transformed into *z'* (5) measures and a *t*-test of significance is made, the difference between the .95 (*U* and *G* correlation) and the .55 (*U* and *F*) is reliable at the 1 per cent level. Thus the *U* group shows reliably more relation to the *G* group than it does to the *F* group.

In English, the correlations are: *U* and *G*, .82; *U* and *F*, .72; and *G* and *F*, .54. None of the differences between the rho's in English are significant. However, if the three groups are ranked in terms of familiarity with the English language, the *G* group should be first, *U* second, and the *F* group third, as is actually the case in terms of provocativeness similarity. Hypothesis *C* is confirmed.

Hypothesis D: As bilinguals progress in experience with a particular language, their associational responses will be more affected by the habitual word-order of that language.

In a study of word associations, Crane (2) points out that in each language there exists an habitual word order which is evident in associations. In English, adjectives generally precede nouns while in French adjectives generally follow nouns. The prediction was made that as experience with French progresses the evidence of French word-order in associational responses would increase.

Each *S* was given a score indicating his percentage of adjective responses to noun stimulus words. The average percentage scores for each group are listed in Table 1. Note that the noun-adjective pattern becomes increasingly evident in both French and English as experience with the French language increases. It is reasonable that the *F* group's marked use of this order in English is due to a carry over of the French pattern into their use of English. It seems equally probable that as one progresses in skill with French, acquired secondarily, the influence of the French habitual word-order will become increasingly apparent in the French as well as in the English wording.

TABLE 1
Percentages of Adjective Responses to Noun Stimuli, Group Averages

U Group		*G* Group		*F* Group	
French	English	French	English	French	English
11.36	8.43	14.57	10.50	18.28	15.71

The differences between the groups, combining the means of both languages, were tested using analysis of variances after the variences were tested for homogeneity and found significant. However, the U and G groups do not differ reliably, $t = .91$, where 2.00 is needed at the 5 per cent level. The two American groups were therefore combined and tested against the F group. On the average, the American *S*s gave 11.21 per cent adjective responses to noun stimuli, while the F group gave 17.00, a difference significant at the 2 per cent level, $t = 2.50$. The general conclusion is that the two American groups are equally affected by the habitual French word-order, both groups being less affected than the F group. Hypothesis D is not confirmed.

In two continuing articles,* further developmental characteristics of second-language acquisition will be analyzed and the whole series of linguistic measures will be compared, making way for a general description of developmental changes in language skill.

D. SUMMARY AND CONCLUSIONS

Three groups of *S*s at different stages of skill in the French language—an undergraduate major group, U; a graduate major group, G; and a native French group, F—emitted continuous associations to French and English stimulus words and their performances were compared.

1. With respect to the total number of French associations given, the U group, as predicted, emitted reliably fewer than the G or F group whereas the latter two groups did not differ reliably. This finding was interpreted as a change in the "meaningfulness" of French concepts.

2. It was predicted that as one becomes more proficient in a second language, he would approach the ranking pattern of "provocativeness" of those who are native users of the language. (A stimulus word which calls forth more associations than another is more "provocative".) Using a ranking method of correlation, this prediction was verified in French and in English.

---

*Sections II and III in this chapter, pp. 16-30.

3. It was predicted that as experience in French progresses *S*s would give a larger proportion of their associations in French when given a choice of languages to use. The U group gave a reliably smaller proportion of their associational responses in French than did either the G or F groups. The latter groups did not differ reliably on this measure.

4. It was predicted that as experience in French progresses, associational responses would be more affected by the French habitual word-order, i.e., adjective responses would more frequently follow noun stimulus words. The results indicated a progressive increase in the frequency of noun-adjective combinations in both French and English languages. Combining languages, the U and G groups gave reliably fewer noun-adjective combinations than did the F group.

II. ASSOCIATIONAL STEREOTYPY, ASSOCIATIONAL FORM, VOCABULARY COMMONNESS, AND PRONUNCIATION

A. THE PROBLEM

In an attempt to isolate the differentiating variables in the linguistic behavior of those who are at various stages of skill in a particular language, a preceding section has analyzed several such variables and the techniques utilized to measure them. This report is concerned with additional variables, each following from a particular hypothesis.

The details of the method including a description of the *S*s and the procedure have been discussed. In general, continuous associations to French and English stimulus words were solicited from three groups of bilingual *S*s differing in experience with the French language. Group U is made up of American undergraduate majors in French, Group G, American graduate majors in French, and Group F, French natives living in this country who know and daily use English.

B. RESULTS AND DISCUSSION

Hypothesis E: As bilinguals progress in experience with a particular language, they will exhibit a decrease in the stereotypy of associational responses in that language.

It was predicted that more stereotypy of response (more repetition of the same associational responses among the *S*s of a group) would be found for those *S*s who had a relatively limited vocabulary, since the range of possible associations would be smaller. As the vocabulary enlarges, a greater range of possible associations is made available—a condition which should reduce stereotypy. Therefore, the U group should display more stereotypy in French and the F group least.

In addition to investigating differences in stereotypy between groups, the possibility of examining a cultural difference in the extent of linguistic conformity presented itself. The generalization is often made that the French are individualists, comparatively. The multitude of political parties and the existence of different philosophical points of view are usually mentioned as evidence of this characteristic. Likewise, Americans are said to strive for conformity, comparatively. These generalizations may be tested indirectly by comparing the conformity or stereotypy of associational responses. The prediction was made that the French natives would give more individualized responses than the Americans, i.e., they would less often give the same associations to particular stimulus words.

To investigate these problems, each *S*'s first two associations were listed. If "flowers" were given as a response to "garden" by all 14 *S*s in a group, either as first or second response, then "garden" would be rated with a stereotypy score of 14. A maximum score of 28 would be attained if all *S*s in a group gave exactly the same first two responses, a minimum of zero if no responses coincided.

The mean stereotypy scores for the three groups in French are: U, 18.80; G, 17.81; and the F group, 15.00. The over-all F-test of the reliability of the differences between the means was applied (after the variances were tested and found homogeneous), and was found significant at the 2 per cent level. The t-tests indicate that the U and G means are not reliably different while the F mean is reliably smaller than either of the other two; $t = 2.11$ when the G and F means are compared, reliable at the 3 per cent level. This finding is in agreement with the prediction that stereotypy will decrease as familiarity with French progresses. Note, however, the following analysis.

The mean stereotypy scores in English for the groups are: U, 18.10; G, 17.25; F, 12.81. The F group which is comparatively least experienced in English again shows least stereotypy to English stimuli. The F-test is 9.51, significant at the 1 per cent level. Thus the differences in stereotypy are better accounted for by the cultural differences of the French and American Ss or by the differences in method of acquiring languages than by the differences in experience with the French language, since the French Ss are less stereotyped in response in both languages. Hypothesis E is not confirmed.

It was possible to examine the difference between the number of stereotyped responses given in English and in French, disregarding groups, i.e., combining all subjects. The French stimuli elicit more stereotyped responses; the mean number for French is 16.02 and for English, 15.48. The t-test indicates that this is a difference reliable at the 6 per cent level, using the appropriate two-tailed test, ($t = 1.97$ where 2.01 is needed at the 5 per cent level). Considering the F group alone, the French language calls forth more stereotyped responses than does the English language and the difference is reliable at the 3 per cent level with the two-tailed test ($t = 2.27$ where 2.16 is needed at the 5 per cent level). Thus, we have found that the French Ss give reliably fewer stereotyped responses but that the French language tends to provoke more stereotyped responses. Conversely, the American Ss give more stereotyped responses whereas the English language provokes less stereotyped responses. The following interpretation of these findings should be considered primarily as an hypothesis to be further tested by an experimental design made-to-order for this purpose.

Assume that the words of different languages differ with respect to the amount of "information" they convey, using the reasoning of communication theorists as presented by Miller (12). If language A is made up of words which convey comparatively little "information" (there is little "uncertainty" as to what response should follow from the use of such words), then those individuals who have mastered Language A may be allowed more freedom in their responding because of the certainty of stimulus-response relationships. Conversely, if Language B is made up of words which convey a great deal of "information" (there is much "uncertainty" as to what response should follow from the use of such words), then those individuals who have mastered

Language B may, as a consequence of the uncertainty of the stimulus-response relationships, tend to congregate on similar responses for the purpose of cutting down on the "information" available and thereby increase communicational precision. The findings from this analysis would suggest that French is a Type A language and English a Type B, since the French language has shown more stereotypy than English, yet the French natives have shown less stereotypy than the English natives with respect to associational responses.

Hypothesis F: As bilinguals progress in experience with a particular language, they will exhibit a difference in the form of associational responses given in that language.

Each of the first two associations elicited by each stimulus word for all *S*s was assigned to one of the following six categories:

1. Definitions, broadly conceived, including synonyms and superordinates.
2. Subordination, or giving a particular example of the stimulus word.
2+. Noun-adjective or noun-verb combination.
3. Correlated response, new idea but related.
3+. Contrasts.
4. Evaluational or personal response.

This classification is a modification of that developed by Woodworth (17) after an extensive study of the research concerned with associational responses.

The purpose of this aspect of the study is to investigate the changes in the form of associational responses which may be related to differences in experience with a language. The findings of the research in this area do not give a clear direction of prediction for the present hypothesis. Jung (6) found that he could differentiate between "educated" and "non-educated" subjects by an analysis of their associational responses; he could also differentiate feeble-minded from normal responding. Woodworth (17) compared the associations of children and adults and found "striking and curious" differences. Children gave very few coördinates but instead "stayed by" the thing mentioned as stimulus word, telling something about the thing or completing

TABLE 2

Associational Form Analysis

Frequency (F) and percentage (P) scores are given for each category of response. Category 1 includes synonyms and definitions; 2, subordinations; 2+, word combinations; 3, correlated responses; 3+, contrast responses; and 4, personal and evaluative responses.

		Undergraduates Categories						Graduates Categories						French Categories					
		1	2	2+	3	3+	4	1	2	2+	3	3+	4	1	2	2+	3	3+	4
FRENCH																			
Total	F	80	109	109	50	52	49	98	92	96	43	57	61	91	126	120	38	40	79
	P	18	24	24	11	11	10	22	20	21	10	13	14	20	28	27	8	9	18
Concrete Nouns	F	20	43	23	12	5	9	21	36	31	9	6	9	22	30	23	11	2	24
	P	18	38	20	11	4	8	19	33	27	8	5	9	19	27	20	11	2	20
Abstract Nouns	F	14	47	21	5	9	16	12	42	25	3	8	21	14	28	43	1	8	18
	P	12	43	18	5	8	15	11	38	22	3	7	19	12	25	35	1	7	17
Adjectives	F	46	19	63	33	38	24	65	12	40	31	43	31	55	22	54	26	30	37
	P	21	8	29	15	16	11	30	6	17	14	19	13	24	10	24	12	13	16
ENGLISH																			
Total	F	137	123	66	44	43	35	149	99	68	42	42	47	99	104	105	30	27	81
	P	30	27	15	10	10	08	33	22	15	09	09	10	22	23	23	06	06	18
Concrete Nouns	F	24	54	9	20	0	5	15	53	14	25	0	5	9	48	23	15	0	17
	P	21	48	07	18	00	05	13	48	12	22	00	04	08	44	19	13	00	16
Abstract Nouns	F	25	37	12	20	7	11	25	22	26	13	7	19	12	32	30	7	6	24
	P	22	32	12	18	06	10	22	19	24	13	06	17	11	29	26	06	05	22
Adjectives	F	88	32	45	4	36	18	109	24	28	5	35	23	78	24	52	8	21	40
	P	39	14	21	02	16	08	48	11	13	02	16	11	35	11	23	03	09	18

and enlarging upon the idea conveyed by the stimulus. Adults jumped to related or parallel ideas. Murphy (13) compared university students and teachers, some of whom were in literary specialties and others in scientific. The scientists gave associations more in the form of contrasts and coördinates, while the literary men gave more contiguous associations, making the latter more like Woodworth's children and the former like Woodworth's adults.

The frequencies and percentages of associational responses assigned to each of the categories are given in Table 2. First, the frequencies of responses to all French and English stimuli are listed; then concrete nouns, abstract nouns, and adjectives as stimulus words are considered separately. The more outstanding results will be discussed.

The *F* group displays more similarity between its French and English patterns of associations than the other two groups. The *F* group gives more personal and evaluational responses (Number 4) in both languages than the other groups, which is consistent with its smaller amount of stereotypy of response. The two American groups give more definitions (Number 1) than the *F* group.

Comparing the three groups with respect to their responses to French stimuli, the trend indicated by the research of Woodworth and Jung is clear, i.e., the two American groups give more definitions, fewer verbal combinations, and fewer personal responses. Jung might consider the Americans less educated in French than the *F* group. Woodworth might consider them more "child-like" in French since they stay by the stimulus idea in comparison to the *F* group. These interpretations seem inadequate however, since the *F* group *S*s show the same type of responding in English where they give comparatively more personal associations, more verbal combinations, and fewer definitions, making them more "educated" and less "child-like" in their responses to English stimuli than the American subjects. Thus, the *F* group exhibits a similar pattern of responding in both its native and in its acquired languages and this form of responding is characteristically different from that of the *U* and *G* groups. There is little indication of a difference between the *U* and *G* groups. Hypothesis *F* is not confirmed.

Hypothesis G: As bilinguals progress in experience with a particular language, the commonness of the words used in that language will decrease.

Each word was given as an association was assigned a rating determined from word-frequency tabulations for French and English as listed in Eaton (4). The ratings indicated whether the word in question was commonly or rarely used in the language. For the elementary student of a language, those words which are frequently encountered in the written and spoken aspects of that language are likely to be learned first; whereas more experience with the language would be necessary in order to learn and incorporate into one's active vocabulary the less frequently encountered words. Consequently, it was reasoned that this measure would differentiate between levels of experience with a language, and the F group would use words in associating of a less common frequency rating than those used by the G or the U groups.

The first three and last three words given by each *S* for each stimulus were used as a sample of that *S*'s responses. Since there are 16 stimuli in each language, each *S*'s final commonness rating for that language was an average of the individual ratings of 96 words. A rating of 1 was given a response word if it was among the first 500 words (the most commonly used words in the language), a rating of 1.5 for words falling among the second 500, and so on up to the least frequently used. The average word-frequency ratings for each group are listed in Table 3.

TABLE 3
Mean Word-Frequency Ratings

U Group		G Group		F Group	
French	English	French	English	French	English
2.23	3.03	2.97	3.32	3.00	3.01

The difference between the means in English is not reliable, (H = 1.40, where 3.84 is needed at the 5 per cent level). For the French language, there is a progression of means in the order predicted and the over-all H is significant at the 1 per cent level, (H =

21.96). The H between the U and G means was 8.64, also better than the 1 per cent level, indicating that the U group gives reliably more common words as responses than the G group in French. The G group, however, does not use words in French which are reliably more common than the F group. Hypothesis G is confirmed.

Hypothesis H: As bilinguals progress in experience with a particular language, their pronunciation of the words in that language will improve.

It was reasoned that the style of pronunciation of the words of the French language should approach that of the native user of the language as experience with French increased. A native French judge rated the pronunciation of each *S* as the *S*'s responses were played back from a tape recorder. Four categories were used for rating: number 1 for pronunciation style indistinguishable from that of a native French speaker; 2 for good style but distinguishable from that of a native; 3 for a fair style and distinguishable; and 4 for poor pronunciation. All *S*s in the F group were given a number 1 rating. The mean pronunciation rating for the three groups were: U, 2.64; G, 2.28; and F, 1.00. The H-test was used to test the reliability of these differences. The U and G groups were not reliably different, H = .80. The difference between the G and F groups was highly significant, H = 10.34 where only 6.64 is needed at the 1 per cent level. Thus, the style of pronunciation between the undergraduates and graduates was not reliably different, whereas the French group was reliably different from both other groups on this measure. Hypothesis H is not confirmed.

In the concluding section, a general description of developmental changes in second language skill will be presented and the whole series of linguistic measures will be compared.

C. SUMMARY AND CONCLUSIONS

Three groups of *S*s at different stages of skill in the French language—an undergraduate major group, U; a graduate major group, G; and a native French group, F—emitted continuous associations to French and English stimulus words and their performances were compared.

1. It was predicted that as experience in French increases, the total range of vocabulary would increase, a condition which should permit less within-group doubling up on the same words used in association ("stereotypy" of response). The F group gave reliably less stereotyped responses in both French and English, suggesting that there may exist a cultural variable which accounts for associational stereotypy.

2. It was predicted that there would be a difference in the form of associations emitted as experience in a language varied. The F group gave associations in both languages which were characteristically different from the American *S*s.

3. It was predicted that the commonness of the words used in associations would progressively decrease as a function of experience in that language. The U group gave reliably more common words than the G or F groups; whereas the latter two groups did not differ reliably.

4. As experience with French increases, pronunciation of French words should improve. There was no reliable difference between the U and G groups in pronunciation; both were poorer than the F group.

III. A DESCRIPTION OF DEVELOPMENTAL CHANGES

A. PURPOSE

The purpose of this report is to interpret and coördinate the series of findings discussed in three previous articles (9, 10, 11). In brief, three groups of bilingual *S*s were chosen to differ in experience with the French language. Group U comprised American undergraduate majors in French, Group G, American graduate majors in French, and Group F, French natives living in this country who know and daily use English. In the first phase of the investigations, *S*s were given directions printed in both English and French to execute, and speed of response was measured. Relative speed of reaction to directions, calculated by correcting for individual differences in absolute reaction-time, was determined for each group. The second phase of the study involved an analysis of continuous associations given by the members of each group to stimulus words presented in the two languages.

For the sake of integration, attention will be directed to a description of the linguistic behavior of an apprentice in a second language in relation to those more advanced in the mastery of this language. The description will be limited to the measures used in this investigation as seen in the analysis of the three groups, U, G, and F. The apprentice, representing the U group, has been studying a second language, French, for approximately 36 quarter hours at the college level.

The amount of time necessary for a printed direction to be recognized or perceived and finally carried out takes reliably longer in the second than in the basic language for the apprentice. Compared with his basic language, he probably does not think in the second language, but translates into the more efficient or dominant language. The second language has not become enough of a competitor with the basic to be a system which can be used efficiently for thinking. A central characteristic of the process of thinking in a language is its automaticity as seen in behavior, a characteristic which the apprentice lacks in his second language. Dunkel (3) discusses automatic language behavior from both the hearer and speaker points of view. In hearing one's native language, he says, one spends little time or attention on perceiving or recording the sounds but concentrates on interpretation. The speaker attends to what he is going to say and to listening to himself, but the sounds roll out automatically. With a newly acquired language, one substitutes the symbols of the old for the new language symbols, he attends to the sounds and perceives and records them, but does not use the language automatically. In terms of the reaction-time measure developed here, the apprentice is not automatic, comparatively, in the second language. He proves himself to be an English-dominant bilingual.

In terms of the number of associations given in the second language, the apprentice is relatively slow. This may be interpreted as an indication that words are less "meaningful" to him [cf. Noble (14)] or it may indicate again that the apprentice is translating, via the second language, into the native language, and in a limited time period, consequently, must emit fewer associations. It may also indicate that his reservoir of associations is being depleted relatively soon, making the rate of emission slow.

With respect to the apprentice's ability to deal with abstractions in the second language, as measured,[1] he does not differ from the advanced student or the native user of that language. This may indicate that his training in the second language has been such as to direct attention toward the abstract aspects of the language; or, that being skilled in the abstract aspects of English, he is able to utilize the same skill in his second language by means of translating into his basic language.

When the stimulus words in the second language are ranked for the apprentice from high provocativeness to low, the pattern of ranks is less similar to the native's pattern than is the advanced student's. In Noble's terms the words in the language are ranked differently by the apprentice with reference to "meaningfulness" in comparison with the native user of that language.

When given a situation wherein a choice of the two languages may be exercised, the apprentice will associate more in his basic language. This seems to indicate another phase of dominance as well as a facility of thinking in the basic language when experience in the second has not placed the two languages in competition.

The content of the apprentice's associations in the second language will tend to be predominantly non-French when compared with the native user's associations. The apprentice will tend, also, to give associations which are more frequently given by others at his level of experience than is the case of native French subjects, i.e., the apprentice will be more stereotyped in his associations in both his basic and his second language.

With reference to the structure or form of his associations, the apprentice does not differ from the advanced student whereas both show a characteristically different pattern of associations in comparison with the native French speaker. The American (both apprentice and advanced student) "stays by" the stimulus word in his associations, to use Woodworth's terminology and is more of a "literary specialist" according to Murphy's findings.

The apprentice is less affected by the second-language's habitual word order as measured, than are the native users of that language. This fact is evident in both his basic and the second language, indicating that he has not internalized certain aspects of the new language to the extent that these aspects affect his linguistic behavior.

The words used in the apprentice's associations are more common ones than are those used by the more advanced students. This finding may indicate that the words which occur frequently in the language have been incorporated in his linguistic reservoir whereas the less common ones have not.

Finally, the pronunciation of the apprentice in the second language is clearly distinguishable from that of the native user of that language.

The <u>advanced</u> student, representing the <u>G</u> group, differs from the apprentice in terms of the relative speed of response in the second language. The chances are much greater that he will be a balanced bilingual in comparison to the apprentice. The advanced student will be able to give as many associations in his second language as the native user of the language. He will not differ, however, from either the apprentice or the native French in terms of associational facility to abstract stimulus words in his second language. The advanced student will not have progressed much past the apprentice stage in terms of his ranking of the provocativeness of the words in the second language. When given a situation where he may choose between languages, the advanced student will show competition between his basic and his second languages. In terms of stereotypy of responses, the advanced student will not have changed from the apprentice stage. He will be just as much a "literary specialist" in the form of his associations as he was at the apprentice stage. He will not have progressed past the apprentice stage in terms of use of the French habitual word-order in his associations. The words he uses will be the same as those of the native in terms of word-frequency ratings. He will, however, give responses which are predominantly non-French in content as are those of the apprentice. The advanced student's pronunciation will not have advanced reliably past that of the apprentice's when compared with a native's pronunciation.

B. COMPARISON OF MEASURES

A schematic means of summarizing the main findings in this investigation is presented in Table 4. We shall consider each measure as a dimension along which the three groups of subjects may be placed. The groups, *U*, *G*, and *F*, will be placed according to the differences in their mean performance. Both ends of the dimensions are artificially tied down in order to point out the placement of the *G* group. This summary is important, for although we have been able to differentiate the linguistic behavior of these three groups of subjects with respect to a series of dimensions, the dimensions, *per se*, have differed in their *degree* of differentiation. The comparison of dimensions adds significance to the findings.

By way of explanation, the placement of the three groups on Dimension 1 indicates that the means were in the order *U*, *G*, *F*, but that there was not a reliable difference between the means. On Dimension 3, the *U* group mean was reliably different from the *G* and *F* means. On Dimension 6, the *F* group mean was reliably different from the *U* and *G* means.

TABLE 4

Schematic Comparisons of the Series of Dimensions

		U G F		
1. Facility With Abstractness	U		G	F
2. French Word-Frequency Ratings	U		G	F
3. Choice Situation	U		G	F
4. Word Fluency in French	U		G	F
5. Habitual Word-Order	U	G		F
6. Rankings of Provocativeness	U	G		F
7. Stereotypy of Response	U	G		F
8. Associational Form	U	G		F
9. Associational Content	U	G		F
10. Pronunciation Rating	U	G		F

Note that the dimensions fall into two groups. Dimensions 2, 3, and 4 fall into one cluster. "Word-frequency ratings" deals with the commonness or rarity of vocabulary; "Choice" deals with the comparative size of vocabulary in a free-choice situation; and "Word fluency" indicates the extent of French vocabulary. These three dimensions have in common the measurement of vocabulary characteristics. Cluster I is accordingly labeled the "Vocabulary" cluster. Cluster II stands apart from the other in that Dimensions 5 through 10 are all dependent upon cultural differences in linguistic behavior of the French group in comparison with the American groups. This grouping of dimensions is labeled the "Cultural" cluster.[2]

This simple breakdown offers some interesting insights. First, let us consider the acquisition of a second language as entailing a series of barriers to overcome. In these terms, the vocabulary barrier would be the easier to overcome as experience with the language progresses. The cultural barrier is more resistant. To overcome this barrier, one must assimilate those aspects of a different culture which influence language behavior.

Secondly, we may interpret the schematic diagram above in the following manner. It was mentioned earlier that those who have attempted to measure extent of bilinguality or dominance have had to concern themselves with singling out particular variables which would differentiate individuals at various stages of experience with a language. It was mentioned that several isolated attempts have been made to measure bilinguality; e.g., Gali proposed the use of total number of associations as an index of extent of bilinguality and dominance. The present research indicates that two individuals who have recently acquired a second language might differ on the measures falling within the vocabulary cluster, therefore these measures would be sensitive to changes in linguistic performance when extent of bilinguality is not great. Individuals more advanced in a second language, however, might perform the same in terms of the vocabulary measures but differ importantly with respect to performance on measures falling within the cultural cluster. Accordingly, the most comprehensive measure of bilinguality would involve a group of tests selected from both clusters.

The relative speed of response measure developed here states the statistical extent of dominance or balance and is a brief and simple test to administer, as well as an interesting one to perform. It may fruitfully be used either as a single test of bilinguality or in conjunction with a complete battery of tests.

A third interpretation emerges from the schematic diagram above. A general question which adds coherence to this study was mentioned in the introduction: When one acquires a second language, are the same or similar processes involved as when a child learns the first language? From the summary of the findings here one notes a trend from Cluster I to II, which is related to "growth" in a second language due to experience with that language. This progression does seem analogous with that of the child acquiring skill in the first language. First the task of amassing a vocabulary is basic for both cases and seems to come first in the sequence. The incorporation of the cultural aspects of the linguistic community seems to be the most advanced stage of skill for both the child with his first and the adult with his second language. The process of socialization of the child (or enculturation) takes place largely in a linguistic medium, and the language behavior of the child is continuously modified by the influences of socialization long after he has developed the vocabulary needed for expression. The same problem seems to face the adult with his second language, i.e., the process of linguistic enculturation takes most time.

NOTES

The writer is pleased to acknowledge his gratitude to Dr. Harold G. McCurdy for the latter's direction and advice. The Organizational Research Group at Chapel Hill kindly offered typing assistance.

[1]This measure is discussed in (8). In brief, the numbers of associational responses given to abstract stimulus words were compared for the three groups. The group means did not differ reliably from one another.

[2]From an analysis of the three groups' speed of response to directions given in the two languages, there is a suggestion of an intermediate "cluster," lying between the two discussed here, which concerns linguistic automaticity as explained in (9). Research is being planned to study several likely intermediate clusters or levels.

REFERENCES

1. Bovet, P. Bilinguisme et Education. Report fait pour la Commission du Bilinguisme, Genève, 1932.
2. Crane, H. E. A study in association reaction and reaction time. Psychol. Monog., 1915, 18, No. 4.
3. Dunkel, H. B. Second-Language Learning. New York: Ginn, 1948.
4. Eaton, H. S. Semantic Frequency List for English, French, German, and Spanish. Chicago: Univ. Chicago Press, 1940.
5. Edwards, A. D. Experimental Design in Psychological Research. New York: Rinehart, 1950.
6. Jung, C. Studies in Word-Association. London: Heinemann, 1918.
7. Kruskal, W. H., and Wallis, W. A. Use of ranks in one-criterion variance analysis. J. Am. Statist. Ass., 1953, 47, 583-621.
8. Lambert, W. E. An exploratory study of the developmental aspects of second-language acquisition. Unpublished doctor's dissertation, Univ. North Carolina, 1953.
9. ________ Measurement of the linguistic dominance of bilinguals. J. Abnorm. Soc. Psychol., 1955, 50, 197-200. [In this volume, pp. 1-8.]
10. ________ Developmental aspects of second-language acquisition: I. Associational fluency, stimulus provocativeness, and word-order influence. J. Soc. Psychol., 1956, 43, 83-89. [In this volume, pp. 9-16.]
11. ________ Developmental aspects of second-language acquisition: II. Associational stereotypy, associational form, vocabulary commonness, and pronunciation. J. Soc. Psychol., 1956, 43, 91-98. [In this volume, pp. 16-24.]
12. Miller, G. A. What is information measurement? Amer. Psychol., 1953, 8, 3-11.
13. Murphy, G. An experimental study of literary versus scientific types. Am. J. Psychol., 1917, 28, 238-262.
14. Noble, C. N. An analysis of meaning. Psychol. Rev., 1952, 59, 421-431.
15. Thorndike, E. L., and Lorge, I. The Teacher's Word-Book of 30,000 Words. New York: Columbia Univ. Press, 1943.
16. Vander Beke, B. E. French Word Book. New York: Macmillan, 1929.
17. Woodworth, R. S. Experimental Psychology. New York: Holt, 1938.

3 The Influence of Noun-Adjective Order on Learning

In Collaboration with Allan Paivio

The general theory of communication developed by Shannon (4) presents a model which may prove useful to psychologists studying linguistic phenomena. The model has received most attention to date in analyses of amounts of information transmitted through communication channels. The purpose of the present study is to compare experimentally the communicational efficiency of two codes which differ in their habitual ordering of signals. The possible importance of such code differences on information transmission has been alluded to by several psycholinguists (1, 2, 3).

If approached as a learning problem, a familiar syntactical difference (signal order) between the English and French languages (codes) can be compared for ease of learning (information transmission). In English, an adjective-noun order is generally observed (e.g. "the red, white, and blue flag"), while in French the order is usually reversed (e.g. "le drapeau bleu, blanc, rouge"). What are the behavioral implications of this difference? Does noun-adjective order affect fidelity of information transmission through a channel?

Using English words and English-speaking subjects, it was hypothesized that, in spite of habitual word order, the noun-adjective order would be learned more easily because the noun acts as a conceptual "peg" from which its modifiers can be hung.

METHOD AND PROCEDURE

Twenty English-speaking subjects, 11 women and 9 men, were used. Subjects memorized two different lists of words, each to a criterion of two errorless runs. The words were presented on a Ranschburg exposure apparatus and the subject was required to call out the word before it appeared (anticipation method).

Each subject was given the following instructions:

> You are to memorize a list of twenty-eight words. The words will appear one at a time in this space, each for approximately two seconds. There will be a slightly longer pause after every fourth word—that is, the words are in groups of four. The first time will be a practice run. After the first run we will go through the list again; this time, and each time thereafter, you will try to tell me what the word will be before it appears. Don't wait until you think you know them all, but start immediately to call out any you feel you remember.

At no time was anything said about the nature of the words to be presented. A pause of approximately five minutes was allowed after one list had been learned before starting on the other. One practice run was allowed on each list.

The list words ranged in frequency of usage from ten to twenty occurrences per million, as determined by Thorndike and Lorge (5), with the mean frequency the same in both lists. Each list consisted of seven groups of four words (one noun and three relevant adjectives per group). The total number of letters in the two lists was approximately the same. The lists are presented in Table I.

The subjects learned one list in the adjective-noun (A-N) order, the other in the noun-adjective (N-A) order. To counteract any practice effects from the first list to the second, and also any differences between lists which might favour differential learning, four different orders of presentation were used. A subject could start with either list and with the words in that list either in N-A or A-N order. Each possible order of presentation was used with an equal number of subjects.

RESULTS AND DISCUSSION

The results shown in Table II clearly support the hypothesis that the noun-adjective order is learned more quickly and with less errors.

TABLE I
Noun-Adjective Lists Used*

List A	List B
magician	actor
skilled	superb
impressive	expressive
subtle	emotional
accent	sensation
pronounced	intense
harsh	icy
artificial	lasting
athlete	dancer
speedy	artistic
agile	graceful
muscular	charming
maple	lettuce
stately	crisp
lofty	leafy
sturdy	nutritious
hermit	bachelor
bearded	bald
shabby	respectable
harmless	homely
melody	scenery
pleasing	colourful
vivid	cloudy
memorable	picturesque
scientist	burglar
eminent	clumsy
critical	sly
efficient	greedy

*The above lists are shown in the noun-adjective order. For the adjective-noun trials the nouns were placed at the ends of the word-groups instead of the beginnings.

TABLE II
Trials and Errors to Criterion
For Noun-Adjective and Adjective-Noun Order

	N-A order mean	A-N order mean	SD of diff.	t ratio	df	Significance
Trials	16.65	22.0	7.25	3.30	19	.005
Errors	136.60	183.35	96.75	2.16	19	.025

Table III shows the total number of errors at each position within the four-word groups of each list. Certain factors favouring the learning of the noun-adjective order appear.

TABLE III
Frequency of Errors at Each Position
Within Groups of the Lists
(N = Nouns, A = Adjectives)

Position	N-A order error frequency	Percentage of total errors	Position	A-N order error frequency	Percentage of total errors
N	714	26.13	A	1396	38.07
A	688	25.18	A	996	27.16
A	731	26.76	A	778	21.22
A	599	21.93	N	497	13.55
Total	2732	100.00		3667	100.00

(1) A disproportionately large number of errors are made with the first adjectives in the A-N order. (2) More errors are made with each adjective within the A-N groups (A_1, A_2, A_3) than with any adjective in the N-A groups. (3) There is an almost linear decrease in errors from the first adjective to the noun in the A-N groups, which is not apparent in the N-A order where errors are clustered around what would be chance distribution for each position.

Differences in the amount of interference involved would seem to account for the comparative difficulty with first adjectives over first nouns. The only interference to learning the noun comes from the nouns of other groups, whereas for the adjective there is interference not only from other first adjectives, but also from the other adjectives within the same group.

Why are there more errors with second and third adjectives in the A-N list than in the N-A list? A_1 should act as a cue for A_2 and A_2 for A_3 as well in one list as in the other. Apparently the noun's position is crucial, for when it appears first it serves as a cue for each adjective, not only for the one immediately following. When the noun comes last in a group, however, it appears to facilitate the retention of adjectives differentially, depending on their nearness to the noun. The words are recognized as nouns or adjectives, and as being related in the groups. The relatedness of group members is determined by the noun; relatedness is high when the noun appears early and low when the noun appears late. In other terms, the adjectives are meaningfully associated with the noun concept, and when the associations are forward (N-A order) rather than backward (A-N order) the adjectives are more easily learned.

Note, however, that one pays a certain price for the over-all communicational efficiency of the noun-adjective order. The nouns in the N-A order are both relatively and absolutely more difficult to learn than are the nouns in the A-N order, and this difference is apparently due to the cue properties of the three preceding adjectives in the A-N order. When a noun is first in a group, the only cue possible is its position in the series of groups. The communicational disadvantage of being first in the group, however, is less detrimental for the noun than for the adjective.

SUMMARY

Subjects learned two lists of noun-adjective word groups, the words in one list having a noun-adjective order, and the other, an adjective-noun order. The noun-adjective order was learned significantly more easily, this communicational advantage depending on the comparative ease of learning adjectives rather than nouns in the noun-adjective order.

REFERENCES

1. Miller, G.A. Psycholinguistics. In G. Lindzey (Ed.), *Handbook of social psychology*, pp. 693-708. Cambridge: Addison-Wesley, 1954.
2. Miller, G.A. Speech and language. In S.S. Stevens (Ed.), *Handbook of experimental psychology*, pp. 798-810. New York: Wiley, 1951.
3. *Psycholinguistics: a survey of theory and research problems*. Supplement to *J. abnorm. soc. Psychol.*, 1954, 49, No. 4, part 2.
4. Shannon, C.E. A mathematical theory of communication. *Bell Syst. tech. J.*, 1948, 27, 379-423, 623-656.
5. Thorndike, E.L., and Lorge, I. *The teacher's word book of 30,000 words*. New York: Bureau of Publications, Teachers Coll., 1944.

4 The Use of Pareto's Residue-Derivation Classification as a Method of Content Analysis

The purpose of this paper is to demonstrate the use of Pareto's residue-derivation scheme (3, 5) as a method of content analysis. The method emphasizes first the latent (rather than manifest) aspects of communication content and secondly, the theory of motives developed by Pareto. The originality of the study consequently runs counter to suggestions of experts in the two pertinent fields of research. First, Berelson defines content analysis as "a research technique for the objective, systematic and quantitative description of the manifest content of communication" thereby excluding analysis of "latent intentions which the content may express or the latent responses which it may elicit" (2, p. 489). Berelson's implication is that latent aspects cannot be systematically, objectively and quantitatively analyzed.

Secondly, G. W. Allport believes that alternative theories of motives have general advantages over Pareto's. Allport explains that Pareto, the irrationalist, "offers a theory of the real motives of men (residues) and of fictitious motives (derivations). Residues bring men under the domination of 'sentiments' which clever people manipulate by the use of 'nonlogical' appeals. The resulting social conduct is 'explained' and prettified with the aid of verbal illusions (derivations). Derivations spread widely in society through devices that psychologists to-day recognize as principles of propaganda. The true motives lie in classes of mental processes to which Pareto gives such labels as 'the instinct of combinations,' 'need of manifesting one's feelings by exterior acts,' 'sexual residues,' and the like . . . Both doctrines (residues and derivations) are handled in a more orderly fashion by various other systems of irrationalist psychology (*e.g.*, Freudian, McDougallian)" (1, p. 17).

In defense of this study, however, it is my belief that "latent" analysis can be objective, systematic and quantitative particularly with the use of Pareto's system, and that the residue-derivation system is especially suited for communication analysis. This study will serve as an illustration of the use of Pareto's system for content analysis and will not test the comparative power of his theory. The preliminary test of this procedure's value will be seen in its face validity or reasonableness.

In Pareto's diagram, A represents the drive, attitude, or

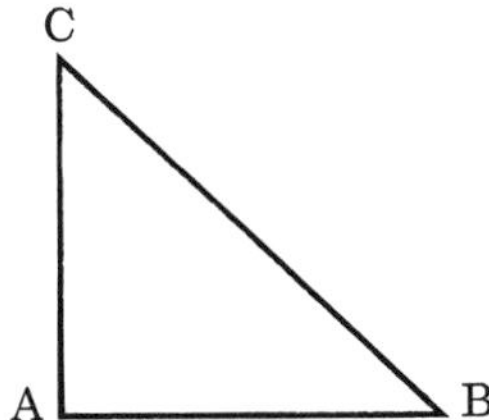

sentiment which underlies any particular "hypothetical psychic state." B represents the behavior of an individual under analysis, his particular acts. C, the important factor to be scrutinized represents the theories which are given verbally to account for the behavior. With this conceptualization, Pareto searched for the relationships between what people say and do, and between what people feel and do and say.

The C of the diagram is analyzed into parts a and b, standing respectively for residues and derivations (a plus b being the derivative or the theory). Residues are the more stable, recurring elements in theories, most closely related to the hypothetical psychic state of the individual. Pareto chooses not to define residues with precision, but refers to them as instinctual or "fundamental notions" of man. The present writer projects his own meaning by considering the residues as generalized perceptual-need schemes. Derivations are the arguments used to explain, justify or rationalize behavior. Thus, other residues may be used as derivations. Pareto differentiated derivations as a separate classification, because of their function—explaining one's behavior, and their comparative non-stability. For example, the expression of a belief in a particular practice (the residue) would recur in several different cultures, but the justification of the practice or the belief (the derivation) would differ among cultures.

By an analysis of the residues, we are given leads to the basic motives or sentiments of man. In practice, we can analyze the verbalizations of man which are facts and observable and work under to the motivation which led to the verbalization. Pareto's technique of analysis is concerned only with the non-logical or non-experimental aspects of human thought and action, that ruled by the sentiments.

The purpose of this paper is to try out Pareto's classifications on editorial materials, thereby illustrating the usefulness of the technique as a means of content analysis. The interested are, of course, urged to consult the volumes of Pareto for the logical development of his final classification.

In 1949, Liebling (4) translated a series of editorials covering the range of sentiments displayed by the French press. This material lends itself easily to a Paretian analysis, and offers a variety of points of view. The plan here is to compare the residues and derivations found in the editorials of left and right wing papers in France.

A murder was being reported, the details of which were obscured by the use made of the incident by the many parties in France to grind their respective axes. The main outline of the case probably is as follows: Madame Paule Schlumpf killed Mr. Raoul Simha, an oriental and possibly a Jew. Paule used the apartment of a friend for the rendez-vous she frequently had with Simha. Paule's husband was aware of the love affair and was extremely "tolerant." (Paule's husband was a Swiss citizen who lived in Alsace during the Occupation and was possibly a Nazi-party member). One night, Paule shot Simha, possibly in self-defence—her own interpretation. After the killing, she called a friend who assisted her in hiding the gun and calling the police.

The French papers represent a left-right political range of opinion in a pattern somewhat like:

1. *Humanité*	(Left)	11. *L'Epoque*	(Right)
2. *Libération*		10. *L'Aurore*	
3. *Franc-tireur*		9. *Ce Matin—Le Pays*	
4. *Le Populaire*		8. *Le Figaro*	
5. *Combat*	6. *L'Aube*	7. *Le Parisien Libéré*	

For this analysis, excerpts from L'Humanité and Libération will present the left-wing point of view, and Le Figaro and L'Aurore the right. L'Humanité presents this story:

> The second session of the trial of the depraved Mme Schlumpf was, if possible, still more fashionable than the preceding one. Even more jewels, more feathers, and more fur coats were on display than the day before, to the point that at one o'clock, newsmen could hardly get through the crowd of fashionable females palpitating with anticipation while they munched little cakes. . . The accused forgets, this time, to hide her tearless eyes behind a handkerchief. She displays her true face, cold, calculating and ill-tempered. There is a great silence when her husband enters, the billionaire collaborateur whose complaisance makes him virtually an accessory to the crime. Quite self-possessed, this singular Helvetian blushes a little when Attorney General Turland refers to his conduct—worthy of a Teuton—during the Occupation, and shows him the oath of allegiance to Hitler he signed in 1944. By what maneuvers was this traitor able to have the damning evidence against him quashed? Nobody has the curiosity to ask him. But one witness, Mr. Diffort, who upon the orders of the resistance had simply kept a record of Mr. Schl.'s actions, was discharged from his factory job and threatened. For 16 months, he was unemployed. Think, he had had the courage to tell of the Nazi galas and receptions for S. S. colonels given by the husband of the criminal. . . A witness casts a clear light upon the nature of the accused: "If you quit me, I'll turn you over to the Gestapo," Paule said to her lover in 1940. . . And this is what Simha told a friend: "Look, here's a pistol I took from her yesterday. She gets new ones all the time." Fifteen minutes after midnight, Judge Loser reads the sentence: "eight years in prison," which the murderer greets with faked sobs for the benefit of her "chic" girl friends. All the same, eight years for a murder is getting away with murder!

What residues[1] are expressed by this Communist-controlled paper? The last sentence is an example of the need for uniformity, *imposed on others*, for the author feels obliged to point out emphatically that this crime should not go unnoticed, that *everyone* should get punished for such a crime. Throughout the editorial, a *sentiment opposing alterations in the social equilibrium* is stressed, *i. e.*, "even" Paule should get the punishment which fits the crime. The author expresses the sentiment of *reestablishment of integrity by operations on the agent of change*—*i. e.*, Paule, the agent of change, should be punished so that others will not kill. Pareto uses this residue in describing the doctrine of "an eye for an eye" or in describing social punishment for offenders.

One might assume that the Left's immediate interest is in change, following the Communist party lines. However, the residue-in-chief is that of *persistence of aggregates*, Pareto's term for the expression of a firm faith in institutions, traditions, morals, mores. Perhaps the Communists feel that their way of life is the oldest and that a change *back* to their way of life is necessary, or that the need for the changes advocated follows from their "old time" values. The residues used to derive are: *morality*, as seen in the insistence on justice being done to a "murderess," and the indignation shown to Schlumpf's complacency; *reestablishment of integrity by operation on the agent of change*; *sentiments opposing alterations in social equilibrium*; *need for uniformity*. These attitudes help account for the Left's emotion noticed in their attack on the "haves", who in this case are "getting away with murder" and are attacking institutions in which the Left have faith.

In addition, it fits their long-ranged plan to have each reader draw a connection between the rich with fur coats, the collaborator, and the murderess—an example of the tendency to *combine bad things with unfortunate events.* To emphasize this residue, a combination of residues is rather effectively brought together. Note the reference to *the repugnance to suffering in general* when mention is made of those connected with Mr. Schlumpf's Nazi activities, and the reference to *self-pity and pity for others*.

The residues used by *L'Humanité* are explained or justified by a series of derivations. Note the use of *terms exciting accessory sentiments*, *i. e.*, "billionaire," "collaborator," "crime," "Helvetian," "damning," "Nazi galas," "Gestapo," "Murderess," "chic." Pareto would argue that the fundamental notions or sentiments of the Left are justified by their thinking in terms of such derivatives, i. e., punishment should be given Paule because she is involved with collaborators and billionaires.

Many affirmations are found, a good example seen in the last sentence. Authority of one or many men is employed in the statement of the witness, Diffort, who develops the argument that Paule's husband was not much good. The argument is quite irrelevant to the case in process, but when the Rightist papers state that it is irrelevant and substitute something equally so, we then see the non-logical aspects of the whole range of papers and their editorializing.

Libération, a paper nearly as far Left as L'Humanité, has this story:

> An audience that looks as if it had been painted by Albert Guillaume. They are incredible. Not one is missing. They have even brought oranges to keep up their strength. . . To the attraction of seeing Paule Schlumpf, the murderess with the golden mane and the mink coat, there is the added (attraction) of seeing and hearing her husband, and perhaps of hearing in the bargain some scandalous alcove secrets.
>
> Fritz Schlumpf enters. He looks the way his name sounds: Fritz Schlumpf. Born Swiss. Perfect German type. He admired them so, cold, filled with anger that he controls. Anger against his wife? No. Against the magistrates' curiosity about his "occupations," as Sacha Guitry would say. He has picked his role. He presents himself as the magnanimous husband. The man is elegant. He is detestable in every element of his personality, the part that shows, the part that doesn't. But he has decided to dazzle by his sophisticated generosity. . . "She told me she was in love with a younger man and wanted to leave me. I asked her to wait. . . When I came to Paris, I did not stay with her, but stopped at the Grand Hotel." Let us note at once that the Grand Hotel at this period of the Occupation was reserved for officers of the Wehrmacht.

> "Simha said that he was madly in love with my wife, that he was her ideal lover. . . 'Yes or no, will you give me your wife?' he said. I explained to Simha that my wife was not an article of merchandise, but a human being. . . To love a woman, Your Honor, is not to keep her selfishly for oneself, but to give her happiness in the form she desires." All the elegant females shivered with pleasure. For the rest, Schlumpf—who used to salute crying: "Heil Hitler" at Mulhouse, in his factory, in the Grand Hotel at Paris; who is tempted many times during his cross-examination to say "the Great Reich" instead of "Germany,"— says that since Alsace had been officially annexed to "Germany,"— his wartime conduct was the only conduct possible. . . One senses in him the wartime economic collaborator and collaborator in every respect of the type still all-powerful today. But that is another story. . . . Maître René Floriot, for the defence, puts on one of his brilliant sleight-of-hand performances. With what result? . . . At a quarter of twelve, the guards bring Paule Schlumpf back to the box. Very pale, staring with dilated eyes, she seems in a trance. Is she drugged? Possibly.
>
> The jurors having answered yes to all questions, Paule Schlumpf is condemned to eight years' imprisonment.

The author's sentiments have taken her from the case at hand to Mr. Schlumpf. She "senses" the collaborator in him—an example of a <u>sentiment transformed into an objective reality</u>. Schlumpf's past activities have been habitually bad, and by extension, his wife is equally bad, an example of the residue <u>persistence of relations of men with other men</u>. The weaknesses and wickedness of the elite clearly include Paule Schlimpf.

However, her technique seems to be to anticipate or review the residues used by the opposing point of view and to ridicule each in turn. She alludes to the <u>sex residues</u> and makes fun of the sexual relations and the mixed-up love affair, whereas the papers on the Right take this point seriously. She is also expressing her faith in <u>morality</u>. Next, she ridicules the husband's <u>self-sacrifice</u> as something to make the girls in the audience "shiver". The sentiment of <u>hierarchy</u> (faith in status and class differences), is ridiculed as well. If she has anticipated or analyzed the opponent's sentiments, her awareness and manipulation of them takes the sentiments out of the realm of the non-experimental. However, she does introduce her own obvious sentiments.

The derivations employed include many terms exciting accessory sentiments, such as: "oranges" (a luxury even after the war), "Wehrmacht," "murderess," "mink coat," "German type," "Heil Hitler," "collaborator." Analogies, the "golden mane," and affirmations, "not one is missing," are skillfully employed.

Le Figaro, the right-wing[2] paper, presented this story:

> But what a success this magnificent husband would have had before the elegant attendance of the previous days. . . The personality of this generous spouse gained by the attack that the prosecutor, Turland, inexplicably insisted upon making on him with regard to his conduct during the war. That conduct may have been, probably was, from our point of view, gravely reprehensible, but it has absolutely nothing to do with the case before us. It is for the special courts to rule on it. It makes Mme Schlumpf neither more nor less guilty.

Here residues used by the papers of the Left have been ruled out as not pertinent and other equally non-pertinent ones substituted, e.g., the sexual residue and the residue of self-sacrifice with respect to the husband.

Derivations of a different type are used by the Right. Indeterminate terms are effectively placed, e.g., "personality," "generous spouse," "conduct," "gravely reprehensible." "Magnificent husband" is a good example of an ambiguous term, especially in relation to his other descriptions.

L'Aurore, an extreme Right and formerly pro-Vichy paper, presents this story:

> There is, incontestably, love involved in this affair that Attorney General Turland, with all his skill, wishes to present as a drama of sordid selfishness. It remains certain that a great tourney of the flesh impelled Paule Schlumpf and

her victim, Raoul Simha, to fight, to insult each other, to separate, to reconcile. For me, what pleaded for the woman condemned yesterday was not her declarations, her tears, but the testimony of her husband. I know nothing of what this Swiss citizen, living in a provisionally annexed Alsace, may have done, considered from a French national point of view. What I remain sure of, per contra, is that from a human point of view, I will always remember him as a gentleman, for the literally unheard-of way he defended his cruel and unfaithful wife. I take my hat off to him for having launched these words at his detractors in open court: "One does not put a Parisienne in a cage, even a golden cage. To love a woman does not mean to try to keep her to oneself alone."

The brilliant orator of the state prosecution flung himself with dialectal felicity upon this neutral industrialist and, if I understood him correctly, even insinuated that he had shot the unfortunate Simha in the back of the neck, and even implied that it was doubtless because the victim knew too much about the suicide of a former mistress of the gentleman whom I so admire that the Oriental (Simha was a Jew) met his death. He did not persuade me.

Should one set down exactly what one thinks? I almost regret now to have written the qualification that I just attached to the name of the victim in this story. A voyage in the heart of a long, amorous adventure, that is what I should have liked to entitle my impressions of this enthralling trial whose slightest developments were followed yesterday by so many pretty women.

Maître Charpentier of the prosecution was astonishing, in moderation and logic. He told us that the heroine of this drama had had a weakness for the green-uniformed invaders. That, of course, is deplorable. The defence, later, swore to the contrary. But that has only a distant relation to the case.

One word now about the jurors. I sat next to them. I observed them with passionate attention. They are probably decent people, but incapable "socially," intellectually, of weighing all the factors in the problem submitted to them. There is, then, something limping, imperfect, in the present

> organization of our criminal courts. . . Is it my fault if the procession of prosecution witnesses left me cold? I wasn't even moved much by the star witnesses for the defence. And nevertheless, Maître Floriot, the defence attorney, was always there to shove with his index finger—a marvellous sharpshooter who defends his clients by attacking when the opportunity offers. His pleading seemed to me to give off sparks. We saw him, turn by turn, comical, logical, sensitive—serious, too—and always relaxed, like a great athlete, who always keeps something in reserve. I find no words to express the satisfaction, the joy, that he produces when he really lets himself go. You say to yourself, "It is a pleasure, all the same, to know that there exist in our country men so brilliant, so blessed by the gods." Paule Schlumpf was lucky that he consented to take her case on August 8, 1946.

The Right expresses a desire for social change. They want a "new jury system" and "more intelligent rule." Their residue-in-chief is the residue of combinations, used by Pareto to refer to a faith in clever techniques of manipulation, implying a higher grade intelligence in the elite. Note the admiration for the "brilliant" defense attorney of whom "all France could be proud"—the same man who was described as sleight-of-hand by the Left. Examples of residues used to derive are: sexual residues (amorous adventure), the residue of hierarchy (the intellectual inferiority of the jurors), and the residue of self-sacrifice for the sake of others (the magnificent husband defending his cruel wife and offering her freedom).

No allusions are made to Mr. Schlumpf's proclivities nor to his wife's probable guilt. The lack of reference to the reestablishment of integrity by operations on the agent of change is noticeable. The technique here is to dodge many aspects of the case in defending the elite.

L'Aurore lacks aggression and definiteness in the derivations used. Indeterminate terms, ambiguous, and non-concrete terms, are freely employed, e.g., "love," "human point of view," "voyage in the heart of a long and amorous adventure," "heroine of this drama," are examples. The choice of words is comparatively smooth and pleasingly vague. Several affirmations are used, *e.g.*, the jurors are called "incapable." To present their point of view, a direct reference is made to the dead man's being a Jew, a term exciting accessory sentiments, not inconsistent with a Vichy point of view. This reference also makes the death something less than a murder in their thinking. The next to the last sentence is a good example of the derivation accord with sentiments of collective interest—the defending attorney is presented as a man of whom all France can be proud.

In summary, the Left made use of the following residues: need for uniformity imposed on others; opposition to alterations in in the social equilibrium; reestablishment of integrity by operation on the agent of change; morality; combination of bad things with unfortunate events; repugnance to suffering in general; sentiments transformed into an objective reality; and, persistence of relations of men with other men. In contrast, the Right employed the following residues: combinations; the sexual residue; hierarchy; and self-sacrifice for the sake of others. The Right differentiates itself by using indeterminate, ambiguous and non-concrete terms as derivations.

The chief residue expressed by the Left was Persistence of Aggregates referring to a faith in old institutions, traditions and morals. The residue-in-chief of the Right was the residue of Combinations, referring to a faith in imagination, ingenuity or clever techniques of manipulation. Pareto stated that Persistence of Aggregates was usually an associate of social conservation while the "instinct" for Combinations was usually associated with social progress.

Up to this point, we have been relying on the classification system of Pareto as a means of content analysis, and as such, it has pointed out the emotional tender spots which can be effectively touched to meet editorial purposes. It should be emphasized, however, that the residues used in the editorials do not necessarily correspond to the basic sentiments of the authors. In fact, Pareto makes clear that residues are often most effectively used as derivations especially in emotional speech and writing. Thus, the morality residue might be used by the Left in one situation, and be ignored in another depending upon the propaganda purposes of the writer, with no relation to the basic residues involved. The content analysis has noted the Left's use of residues associated with conservatism and the Right's association with social change. In view of historical facts, these residues were likely used to assist in meeting desired propaganda goals. If Paule Schlumpf were the wife of a coal miner and a member of the Communist party, the positions taken by the Left and Right would very likely be changed.

SUMMARY

An attempt has been made to develop and illustrate a new method of content analysis by making use of Pareto's residue-derivation scheme. The editorial materials analyzed were easily placed into Pareto's classifications, and the patterns of residues expressed by both political positions appear logically consistent. A further test of the method would involve measurement of the agreement among judges in categorizing materials. The method should prove useful in discovering consistencies of expression of particular sentiments over extended periods of time by different political or cultural groups. The recorded debates in United Nations meetings, for example, would offer rich material.

NOTES

[1]Residues and derivations are given the labels used by Pareto with an example to define the terms. Residues and derivations are in italics.

[2]The middle of the road paper, L'Aube, representing Bidault's middle-class, Catholic party, stayed out of the arena and gave the case one factual paragraph on a back page.

REFERENCES

1. Allport, G. W., The Historical Background of Modern Social Psychology, in G. Lindzey (Ed.), Handbook of Social Psychology. Addison-Wesley Press, Cambridge, 1954.
2. Berelson, B., Content Analysis, in G. Lindzey (Ed.), Handbook of Social Psychology. Addison-Wesley Press, Cambridge, 1954.

3. Homans, G. C., and Curtis, C. P., An Introduction to Pareto. Alfred Knopf, New York, 1934.
4. Liebling, A. J., The Wayward Press. New Yorker, March 19, 1949.
5. Pareto, V., The Mind and Society (4 vols.). Harcourt Brace and Co., New York, 1935 (Translated by L. J. Henderson).

5 The Influence of Language-Acquisition Contexts on Bilingualism

In Collaboration with J. Havelka and C. Crosby

The bilingual person presumably must learn two different verbal responses for each referent, a requirement analogous to learning different responses to the same stimulus in experimental studies of negative transfer. It is of psychological interest, therefore, that bilinguals are so often able to communicate freely in either language without interference from the other. As yet, no adequate psychological theory has been offered to account for bilingualism. In his review of various limited explanations, Weinreich concludes that "a comprehensive psychological theory of bilingualism ought to account for both the effectively separated use of the two languages and for interference of the languages with one another" (9, p. 71). It is the purpose of the present investigation to contribute to such a theory by analyzing conditions that are presumed to affect both the "effectively separated use" of the bilingual's two languages and the "interference of the languages with one another."

As a first step, it may be profitable to apply certain principles derived from paired-associate learning and transfer phenomena to the case of learning two languages.[1] In the experimental study of retroactive inhibition, the learner must first link S_1 to R_1 and, in the later interpolated phase, S_1 to R_2. When alternative responses are associated with a common stimulus, interference between the two associations is the usual consequence. The bilingual is confronted with an analogous learning problem when, for example, the symbols "church" and "_église_" are both associated with the appropriate environmental event.

One general means of minimizing interference in learning situations is to increase the distinctiveness of the two tasks to be learned.[2] In studies of retroactive inhibition, for example, interference is effectively minimized by increasing the degree of learning of original and interpolated tasks or by decreasing the associative similarity between the competing responses. Both these variations enhance the distinctiveness of the tasks. If distinctive secondary cues, such as differently colored backgrounds, are associated with the two tasks to be learned, the functional separation of the tasks should be increased.

Following the logic of interference theory, we can reason that response competition in bilingualism is functionally related to the distinctiveness of contexts in which the bilingual's two languages are acquired; the more "separated" the contexts of acquisition, the less the bilingual interference. Acquisition contexts are considered to be separated when the association between a symbol such as "church" and the appropriate environmental event has consistently taken place in a setting distinct from that in which the association between "église" and its corresponding environmental event occurs. On the other hand, in "fused" acquisition contexts, members of a linguistic community can and do use both symbols for any particular environmental event, thereby increasing the interchangeability of the symbols.

Recently, Ervin and Osgood (4) attempted a theoretical interpretation of bilingualism that indicates the potential importance of language-acquisition contexts. They suggest that bilinguals could theoretically acquire "compound" or "coordinate" language systems. The compound system would be developed through experience in fused contexts, as with vocabulary training in school, or where the same family members use two languages interchangeably to refer to the same environmental events. The coordinate system would be developed through experience in different linguistic communities where languages are rarely interchanged. They suggest that the alternative symbols in his two languages have a single meaning for the compound bilingual whereas the coordinate bilingual, presumably because of the distinctiveness of his language-acquisition contexts, develops separate meanings for each of his alternative symbols.

Accepting this theoretical position, we hypothesized that experience in "separated" language-acquisition contexts enhances the functional separation of the bilingual's two languages while experience in "fused" contexts reduces the functional separation of the two language systems. We predicted that bilinguals with experience in separated contexts would show comparatively greater semantic differences between symbols in one language and their translated equivalents in the other, more associative independence of translated equivalents in their two languages, and less facility of switching from one language to the other.

METHOD

Classification of Subjects

The *S*s were college or university students with extensive experience in both English and French languages. Since all but four were either preparing for or actually in graduate schools, it can be assumed that the group was relatively homogeneous in intelligence. Each *S* was tested for extent of bilingualism (5, 6) and the 32 who met our criterion for bilingual "balance" will be discussed here. "Balance" implies a high level of second language competence, high enough, in fact, that no dominance of one language over the other is measurable with the technique employed.

Our primary task was to classify *S*s according to their language-acquisition contexts and, to this end, detailed information was obtained from each *S* concerning how, when, and where his languages were acquired. Acquisition contexts were considered separated when one language was learned exclusively in the home and the other exclusively outside the home, when one parent consistently used one language and the other parent a different language, or when one language was acquired in a particular national or cultural setting distinct from that in which the second was acquired. Acquisition contexts were considered fused when both parents used the two languages indiscriminately, when both languages were used interchangeably inside and outside the home, or when an individual acquired his second language in a school system stressing vocabulary drill and translation and where the first or native language was used as the medium of instruction. This scheme of classification is derived from that used by Ervin and Osgood (4) in their definitions of compound and coordinate systems. The actual classification of *S*s as having separated or fused contexts for acquisition is essentially an arbitrary one in spite of the rather explicit criteria for placement. In five cases, for example, a problem arose in deciding whether to give credit for some experience with separated contexts when an *S* had early experience in a fused context, as when as English *S* acquired French in a school system but later used this language exclusively in France for some period of time. Our decision was to classify such an *S* as separated if he spent at least an entire year using the acquired language either exclusively or primarily. Using this scheme, 23 *S*s were classified as "separated" and 9 as "fused."[3]

It was also possible to further subdivide the "separated" group according to the following line of reasoning. An *S* could be classified as "separated" if he had experience either in distinctive acquisition contexts within a particular national setting, as in Quebec, or in two geographically different cultures, as from living many years in France before coming to America. We predicted that separated contexts based on "bicultural" experiences, as in the latter example, would particularly enhance the distinctiveness of the two contexts. In this case, the environmental events themselves may often not be common for the two sets of symbols. For example, "*église*" could mean a gothic cathedral while "church" could mean a tall wooden building used on Sundays, and "ami" and "friend" could take on quite different meanings. A recent study by Ervin (3) demonstrates how such environmental differences affect the perceptual and personality functionings of bilinguals. With these considerations in mind, the "separated" group was subdivided into 15 *S*s with bicultural and 8 *S*s with "unicultural" experiences.

Behavioral Indices of the Influence of Acquisition Contexts

As a measure of the differences in meanings of concepts in the bilingual's two languages, we made use of Osgood's "semantic differential" (7), a method of scaling stimulus-words on a standard set of meaning dimensions. For example, an *S* is presented with a stimulus-word, such as "house," and is asked to rate it along a seven-point dimension, such as "fast-slow" or "pleasant-unpleasant." In the present case, the stimulus-words were four common English concepts ("house," "drink," "poor," "me") and their French translations. They were presented in a fixed order so that any word was maximally separated from its translated pair. Ten standard dimensions (see 8) were used and their order of presentation was continually changed to eliminate any patterning of ratings. The *S* might rate "house" at Position 3 on the "fast-slow" dimension, and later "maison" might be rated at Position 5 (more slow) on the same dimension, which had been translated into French. Since both stimulus-words and the anchors of each dimension were translated, we can only make statements about differences in meanings of both stimulus-words and dimensional attributes, or their interaction. The average degree of difference between the French and English semantic ratings for the four pairs of stimulus words was determined for each *S* using Osgood's D score (7); the larger the D score, the greater the semantic differences between translated equivalents in French and English. We predicted that *S*s with experience in separated language-acquisition contexts would show comparatively greater semantic differences between translated equivalents in their two languages.

As a measure of the degree of associative independence of translated equivalents, we made use of the retroactive inhibition design. If an *S* learns list A, then list B, then re-learns list A, one can determine the amount of associative interference imposed by the interpolated material. If the interpolation has no effect on the previously memorized material, then the two can be considered functionally independent. Interference and facilitation from the interpolated material may be thought of as indices of the functional dependence of the first-learned and interpolated tasks.

Each *S* learned a list of 20 commonly occurring English words by the anticipation method. A criterion of 8 correct responses out of 20 was chosen so as to permit improvement following the interpolated task. This was followed by three presentations of a list of 20 three-letter nonsense words. Then the English list was re-presented and the *S*'s retention was measured. Finally, *S*s were asked to relearn the nonsense list, but these data will not be discussed here. This preliminary test gives a measure of the associative interference or facilitation imposed by a meaningless task, one assumed to be semantically independent of the original task. After a rest period, the same procedure was repeated, but this time a second, similar list of 20 English words, learned to the same criterion, was followed by a list of their exact translations in French, presented for three trials. A score was assigned to each *S* which indicated the degree of associative interference or facilitation imposed by the interpolated French material in relation to interpolated meaningless material. The following illustrative case indicates some facilitation from both interpolated tasks but more from the interpolated French. The number of correct responses for the criterion trials are placed in Column A, and the number of correct responses for retention trials are given in Column A', for the English-Nonsense-English and the English-French-English series:

	A	I	A'	A - A'
Series I:	E_1 = 10	N(3 trials)	E_1 = 11	-1
Series II:	E_2 = 10	F(3 trials)	E_2 = 15	-5
		I - II = +4		

Positive scores indicate that the interpolated French translations facilitate retention of English words more than do interpolated nonsense words. Negative scores indicate that interpolated French translations interfere with the retention of English words. A zero score would indicate that the interpolated French translations offer no more facilitation than interpolated nonsense words. Following the reasoning outlined above, the closer the scores approach zero, the more associatively independent the translated equivalents. We predicted that *S*s with experience in separated acquisition contexts would show more associative independence between translated equivalents in their two languages than those with experience in fused contexts.

Finally, we predicted that experience in fused as compared to separated contexts would express itself in a greater facility of switching from one language to the other. As a measure of such facility, we made use of a speed of translation test described elsewhere (6). Each *S*, given 20 French and 20 English words to translate, was assigned a score for his average speed of translation from English to French and from French to English. Speed was measured by a voice key in circuit with a chronoscope.

RESULTS AND DISCUSSION

As predicted, those bilinguals who acquired their languages in separated contexts showed a significantly greater difference in meanings of translated equivalents than did those who acquired their two languages in fused contexts (see Table 1). However, when a comparison was made between those who acquired their two languages in geographically distinct cultures (bicultural experience) and those who acquired both languages in separated contexts within one geographical region (unicultural experience), it became clear that bicultural experience accounted for the over-all difference between fused and separated groups. In fact, *S*s with unicultural experience are not essentially different from either of the other two groups with respect to similarity of meanings of translated equivalents. It appears, therefore, that the difference in meanings of translated equivalents is not a simple function of experience in separated acquisition contexts. Experience in bicultural acquisition contexts, where there is a greater likelihood that the actual referents of translated symbols are different, does appear to affect the semantic aspects of the bilingual's two languages.

Bilinguals with experience in separated acquisition contexts also showed significantly more associative independence of translated equivalents in their two languages than did those with experience in fused contexts (see Table 2). An interpolated list of French translations had about the same influence for the separated group as an interpolated list of nonsense syllables. *S*s in the fused group, on the other hand, clearly benefited from the interpolated French list.

These findings are consistent with those summarized above for semantic differences. Since translated equivalents were semantically more similar for the fused *S*s, the interpolated translations in the learning problem were more like an extension of the original English list. It is logical therefore that these *S*s were helped more by the interpolated French than were the separated *S*s. Since translated equivalents have comparatively different meanings for the separated *S*s, interpolated translations should have shown less associative facilitation and possibly more interference with the original English list, as was the case.

This interpretation has its limitations, however, since the data in Table 2 indicate that there is no difference in degree of

TABLE 1
Semantic Differential Comparisons

Contexts	N	Mean English-French Profile Separations[a]	Variance		t tests[b]	p values
Fused (F)	9	3.19	0.38	F-S:	2.24	<.05
Separated (S)	23	3.93	1.23	F-B:	2.64	<.03
Bicultural (B)	15	4.22	1.47	F-U:	<1	n.s.
Unicultural (U)	8	3.39	0.33	B-U:	2.13	<.06

[a]Entries are mean D scores (7). The larger the mean, the greater the semantic differences between languages.

[b]Where the variances were not homogeneous, p values were determined according to a formula suggested by Edwards (1, p. 273 ff). All t tests in this and the following tables are 2-tailed tests of significance.

TABLE 2
Associative-Independence Comparisons

Contexts	N	Mean Independence Indices[a]	Variance		t tests	p values
Fused (F)	9	+3.44	9.75	F-S:	2.65	<.02
Separated (S)	23	+0.13	11.23	F-B:	2.12	<.05
Bicultural (B)	15	+0.60	10.86	F-U:	2.55	<.02
Unicultural (U)	8	−0.75	12.28	B-U:	<1	n.s.

[a]The closer the scores approach zero, the more between-language associative independence indicated. A constant of 8 was added to each score to eliminate negative values before variances were computed.

associative independence between bilinguals with bicultural and those with unicultural experiences. In fact, both these subgroups means are significantly different from that of the fused group. This finding suggests that experience in separated contexts of either a bicultural or unicultural nature enhances the associative independence of translated equivalents in the bilingual's two languages, as compared to experience in fused acquisition contexts.

TABLE 3
Switching Facility Comparisons

Contexts	*N*	Mean Translation Speed[a]	Variance		*t* test	*p* values
Fused (F)[b]	7	125.08	112.43	F-S:	<1	n.s.
Separated (S)	23	125.69	288.65	F-B:	<1	n.s.
Bicultural (B)	15	124.59	303.42	F-U:	<1	n.s.
Unicultural (U)	8	127.76	254.62	B-U:	<1	n.s.

[a]Entries, in hundredths of a second, are group means. The larger the mean, the slower the group is in translating into French and into English.

[b]Two *S*s were not available for this test.

Table 3 makes it clear that there were no differences between groups in facility of switching from one language to the other, a finding contrary to predictions. There is no immediately obvious interpretation for this lack of difference between groups, other than the possible lack of sensitivity of our measuring device. Accepting the finding as reliable, one may speculate that *S*s in both groups have had equal experience in translating but possibly different types of experience. The fused *S*s, by definition, have learned their two languages in contexts that encourage translation. On the other hand, a bilingual who has contacts with two separate linguistic communities may often be called on to recount his experiences with members of both communities. In a sense, he becomes the liaison between two linguistic communities and he may learn to use concepts which have meaningful equivalents for members of both communities.

When requested to translate, *S*s in the two groups demonstrate similar facility to switch. In view of the other findings, however, the fused and separated *S*s appear to make different use of the translation process. The fused *S*s made use of the interpolated translations in the learning task and accordingly showed improvement in their retention scores. It is possible, although no attention was paid to this feature in the collection of data, that the separated *S*s were less aware that actual translations were being interpolated than were the fused *S*s. Stated differently, the fused *S*s may have been more set to translate than were the separated *S*s.

In conclusion, we have been able to demonstrate, within the limitations of the small sample of *S*s studied, that language-acquisition context does influence the functional separation of the bilingual's two languages in certain respects. The theory of coordinate and compound language systems has been given empirical support and the defining characteristics of these systems have been extended. The co-ordinate bilinguals, in contrast to the compound bilinguals, appear to have more functionally independent language systems. If their coordinateness has been developed through experience in culturally distinctive contexts, they will have comparatively different meanings for concepts translated into their two languages. Coordinate and compound bilinguals, however, appear to have equal facility in switching from one language to the other.

SUMMARY

Bilinguals were classified as having learned their two languages in either separated or fused contexts. It was hypothesized that experience in separated as compared with fused language-acquisition contexts comparatively enhances the effectively separated use of the bilingual's two languages.

It was found that experience in separated contexts comparatively increases the associative independence of translated equivalents in the bilingual's two languages. If the bilingual has learned his two languages in culturally distinctive contexts, the semantic differences between translated equivalents is comparatively increased.

There was no difference found in facility to switch from one language to the other that can be attributed to contextual influences.

The findings were related to the theory of compound and coordinate bilingual language systems.

NOTES

This research was supported in part by the Canadian Defence Research Board, Grant Number D77-94-01-10, and in part by N. R. C. Grant A. P. 17.

[1]In 1915, Epstein (2) considered bilingualism in terms of such a psychological theory, but did not experimentally test its applicability.

[2]Essentially the same reasoning underlies the "direct method" of language teaching. The direct method theorists maintain that the acquired language should be learned directly from association with environmental events without the mediation of the native language. When learning French as a second language, one should never link "pomme" with "apple" but should link "pomme" directly with the perceived environmental event. In contrast to the "indirect" method which utilizes translation as an aid in acquisition, the direct method is purported to develop "pure" bilingualism, the ability to move from one linguistic and semantic world of experience to another with comparatively little interference.

[3]In view of our method of selecting *S*s (see 6) where an attempt was made to draw equal numbers of both types, one may safely generalize that it is comparatively easier for bilinguals with separated acquisition contexts to attain bilingual balance.

REFERENCES

1. Edwards, A. L. Statistical methods for the behavioral sciences. New York: Rinehart, 1954.
2. Epstein, I. La pensée et la polyglossie. Paris: Payot, approx. 1915.
3. Ervin, S. M. The verbal behavior of bilinguals: the effect of the language of report upon the T. A. T. stories of adult French

bilinguals. Unpublished dissertation, Univer. of Michigan, 1955.
4. Ervin, S. M., and Osgood, C. E. Second language learning and bilingualism. In C. E. Osgood and T. A. Sebeok (Eds.), *Psycholinguistics*. *J. abnorm. soc. Psychol.*, *Suppl.*, 1954. Pp. 139-146.
5. Lambert, W. E. Measurement of the linguistic dominance of bilinguals. *J. abnorm. soc. Psychol.*, 1955, 50, 197-200.
6. Lambert, W. E., Havelka, J., and Gardner, R. C. Linguistic manifestations of bilingualism. *Am. J. Psychol.*, 1959, 72 77-82. [In this volume, pp. 63-71.]
7. Osgood, C. E. The nature and measurement of meaning. *Psychol. Bull.*, 1952, 49, 197-237.
8. Osgood, C. E., and Luria, Z. A blind analysis of a case of multiple personality using the semantic differential. *J. abnorm. soc. Psychol.*, 1954, 49, 579-591.
9. Weinreich, U. *Languages in contact*. New York: Linguistic Circle of New York, 1953.

6 Linguistic Manifestations of Bilingualism

In Collaboration with J. Havelka and R. C. Gardner

Social scientists are beginning to recognize that bilingualism offers a unique opportunity for the study of language-behavior. Second-language acquisition, in contrast to the infant's learning of his first language, permits closer experimental observation, as well as phenomenological analysis by the learner himself, of the development of linguistic skills. In this sense the bilingual condition places one type of language-acquisition in slower motion for the observer. Before social scientists can take full advantage of bilingualism, however, the phenomenon must be systematically defined and its influence on verbal behavior assessed.

Analysts of the acquisition of a second language have used the term 'automatic' to describe the linguistic behavior of those using a language with fluency in contrast to the hesitancy of others beginning the study of a second language.[1] As one develops skill, he becomes less dependent on translation and reacts automatically in the new language. When we use a language automatically, it appears, we do not attend to the language-process itself but to the organization and appropriateness of content.

The chief characteristic of automatic behavior is speed of response, a commonly accepted index of habit-strength. In an earlier study with English-French bilinguals we have made use of this speed-variable as a behavioral measure of bilinguals' comparative automaticity in their two languages.[2] The actual technique involved the use of eight finger-keys, the stems of which were differently colored, an exposure-apparatus which directed *S* to depress a particular key with directions appearing randomly in either of two languages, and a chronoscope measuring speed of response. The direction 'left, red,' for example, is presented and *S*'s speed of response is measured; later in the series, *S* is directed in French to push the same key. After 12 practice-trials, 32 directions are given and *S*'s comparative speed of response in his two languages is determined.

The measuring-technique is a behavioral analogue of linguistic automaticity as described by language-theorists. With respect to reliability, two measures of automaticity were obtained from 16 *S*s on different days and the product-moment correlation of mean difference-scores (French speed minus English speed) was 0.74.[3] The technique distinguishes *S*s whose language-histories suggest probable differences in their comparative linguistic skills and it also correlates significantly with *S*'s comparative associational fluencies in their two languages.[4]

Making use of this measure, bilinguals can be conveniently grouped as dominants, those showing a statistically significant difference in speed of response between their two languages, and balanced, those showing similar speed of response in both native and second languages. Earlier research focused attention on those linguistic characteristics which differentiate the dominant from the balanced bilinguals, allowing us to describe the changes which occur as one develops skill in the use of a second language.[5] Various developmental stages of skill have been isolated by analyzing the associations *S*s give to stimulus-words presented in the two languages. These stages of development, which may be considered as successive steps in the acquisition of a second language, have indicated that a vocabulary-skill, as defined by a cluster of tests, is the easiest to develop, while a factor involving acquaintance with the second culture, defined by a different grouping of measures, constitutes the most resistent barrier to full mastery of the second language.

The purpose of the present study is to develop further a series of behavioral measures of bilingualism.

Procedure. The *S*s used in the present investigation were 43 English-French bilinguals, all college- or university-level students who had not only studied both languages but had had some experience speaking in both. This restriction on speaking ability was introduced to eliminate those extremely dominant in one language whose inclusion would unduly emphasize differences between balanced and dominant *S*s.

The *S*s were recruited by asking members of the French Department of McGill University for students who appeared bilingual and by contacting other departments for known bilingual students. These *S*s, who were paid for their time, willingly gave names of other appropriate *S*s. Each *S* was tested for a total of 3 to 4 hr., distributed over different days. The directions and procedures were read by each *S* and were summarized orally by E. The directions were given in English, but the procedural examples were always repeated in French.

Thirty *S*s met our criteria for bilingual balance and 13 were dominant in either French or English. For the purpose of the present analysis, the *S*s were considered as varying in extent of bilingualism along a continuum ranging from dominance in one language through balance to dominance in the other language. For each *S*, the mean reaction-time to English directions was subtracted from the mean time of responding to French directions. The *S* with the largest difference-score fell at one dominant extreme, depending on which language was dominant, and the *S* with the smallest difference-score fell nearer the balance point on the continuum. Pearson product-moment correlations were calculated between the degree of bilingualism and other linguistic measures to be described below. 'Degree of bilingualism' refers to the difference-scores which reflect the direction and the magnitude of the difference between reaction-times to French and English directions, indicating in which language *S* responds more quickly. Thus, the perfectly balanced bilingual would obtain a difference-score of zero, and the person more proficient in French would have a negative score.

Results. (1) Speed of word-recognition. In the light of studies relating recognitive thresholds to familiarity of words, our first speculation was that extent of bilingualism should manifest itself in perceptual as well as response-processes.[6] As a test, each *S* viewed tachistoscopically 20 English and 20 French words presented in a shuffled order. Thresholds of recognition were determined by the common procedure of increasing the time of presentation until a word was correctly reported. The words varied in content between languages but were matched for length and frequency of occurrence. The *S*s were given four practice-words and were encouraged to guess or to spell the word if it was difficult to pronounce. It was our prediction that the closer bilinguals approach balance in the test of speed of responding, the more likely they are to have similar recognitive thresholds for words in their two languages. Average thresholds for each language were determined and difference-scores between-language (French exposure-time minus English exposure-time) computed for all *S*s. The product-moment correlation between degree of bilingualism and comparative recognitive thresholds is 0.46, significant at beyond the 1% level. It appears, then, that the degree of bilingualism is reflected in the perceptual processes.

(2) Facility in word-completion. In an earlier study, a different group of bilinguals were asked to give continuous free associations to French and English stimulus-words with the restriction that associations be made in the same language as the stimulus-word.[7] A high positive correlation, $r = 0.82$, between degree of bilingualism and degree of bilingual fluency was obtained. Since such a high correlation had been found, it seemed advisable to examine further the relation of bilingualism to associational fluency. Word-completion tasks, such as crossword puzzles, call for an ability to make active use of one's vocabulary. We predicted that the closer a bilingual approaches balance, the more nearly equal will be his use of his vocabularies in both languages. As a test, we presented *S*s with a series of two-letter sequences which are common beginnings for words in both languages, such as 'vi', common to 'ville' or 'victory.' The *S*s were requested to make as many completions of each stimulus as possible in a 60-sec. period and were encouraged to make their completions in both languages. Differences between the total number of English and French responses were computed for each *S*. As predicted, there was a positive correlation between degree of bilingualism and comparative word-completion facilities; $r = 0.58$, significant at beyond the 1% level.

(3) Facility in word-detection. We speculated further that bilingualism would express itself in the facility of finding embedded English and French words. The *S*s were instructed to find English or French words in a series of letters, e.g. DANSONODEND where dans, ans, de, en are meaningful French words, no, nod, node, ode, end are meaningful English words, and an, son, on could be meaningful in either language depending upon how they are pronounced. In constructing these stimulus-series of letters, attention was given to the commonality of words embedded, their number in each language, and their position in the series. After a practice-example, where the *S*s

were instructed to read from left to right, four test-stimuli were presented tachistoscopically for four consecutive 1-sec. intervals. The score assigned each *S* was the percentage of English words detected minus the percentage of French words detected. We predicted that comparative facility in the detection of words would correlate positively with degree of bilingualism. It did, with an $\underline{r} = 0.42$, significant beyond the 1% level.

(4) Facility in reading. We reasoned that bilingualism should express itself in the comparative speed of reading words in both languages. Whereas word-recognition was measured by the time for a stimulus-word to take on meaning, reading-speed involves the time to make verbalized responses to words above the recognitive-threshold. Twenty commonly-occurring English words intermixed with their French equivalents were presented one at a time in a Rantchburg exposure-apparatus. The *S*s were asked to read each word as quickly as possible. The verbal response was picked up by a sensitive microphone in circuit with a chronoscope. The time taken to start each response was measured in hundredths of a second.[8] As predicted, the comparative facility in reading (French reaction-time minus English reaction-time) was positively correlated with degree of bilingualism, with $\underline{r} = 0.46$, significant beyond the 1% level.

(5) Verbal-response set. French-English bilinguals are often confronted with stimulus-words common to both language-systems, such as 'silence,' 'chance,' 'important,' which have quite different pronunciations. An individual dominant in English would be likely to perceive and read these words in English and a French dominant would be likely to read them in French. We presumed that the more closely an individual approaches bilingual balance, the less would he be set to respond in one language rather than the other. Given a series of such stimulus-words, he should respond equally often in both languages. To test for this type of verbal-response set, 14 stimulus-words which are spelled the same in both languages were randomly placed in the longer list of French and English words described in the immediately preceding section. It will be recalled that the *S*s were instructed to read these words as quickly as possible. For the 14 stimulus-words common to both languages, note was taken of whether a French or an English pronunciation was given to them and difference-scores (the number of English minus the number of French responses) were presumed to indicate in which language, if either, an *S* was set to respond.

As predicted, the degree and direction of response-set was positively correlated with the degree of bilingualism; $\underline{r} = 0.45$, significant beyond the 1% level.

(6) Facility in translation. Bilinguals, by definition, have learned two symbols for each referent and there should be some functional connection between the bilingual's two sets of symbols. We argued that bilingualism should express itself in the facility of switching from one symbol to the other; the more balanced a bilingual, the more similar should be his translation times into French and English. To measure this facility in translation, the procedure used for determining skill in reading, as described above, was extended. After the *S*s had read the 40 English and French words, the list was presented again and they were asked to translate each word into its other-language equivalent. Speed of translation was measured in terms of the resulting reaction-times. The score assigned each *S* was the average time for translation from English to French minus the average time for translation from French to English. The correlation between degree of bilingualism and comparative speed of translation is not significantly different from zero, with $\underline{r} = 0.18$.

Because our prediction was not supported by the data derived from facility in translation, we looked more carefully at the logic underlying the process of translation as well as the data themselves. Not all the *S*s showed the same direction of difference in both reading and translating. In fact, 23 *S*s showed a greater average speed of reading in one of their languages and also a greater average speed of translation into that language, but 20 *S*s with a greater average speed of reading in one language were faster translating into their other language. The obvious assumption is that one would be faster translating into his dominant language (or, if balanced, his native language) since response in the dominant language is the more automatic, and since the response takes more time than perceiving. It appears, however, that a good proportion of bilinguals are more skilled in translating into the acquired language.

We can only speculate about the reasons for this phenomenon until it is systematically studied. In brief, our speculation is that an individual may be passive or active in the acquisition of a second language. If passive, he may learn to translate into his dominant language and thereby transform unknown symbols, when encountered, into known ones. An active learner may attempt to reduce the number of unknown symbols and learn to translate into the acquired or less-dominant language. The passive learner, dominant in English, would look up the word 'chien' when he encounters it, while the hypothetical active learner would ask himself how the French say or write 'dog,' and look it up. The former would use a French to English and the latter an English to French dictionary. Our guess is that differences in attitudinal and motivational variables underlie the two types of orientation. The data on hand, of course, were not collected with this idea in mind, but we are encouraged to note that the five *S*s who show a greater mean speed of reading in French and who have a greater mean speed of translation into English are all French natives who have come to an English university for training. For these *S*s, acquiring English in an active manner is of clear instrumental value.

In conclusion, it appears that bilingualism has a pervasive influence throughout various aspects of verbal behavior. It is exhibited in thresholds of word-recognition, facility for word-completion and word-detection, response-sets, and speed of reading, but not in speed of translation. The closer an individual approaches bilingual balance, the more he will be able to perceive and read words in both languages with similar speeds, to associate in both languages with similar fluency, to make active use of his vocabularies in both languages, and to be set to verbalize in both languages. If he is dominant in French, let us say, on one of these measures, then he will be dominant in French on all of them.

When consideration is given to the potential usefulness of these findings for measuring bilingualism, the question of the independence of the various measures arises. Table I gives the intercorrelations of all seven measures.

The range of correlations is generally small, except for the measures involving translation, and an examination of the correlation-matrix indicates that a single factor is sufficient to describe all associations. Factor loadings, computed by the centroid method, are presented at the right of Table I. Although a second factor was extracted, it is doubtful that this factor is amenable to any meaningful interpretation. It seems appropriate to conclude that the seven measures developed here are common tests of the relative strength of

TABLE I
Correlation-Matrix of Bilingual Measures
(All correlation are based on an N of 43.)

Measures	Measures 2	3	4	5	6	7	Centroid factor loadings I	II
(1) Automaticity	.46*	.45	.58	.46	.18	.42	.68	.04
(2) Recognition-Speed		.40	.58	.45	.12	.38	.65	.09
(3) Response-Set			.68	.68	.06	.46	.75	.22
(4) Word-Completion				.53	.35	.65	.88	-.22
(5) Reading-Speed					.02	.31	.68	.44
(6) Translation-Speed						.15	.27	-.37
(7) Word-Detection							.66	-.26

*With 40 df., an r of 0.30 is significant at the 5% level of confidence and an r of 0.39 is significant at the 1% level.

English and French in this group of bilinguals. The factor loadings indicate that word-completion and response-set are direct measures and easily administered indices of bilingualism which are convenient substitutes for measurement by automaticity.

SUMMARY

English-French bilinguals were given a series of tests to determine the degree of correlation among various aspects of their linguistic behavior. It was found that their relative superiority in French or English is manifested in comparative thresholds for word-recognition, facility in word-completion and word-detection, response-sets, and speed of reading, but not in speed of translation. Intercorrelations indicate that a single dimension underlies these various measures, suggesting that bilingualism is reflected in many aspects of linguistic behavior.

NOTES

This research was supported in part by the Canadian Defence Research Board, Grant D77-94-01-10, and in part by N.R.C. Grant A.P.17. Our thanks are due Dr. G.A. Ferguson for his assistance in this study.

[1] H.B. Dunkel, Second-Language Learning, 1948, 46 ff.; J. Warshaw, Automatic reactions in practical foreign language work, Mod. Language J., 9, 1924, 151-158.

[2] See W.E. Lambert, Measurement of the linguistic dominance of bilinguals, J. abnorm. soc. Psychol., 50, 1955, 197-200.

[3] From a comparison of the first and last 16 responses of a larger group of *S*s it appears that reliability can be increased by giving much more practice; the last 16 responses are typically more stable and indicate more distinctly the comparative extent of experience with the two languages.

[4] Lambert, op. cit., 199.

[5] Lambert, Developmental aspects of second-language acquisition, J. soc. Psychol., 43, 1956, 83-104.

[6] D.H. Howes and R.L. Solomon, Visual duration threshold as a function of word probability, J. exp. Psychol., 41, 1951, 401-410; K.A. Preston, The speed of word perception and its relation to reading ability, J. gen. Psychol., 13, 1935, 199-203.

[7] Lambert, op. cit., 1955, 83-90.

[8] Although the voice-key was constructed for this investigation by an electronics specialist, pretests indicated that the results would depend on the types of words used as well as *S*'s manner of pronunciation. We chose words for both languages which start with explosive consonants and the *S*s were trained to enunciate clearly, but the results were still not as precise as desired. Nevertheless, we are confident that mean scores for 20 stimulus-words in each language are comparable for the present purpose.

7 A Pilot Study of Aphasia Among Bilinguals

In Collaboration with S. Fillenbaum

The study of aphasia among people who speak more than one language has been undertaken in the main by specialists in aphasia, and several case reviews have been compiled. The course of aphasia among polygots has been interpreted in terms of several different principles. First, cases have been reported which support the "rule of Ribot" (6, p. 76), which states that linguistic habits acquired early, as in childhood, are more resistant to aphasic damage than those acquired subsequently. The "mother tongue" is not only learned first but presumably is built up with more emotional meaning, thereby increasing its relative strength. An important paper by Pitres (5) offered a different generalization in order to account for his own observations of the effect of aphasia on polygots. In essence, Pitres' is a habit strength principle which states that the language or languages most used before the aphasic insult will be the first to recover. The less well practised languages will be recovered less quickly and, if a language has been used very little before aphasia, that language might not be remembered or used at all afterward. Minkowski (4) presented several cases of bilingual aphasics which he proposed as exceptions to Pitres' principle and which also appear to be exceptions to the Ribot rule. Minkowski showed that an emotional or affective factor related to the use of one language might account for the survival of that language after the polyglot had suffered an aphasic insult. In short, cases have been presented which agree, and others which conflict with each principle. The conservative conclusion must be that aphasia can have various effects on the bilingual's languages, the particular post-aphasic pattern probably depending in some complex fashion on: the order in which the languages were learned, the comparative levels of skill attained in each, and the affective value each language has for the individual.

The study of the effects of an aphasic insult on the languages of a polyglot is also of interest and value to those who are primarily concerned with bilingualism itself. Thus, for example, the recent work of Weinreich (6), which indicates the relevance of data from polyglot aphasics to various theories about the verbal behavior of the "bilingual individual," makes it clear that our understanding of bilingualism would be greatly improved if data were systematically collected about the course of aphasia in bilingual patients.

Certain findings from our own and other research on bilingualism led us to a consideration of the data on aphasics. The point of departure was an hypothesis, developed by Weinreich (6) and Ervin and Osgood (1), which maintains that some bilinguals develop the same meaning for translated equivalents in their two languages, while others develop a different meaning for the concept in each language. The former would be characteristic of the "compound" bilingual and the latter of the "co-ordinate" bilingual for whom, theoretically, the two languages, or certain elements of the languages would function independently. This hypothesis is of value in understanding differences among bilinguals in their ease of switching from one language to the other, their control of interferences from the other language in any verbal situation, and their abilities to think and behave appropriately in the different linguistic contexts. This hypothesis was extended in a study by Lambert, Havelka, and Crosby (2) where it was concluded that the learning contexts in which the bilingual's two languages are acquired may well determine the functional independence of the languages. The more the learning contexts are "separated," either in time, cultural distinctiveness, or in distinctiveness of the setting of habitual usage, the more likely it is that bilingual "co-ordinateness" will develop.

There is the possibility that the functional relations of the bilingual's two languages have some systematic neural representation in those areas of the brain necessary to the functioning of language. The nature of this neural representation is necessarily largely a matter for speculation in view of how little is now known about language centres in the human brain. Our notion was that co-ordinate bilinguals should have more functionally separated neural structures underlying their languages than should compound bilinguals. Thus, the concepts "house" and "maison" which are more functionally independent for co-ordinate than for compound bilinguals would be "stored" in neural elements which have some sort of greater functional discreteness for the co-ordinate bilinguals.

It follows from this line of reasoning that any specific brain damage resulting in aphasia would be likely to affect all languages of the compound bilingual, but should lead to more selective disturbances for co-ordinate bilinguals. Thus, one would predict that if factors such as size and locus of brain damage could be held constant, co-ordinate bilinguals would be more likely to show aphasic damage in one language system, while compound bilinguals would be more likely to show aphasic damage in all languages known. It should be recognized that factors of size and locus of damage can never be "held constant," and that even with a large sample of patients only general trends can be expected to emerge from a study of bilingual aphasics.

The present work sought to examine some data on aphasia in polyglots, to determine (a) if any relation exists between language learning contexts and the nature of the aphasic disorder, and (b) to what extent these data fit the general principles previously suggested, particularly the principles of primacy and "habit strength." Most reported cases on polyglot aphasics are anecdotal and incomplete: factual information on the language proficiencies of a patient before brain damage is rarely available. Such information as there is, in nearly every case, is based on the recollections of the patient or his family. Furthermore, the hospital environment in most communities is unilingual and the bilingual aphasic's first speech efforts may be forced into the language spoken in the hospital, with relearning taking place in that language only.

As source material we used the cases of European polyglot aphasics presented in a recent review by Leischner (3), and cases of polyglot aphasics obtained from several hospitals and rehabilitation centres in Montreal. In the collection of our own fourteen cases we were no more successful in obtaining complete information than other researchers. Interviews were held with the patient and with members of his family in an attempt to elicit data on his premorbid and present language skills. Information was obtained as to the language history of the patient, the times, conditions, and circumstances of acquisition, and use of the different languages, and the relative fluencies of the patient in each language. Each patient was interviewed to determine the present state of his language skills. Conversation was carried out in both (or all) languages known, and attention was paid to his expressive and receptive difficulties in each, his ability to switch languages spontaneously or on demand, to answer questions, to use words, and to read in each language.[1]

The extent to which the data fit such rules as a habit strength or primacy principle is summarized in Table I, where European and Montreal cases are kept separate. It can be seen that the Montreal cases and European cases fall into substantially different patterns. The European cases in most instances fail to support either a primacy or a habit strength principle, while in contrast most of the Montreal

TABLE I
Summary of Instances of Support for Various Principles

	Primacy (Ribot)		Habit strength (Pitres)		Affective (Minkowski)
	Pro	Con	Pro	Con	Pro
European cases	5	17	6	14	7
Montreal cases	8	2	9	2	1

cases are consistent with both principles (χ^2 values, corrected for continuity, for the difference between European cases and Montreal cases are 7.13, $p < .01$ (primacy) and 5.70, $p < .02$ (habit strength) respectively). In the European data there is evidence in seven cases for some affective factor which might account for the better survival of the language not first or better learned; in the Montreal data the one instance clearly involving some affective factor supports the importance of the first learned language. These apparent differences might be due to differences in the selection of cases: we investigated all bilingual aphasics available, cases reported in the literature may be the more dramatic ones taken as exceptions to expectation. We have no way of testing such a possibility.

The differences may also be interpreted, however, as evidence in favor of our original hypothesis. The typical pattern in the

European patients is that the first learned language had been used for the greater (or greatest) period of time prior to aphasia, but a second language had also been acquired and used in the period prior to the aphasia. The language surviving aphasia best is characteristically a secondarily acquired language, a fact which conflicts with Ribot's generalization (primacy principle) and, to the extent that the second language is less known and used with less facility, with Pitres' (habit strength) principle as well. For the European patients the second language is typically learned in a context distinctly separated from the first, that is, the two languages are characteristically learned in a co-ordinate fashion. In Europe the polyglot may be forced to master the language of the new country of residence (its only language) and accordingly its acquisition (and retention after aphasia) will be of great personal importance. The seven cases in which an affective factor is evident suggest that a language which is emotionally important to the individual, although not used as often as another, may be the only language retained, or the one least damaged after aphasia. The typical Montreal case indicates that the first-learned language is also the one most used until the time of aphasia while the other language, learned early in life and used concurrently with the first, typically is not used as frequently as the first language. After aphasia, both languages are damaged but retain the order of dominance which was developed prior to aphasia. The affective factor is less apparent, perhaps because in Montreal a greater freedom of use of all languages known is possible. It is likely that the Montreal scene encourages the development of bilingual compoundedness since essentially the same context for language learning is probably more likely to be used for all languages acquired. If we assume that the European and Montreal scenes encourage co-ordinate and compound bilingualism respectively, then the data offer some support for our hypothesis since the Montreal cases typically show a generalized disorder affecting both languages, while the European cases typically show a more specific-language disorder following aphasia.

A set of cases collected before the turn of the century by Pitres (5) was not mentioned or included in Leischner's 1948 review. Pitres' cases are of particular interest for our purposes because they were gathered in the southwest section of France, and because they include in all instances people who used French along with one or more languages, such as patois, Basque, Spanish, and Italian. In six cases, French was used most frequently and, with the exception of brief periods in two cases, was used continually throughout the patients' lives in France. It will be noted in Table II that these cases

TABLE II
Pitres' Cases of Polyglot Aphasics

Primacy (Ribot)		Habit strength (Pitres)	
Pro	Con	Pro	Con
5	1	6	0

are strikingly similar to the Montreal cases in that both the Ribot and the Pitres principles are consistently supported, that is, the first learned language is the most used and also the one which returns first after aphasia. The generalization therefore seems appropriate that the language (or languages) which bilinguals use continuously from early life will probably be least vulnerable to aphasia. The Montreal cases are also consistent with this generalization in that two languages are more likely to be learned early in life and used concurrently in Quebec.

The Pitres cases also allow one further observation. The French people in the southwest section of France may learn a local patois and French in essentially the same context, much as Canadians may learn two languages in Montreal. That is, the patois and French may become "compounded" for these bilinguals. We would predict, then, that these two languages should be similarly affected by aphasia. Three of Pitres' patients are polyglots with French and patois as two of their languages. Two of the patients suffered complete aphasic loss for a long period during which both languages did not return, and after three years, in each case, French was only poorly used while the patois was not used at all. It appears that language training after aphasia was carried out in French, and the difference between the ability to use the two languages after this long period may have been due to the training only. It is possible that these languages were learned as a compound system and that both were similarly affected (in this case equally damaged) by the aphasia, as our theory would predict. The third case is also consistent with expectations. This person learned French and patois from early years and later acquired several other languages in work situations. Six months following aphasia this patient was able to use both French and the patois fairly well, but still could neither understand nor use the other languages.

In conclusion, although the results are consistent with the theoretical analysis of compound and co-ordinate bilingualism, much more detailed information about the language history of each patient is needed before alternative interpretations of the results can be excluded. For example, we argued that Montreal and that region of France where a local patois is used are likely to be situations which encourage the development of compound bilingualism. These social environments also allow the continual and concurrent use of two or more languages, and the difference in freedom of usage of languages known may also account for the differences in the effects of aphasia noted when Leischner's "European" cases are compared with our own cases and with those of Pitres.

SUMMARY

Several studies of the effects of aphasia among people who use more than one language were reviewed and three generalizations about the effects of aphasia in these cases were discussed. Classical cases of polyglot aphasics and new cases compiled in Montreal were analysed in order to test the hypothesis that the functional dependence or independence of polyglots' languages, determined by the manner in which the languages were originally learned, will determine, in part, how the languages are affected by an aphasic insult. Although the findings, derived from the analysis of cases, are consistent with the theoretical analysis, alternative interpretations cannot be excluded with the data available at present.

NOTES

This research was supported by the Defence Research Board of Canada Grant D77-94-01-10. The members of the S. S. R. C. seminar on aphasia, held in Boston in 1958, assisted us with criticisms and suggestions for expanding an earlier version of this paper.

[1] All case materials analysed for this study will be found in Appendices (I-III) which can be obtained from the first author. Translations of the cited works of Minkowski (4) and Pitres (5) are also available.

REFERENCES

1. Ervin, S. M., and Osgood, C. E. Second language learning and bilingualism. In C. E. Osgood and T. A. Sebeok (Eds.), Psycholinguistics. J. abnorm. soc. Psychol., Suppl., 1954, 139-146.
2. Lambert, W. E., Havelka, J., and Crosby, C. The influence of language-acquisition contexts on bilingualism. J. abnorm. soc. Psychol., 1958, 56, 239-244. [In this volume, pp. 51-62.]
3. Leischner, A. Ueber die Aphasie der Mehrsprachigen. Archiv für Psychiatrie und Nervenkrankheiten, 1948, 180, 731-775.
4. Minkowski, M. Sur un cas d'aphasie chez un polyglotte. Revue neurologique, 1928, 35, 361-366.
5. Pitres, A. Etude sur l'aphasie chez les polyglottes. Revue de médicine, 1895, 15, 873-899.
6. Weinreich, U. Languages in contact. New York: Linguistic Circle of New York, 1953.

8 Evaluational Reactions to Spoken Languages

In Collaboration with R. C. Hodgson, R. C. Gardner, and S. Fillenbaum

Spoken language is an identifying feature of members of a national or cultural group and any listener's attitude toward members of a particular group should generalize to the language they use. From this viewpoint, evaluational reactions to a spoken language should be similar to those prompted by interaction with individuals who are perceived as members of the group that uses it, but because the use of the language is one aspect of behavior common to a variety of individuals, hearing the language is likely to arouse mainly generalized or stereotyped characteristics of the group. Thus, when one hears a radio broadcast of an international meeting and encounters passages of a foreign language, one's evaluational reactions to the communication are attributable, in part, to the language used and likely reflect generalized attitudinal reactions to the group that uses it.

The purpose of the present investigation was to determine the significance spoken language has for listeners by analyzing their evaluational reactions to English and French. Since we were interested in reactions that are attributable primarily to the language itself, we attempted to minimize the effects of both the voice of the speaker and his message by employing bilingual speakers reading the same message in two languages. In view of previous studies (see Licklider and Miller, 1951, p. 1070f) which have shown that evaluations of personality based solely upon voice have little or no reliability, it was predicted that the differences in the favorableness of any *S*'s evaluations of the French and English guises of speakers would reflect his attitude toward members of his own and members of the other language group. The study was carried out with *S*s living in Montreal, a community whose history centers largely in a French-English schism which is perhaps as socially significant for residents of the Province of Quebec as that between the North and the South is for Southerners in the United States.

METHOD

Procedure

A 21/2 min. passage of French prose of a philosophical nature was translated into fluent English and tape recordings were made of the voices of four male bilinguals each of whom read both French and English versions of the passage. Recordings were also made of the voices of two other men, one reading the passage in English, the other in French. There were, then, 10 taped voices, four of which were "matched," each speaker using both languages, and two used as "filler" voices and for practice. The 10 voices were presented to *S*s in alternating French-English order starting with the two filler voices and allowing the maximum possible interval between successive presentations of the English and French guises of any speaker. Evaluational reactions to the matched voices only were examined.

The study was introduced as an experimental investigation of the extent to which peoples' judgments about a speaker are determined by his voice and *S*s were reminded of the common phenomenon of having a voice on the radio or telephone summon up a picture in the listener's mind of the person speaking. *S*s were <u>not</u> told that they were going to hear some of the voices twice, but rather that they would hear 10 recorded male voices, all reading the same passage, five in French and five in English. The two languages, it was said, were being used to give greater scope to the experiment. In this regard, *S*s were given copies of the French and English versions of the text they were to hear so that they could be acquainted with the message and the languages and be better prepared to pay attention only to the voices of the speakers. There was no indication that any *S* became aware of the fact that bilingual speakers were used.

The *S*s were also given a response sheet for each voice which directed them to rate each of 14 traits on 6 point scales ranging from "very little" (fort peu, for French *S*s) to "very much" (beaucoup). The traits used were: height (taille), good looks (attrait physique), leadership (apte à diriger), sense of humor (sens de l'humour), intelligence (intelligence), religiousness (pieux), self-confidence (confiance en soi), dependability (digne de confiance),[1] entertainingness (jovialité), kindness (bonté), ambition (ambition), sociability (sociabilité), character (caractère) and general likeability (est-ce qu'il est sympathique ?). Each voice was played once and *S*s rated that voice on the scales both while it was playing and during the 90 sec. interval between voices. At the bottom of each response sheet *S*s were asked to indicate in what occupation this man would likely be found.

Attached to the back of the 10 response sheets, facing down and covered by a blank sheet, were several questionnaires to be completed. This packaging of questionnaires and response sheets discouraged *S*s from looking ahead in the booklet and also permitted them to answer all items anonymously. *S*s were asked only their age, place of birth and religious affiliation. After the ratings were obtained on all voices, *S*s were directed to turn to the first questionnaire.

Importance ranks of traits. The list of traits used to describe each voice was presented again and *S*s were asked to rank the traits in terms of their desirableness in friends. It was felt that this information would offer a more personally relevant set of traits for analysis.

Prejudice scale. In view of its wide use as an index of generalized prejudice and ethnocentrism, we incorporated Forms 40 and 45 of the California F Scale (Adorno, Frenkel-Brunswik, Levinson, and Sanford, 1950) as one of the independent measures of attitude toward outgroups.

Attitude scales. *S*s were asked to complete 14 incomplete sentences designed to elicit attitudes toward both their own and the other language group. Examples are: English Canadians think. . ., Children of French Canadian parents. . .; The more I get to know French Canadians. . .; French Canadians. . .; English Canadians . . .; and The more I get to know English Canadians. . . . The items were translated into French for the French speaking *S*s. Two separate scores were assigned each *S* on the basis of his completions: an "attitude toward English group" score and an "attitude toward French group" score each comprising the number of favorable statements made minus the number of unfavorable statements made about each group. Two judges independently scored the items for each sample and the interjudge reliabilities are, for the English sample, r = .69 and r = .86 for attitudes toward English and French respectively and for the French sample r = .75, and r = .80.

Preference scale. *S*s indicated their preference for English or French Canadians as: marital partners, friends, neighbours, tenants, colleagues, and political candidates, by ranking which they would rather have for each case. Preference scores were the sum of differences in ranks given to French and English Canadians for all items.

Degree of bilingualism. We reasoned that differences in evaluational reactions to the English and French guises would be less pronounced for those *S*s who had experience with both languages and presumably both linguistic communities as well. *S*s checked their degree of facility in the use of the other group's language by indicating how well they could speak, read, and write, and whether they could do so: not at all, a little, fairly well, or fluently. An index of bilingualism was computed for each *S* by assigning zero to "not at all" 3 to "fluently." We doubled the score for ability to speak the language on the assumption that speaking experience was most important for the purpose of the study. A maximum score would be 12. A bimodal distribution of scores was obtained from both samples and both were split at the same point so that *S*s with scores 0 to 7 are categorized as being less bilingual and those with scores 8 to 12 as being more bilingual.

Subjects

The English speaking sample comprised 64 students, taking the first course in Psychology at McGill University, who volunteered to participate. The average age for the group was 18.8 years and both sexes were approximately equally represented.[2] The introduction and procedures were presented to the group by the first two authors in English. All *S*s used English as their school and primary social language, and all but nine who were born in Europe learned English as their first language.

The French speaking sample was made up of 66 male students in their final year at a classical French collège in Montreal who were at approximately the same educational level as the English sample, with an average age for the group of 18.2 years. The study was presented to the students by a professor of the collège and Wallace Lambert, in French. The experiment took the place of a regular lecture. All but one of these *S*s were born in Canada and all but four in the province of Quebec. All used French as their home, school, and primary social language. The faculty and students speak grammatically correct French, of course, but in general they have a distinctive French Canadian accent.

Speakers

Much care was taken to select appropriate speakers who could take on both French and English guises (in the sense of habitual manners of speaking). We chose from acquaintances in the English speaking community three bilinguals (Bla, Cou, and Leo) who spoke faultless English and yet were trained in French schools in Canada through the graduate level and used French in their homes, or, in the case of Leo, in social or work situations. Several recordings had to be made of each speaker to have errorless readings and in the case of Bla to perfect the pronunciation of a few English words. The final recordings of all four speakers were judged to be spoken in perfect French and English by three bilingual judges. The judges agreed that speakers Bla and Cou spoke with French Canadian accents and that Leo spoke with a marked French Canadian accent characteristic of those who work "in the bush" where, in fact, his style of pronunciation was acquired. The fourth speaker, Tri, spoke French with an accent that was judged as indistinguishable from that used in France. It was felt that these variations in accent and style would not only make the task more interesting for *S*s but would also lead to new aspects of the problem for further study, e.g., the reactions of both samples to Parisian French (Tri) and to caricatured French Canadian French (Leo). However, since the present study was not

TABLE 1

_t_ Values for Significance of Differences in Evaluations of English and French Guises of Speakers

Trait	English *S*s' Judgment of Speakers					French *S*s' Judgments of Speakers				
	Cou	Bla	Leo	Tri	Over-all	Cou	Bla	Leo	Tri	Over-all
Height	8.63**	4.67**	4.05**	2.59*	8.83**	5.50**	2.32*	2.41*	1.04	4.58**
Good Looks	7.16**	4.10**	2.66**	-.90	5.78**	7.50**	6.00**	7.26**	1.73	9.77**
Leadership	1.72	.69	1.41	-1.82	1.20	4.05**	9.32**	12.10**	.82	11.06**
Sense of Humor	-.58	-.14	2.25*	-3.48**	-2.16*	2.67**	.58	.64	-.30	1.40
Intelligence	1.44	.11	2.25*	1.98*	2.40*	4.54**	9.17**	11.73**	1.00	10.22**
Religiousness	-.67	-.33	-.26	1.81	.27	-1.79	-3.11**	-1.60	-1.14	-2.94**
Self-confidence	-.50	-.47	1.13	-1.33	-.69	5.37**	7.56**	10.00**	-2.00*	8.28**
Dependability	1.61	-.15	3.51**	2.74**	3.11**	2.89**	4.36**	7.50**	1.89	6.44**
Entertainingness	1.77	1.67	.00	-4.44**	-.84	.44	-.27	-.81	.22	-.21
Kindness	2.40*	2.47*	1.67	.74	3.37**	.10	-4.12**	-2.65*	-.74	-2.96**
Ambition	.45	2.43*	2.33*	.84	2.83**	3.06**	4.64**	7.53**	-1.53	5.89**
Sociability	.24	-.16	-.17	-4.13**	-1.44	3.44**	2.10*	3.47**	.29	3.72**
Character	3.07**	1.00	3.17**	.12	3.08**	3.95**	6.81**	8.68**	.31	8.51**
Likability	2.38*	.26	1.38	-1.21	1.22	1.83	.80	2.05*	.79	2.00*

Note.—Positive entries indicate that English guises are evaluated more favorably than French, and minus entries indicate a more favorable evaluation for French guises. This is so for both French and English *S*s' judgments.

*Significant at .05 level.

**Significant at .01 level, two-tailed tests.

designed to deal comprehensively with variations in accent, attention will be mainly given to over-all comparisons of French and English languages until the final section where accent differences will be discussed.

RESULTS

Favorableness of reactions: English *S*s' judgements. For each *S* on each of the 14 traits the difference (D) between the evaluations of the English and French guises of each speaker was noted, with account taken of the direction of the difference. These D values were then summed over the 4 speakers and over *S*s and the departure of the D scores from zero was examined. As can be seen in the over-all column of Table 1, the English *S*s evaluated the following seven traits significantly more favorably for the English than for the French guises: Height, Good looks, Intelligence, Dependability, Kindness, Ambition, and Character.[3] There were no significant differences in evaluations of Leadership, Religiousness, Self-confidence, Entertainingness, Sociability, and Likability. The French guises were evaluated significantly more favorably on Sense of Humor, but this finding is not clearcut since for one speaker the English guise was evaluated significantly more favorably on this trait. There was considerable consistency in the data for three of the four voices but the fourth (Tri) differed from the others on a number of traits.

*S*s had ranked the 14 traits for their desirability in friends. For each *S* two ΣD scores were obtained, one for the three traits judged most desirable and one for the three traits judged least desirable, by noting the difference in evaluations of the English and French guises for each set of traits. English *S*s evaluated the English guises significantly more favorably both for desirable traits ($\underline{t}_{55df} = 2.13$) and the less desirable traits ($\underline{t}_{53df} = 4.33$). There was no difference between the most and least desirable traits with regard to this preference ($\underline{t}_{49df} = 1.72$).

<u>Favorableness of reactions: French *S*s' judgments</u>. A similar analysis was carried out for the French *S*s. They evaluated the English guises of the speakers significantly <u>more</u> favorably than the French guises for the following 10 traits: Height, Good looks,

Leadership, Intelligence, Self-confidence, Dependability, Ambition, Sociability, Character, and Likability (Table 1). There was no difference in evaluations with regard to Sense of Humor and Entertainingness, and the French guises were evaluated significantly more favorably on Religiousness and Kindness. The results for three of the four speakers were consistent and again speaker Tri was the exception. The English guises were evaluated significantly more favorably both for the three most desirable traits ($t_{37} = 7.17$) and for the three least desirable traits ($t = 7.58$) and, as in the case of the English *S*s, there was no difference between the most and least desirable traits ($t < 1$).

TABLE 2

t Values for Significance of Mean Differences in Evaluations, English vs. French Judges

Trait	English Guises	French Guises
Height	3.76**	0.30
Good Looks	1.78	4.59**
Leadership	-2.55*	6.19**
Sense of Humor	0.62	3.10**
Intelligence	-2.87**	2.82**
Religiousness	2.44*	-0.15
Self-confidence	-3.02**	4.85**
Dependability	-1.32	1.97*
Entertainingness	-0.52	-0.42
Kindness	1.82	-3.18**
Ambition	-0.57	2.28*
Sociability	-1.87	2.14*
Character	-1.22	3.60**
Likability	-1.34	-0.31

Note. —Positive entries indicate that English judges evaluated a particular trait more favorably on the average than did French judges; minus entries indicate more favorable evaluation for French than English judges.

*indicates a *t* is significant at the .05 level, on two-tailed tests.

**indicates a *t* is significant at the .01 level, on two-tailed tests.

Favorableness of reactions: English *S*s' vs. French *S*s' judgments. The evaluations of the English guises given by the English judges were compared with the evaluations of the English guises given by the French judges, and a similar analysis was carried out for the evaluations of the French guises by the two groups of *S*s. Table 2 shows that for the English guises the English *S*s evaluated Height and Religiousness significantly more favorably than did the French *S*s. There were no differences between English and French *S*s with regard to: Good Looks, Sense of Humor, Dependability, Entertainingness, Kindness, Ambition, Sociability, Character, and Likability, and the French *S*s evaluated the English guises significantly more favorably than did the English *S*s on Leadership, Intelligence, and Self-confidence. The comparisons with respect to the French guises are also given in Table 2. It can be seen that the English *S*s evaluated the French guises significantly more favorably than did the French *S*s on the following nine traits: Good looks, Leadership, Sense of Humor, Intelligence, Self-confidence, Dependability, Ambition, Sociability, and Character. There were no differences in evaluations for: Height, Religion, Entertainingness, and Likability, and the French *S*s evaluated the French guises significantly more favorably than did the English *S*s on Kindness.

Attitudinal measures. The correlations between the various measures of attitude and the comparative favorableness of evaluations of guises are given in Table 3 for the English *S*s. It is striking that none of the attitude measures correlate with the degree of favorableness of reactions to English and French guises, with the exception of attitudes to their own group as reflected in responses to the incomplete sentences, a measure that just meets significance requirements.

Although the pattern of correlations is also low for the French *S*s, the comparative favorableness of evaluations of guises for this sample is somewhat more clearly related to both attitudes toward and preference for own group. It should be noted that the French *S*s on the average clearly showed more favorableness to English than French guises, in fact only 14% of the *S*s showed the expected trend of more favorable reactions to French over English versions. This was not the case for either the preference or attitude measures where the majority of *S*s (85% and 62% respectively) preferred and showed more favorable attitudes toward the French over the English

TABLE 3
Relation of Attitudinal Measures to Other Variables; English Sample

Variables	1	2	3	4	5	6
Prejudice (F scale)	X	.29*	-.22	-.01	.20	.19
Preference (Bogardus)		X	-.40**	.17	.13	.13
Attitudes to French (incomplete sentences)			X	-.18	-.04	-.08
Attitudes to English (incomplete sentences)				X	.26*	.25
Favorableness of evaluations (English over French; all traits)					X	.77**
Favorableness of evaluations (English over French; desirable traits)						X

Note.—The N's vary around 55 for all entries except Variable 6 where they drop to around 50.

*Significant at .05 level.

**Significant at .01 level.

TABLE 4
Relation of Attitudinal Measures to Other Variables; French Sample

Variables	1	2	3	4	5	6
Prejudice (F scale)	X	.17	.03	-.07	-.05	-.11
Preference (Bogardus)		X	.38**	-.45**	.26*	.27
Attitudes to French (incomplete sentences)			X	-.43**	.25*	.45**
Attitudes to English (incomplete sentences)				X	-.21	-.20
Favorableness of Evaluations (French over English; all traits)					X	.72**
Favorableness of Evaluations (French over English; desirable traits)						X

Note.—The N's vary around 55 for all entries except Variable 6 where they drop to around 35.

Since the French *S*s in general showed more favorableness to English than French guises, Variables 5 and 6 mainly represent degrees of nonfavorableness to English guises.

*Significant at .05 level.

**Significant at .01 level.

group. The significant correlations in Table 4 therefore indicate that the more the French *S*s show preference for and favorable attitudes toward their own group the less they overrate English guises.

The relation of bilingualism to other variables. *S*s categorized as having a high degree of bilingualism were compared with those having little experience or skill in the other group's language on all attitudinal variables as well as the comparative favorableness of evaluations to the spoken languages. For the English sample, the more bilingual subgroup had a reliably lower mean F score than did the less bilingual group, $t_{60} = 2.20$, a finding consistent with another study (Gardner and Lambert, 1958) on the relation of bilingualism to attitudes. The two bilingual groups did not differ reliably on any other variable, however. For the French sample, the only significant difference between the more and less bilingual subgroups was on the modified Bogardus scale: the more bilingual group showed reliably less own group preference than did those with little facility in English, $t_{62} = 2.43$.

DISCUSSION

Evaluational reactions. It is not unexpected that English speaking *S*s should show more favorableness to members of their linguistic group, but the finding that French *S*s also evaluate English guises more favorably is as unexpected as the finding that these *S*s judge French guises less favorably than do the English *S*s.

The traits given to *S*s for evaluation included several of those commonly considered necessary for social and economic success (e.g., looks, leadership, confidence, ambition), but we attempted to balance these with personality characteristics generally considered of greater value such as likability and kindness. It is possible that we were biased in the selection of traits and, through ignorance, presented a list which omitted characteristics which have value for French-speaking Canadians. However, the French sample chose dependability, intelligence, and kindness as the most desirable traits for friends of those given them for consideration, and two of these were rated more favorably with the English guises, a fact which argues against the view that no opportunity was given the French sample to evaluate the speakers on culturally important traits.

In view of the greater probability of finding English people in more powerful social and economic positions in the Montreal community, both samples of *S*s might more likely think of an English speaker as having higher status and then evaluate the English voice of the putative lawyer as having more ambition, intelligence, etc., than the French voice of the putative store employee. If the French *S*s had a greater tendency to do so, this might account in part for their evaluational reaction pattern. Data were available to test this notion in an indirect fashion by making use of *S*s' estimations of each speaker's likely occupation in his French and English guises. These occupational assignments were categorized as either professional or nonprofessional by two judges working independently. For the English sample, the ascribed status of English guises was markedly higher than for French guises, $\chi^2 = 38.14$ with 1 df. For the French sample, the same trend was noted but was much reduced in magnitude, $\chi^2 = 5.38$. The fact that the French *S*s ascribe higher status to a larger proportion of French guises (44%) than do English *S*s (33%) and also evaluate the French guises less favorably than do English *S*s argues against an interpretation in terms of differences in perceived status of the two groups.

The findings can also be interpreted as meaning that the French *S*s actually perceive members of the English speaking group as having various desirable personality traits. The characteristics ascribed to the English speakers are generally the same as those ascribed by the English *S*s to the same guises with the exception of the English-French conflict over which group is more kind. The French *S*s may well regard themselves as members of an inferior group, one that is nonetheless kind and religious. Several recent studies (Adelson, 1953; Sarnoff, 1951; Steckler, 1957) which document the manner in which minority groups sometimes adopt the stereotyped values of majority groups indicate that a parallel process may be taking place in the French Canadian community (cf. Stewart and Blackburn, 1956).

An examination of the common descriptions given by the French *S*s in the open-ended questionnaire suggests that they have ambivalent feelings about both French Canadians and English Canadians, an interpretation that is analogous to the attitude of American Jews toward both Jews and non-Jews as described by Lewin (1948, p. 145ff). The French *S*s describe their own group as progressing and having a potential (18 occurrences); feeling inferior or without confidence (16); having good qualities and being likable (16); being uninformed or uneducated (16); being intelligent or as intelligent as English Canadians (14); being individualistic or disunited (11); lacking ambition (11); and as being prejudiced or narrow-minded (10). They describe the English Canadians as being likable, good, or nice (27); thinking badly of French Canadians (19); feeling superior to French Canadians (13); being too Americanized (12); lacking knowledge of or appreciation for French Canadians (11); and as being less mannered or more rude (11).

The findings presented here take on somewhat more significance in view of two pilot studies using other samples of *S*s which show essentially the same results. In the first study, 17 English speaking college students listened to three of the four speakers used in the present study. In this case, English guises were evaluated more favorably on all five traits presented. In the second study, 22 male and 25 female French speaking members of Catholic religious orders were *S*s and three of the four speakers and 12 of the 14 scales used in the present study were administered. *S*s evaluated the English guises significantly more favorably on most traits except for kindness (bonté) on which French guises were more favorably evaluated. Speaker Tri, as in the present study, was not subject to this trend.

Attitude data. The general trend of correlations indicates that certain measures of attitude, particularly attitudes toward one's own group, are associated with the favorableness of evaluational reactions to the spoken languages, but this relation is clearly not a marked one, especially for the English *S*s. Furthermore, the prediction was not supported that more skill with the other group's language, which would permit more intimate interaction, would lead to smaller differences in favorableness of evaluational responses to the guises.

In view of the striking tendency for both English and French speaking *S*s to evaluate the English guises more favorably, a possible reason for the generally low correlations may be that generalized characteristics of French speaking and English speaking people are so widely accepted in the Montreal community that even those English *S*s with positive attitudes toward French may still perceive them as inferior on many traits. Likewise, French *S*s with negative attitudes toward English speaking people may still perceive them as superior in many respects. That is, both French and English *S*s regardless of their attitude may have come to believe that English speaking Canadians are taller and possibly more "intelligent" in the sense that they have more educational opportunities. To this extent, the attitude factor would be submerged by powerful community-wide stereotypes. This argument is limited, however, in that attitudes would certainly be expected to play the dominant role when the two guises are compared on such traits as good looks or character. To check this possible interpretation, correlations for the English sample were computed between the comparative favorableness of reactions to the guises and attitudes toward English Canadians for each trait examined separately. The correlations for character, intelligence, and dependability reach significance at about the .05 level but none of the others do, even those for good looks or kindness which would also be expected to reflect an attitude factor. We conclude, therefore, that the comparatively unfavorable perception of French speakers is essentially independent of the perceivers' attitudes toward French and English groups. The correlations for the French sample are not large or consistent enough to make French *S*s an exception to this generalization. Furthermore, experience with both groups, as inferred from the degree of skill in using both languages, also appears to be independent of the tendency to downgrade French speaking individuals. Further research is necessary to determine the influence of community-wide stereotypes and majority-minority feelings of members of the two language groups in Montreal.

Although the findings may be considered consistent and reliable, the generality of the results will become clear only after extensions to other samples of *S*s and a larger sample of speakers. It will be recalled that the four speakers used here were chosen to represent different linguistic communities: three speakers were educated in French Canadian universities but Leo spoke more naturally with a caricatured French Canadian accent. Only speaker Tri spoke French with a Parisian accent. A comparison of the evaluational reactions made to these speakers suggests that further study of accent differences of speakers from different linguistic communities may well extend the usefulness of the technique developed here. It can be seen in Table 1 that speaker Tri was not downgraded by the French *S*s when speaking French as were the other speakers; in fact he was considered significantly more self-confident in French than in English. Nor do the English *S*s treat him adversely in French, for they perceive him as having reliably more humor, entertainingness, and sociability in French than English. Clearly more than one speaker with a Parisian speech style is needed to test this notion but the data suggest that the Montreal community may differentiate between Parisian and Canadian French in their attitudes. Note also in Table 1 that speaker Leo, the caricatured French Canadian, is particularly downgraded in his French guise by both English and French *S*s, if we interpret the size of $\underline{t}$ values as an index of differential favorableness of evaluation.

SUMMARY

Samples of French speaking and English speaking Montreal students were asked to evaluate the personality characteristics of 10 speakers, some speaking in French, others in English. They were not made aware that actually bilinguals were used as speakers so that the evaluational reactions to the two language guises could be matched for each speaker. The comparative favorableness of evaluations of the two guises was correlated with various measures of attitudes toward French and English Canadians for both samples of *S*s.

The results indicate that English *S*s evaluate the English guises more favorably on most traits. French *S*s not only evaluate the English guises more favorably than French guises, but their evaluations of French guises are reliably less favorable than those of English *S*s. This finding is interpreted as evidence for a minority group reaction on the part of the French sample.

The correlations between comparative favorableness of English and French guises and measures of attitude toward own and other groups were generally low and insignificant, especially for the English sample. The essential independence of evaluational reactions to spoken languages and attitudes is interpreted as a reflection of the influence of community-wide stereotypes of English and French speaking Canadians.

NOTES

This research was supported by the Canadian Defence Research Board, Grant Number D77-94-01-10, and by a Ford Foundation grant to D. O. Hebb. We are grateful to Henri Barik for his computational assistance.

[1]Digne de confiance translates to both "dependable" and "trustworthy."

[2]Thirty-two *S*s indicated that their religion was Jewish, and, to determine their comparability with the rest of the sample, a separate analysis was carried out for Jewish and non-Jewish *S*s. For both subgroups, correlations were calculated between each of the four attitude measures and the comparative favorableness of evaluations of the English and French guises considering all traits as well as those most desirable for friends. The comparison of correlations indicated that there were no statistically significant differences between the two subgroups at any point and therefore the Jewish and non-Jewish *S*s were combined.

[3]Although a rating toward the upper end of the scale does not necessarily indicate favorableness in the cases of "height" or "ambition," the term "favorableness" is a meaningful description for the majority of the judgments.

REFERENCES

Adelson, J. B. A study of minority group authoritarianism. J. abnorm. soc. Psychol., 1953, 48, 477-485.

Adorno, T. W., Frenkel-Brunswik, E., Levinson, D. J., and Sanford, R. N. The authoritarian personality. New York: Harper, 1950.

Gardner, R. C., and Lambert, W. E. Social-motivational aspects of second-language acquisition. 1958. (Mimeo.)

Lewin, K. Resolving social conflicts. New York: Harper, 1948.

Licklider, J. C. R., and Miller, G. A. The perception of speech. In S. S. Stevens (Ed.) Handbook of experimental psychology. New York: Wiley, 1951.

Sarnoff, I. Identification with the aggressor: Some personality correlates of anti-semitism among Jews. J. Pers., 1951, 20, 199-218.

Steckler, G. A. Authoritarian ideology in Negro college students. J. abnorm. soc. Psychol., 1957, 54, 396-399.

Stewart, J., and Blackburn, J. Tensions between English-speaking and French-speaking Canadians. Contributions à l'Etude des Sciences de l'Homme, 1956, 3, 145-167.

9 Verbal Satiation and Changes in the Intensity of Meaning

In Collaboration with Leon A. Jakobovits

Several investigators have demonstrated that *S*s experience a change or loss of meaning for words which have been continuously repeated or fixated for a certain period of time (Basette and Warne, 1919; Mason, 1941; Smith and Raygor, 1956; Wertheimer and Gillis, 1956). For instance, Basette and Warne (1919) reported that the meanings of familiar nouns which were repeated aloud "dissipated" for their *S*s within 3 or 4 sec. More recently, it was found that if *S*s fixated a word exposed on a screen for 20 sec., their first association to the word is uncommon as measured by the Kent-Rosanoff Word Association Test (Smith and Raygor, 1956). The lapse or radical change of the meaning of a word as a result of its continued repetition is known as verbal satiation. Before the full implication of this concept for theories of learning and meaning can be determined, it is necessary to develop a method for reliably measuring the extent of meaning change which can be attributed to the satiation experience. The purpose of the present study is to extend the significance of the concept of verbal satiation by introducing a more comprehensive method of measuring the phenomenon and thereby relating it to a contemporary theory of meaning.

Osgood, Suci, and Tannenbaum (1957) have proposed an objective and reliable instrument for the measurement of certain aspects of connotative meaning. This instrument, the "semantic differential," consists of a series of scales each representing a 7-point, bipolar dimension. The meaning of a word, such as "father," is given by its position on an evaluative factor (its degree of goodness or badness), on an activity factor, and on a potency factor. The theory underlying this method assumes that the meaning of a word has a place in a multidimensional semantic space. A word without

TABLE 1
Illustration of a Semantic Profile

Father								
Good	X		Y					Bad
Strong				Y	X			Weak
Passive					Y	X		Active
	3	2	1	0	1	2	3	

Note.—*S* rates the concept "father" by indicating on each scale the position considered most appropriate. The polarity score in the present example is 6 for the X ratings and 2 for the Y ratings. The polarity-difference score for this example using one concept and three scales is -4, indicating that the second ratings (Ys) moved 4 scale units closer to the zero point.

meaning would rest at the point of origin for all dimensions. Each scale has three degrees of polarity (see Jenkins, 1959) which describe the appropriate placement of the word along the scale. The middle position indicates lack of applicability of the word to either polar adjective, or "meaninglessness" on one dimension. A semantic profile is illustrated in Table 1.

In the present studies, the semantic differential is used as a method of indexing changes in meaning induced by means of verbal repetition of words. The study was carried out in several independent steps and the present report describes two separate experiments.

EXPERIMENT I

If *S* is requested to indicate the placement of a word on a semantic dimension immediately after continuous repetition of the word, his responses should fall on the zero point of the dimension if a total lapse of meaning has occurred. The semantic differential permits one to assess decreases of meaning short of total lapses. Thus, if under normal conditions *S* considers the word "father" and assigns it to Position 1 on an evaluative dimension ("extremely good") and then, after continuous repetition of the word (father) assigns it to Position 3 ("slightly good"), we will infer, when consideration is given to various controls, that the connotative meaning of the concept "father" has decreased (by about two-thirds) on this dimension.

Procedure

Three groups of college students were tested individually under several different conditions. As each *S* (with the exception of those in the retest control group, see below) came to the experimental room, he was asked to fill out a booklet in which he rated five words (child, me, rich, truth, family), each one on nine semantic scales (three scales for each of the three most prominent factors determined by Osgood et al., 1957). Then each *S*, depending on the condition to which he was assigned, followed a procedure outlined below. Each of the five words and each scale was printed on a separate 5 x 3-in. card. The cards were placed in a Kardex folder so that E could expose them in a predetermined order.

Experimental satiation.—For each of the 22 *S*s in this group, a word was first exposed for about 1 sec. and *S* was asked to say the word aloud for 15 sec. at a rate of 2-3 repetitions per second. Then E immediately exposed a scale and *S* made his rating by pointing to one of the positions on the 7-point dimension. This was done for all words on all scales, a total of 45 responses per *S*. The order of presentation maximized the separation of the reoccurrence of each word and each scale. The initial and final ratings were subsequently compared.

Silence control.—The same procedure was used with 19 other *S*s with the exception of one change: the *S*s did not repeat aloud the words during the 15-sec. interval which elapsed between the time of exposure of the word and the semantic rating. They were initially instructed to "sit and wait" until a dimension was presented. No reference to "thinking about" the word presented was made in the instructions.

Different-word control.—The same 19 *S*s participating in the previous phase also took part in this second control condition. Four additional words (war, death, teacher, athlete) were added to the booklet which was completed at the beginning of the experimental session. Using the same general procedure, the *S*s repeated aloud a particular word during the time interval, but were then presented with a different word to rate. For example, the word "key" was exposed (the words used for repetition in this case were: key, moon, shoe, and book) and *S* repeated it aloud for 15 sec.; then the word "war" was exposed, read out loud by *S* who immediately gave a semantic rating on "war." This control condition was introduced to determine what effect the act of repeating words aloud had upon the stability of the ratings. Whereas the previous condition is a "unfilled-interval" control, the present condition is a "filled-interval" control.

Retest control.—the 22 *S*s in this group did not fill out a booklet at the start of the experiment. In this case, ratings were taken immediately after the exposure of the words, with no repetition or interval interposed. Furthermore, after the first 45 ratings were obtained, the same complete series was repeated, and the ratings for the two series were compared.

Results

Mean polarity-difference scores were computed for each *S*. These represent the changes in degree of polarization (see Table 1) from the first testing under normal conditions and the second testing under experimental or control conditions. The changes are presented as average changes per word summed over all scales (in this case, nine). Thus, one *S* with a mean polarity-difference score of −3.6 had a total polarity score for the first testing of 102 (based on 45 ratings, 5 words on 9 scales) compared to 84 for the second testing under the satiation condition. The difference between these two totals, or 18, is 3.6 scale unit changes per word. A minus sign indicates a change from a higher to a lower score, i.e., a decrease in the intensity of association between the word and the bipolar adjective. Values of zero would indicate no change and positive scores would indicate an increase in intensity of connotative meaning.

Table 2 shows that the decrease in the intensity of meaning occuring under the experimental satiation condition was significantly greater than zero. Tests of significance between the experimental and control conditions on meaning change are presented in Table 3.

TABLE 2
Average Change in Polarity per Word over the Sum of 9 Scales: Exp. I

Condition	Change in Polarity			
	N	Mean	SD	t
Satiation	22	−2.85	2.93	4.45*
Silence control	19	0.03	1.41	0.09
Diff.-word control	19	−0.66	1.91	1.46
Retest control	22	−0.21	0.73	1.31

*Significantly different from zero beyond the .01 level.

TABLE 3
H Tests of Significance Between Conditions: Exp. I

Condition	Silence Control	Diff.-Word Control	Retest Control
Satiation	12.83	6.56	11.10
Silence control	——	0.92	0.69
Diff.-word control	——	——	0.03

Note.—If $H > 6.63$, $P \leqslant .01$; if $H < 3.84$, $P > .05$.

The differences between the experimental and each of the three control conditions are significant, while none of the differences among the control conditions reaches significance. We conclude, therefore, that the decrease of meaning (verbal satiation) obtained with the experimental treatment is attributable to the continuous repetition of the word just before semantic ratings were made, and not to either of three other possible features of the experiment, namely, the unreliability of the measuring instrument, the 15-sec. interval period, or the interpolated task of repetition.

Examination of the data reveals that verbal repetition of a word may lead to small decreases of meaning as well as total lapses. In fact, when we calculate scores which each *S* would have obtained had there occurred a total loss of meaning, the obtained scores represent only 21% of those values that would have been obtained had there occurred a total loss of meaning as measured by the semantic differential. It is left for further studies to determine what amount of repetition would yield maximum satiation effects.

The results are consistent with Osgood's (1953, p. 410 ff.) interpretation of meaning. In this framework, the meaning of a symbol (or sign) is some replica of the actual reactions elicited by the environmental event which serves as a referent for the sign. These mediating reactions should follow the same principles as any other response. During verbal repetition, the mediating reactions are repeatedly and rapidly elicited. Under such circumstances we would expect that a form of reactive inhibition would be generated which would temporarily decrease the availability of the mediators. Since Osgood's semantic differential is designed to index the strength as well as the kind of mediating reactions elicited by a sign, the development of inhibition during verbal repetition should be exhibited as a decrease in the extremeness of the ratings on the semantic differential, as indeed the present experiment has demonstrated.

The second experiment to be described was meant to replicate the above findings and to study further the nature of mediating reactions. One might argue that the changes in intensity of meaning noted above may be due in large part to the muscular components of the act of continuous verbal repetition. The following study bears directly on this point.

EXPERIMENT II

For Osgood, the mediation process is the meaning of a symbol. He leaves the question open as to the possible locus (loci) of mediational responses. They may be peripheral ("muscular or glandular reactions") (Osgood, 1953, p. 697) or central ("purely neural responses") (Osgood, 1957, p. 7). In this study, we presume that the mediation process that transmits significance to a symbol is inhibited by the continual verbal repetition of that symbol. The fact that the satiation effect was noted only for the experimental *S*s, those who continuously repeated a symbol before it was rated, suggests that the mediation process may in large part be dependent on muscular reactions. In order to test the comparative importance of peripheral and central components of mediation processes, one might compare the behavior of the experimental *S*s described above with another group of *S*s who would be directed to "think about the word presented" but not to repeat it aloud. Should such a group display the satiation effect, however, one could still argue that they actually had said the words subvocally and no conclusive evidence would be given either the central or peripheral possibilities.

We attempted to circumvent this ambiguity by using another procedure which indirectly tests the comparative influence of peripheral responses and a central cognitive process on verbal satiation. We assume that saying aloud a meaningful word involves both muscular-glandular activity as well as some more central cognitive response as the meaningful nature of the symbol is registered. On the other hand, saying aloud a meaningless word with low association value involves peripheral muscular response accompanied by diversified cognitive activity, such as searching for possible significance in the word or for associations with the sound or form of the word, etc. In the case of the meaningful word, there is a relation between the peripheral and cognitive activities which is mediated by the meaning of the symbol. We argue that the cognitive activity is only distantly or not identifiably related to the peripheral in the case of the saying aloud of a meaningless word. The muscular reactions brought into play in the continual repetition of the words "canoe" and "nuka" (with the accent on the first syllable) are identical. (This assertion is supported by the fact that a listener cannot determine whether *S* is repeating "canoe" or "nuka," once the sequence of repetition is underway. The fact that the original peripheral feedback of the sequence "nu-ka-nu-ka" is different from that of the sequence "ca-noe-ca-noe" does not invalidate the present argument since the rest of the two sequences are essentially identical, and hence both should have the same effect on the peripheral responses). The representational mediating processes which are elicited in the two situations, however, must be quite different since only one is a meaningful English word. The peripheral theory maintains that motor responses are both necessary and sufficient for thinking. Thus, the continuous repetition of "nuka" and "canoe," involving identical muscular reactions, should have a similar satiation effect on the meaning of "canoe." For Osgood, whether the mediators are peripheral or central, they are not of the same form as the overt verbal response, since their character depends entirely upon the total reactions made to the thing signified and not the mediated verbalization. Since thinking of "ca-noe-ca-noe" and of "nu-ka-nu-ka" involve different cortical processes, repetition of "nuka" should not lead to satiation of "canoe."

Procedure

Twenty-three *S*s (male and female public school teachers enrolled in a summer school) were tested under three different conditions. These are described below.

Satiation.—The procedure was identical with that used in the experimental satiation condition in Exp. I, except that words and scales have been changed. The purpose of this condition was to attempt to reproduce the results obtained previously as well as to serve as a comparison condition to the other two conditions described below.

Peripheral control.—The "centrality" hypothesis was tested by requiring *S*s to repeat the words "grony" (accent on second syllable) and "nuka" before semantic ratings of the words "negro" and "canoe," respectively. The procedure was thus identical with the Different-Word Control in Exp. I. At the end of the experiment each *S* was asked whether he had "caught on" to the fact that "grony" and "nuka" were actually "negro" and "canoe" repeated backwards.

Nonsense control.—The effect of the repetition of a nonsense word on semantic ratings was determined by having *S*s repeat "troga" and "blatu" before ratings of "house" and "soldier."

There were six words used in all (two words for each condition) and eight scales, six of these representing the three standard factors, and two scales representing a Familiarity factor (meaningful-meaningless; comprehensible-incomprehensible). The ratings given for the last factor were separately analyzed and will be discussed below.

Each *S* took part in three testings. The first was an assessment of *S*'s meaning of words under normal conditions. The words and scales were individually exposed in the Kardex folder and responses were recorded by E (no booklets were used in this experiment). The second testing consisted of the three conditions described above. The third testing, identical with the first, was given after a rest period of 5 min. to determine whether the satiation effect dissipates with time.

Results

The polarity-difference scores in Table 4 are averages for the group and represent mean changes of polarity per word on all six scales (absolute values cannot be compared with those in Table 2 since a different number of scales was used in Exp. I and II). Entries under the Exp. column are differences in polarity scores between the first and second testing, whereas entries under the Dissipation column are differences in polarity scores between first and third testings. It can be seen that the only significant changes in meaning took

TABLE 4
Average Changes in Polarity per Word over the Sum of 6 Scales: Exp. II
(N = 23)

Condition	Experimental			Dissipation		
	Mean	SD	t	Mean	SD	t
Satiation	-1.95	2.06	4.43*	-1.76	2.11	3.91*
Peripheral control	0.19	1.37	0.65	-0.02	1.17	0.08
Nonsense control	-0.06	1.22	0.23	0.45	2.05	1.02

*Significantly different from zero at the .01 level.

TABLE 5
$\underline{H}$ Tests of Significance Between
Conditions: Exp. II

Condition	Satiation, Exp.	Peripheral Control, Exp.	Nonsense Control, Dissip.
Satiation, Exp.	—	13.78	—
Satiation, Dissip.	0.21	—	10.14
Peripheral control, Dissip.	—	0.71	0.75
Nonsense control, Exp.	11.96	0.81	1.35

Note.—If $\underline{H} > 6.63$, $\underline{P} \leqslant .01$; if $\underline{H} < 3.84$, $\underline{P} > .05$.

place under the Satiation condition. The possibility exists that the failure to obtain a satiation effect in the Peripheral Control and Nonsense Control conditions was due to the fact that the initial polarity of the particular words used under these conditions was already low, and hence could not decrease further. We therefore have calculated the mean initial polarity per word over the sum of six scales, as measured during the first testing, for all three conditions. These were as follows: 8.89 for the Satiation condition, 8.76 for the Peripheral Control and 9.17 for the Nonsense Control. None of these means was significantly different from another when a signed rank test was applied. It is evident, then, that differences in initial polarity of the ratings cannot account for the obtained results.

Table 5 shows that there is no significant difference between the Exp. and Dissipation scores under the Satiation condition, suggesting that the loss of meaning as a result of repetition persisted after a 5-min. rest (the mean dissipation score for the group obtained by subtracting the Exp. from the Dissipation scores is 0.19 ($\underline{t} = 0.35$). The other differences in Table 5 are in harmony with a centrality hypothesis of meaning.

All but one of the 23 *S*s reported that they became aware of the fact that "grony" and "nuka" were actually "negro" and "canoe" repeated backwards. It appears from *S*s' reports that repetition of "grony," even though it involves the same muscular reactions, was not the same task as repetition of "negro." As one *S* put it, "When I was repeating 'grony' I was trying not to think of 'negro.' But when I was repeating 'father' I kept on thinking of 'father.'" Translating this into our terminology, we can say that, given instructions to repeat "grony," the mediating processes identified with "negro" were not consistently and reliably elicited. In view of these findings, we contend that in order to satiate the meaning of a symbol through continuous repetition one must consistently call into play some particular cognitive activity which is related to the symbol.

DISCUSSION

The continuous repetition of words reduces the intensity of their connotative meanings. The effect appears to be reliable and to persist for at least a period of 5 min. The effect also appears to depend on a consistent reactivation of some type of cognitive activity which is related to the word repeated. We conceptualize this phenomenon as a type of "semantic satiation" and consider the findings as support for a central interpretation of representational mediation processes.

The results show that by dint of continuous verbal repetition of words the semantic ratings *S*s made moved closer to the point of meaninglessness on the scales. It is not clear from the above results whether the satiation effect is restricted solely to the words which are repeated or if the effect is generalized, affecting the intensity of meaning of both the words and the bipolar adjectives, as well as the task of making a judgment. The finding of a decrease in intensity of meaning across the standard semantic scales is not inconsistent with the notion of a generalized satiation effect; if the bipolar adjectives were also satiated, they would have contributed to the decrease in the degree of association between the repeated words and the adjectives. If it could be shown, however, that *S*s were also able to perceive increases in intensity of meaning on certain scales at the time of rating, we could argue that the inhibition effect is primarily restricted to the words which are repeated. As a test, we presented *S*s in Exp. II with two additional scales: "meaningful-meaningless" and "comprehensible-incomprehensible" and all words were rated along these scales as on the standard scales. These two scales should elicit a movement of ratings toward the "meaningless" and "incomprehensible" poles following the satiation treatment. Scores were assigned to *S*s for the amount of movement of ratings, comparing the first testing under normal conditions with the experimental and control condition testings, toward or away from the "meaningless" and "incomprehensible" poles. It was found that there was an average movement in the predicted direction of 1.43 scale units for the group under the satiation condition, a change which is reliably different from zero ($t = 3.25$, $P < .02$). No reliable change was noted for the other two control conditions ($t = 0.02$ for the satiation and peripheral control conditions and $t = 0.15$ for the satiation and nonsense control conditions).

One last point should be made about an alternative interpretation of our results; namely, that *S*s "caught on" to the fact that repetition of a word renders it less meaningful and consciously "played along" with E by making neutral judgments. There are several arguments against such an interpretation. Firstly, in the discussion which followed the experiment, *S*s were asked whether they thought that they had changed their judgments as the experiment went on and whether repetition influenced their ratings. The typical answers were "maybe" or "slightly," but the reason given for the change was ". . .because I forgot which judgment I had made previously." (In a current experiment using the same procedure, the question period at the end of the experiment was standardized and *S*s' answers were recorded. Only 1 out of 31 *S*s stated that repetition rendered the word more "meaningless." The typical answers were again "slight changes because I forgot what I had done before," or ". . .because I thought of something else.") Secondly, had *S*s wanted to please E by making neutral judgments, it is difficult to understand why they did not go all the way and give neutral ratings all the time. Thirdly, the dissipation scores in Exp. II exhibit the satiation effect on the words used under the Satiation condition only. Since the ratings of these words were mixed with those of the other conditions, it is improbable that *S*s could remember which were the satiation words and which were not. (In the current study mentioned above, only 3 *S*s could recall the words used for each condition.)

SUMMARY

The phenomenon of verbal satiation—the decrease in the meaning of symbols—was studied by having college *S*s continuously repeat a word and then rate the word along scales of the semantic differential. Changes in semantic ratings, comparing normal and satiation conditions, indicate that there is a reliable movement of ratings toward the meaningless points of scales. Control group comparisons suggest that this movement is not due to the unreliability of the measuring instrument, to the time interval involved in repetition, nor to the activity of repetition per se. The phenomenon is conceptualized as a cognitive form of reactive inhibition and is related to Osgood's theory of representational mediation processes.

A second experiment sheds light on the nature of mediation processes, presenting evidence that they depend more on central than peripheral-muscular activities. In order to satiate the meaning of a symbol through continuous repetition, some particular cognitive activity which is related to the symbol must consistently be called into play. Further findings suggest that the satiation effect is not generalized but stems primarily from changes in the symbol which is continuously repeated.

NOTE

This research was supported in part by the Canadian Defense Research Board Grant D77-9401-10. We are particularly grateful to C. E. Osgood for his assistance and advice in the planning as well as the presentation of this study. R. C. Gardner and D. O. Hebb helped us by their suggestions and criticisms.

REFERENCES

Basette, M. F., and Warne, C. J. On the lapse of verbal meaning with repetition. Amer. J. Psychol., 1919, 30, 415-418.

Jenkins, J. J. Degree of polarization and scores on the principal factors for concepts in the semantic atlas study. Studies of Verbal Behavior, Rep. 1, Univer. Minnesota, 1959. (Mimeo.)

Mason, M. Changes in the galvanic skin response accompanying reports of changes in meaning during oral repetition. _J. gen. Psychol._, 1941, 25, 353-401.

Osgood, C. E. _Method and theory in experimental psychology_. New York: Oxford Univer. Press, 1953.

Osgood, C. E., Suci, G. J., and Tannenbaum, P. H. _The measurement of meaning._ Urbana: Univer. Illinois Press, 1957.

Smith, D. E. P., and Raygor, A. L. Verbal satiation and personality. _J. abnorm. soc. Psychol._, 1956, 52, 323-326.

Wertheimer, M., and Gillis, W. M. Some determinants of the rate of lapse of verbal meaning. Paper read at Rocky Mountain Psychol. Ass., Moran, Wyoming, 1956. (Mimeo.)

10 The Relation of Bilingualism to Intelligence

In Collaboration with Elizabeth Peal

Psychologists and linguists have wondered whether bilingualism affects intellectual functioning since as early as the 1920's when Saer (1923) and Smith (1923) reported research on the topic. Numerous studies since then have attempted to determine whether monolingual and bilingual young people differ in intelligence as measured by standard tests. A large proportion of investigators have concluded from their studies that bilingualism has a detrimental effect on intellectual functioning. The bilingual child is described as being hampered in his performance on intelligence tests in comparison with the monolingual child. A smaller proportion of the investigations have found little or no influence of bilingualism on intelligence, in that no significant difference between bilinguals and monolinguals on tests of intelligence was apparent. Only two empirical studies were encountered which suggest that bilingualism may have favorable intellectual consequences.

An attempt will be made to understand these seemingly contradictory findings by critically reviewing representative studies reporting each type of effect. The studies will be evaluated mainly in terms of how well other relevant variables were controlled, particularly certain personal characteristics which are known to be related to intelligence and which should be taken into account when the effect of bilingualism on intelligence is examined.

In the design typically used, where two groups of subjects are being compared on intelligence, it is necessary to match the groups on as many features known or suspected to correlate with intelligence as possible so that the difference between the groups, if any, may be attributed to linguality itself. This model requires a clear definition of monolingualism and bilingualism in order that the two can be objectively determined without risk of overlap or confusion. Socioeconomic status has been repeatedly found to be related to intelligence and linguistic development (Jones, 1960; McCarthy, 1954). McCarthy states that "there is considerable evidence in the literature to indicate that there exists a marked relationship between socioeconomic status of the family and the child's linguistic development" (p. 586). From past research it is well established that girls are more advanced than boys in language development, especially in the early years. They have a larger vocabulary and are more skilled in the use of words. Since most intelligence tests draw heavily on verbal skills, it would be advisable to have approximately equal numbers of boys and girls in the groups to be compared. Furthermore, groups should also be matched for age. The educational background of children may also affect their performance on standardized tests of intelligence. This variable could be approximately controlled by using subjects from the same schools or school system. The intelligence tests should be constructed and standardized on a population similar to the one being tested, especially with respect to language. A translation of a test from one language to another, without standardization, might bias the results for or against one group. Also, the tests should be given in the language in which the bilinguals are most proficient.

Studies Supporting the Detrimental Effects of Bilingualism on Intelligence

The studies in this category may be arbitrarily divided into two subgroups. The first of these consists of those which found that monolingual groups performed better than bilingual on both verbal and nonverbal intelligence tests. Can the depressed scores of the bilinguals be attributed to bilingualism itself, or were there uncontrolled variables which might account for the obtained differences between groups?

After testing 1,400 children in Wales, Saer (1923) reported a statistically significant inferiority of rural bilingual children when compared with rural monolingual children on the Stanford-Binet scale. This inferiority became consistently greater in degree with each year from 7 to 11 years of age. Saer attempted to explain this trend in terms of the "mental confusion" encountered by the bilingual children. When urban children only were compared he found no significant difference between monolinguals and bilinguals. It should be noted that socioeconomic class was not controlled in this research and that a Welsh translation of the Stanford-Binet test was used.

Pintner (1932) administered the Pintner Language and Non-language tests to monolingual and bilingual groups in each of three schools in New York City. The results obtained are inconclusive in the sense that in one school monolinguals were superior on both tests while in another they were inferior and in the third, there was no difference between the groups. There was no control for socioeconomic class in this study and bilingualism was determined by looking at the child's name!

The most important study in this grouping was the one by Jones and Stewart (1951). After surveying the studies done prior to 1951 in Wales, they concluded that bilingual and monolingual groups differed little in nonverbal intelligence tests and that monolingual groups were usually superior to bilingual groups in verbal tests. The design of their experiment was based on these conclusions. A verbal test and a nonverbal test were given to monolingual and bilingual groups in rural districts. The children were between 10-6 and 11-6 years of age. The monolinguals were found to score significantly higher on both types of tests. The two groups were equated statistically, by the analysis of covariance, on nonverbal IQ and the differences between them on verbal IQ were then noted. "It was therefore concluded that the bilingual children were significantly inferior to the monolingual children, even after full allowance has been made for the initial difference in the nonverbal intelligence tests" (Jones and Stewart, 1951). It could be argued that the bilinguals may have encountered greater difficulties because for them the tests were translated into Welsh, their vernacular, but not standardized in the Welsh culture. This may have lowered their scores on the verbal test. However, this would not account for the original difference in nonverbal IQ. After further investigations, Jones later conceded that the significant difference in nonverbal test scores observed in all his studies may have arisen from occupational rather than linguistic variations between the groups. Thus the complete work of Jones and his collaborators has, according to James (1960), "drawn attention to the influence of socio-economic factors in comparisons between groups of monolingual and bilingual children and has emphasized the importance of such factors in the correct interpretation of test results."

In his most recent article, Jones (1960) criticized a study published by Lewis (1959) for the inadequate treatment given to socio-economic class. Lewis had reported a statistically significant difference in favor of the monolinguals corresponding to about 8 IQ points on a nonverbal intelligence test. Apart from his failure to control socio-economic class, his method of selecting his groups was an improvement over previous studies. He assessed the linguistic background of 10-year-old children by means of a language questionnaire and attempted to make each group as homogeneous as possible.

Several studies (Graham, 1925; Mead, 1927; Rigg, 1928; Wang, 1926) have found that monolingual American groups performed better than children with various foreign backgrounds on intelligence tests. All these studies lacked controls for age and socioeconomic class, and in some bilingualism was not adequately measured.

The second subdivision of studies showing the unfavorable effect of bilingualism encompasses those which reported that monolinguals scored better than bilinguals on verbal tests, but the bilinguals scored better or as well as monolinguals on performance or nonverbal tests.

A rather well-controlled study by Seidl (1937) found that monolinguals were superior to bilinguals on all verbal tests, but bilinguals were superior to monolinguals on performance measures. The 1916 Stanford-Binet scale and the Arthur Point Scale of Performance were the tests used. The two groups of subjects, whose linguality was determined by a questionnaire, were matched on sex and age. However, the mean occupational level of the monolinguals' parents was in the laboring class while the bilinguals' was semiskilled labor. This difference in social class may partly account for the results. Seidl, however, concluded that the language handicap of the bilinguals interfered with their verbal IQ scores.

Pintner and Keller (1922) gave the Stanford-Binet and the Pintner Nonlanguage Group Test to two groups, one English-speaking and the other of foreign background, and found that the latter group received lower scores on the Stanford-Binet than on tests in which a minimum of English was required. The authors concluded that these children were penalized because the Stanford-Binet was used. However, no measures of bilingualism were used and no mention was made of the social status of the children's families.

Darcy (1946) reported on research carried out with 212 American preschool children of Italian parentage. In this study, the relevant variables were quite well controlled. The subjects were classified as bilingual or monolingual by a rating scale; the groups were matched for age, sex, and social class. The Stanford-Binet (1937 Revision) was used as the verbal measure, and the Atkins Objec-Fitting Test as the nonverbal. Darcy found that the monolingual group scored significantly higher than the bilingual on the Stanford-Binet, but lower on the Atkins test. She concluded that the bilingual subjects of her investigation suffered from a language handicap in their performance on the Stanford-Binet scale. However, the subjects were so young (from 2-6 and 4-6 years) that it would not be advisable to draw any general conclusions from this study. Even if the bilinguals suffered from a language handicap at this age, they might overcome it later. Also the intelligence of infants and pre-school children is known to be somewhat difficult to determine accurately and depends more on performance items than on verbal.

Another study from which generalizations should not be drawn is that by Altus (1953) since both groups used were "dull" school children. They may have been classed as dull for various reasons. The groups were equated on age, sex, and the Performance IQ of the Wechsler Intelligence Scale for Children (WISC). Differences in IQ on the Verbal scale averaged 17 points in favor of the monolingual group. Altus suggests that linguistic difficulties interfered with normal functioning in the bilingual group.

An important technique for objectively measuring bilingualism was introduced by Johnson (1953). His Reaction Time Test, derived from the earlier work of Saer (1931), was a measure of linguistic balance obtained by dividing the number of words produced in English in 5 minutes, by the number of words produced in Spanish in 5 minutes. The subjects for his experiment were 30 Spanish-English bilingual boys in the United States between the ages of 9 and 12 years. The Goodenough IQ for these children was about average for the total population, but the Otis IQ was considerably below average. Johnson's Test of Bilingualism was found to correlate negatively with the Otis (a verbal test) and positively with the Goodenough Draw-a-Man Test (a performance test). The more bilingual the subjects were the better they did on a performance test and the poorer on a verbal test.

Levinson (1959) tested American-born Jewish preschool monolingual and bilingual children of similar socioeconomic level and found them to perform alike on the Goodenough test and most subscales of the WISC. However, on the Stanford-Binet and the WISC Arithmetic, Vocabulary, and Picture Arrangement subtests the monolinguals scored higher.

Many of these studies of the detrimental effects of bilingualism lacked important controls. Taking this into account, the weight of evidence so far presented seems to support the contention that there is no significant difference between monolinguals and bilinguals on nonverbal intelligence, but the bilinguals are likely to be handicapped on verbal intelligence measures. The need for further research with more complete controls becomes evident.

Studies Supporting the Favorable Effects of Bilingualism on Intelligence

The paucity of studies that have found a favorable intellectual effect accruing from bilingualism would seem to suggest that bilingualism may not be as advantageous as has been thought by many language teachers and educators. In a study conducted in London, England, Davies and Hughes (1927) reported the superiority of Jewish over non-Jewish children in arithmetic, English, and general intelligence. However, no measure of bilingualism was used and the Jewish children were assumed to be bilingual. Other controls such as age, sex, and social class were notably absent, as they were in the study by Stark (1940), who found that at 10 and 11 years of age, bilinguals were superior to monolinguals on one form of a test. At a later age, this trend was reversed, but the measurement was made on a different form of the test. Stark concluded that children of "innate verbal facility" may find early bilingualism an asset to their mental development.

Studies Finding No Effect of Bilingualism on Intelligence[1]

From his study of Japanese and American children, Darsie (1926) concluded that the differences in general mental capacity between the two groups were slight. On some tests, the Japanese subjects were inferior while on others the Americans were inferior.

However, the social class of these two groups was not comparable and no measure of bilingualism was employed.

The best controlled study in this category is that of Hill (1936) with Italian-American children. Bilingualism was determined by a questionnaire and on the basis of language background. The two groups were matched on sex, age, IQ, socioeconomic class, and mental age. No reliable differences were found in scores on verbal, nonverbal, and performance tests between monolinguals and bilinguals. However, it should be kept in mind that since the two groups were matched on mental age and IQ, only minor differences between them could be expected on intelligence subtests. Thus, there may have been a selection of brighter Italian-American children in this instance.

Pintner and Arsenian (1937) gave the Hoffman Bilingual Schedule to 459 Jewish children in New York City; all the children were Yiddish-English bilinguals. The 20% receiving the highest scores on the Hoffman test constituted a high bilingual group, and the 20% receiving the lowest scores, a low bilingual group. The mean verbal and nonverbal IQs of these two bilingual groups were compared, and no difference was found between them. The authors concluded that the relationship between intelligence and bilingualism is "practically zero" ($\underline{r}$ = -.059).

Spoerl (1944) tested all the bilingual freshmen enrolled at an American college. These were matched with a group of monolingual freshmen for sex, age, intelligence, and social class. A student was considered bilingual if he had learned two languages before school entrance. No differences were found between monolinguals and bilinguals on the 1937 Stanford-Binet or Purdue Placement Test. A slight inferiority was shown by the bilingual students on five of the verbal items of the Stanford-Binet scale. It is interesting to note, however, that the bilinguals had done consistently better in school work than the monolinguals even though their IQs did not differ significantly. Spoerl mentioned that a compensatory drive arising from a feeling of environmental insecurity may have been a contributing cause of the superiority of the bilinguals in academic achievement.

Arsenian's (1937) experiments with American-born Italian and American-born Jewish children were well controlled from the point of view of age, sex, socioeconomic class, and measurement of bilingualism. However, Darcy (1953) questions the adequacy of the tests used (Pintner Nonlanguage Test, and the Spearman Visual Perception Test), as measures of intelligence. The Spearman test was not even standardized. Furthermore, there were no tests of verbal intelligence. Several different combinations of subjects were used in the analysis; and in the comparison between bilinguals and monolinguals, the number of subjects (38 of each group) was too small to permit definite conclusions. The findings are nevertheless of interest and of some importance. The extent of bilingualism did not vary from 9 to 14 years. There was only a very slight relation between intelligence and socioeconomic class. There was no difference between the two language groups as to intelligence or age-grade status. Arsenian concluded: "it may be stated that . . . there was discovered no retardation or acceleration in the mental development of children from ages 9 to 14 in the groups studied, which might be attributable to bilingualism as such" (p. 120).

In summary, it becomes apparent that it is necessary to control certain variables in this type of study before any conclusions can be drawn. The important variables to control seem to be socioeconomic class, sex, degree of bilinguality, age, and the actual tests used. In view of the weaknesses of the studies reviewed, the best general conclusion is that there is little evidence to suggest that bilinguals differ from monolinguals on nonverbal intelligence, but that there may be differences in verbal intelligence as measured by intelligence tests. At a certain stage in the learning of the second language, a bilingual may suffer from a "language handicap."

Theoretical Considerations

Theoretically, what would be the expected effects of bilingualism on intelligence or mental development? Few of the psychologists who have studied this problem have attempted any explanation beyond rather vague references to a "language handicap" or "mental confusion."

An inquiry into the effects of the learning of two languages on mental development demands a serious consideration of the broader question of the relation between language and thought, and modern psychology has generally eschewed this question. The apparent belief of many is that at least partial answers to the broad question may appear from the study of the interrelation of language and intelligence. Arsenian (1937), after examining various theories of language and thought, hypothesized that language and intelligence are not identical. In line with this hypothesis, he maintained that:

> the influence of bilingualism, whatever for the moment we may suppose it to be, does not extend to the whole area of thinking or intelligence, but to that particular section where linguistic symbolism and schemata are involved in the thinking process.

Susanne Langer (1942) made a distinction between speech and thought. She argued that: "It [speech] is the normal terminus of thought . . . But in fact, speech is the natural outcome of only one kind of symbolic process" (p. 45). Assuming then, that language and thought are not isomorphic, how would the learning of two languages influence scores on intelligence tests, which obviously require thought?

Several writers, assuming a lack of identity between language and thought, suggest that the learning of two languages from childhood has favorable effects on the thinking process. Two writers in particular have made this point. Leopold (1949), after extensive observations of the mental development of his own child, felt that the bilingual child learns early to separate the sound of a word from its referent. He writes:

> I attribute this attitude of detachment from words confidently to the bilingualism. Constantly hearing the same things referred to by different words from two languages, she had her attention drawn to essentials, to content instead of form (p. 188).[2]

S. J. Evans of Wales (1953) also argues that the:

> teaching of Welsh along with English does what the efficient study of any two languages must do: it frees the mind from the tyranny of words. It is extremely difficult for a monoglot

> to dissociate thought from words, but he who can express his ideas in two languages is emancipated (p. 43).

These arguments, suggesting that a bilingual has an intellectual advantage over a monolingual because his thinking is not restricted by language, give support to those few studies which found favorable effects of bilingualism on intelligence and mental development. In view of these arguments, it also seems possible that the type of benefit that comes from bilingualism might not become apparent on standard intelligence tests. It could be argued that the studies finding no difference or a deficit for bilinguals were simply using inappropriate measures.

O'Doherty (1958) suggests that it is necessary in any consideration of the influence of bilingualism on intelligence to distinguish between two types of bilinguals for whom the effects may differ—the pseudo-bilingual and the genuine bilingual. The pseudo-bilingual knows one language much better than the other and does not use his second language in communication. The true bilingual masters both at an early age and has facility with both as means of communication. O'Doherty states that there can be no question that bilingualism of the genuine kind is an intellectual advantage. "The pseudo-bilingual is the real problem, since very often he fails to master either language, while the bilingual by definition has mastered both" (p. 285). Thus, O'Doherty's writings lend additional support to the notion that "genuine" bilingualism may be an asset.

Can we find any theoretical support for the detrimental effects of bilingualism on intelligence? Weinreich (1953) makes the point that any individual who speaks two or more languages will experience interference due to the contact between them. That is, a bilingual's speech in each language will be different than it would have been had he only learned one language. The extent of the interference in any particular case will depend in part on certain linguistic differences between the two language systems.

> The more numerous the mutually exclusive forms and patterns in each, the greater is the learning problem and the potential area of interference. But the mechanisms of interference. . . would appear to be the same whether the contact is between

> Chinese and French or between two subvarieties of English (pp. 1-2).

The language handicap reported for bilinguals could thus be attributed to interlingual interference. The effect of this interference would show up on verbal tests, but could be expected to influence performance on nonverbal tests only in so far as these depend on verbal skills.

It could be hypothesized that bilingualism might affect the very structure of intellect. Such a hypothesis could be developed from a current conceptualization of intellect as consisting of factors. Guilford (1956) and others propose that intelligence is composed of a general factor and many different specific factors, each of which may be isolated by factor analytic methods. Ferguson (1954) has put forth the thesis that human abilities are learned. Stated another way, a large proportion of an individual's intellectual ability is acquired through experience and its transfer from one situation to another. The "factors of intellect" are gradually developed through a series of learning situations. This learning process may proceed in different ways for different individuals depending on their experiences. Thus the structure of intellect will very likely vary from one individual to another. The developmental process for monolinguals and bilinguals is certainly different in respect to language, and the learning of abilities depends greatly on language. Bilinguals could have different and more complex contexts for learning than monolinguals. Arsenian (1937) states that, "The two different words in two different language systems for the same referent may carry different connotations and put the bilingual person in contact with two worlds of experience." We could, therefore, hypothesize that the structure of the intellect of monolinguals and bilinguals might differ in various aspects. Guilford (1956) states: "to the extent that factors [of intellect] are developed by experience, they would appear at such ages as the effects of experience have sufficiently crystallized" (p. 287). That is, the emergence of an intellectual factor is dependent on the accumulation of experiences. From this notion, it seems reasonable to propose that such factors would appear at different ages in monolinguals and bilinguals, since their linguistic and cultural experiences are quite different. It may therefore be important to discover the nature of the effects of bilingualism on intellectual functioning.

Some recent studies have emphasized the importance, for second language learning, of an individual's attitude toward the second language community. Using a language involves personal participation in a second culture. Christophersen (1948) has made the point that a bilingual person belongs to two different communities and possesses two personalities which may be in conflict if the two language communities are in social conflict. Changes in the bilingual's attitude toward a language community may account for the variation in his efficiency in the use of that language which could even effect his performance on intelligence tests. Arsenian (1937) mentions that, "National, religious, and political sympathies or antipathies determine the affective tone or the attitude of a bilinguist toward the second language, and they introduce, therefore, important differences among bilinguists." The studies of Lambert, Hodgson, Gardner, and Fillenbaum (1960), and Anisfeld, Bogo, and Lambert (1961) suggest that certain community-wide negative stereotypes toward speakers of a particular language may have a negative influence on a bilingual who uses that language. He may be aware, for example, of the ridicule coming from others when he uses that language and this may constitute an intellectual interference in that language for him. This could have a detrimental effect for a bilingual when functioning in one of his languages if he had associations of inferiority or shame with that language. However, a bilingual even in Montreal's bicultural community could have favorable attitudes toward the use of both his own and the other language. The fact than an individual becomes bilingual in a bicultural community may be attributable to a favorable disposition toward both the linguistic communities, whereas the monolingual may be retarded in his acquisition of a second language because of his unfavorable attitudes toward both the other culture and its language.

STATEMENT OF THE PROBLEM

The present research was designed to examine more extensively the effects of bilingualism on the intellectual functioning of children and to explore the relations between bilingualism, school achievement, and students' attitudes to the second language community.

In line with previous findings, it was predicted that two groups of subjects, one monolingual and the other bilingual, should not differ significantly on nonverbal IQ, but might differ on verbal IQ as measured by intelligence tests standardized in the native language of both the monolinguals and bilinguals. The monolinguals were expected to perform significantly better than the bilinguals on the verbal tests. The groups were matched on socioeconomic class, sex, and age. They were selected from the same school system and where possible the same school. Several measures of degree of bilingualism were employed to determine objectively the bilingualism of each subject.

It was further predicted that the attitudes of the monolinguals would likely be less favorable to the other language group than those of the bilinguals, and that individual differences in these attitudes would be related to school achievement in the second language. For this purpose, several measures of attitude were used.

It was also thought that a relationship might be found between bilingualism and school grade. This idea stemmed from the work of Morrison (1958) who found that bilinguals were as much as 1 $^1/_2$ years behind their age norm in school.

In line with the hypothesis that the structure of intellect might be different for the two groups of subjects, we used a wide variety of measures of different types of intelligence. It was predicted that bilinguals and monolinguals would perform differently on various types of subtests of intelligence. This is, in effect, an attempt to investigate the _nature_ of the effect of bilingualism on intelligence.

METHOD

Subjects

The subjects were 10-year-old school children from six French schools under the jurisdiction of the Catholic School Commission of Montreal. Three of these schools were located in the western region of Montreal, and the remainder in the extreme eastern region of the island. All were roughly classified as middle class schools by the School Commission. In each school all the 10-year-olds were tested, regardless of school grade.

Procedure

The testing took place in the classroom and was divided into five sessions of 1 hour each, spaced about a week apart. All instructions to the children were given in French by native speakers of French, except for the test of English vocabulary which was administered by a native speaker of English.

In the first session, all the 10-year-olds were administered a questionnaire and several tests to determine degree of bilingualism. The questionnaire sought general information about the child and his family, specific information about his language history, and details about his father's occupation. Three tests were used to determine whether the child was a balanced bilingual, that is, equally skilled in French and English, or whether he was a monolingual. His own self-ratings of his ability in English were also taken into account.

Criteria for Selection of Subjects

Word Association Test. The first test of bilingualism was based on an association fluency technique developed by Lambert (1956). Modifications were introduced to make the technique appropriate for use with children in a group setting. French and English words were presented alternately and the children were asked to write down as many words as they could think of in the same language as the stimulus which seemed to "go with" or "belong with" that word. An interval of 60 seconds was allowed for association to each word. For each subject the sum of the associations to all the French words was calculated (NF). The same was done for the associations to the English words (NE). These two sums were used to form a balance score:

$$\text{Balance} = \frac{NF - NE}{NF + NE} \times 100$$

A zero score indicates perfect balance between the two languages, a plus score means French dominance, and a minus score English dominance.

Word Detection Test. This test was also a modification of one developed by Lambert, Havelka, and Gardner (1959). It was postulated that bilingualism would express itself in the facility of finding short embedded English and French words in a series of letters such as DANSONODEND. The subjects were given four such series and allowed $1^1/_2$ minutes to work on each. Approximately equal numbers of English and French words were embedded in each group of letters. A balance score was obtained here, similar to the one described above.

Peabody Picture Vocabulary Test. This test, derived from Dunn (1959), was used because it made possible a distinction between oral and graphic language skills. It was thought that there might be bilinguals who would nevertheless be balanced bilinguals in the oral sense. Such bilinguals might be at a disadvantage on the two previous tests which required some knowledge of written English. The test consists of a series of plates, each of which has four pictures of objects or actions numbered 1-4. The examiner says one English word aloud and the subject has to point to the picture corresponding to the word. To adapt this for use with a group, we flashed each plate on a screen by means of an epidiascope, and an examiner pronounced the word in English. The children wrote down the number of the picture which corresponded to the English word pronounced. In this way, no graphic skills in English were required of the subjects. Twenty-one plates of increasing difficulty were presented. A score of the number of correct responses out of 21 was obtained for each child.

Subjective Self-Rating Score. The subjects were asked to rate their ability to speak, read, write, and understand English on 4-point scales ranging from "not at all" (scored 1) to "very fluently" (scored 4). For each subject an oral self-rating score was obtained by summing his weights on "speak" and "understand," and a graphic score by doing the same on "read" and "write." The maximum possible score was 8 on each (oral and graphic scores).

On the basis of these tests, the entire sample of 364 subjects originally contacted was divided into three groups: one group composed of monolinguals, a second group of bilinguals, and a third group which could not be unambiguously classified as either monolingual or bilingual. Only the first two of these groups were further tested. The third group was not used again.

The criteria used in the classification of subjects were as follows: (*a*) Monolinguals—Word Association Test, a balance score of at least +75; Word Detection Test, a balance score of at least +75; Peabody Picture Vocabulary, a score of not more than 6; Subjective Self-Rating, a score of not more than 7 in oral and graphic skill in English (combined). (*b*) Bilinguals—Word Association Test, a balance score of 0 ± 30; Word Detection Test, a balance score of 0 ± 30; Peabody Vocabulary Test, a score of at least 15 out of 21; Subjective Self-Rating, a score of at least 13 out of a possible 16 in oral and graphic English (combined).

Two judges consulted on the classification of each subject. In some cases where the different criteria were in disagreement, more weight was given to the Vocabulary score than to the others.

Our selected sample was composed of 164 subjects: 75 monolinguals and 89 bilinguals; 96 boys and 68 girls. These subjects were tested four additional times.

Measures of Intelligence[3,4]

Lavoie-Laurendeau (1960) Group Test of General Intelligence (Variables 6-9; Variables 16-23). Previous studies pointed to the importance of using a test of intelligence standardized in the native language of the subject and preferably prepared for use in that language community. The Lavoie-Laurendeau test, standardized by psychologists at the University of Montreal on a Montreal French-speaking school population, seemed to meet these requirements. It is based on several other well-developed tests (Wechsler-Bellevue, WISC, Barbeau-Pinard) using those sections which could best be adapted for group testing. The nonverbal and verbal sections of this test were administered to each group. Nonverbal, verbal, and total IQ scores were calculated for each subject. A ratio score was obtained by dividing the verbal IQ by the nonverbal IQ and multiplying by 100.

Raven (1956) Progressive Matrices Test (Variable 10). The colored form of this (Sets A, Ab, and B) was administered as a group test. This was included as a measure of basic intelligence (pure "g"). A total raw score was obtained for each subject (maximum 36).

Thurstone (1954) Primary Mental Abilities (Variables 11-15). An attempt was made to select those subtests from the Primary Mental Abilities which draw least directly on verbal skills. The following five were chosen and administered in French: Space, Figure-Grouping, Perception, Number, and Verbal Meaning. This test was translated by a linguist at McGill.

Measures of Attitude

In the final testing session, the children were given a booklet containing a number of different measures of attitude. The complete versions of these are presented in Appendix C.

Attitude-to-English Scale (Variable 33); Attitude-to-French Scale (Variable 34). The first measure was an attitude questionnaire, devised especially for use with children in the Montreal setting, answers to which purportedly reflect social attitudes toward either English Canadians or French Canadians. Two scales were derived from this questionnaire. Each question was defined as belonging either to the Attitude-to-English scale or to the Attitude-to-French scale. Responses to each question were scored on a three-point scale, from favorable to unfavorable. All the responses to the questionnaire belonging to the Attitude-to-French scale were scored and summed, a high score indicating a favorable attitude to French and a low score an unfavorable attitude. The Attitude-to-English scale was scored in the same manner.

Parents' Attitudes to English Canadians (Variable 38); Parents' Attitudes to French Canadians (Variable 39). The questionnaire contained items relating to the parents' attitudes toward the French and the English communities. These were scored in the same way as Variables 33 and 34.

Evaluation of Moi (Me) (Variable 35); Evaluation of French Canadians (Variable 36); Evaluation of English Canadians (Variable 37). A second series of measures made use of the Semantic Differential (Osgood, 1957) as a technique for determining the subjects' attitudes to various groups. The subjects rated several concepts on 18 bipolar scales, each with seven points. The concepts used in the analysis of the data were: Me, les canadiens français, and les canadiens anglais.

Variables 35, 36, and 37 were obtained by summing the ratings assigned by a given subject to each of the concepts on all 18 scales. A high score on these variables indicates a high evaluation of the concept and a low score a low evaluation.

Differential Evaluation of French Canadians (Variable 40); Differential Evaluation of French Canadians and English Canadians (Variable 41); Differential Evaluation of Me and English Canadians (Variable 42). This measure was obtained by subtracting the evaluation of the concept listed second from the evaluation of that listed first. A high score indicates the first concept was evaluated more unfavorably than the second. A low score shows the opposite. A differential evaluation score was calculated between French Canadians and Me (Variable 40), between French Canadians and English Canadians (Variable 41), and between Me and English Canadians (Variable 42).

Identification of French Canadians and Me (Variable 43); Identification of French Canadians and English Canadians (Variable 44); Identification of Me and English Canadians (Variable 45). Osgood Ds were calculated between the subject's ratings of each pair of concepts. These constitute scores on Variables 43, 44, and 45. A high score (D) indicates greater semantic distance between the two concepts or less similarity between them. A low score shows closer identification of the two concepts as discussed by Lazowick (1955).

Voice Study (Variable 46). In an attempt to get at stereotypes which the subjects might hold about French Canadians and English Canadians, a study was carried out using tape recordings of the voices of children reading a passage in French and an English translation of the same passage—an adaptation of a study by Lambert et al. (1960). There were four speakers, each one reading twice, once in each language. The subjects were unaware that they were rating the personality characteristics of only four speakers who were perfectly bilingual. English and French voices were presented alternately, the two voices of any one speaker being maximally separated on the tape. The subjects were asked to rate what they thought each speaker must be like as a person from the sound of her voice. The ratings were made on 15 traits, each one having a 5-point scale. For each subject on each of the traits, the sum of his ratings for all the English voices was subtracted from the sum of his ratings for all the French voices, yielding a measure (D) of the direction of the difference between his ratings of the two. In this case a constant of five was added to all scores. A score of 5 would mean there was no difference perceived between the two guises. A score greater than 5 would mean that the English were perceived more favorably than the French and a score lower than 5 would indicate that the French were perceived more favorably than the English.

Achievement Measures

From the teachers, ratings were obtained of how well each child did in school in relation to the others in his class. The teacher rated each child along a five-point scale in terms of his achievement in general (Variable 24), in French (Variable 25), and in English (Variable 26) if this happened to be one of his subjects. We also obtained the marks in French that each subject received in *dictée* (Variable 27), *lecture* (Variable 28), and *composition* (Variable 29) at midterm.

The following measures were based on information from the original questionnaire filled out by each subject.

Sex (Variable 1); School Grade (Variable 4); Number of Years Speaking English (Variable 5); French skills of Parents (Variable 30). Each subject rated the ability of his father and mother to speak, read, write, and understand French. These were scored in the same manner as his self-ratings of his English ability. The scores for mother and father were summed.

English Skill of Parents (Variable 31). This variable was derived in the same way as above, using the items about English in place of those about French.

Balance between English and French Skills of Parents (Variable 32). The score on Variable 30 was subtracted from the score on Variable 31 and a constant of 100 added. A score of 100 on this variable indicates that the parents are equally skilled in French and English. A score of less than 100 means that the parents are more skilled in English than in French, and vice versa.

Socioeconomic Class (Variable 3). Realizing the relevance of socioeconomic class to language learning, we decided to investigate its role in detail. On the basis of information received from the child, the school records, the school principal, and the parents themselves when necessary, we placed each child into one of seven categories outlined by Warner, Meeker, and Eells (1949). A small sample of 110 children was selected from the large sample so that there were equal numbers of bilinguals and monolinguals in each of the seven classes.

RESULTS AND DISCUSSION

Comparisons were made between the performance of the monolinguals and bilinguals on the various measures employed. Table 1 presents the means, *t* values, and associated probability levels for each comparison for the entire sample of subjects (large sample). The original statement of the problem required that the two groups be matched for socioeconomic class since previous studies had indicated the importance of this variable. Although the subjects in both groups were drawn from the same school system and in many cases the same school, all of which were considered middle class by the school commission, there was a significant difference between the two groups on socioeconomic level (Table 1, Variable 3). Because of this discrepancy, a small sample having equal numbers of bilinguals and monolinguals in each of seven socioeconomic status categories was analyzed separately. Table 2 shows the means, *t* values, and probability levels for this small sample. The general pattern of results for the two samples was highly similar.

For purposes of correlational analysis, 38 out of the 48 variables were chosen and intercorrelated for the bilingual group and the monolingual separately. Thirty-one variables were selected on the basis of their appropriateness for factor analysis. That is, total IQ measures were eliminated and only subtests kept, ratio and balance scores were eliminated because they were composed of two other measures, and only two of the nine rating scales of attitudes were kept, to reduce the possibility of built-in correlations. Each 31 by 31 variable correlation matrix was factor analyzed by Thurstone's (1947) centroid solution and seven factors were extracted. The factors were rotated using the normal varimax rotation program developed at McGill.

The correlation matrices and factor matrices (centroid solution) are presented in Appendix A. The rotated factor matrices appear later in the Discussion section. In these analyses, the large sample was used, with socioeconomic status left free to vary in order that the extent of its influence could be determined.

The main findings of the study will be presented in summary. Following this, each one will be examined separately in more detail. Finally, an attempt will be made to integrate all the findings.

The first hypothesis, that the two groups would not differ significantly on nonverbal IQ, was not supported. The results (Table 2) show that the bilingual group performed significantly better than the monolingual on the Raven Progressive Matrices, and the Lavoie-Laurendeau Nonverbal IQ, and most of the subtests of the nonverbal type.

The finding that the bilinguals also scored significantly higher than the monolinguals on the Lavoie-Laurendeau Verbal IQ, and on all the verbal subtests, is in direct contradiction to the original prediction.

The monolingual and bilingual groups performed differentially on subtests of intelligence, as was expected. On certain subtests of the nonverbal type there were no significant differences between the groups, while on others, both nonverbal and verbal, the bilinguals performed better in differing amounts. However, on none of the subtests did the monolinguals exceed the bilinguals.

The predicted relation between attitudes to English and school achievement in English was found. For example, in the monolingual case, there is a significant correlation (-.51) between achievement in English (Variable 26) and the degree of perceived similarity between Me and English Canadians (Variable 45).

Morrison's observation that bilinguals were often behind in school grade was not borne out in this study. Quite to the contrary, the results show that bilingual subjects who were of the same age as the monolinguals (10 years), were in a higher grade in school, even for the sample which was matched on socioeconomic class.

TABLE 1
Means, t Values, and Probability Levels for Monolingual and Bilingual Groups on All Measures, Large Sample

Name of Variable	Bilingual M	Monolingual M	t value[a]
1. Sex	—	—	—
2. Linguality	—	—	—
3. Socioeconomic class	4.27	3.31	3.71***
4. School grade	4.86	4.42	5.61***
5. Number of years speaking English	5.68	.71	14.44***
6. Lavoie-Laurendeau (L-L) Nonverbal IQ	109.43	95.40	5.78***
7. L-L Verbal IQ	116.26	103.14	6.06***
8. L-L Total IQ	115.01	99.45	6.75***
9. L-L Ratio Score	106.60	110.34	-1.46
10. Raven Progressive Matrices	27.48	22.40	5.44***
11. Primary Mental Abilities (PMA) Verbal Meaning	26.91	24.94	3.13***
12. PMA Space	15.96	14.33	2.48**
13. PMA Figure-Grouping	19.21	17.49	2.62***
14. PMA Perception	22.32	20.19	2.07*
15. PMA Number	36.38	33.13	2.58**
16. L-L Picture Arrangement	8.55	6.19	4.80***
17. L-L Figure Manipulation	10.58	8.77	3.57***
18. L-L Dissimilarities	9.33	8.03	3.57***
19. L-L Picture Completion	10.10	8.43	3.58***
20. L-L Vocabulary	12.74	10.52	4.08***
21. L-L Comprehension	6.23	5.23	3.32***
22. L-L Similarities	9.08	7.70	3.93***
23. L-L Information	12.67	9.44	6.19***
24. Achievement in General	3.43	3.04	2.85***
25. Achievement in French	3.37	3.10	1.86
26. Achievement in English	4.16	2.63	7.61***
27. Marks in French *dictée*	73.65	71.14	1.02
28. Marks in French *lecture*	78.78	75.22	1.97

TABLE 1—continued

Name of Variable	Bilingual M	Monolingual M	t value[a]
29. Marks in French composition	74.93	73.03	1.18
30. French skills of parents	22.15	23.26	-2.34*
31. English skills of parents	21.59	16.36	7.05***
32. Balance between Variables 30 and 31	100.74	106.92	-7.19***
33. Attitude-to-English scale	52.75	38.85	8.91***
34. Attitude-to-French scale	26.71	31.31	-5.46***
35. Evaluation of self	111.18	105.12	2.11*
36. Evaluation of French Canadians (FC)	109.27	110.07	-.34
37. Evaluation of English Canadians (EC)	104.34	95.24	2.87***
38. Parents' attitude to EC	5.00	4.06	5.86***
39. Parents' attitude to FC	4.95	5.40	-2.92***
40. Differential Evaluation of FC—Me	511.58	485.25	2.36**
41. Differential Evaluation of FC—EC	477.75	425.80	2.83***
42. Differential Evaluation of Me—EC	466.55	441.26	1.38
43. Identification of FC and Me	37.55	39.40	-.23
44. Identification of FC and EC	56.63	82.75	-1.53
45. Identification of Me and EC	54.22	90.98	-2.06*
46. Voice Study	4.98	4.65	3.38***

[a]Positive entries indicate that the mean for the bilingual group is higher than the mean for the monolingual group. Negative entries indicate the reverse.

* $p < .05$. ** $p < .02$. *** $p < .01$.

TABLE 2

Means, t Values, and Probability Levels for Monolingual and Bilingual Groups on All Measures, Small Sample[a]

Name of Variable	Bilingual M	Monolingual M	t value[b]
1. Sex	—	—	—
2. Linguality	—	—	—
3. Socioeconomic class	3.80	3.83	.11
4. School grade	4.87	4.48	4.77***
5. Number of years speaking English	5.36	.72	11.24***
6. Lavoie-Laurendeau (L-L) Nonverbal IQ	110.26	95.85	4.84***
7. L-L Verbal IQ	114.98	104.43	4.08***
8. L-L Total IQ	114.62	100.60	5.11***
9. L-L Ratio Score	104.80	111.62	-2.13*
10. Raven Progressive Matrices	27.15	22.12	4.40***
11. Primary Mental Abilities (PMA) Verbal Meaning	26.94	25.35	2.23*
12. PMA Space	15.80	14.31	1.90
13. PMA Figure-Grouping	19.46	17.58	2.39**
14. PMA Perception	22.06	20.33	1.29
15. PMA Number	35.92	33.29	1.65
16. L-L Picture Arrangement	8.50	6.15	4.00***
17. L-L Figure Manipulation	10.42	8.96	2.37**
18. L-L Dissimilarities	9.69	8.08	3.64***
19. L-L Picture Completion	10.35	8.50	3.21***
20. L-L Vocabulary	12.63	10.73	2.99***
21. L-L Comprehension	6.02	5.22	2.17*
22. L-L Similarities	8.77	7.80	2.21*
23. L-L Information	12.81	10.02	4.62***
24. Achievement in General	3.38	3.04	1.97
25. Achievement in French	3.35	3.11	1.29
26. Achievement in English	4.00	2.68	5.24***
27. Marks in French *dictée*	72.73	71.51	.40
28. Marks in French *lecture*	79.04	75.73	1.46

TABLE 2—continued

Name of Variable	Bilingual M	Monolingual M	t value[b]
29. Marks in French composition	75.09	72.49	1.29
30. French skills of parents	22.50	23.10	-1.09
31. English skills of parents	21.13	17.08	4.27***
32. Balance between Variables 30 and 31	101.38	106.05	-4.75***
33. Attitude-to-English scale	51.76	38.85	7.12***
34. Attitude-to-French scale	26.57	31.65	-5.00***
35. Evaluation of self	110.55	105.82	1.24
36. Evaluation of French Canadians (FC)	108.89	110.58	-.60
37. Evaluation of English Canadians (EC)	101.04	98.28	.76
38. Parents' attitude to EC	4.88	4.09	4.11***
39. Parents' attitude to FC	5.14	5.48	-2.03*
40. Differential Evaluation of FC—Me	510.04	492.42	1.24
41. Differential Evaluation of FC—EC	462.94	432.42	1.40
42. Differential Evaluation of Me—EC	453.26	439.66	.63
43. Identification of FC and Me	42.36	35.42	.74
44. Identification of FC and EC	70.64	64.98	.32
45. Identification of Me and EC	66.78	73.93	-.39
46. Voice Study	4.95	4.63	2.33*

[a]Equated for socioeconomic status.

[b]Positive entries indicate that the mean for the bilingual group is higher than the mean for the monolingual group. Negative entries indicate the reverse.

* $p < .05$. ** $p < .02$. *** $p < .01$.

The attitudes of the bilinguals toward English Canadians were significantly more favorable than those of the monolinguals, as indicated by the means on the Attitude-to-English scale. These attitudes appear to be related to socioeconomic class, however, since in the larger sample where the bilinguals were of a higher social class, their favorable attitudes to English became evident on more variables measuring attitudes. It should also be noted that the monolinguals held more favorable attitudes to the French Canadians than the bilinguals.

No significant differences were found between the group means (small sample) for: achievement in general, achievement in French, evaluation of self, and most of the remaining attitude measures, although these do relate differentially to the other variables.

Performance on Nonverbal Intelligence Measures

The finding that a group of bilingual children scored higher on nonverbal intelligence tests than did a group of monolinguals runs counter to most previous findings in this area and to the original expectation of this study. It raises the question as to why the bilinguals scored higher on nonverbal tests.

This problem may be viewed from two perspectives. One may ask whether the more intelligent children, as measured by nonverbal intelligence tests, are the ones who become bilingual, or whether bilingualism itself has a favorable effect on nonverbal intelligence.

In support of the first notion, one could argue that the more intelligent child would be more able to pick up English from his playmates and his schooling than the less intelligent child, given the same opportunities. Previous studies have shown a correlation between intelligence and language aptitude (Gardner and Lambert, 1959; Wittenborn and Larsen, 1944). When a frequency distribution is made of the scores obtained by the two groups on a nonverbal test (such as the Raven) we find that the distribution of bilinguals' scores is negatively skewed. That is, though there were some children of low intelligence who became bilingual, most of the bilinguals scored higher on this intelligence test. Also, there were a few monolinguals who did as well as the bilinguals on the test, but the majority was found near the middle or at the lower end of the distribution. This shape of distribution implies that at least some minimum level of intelligence is necessary to become a really balanced bilingual, at least to meet the requirements for bilingualism set in this study.

In a bilingual community such as Montreal, it is a very great asset and at times a necessity for French Canadians to know English. These advantages may be realized more fully by parents of higher intelligence who may be more inclined to encourage their children to learn English. Parents of higher intelligence may be expected to have more intelligent children. This notion is supported by the following facts. The bilinguals reported significantly more than the monolinguals that their parents encouraged them to learn to speak English and the parents themselves had more skill in English than did the parents of the monolingual children ($p < .01$) who apparently either failed to see the benefits of knowing English or reacted negatively to the English-Canadian community. The more intelligent children may themselves realize the value of knowing English and therefore seek opportunities to learn it. When they do show progress in learning English, one could predict that they would receive parental encouragement for so doing. Even if the less intelligent child should see the advantages, he might encounter difficulties in attempting to learn English and might give up more readily, being accustomed to failure in other areas. Furthermore, he does not receive encouragement from his parents. But for the bright child who is ahead in school, the opportunity to learn anything new may present a challenge, which he is capable of meeting.

An alternative explanation of these results is that bilingualism may in some way influence nonverbal intelligence. It may be that knowing two languages from an early age gives a child an advantage in his performance on nonverbal tests. If this is the case, why did the bilinguals not do better on _all_ the different nonverbal subtests? In her chapter on Performance and Nonlanguage tests, Anastasi (1961) writes:

> An important question to consider regarding nonlanguage tests concerns the extent to which they depend upon spatial and perceptual functions, as contrasted to the symbolic

> manipulation of abstract relations, concepts, and factual information. The latter functions would seem to resemble more closely those required in the traditional verbal tests of "intelligence" . . . Some tests . . . stress spatial and perceptual factors almost to the exclusion of other functions . . . Other non-language tests employ a greater proportion of items calling for ideational or symbolic responses (p. 253).[5]

The nonverbal tests in this study can be subdivided conveniently into two groups in the fashion suggested by Anastasi. The Primary Mental Abilities Space and Perception tests both draw more on spatial and perceptual processes than on symbolic manipulation. The Number test of the Primary Mental Abilities is composed of simple addition questions which do not involve much mental "manipulation." Because this is a timed test, the important requirement is perceptual speed. In the Primary Mental Abilities Figure-Grouping, the Raven, and the Lavoie-Laurendeau Dissimilarities tests the subjects must form a concept or discover relations between elements which cannot be done without cognitive reorganizations. The Lavoie-Laurendeau Figure-Manipulation and the Lavoie-Laurendeau Picture Arrangement tests require reorganizations of relations and concepts. Thus, the different nonverbal tests do logically fall into two categories: (*a*) those with spatial-perceptual requirements: Primary Mental Abilities Space, Perception, and Number; and (*b*) those with symbolic reorganization requirements: Primary Mental Abilities Figure-Grouping, Raven Progressive Matrices, Lavoie-Laurendeau Dissimilarities, Figure-Manipulation, and Picture Arrangement. The Picture Completion test is difficult to categorize, a priori. Further support for the division of nonverbal or performance tests into two subtypes comes from an abstract of a study conducted by Ahmed (1954):

> A factorial analysis study demonstrating that spatial visualization and mental manipulation are independent abilities . . . The author tentatively describes this ability as if it consisted of *mental flexibility* [italics added] which is involved in the process of mentally reorganizing the elements of a problem or situation.

Reference to Table 2 reveals that on the spatial-perceptual type of test, the two groups performed similarly whereas on the mental reorganization type there is a significant difference between them. The bilinguals therefore perform better only on the type of nonverbal tests involving concept-formation or symbolic "flexibility."

Several hypotheses will be proposed as to why bilinguals might have an advantage on these tests. People who learn to use two languages have two symbols for every object. From an early age, bilinguals may be forced to conceptualize environmental events in terms of their general properties without reliance on their linguistic symbols. This would be particularly relevant in the case of those bilinguals who are "compound" (Lambert, Havelka, and Crosby, 1958), that is, bilinguals who learned their two languages in the same setting and therefore have two words for the identical referent. Most of our bilinguals have learned both their languages in Montreal and would likely be compound. Leopold (see the introduction) noted that his bilingual child learned to separate the sound of the word from the thing itself. This ability to think in terms of abstract concepts and relations, independent of the actual word, apparently is required in the symbolic reorganization type tests. The monolinguals may never have been forced to form concepts or abstract ideas of things and may be more likely to think mainly in terms of concretes. They could not be expected, therefore, to be as agile at concept-formation as the bilinguals and they might appear handicapped comparatively. S.J. Evans (1953) implies that monolinguals may be at a disadvantage in that their thought is always subject to language. In summary, it is proposed that bilinguals, because of their training in two languages, have become more adept at concept formation and abstract thinking than the monolinguals, and that this accounts, in part, for their superiority on the symbolic reorganization type tests.

The second hypothesis is that bilinguals may have developed more flexibility in thinking. Compound bilinguals typically acquire experience in switching from one language to another, possibly trying to solve a problem while thinking in one language, and then, when blocked, switching to the other. This habit, if it were developed, could help them in their performance on tests requiring symbolic reorganization since they demand a readiness to drop one hypothesis or concept and try another. Morrison (1958) gives an example of a Gaelic-speaking boy of 11, who had just taken the Raven Matrices test. When asked whether he had done his thinking in Gaelic or in English he replied, "Please, sir, I tried it in the English first, then I tried in the Gaelic to see would it be easier; but it wasn't, so I went back to the English" (p. 288). The monolinguals of course could not have developed a habit of alternating languages, and therefore, of making use of two different perspectives. One might thus expect them to be more rigid or less flexible than the bilinguals on certain tests. This might account for the significant difference between the two groups on these tests. This hypothesis could be more directly tested by giving groups of monolinguals and bilinguals tests of rigidity to see if rigidity-flexibility is a dimension on which they actually do differ.

Nonlanguage or performance tests depend, to a certain extent, on prior exposure to and familiarity with materials similar to those used in the test. The broader a child's experience, the higher the probability that he will have come into contact with the type of ideas and situations that will assist him in his performance. The bilingual child has been exposed to a wider range of experiences than the monolingual, because his experiences stem from two different cultures. This enriched environment may benefit him on nonverbal tests.

The bilingual's contact with the English culture should have put him in an advantageous position on the Primary Mental Abilities Test which is basically an English style test translated into French for present purposes. However, the fact that this was the test on which the bilinguals performed relatively the poorest would seem to justify our use of a translation; that is, it apparently did not give the bilinguals an advantage.

Performance on Verbal Intelligence Measures

The next finding to be discussed is that bilinguals also performed better on verbal tests. We had anticipated that the monolinguals would excel. Why this complete reversal? The superior performance of the bilinguals on the verbal tests may simply be a reflection of their overall superior intelligence. This seems to be the case for the small sample. An analysis of covariance (Table 3) showed that when the two groups were matched statistically on nonverbal intelligence, there was no significant difference between them on verbal intelligence. (The Lavoie-Laurendeau Nonverbal and Verbal IQs were used in this analysis.) For the large sample, this does not hold up (see Table 4). There is still a significant difference ($p = .01$) between the groups in favor of the bilinguals on verbal, even after they have been matched on nonverbal. Arguing from the large sample results, it appears that our bilinguals, instead of suffering from "mental confusion" or a "language handicap" are profiting from a "language asset." A partial explanation of this may lie in our method of choosing the bilingual sample. Those suffering from a handicap may unintentionally have been eliminated. We attempted to select bilinguals who were balanced, that is equally fluent in both languages. However, when the balance measures used did not give a clear indication of whether or not a given child was bilingual, more weight was attached to his score on the English vocabulary test. Thus some bilinguals who might be balanced, but whose vocabulary in English and French might be small, would be omitted from our sample. The less intelligent bilinguals, those who have not acquired as large an English vocabulary, would not be considered "bilingual" enough for our study.

TABLE 3
Analysis of Covariance of Performance of Two Groups of Subjects, Small Sample

Source	*df*	X^2	XY	Y^2
Between groups	1	3998.51	3365.39	2832.52
Within groups	103	34207.89	21629.28	41040.82
Total	104	38206.40	24994.67	43873.34

Analysis of Covariance

Source	*SS* of errors of estimate	*df*	*MS*	*F*
Total	27521.80	103		
Within groups	27364.86	102	268.28	
Adjusted means	156.94	1	156.94	.584

Note.—Sums of squares and cross products for 2 groups of subjects (monolingual and bilingual) on Lavoie-Laurendeau Nonverbal IQ (X) and Lavoie-Laurendeau Verbal IQ (Y).

TABLE 4
Analysis of Covariance of Performance of
Two Groups of Subjects, Large Sample

Source	df	X^2	XY	Y^2
Between groups	1	8284.89	6864.76	5687.94
Within groups	145	32361.41	14500.34	26389.26
Total	146	40646.30	21365.10	32077.20

Analysis of Covariance

Source	*SS* of errors of estimate	df	MS	F
Total	20847.00	145		
Within groups	19892.06	144	138.14	
Adjusted means	954.94	1	954.94	6.91*

Note.—Sums of squares and cross products for 2 groups of subjects (monolingual and bilingual) on Lavoie-Laurendeau Nonverbal IQ (X) and Lavoie-Laurendeau Verbal IQ (Y).

*Indicates significance at the 1% level of confidence.

In O'Doherty's terms, we may have included mainly genuine bilinguals, as opposed to pseudo-bilinguals. The genuine bilingual, having mastered both languages, is believed by O'Doherty (1958) to be clearly in an advantageous position intellectually. But this study does not include information about the other type of bilingual.

The superiority of the bilinguals on the verbal measures might be considered from another point of view. Bilinguals have a more extended total vocabulary than have monolinguals in the sense that they have learned both English and French symbols for most referents in their environment. The overlap of English and French vocabularies is considerable, so that an English-French bilingual may actually be helped when functioning in either language by the positive transfer derived from the other. The difference in the amount of overlap between two languages may, in part, explain the discrepancy between the results reported here and those reported previously from Wales. French and English have many more words derived from common roots than do Welsh and English. A Welsh-English bilingual would not benefit from as much positive transfer in vocabulary as would a French-English bilingual.

Differential Performance on Intelligence Measures

It was suggested in the introduction that bilinguals and monolinguals might be found to perform differently on various types of intelligence subtests and that this performance difference might somehow be related to a difference in the structure of the intellect of the typical students in the two groups. Reference to the factor analyses (Tables 5 and 6) shows that the bilinguals seem to have a greater number of separate or independent abilities on which to draw in completing these tests in contrast to the monolinguals who have fewer. That is, the bilinguals have more independent factors defined by intelligence variables than the monolinguals. For the bilinguals, Factor IV is clearly defined as a verbal intelligence factor. There are several nonverbal intelligence factors—III, V, VI, VII—which are defined by the intelligence measures, but also have loadings of achievement and attitude variables on them. Factor I also has some loadings of intelligence tests on it. For the monolinguals, on the other hand, most of the intelligence variables, both verbal and nonverbal, load together on Factor I which is clearly a general intelligence factor. Factor VI for the monolinguals is roughly equivalent to the verbal factor (IV) for the bilinguals, but it is not so pure and clear. Similarly, Factor VII (monolinguals) has high loadings of both intelligence and achievement in English. The remaining loadings of the intelligence variables on other factors do not play an important role for the monolinguals. Thus some support is given to the notion that bilinguals have developed more independent abilities and skills at an earlier age through their experiences and their learning of a second language. In summary, the structure of intellect of the bilinguals appears to be more diversified than that of the monolinguals. Thus, Guilford's (1956) belief that different experiences might cause different factors of intellect to appear at varying times for different individuals receives support here. Further research on this structure for monolinguals

TABLE 5
Rotated Factor Matrix for Monolinguals

	Variable	I	II	III	IV	V	VI	VII	h^2
3.	Socioeconomic class	.03	−.04	.57	.20	.01	.25	.15	.46
4.	School grade	.14	−.07	.51	.08	.04	.52	.09	.57
10.	Raven Matrices	.71	.24	−.06	.20	−.02	.06	.19	.64
11.	Primary Mental Abilities (PMA) Verbal Meaning	.47	.11	.08	.23	.28	.22	−.10	.43
12.	PMA Space	.29	.06	.01	.32	.15	.26	.40	.44
13.	PMA Figure-Grouping	.40	.05	.06	−.04	.13	−.15	.58	.54
14.	PMA Perception	.35	.20	−.06	.31	.09	.45	.33	.59
15.	PMA Number	.04	.40	−.07	.25	−.05	.49	.16	.50
16.	Lavoie-Laurendeau (L-L) Picture Arrangement	.74	.17	.09	.02	−.08	.06	.04	.59
17.	L-L Figure Manipulation	.57	.22	.17	.21	.11	.16	.24	.54
18.	L-L Dissimilarities	.13	.19	.09	.04	.34	.24	.46	.45
19.	L-L Picture Completion	.64	.09	.15	−.17	−.01	.30	.21	.60
20.	L-L Vocabulary	.50	−.07	.25	−.00	.20	.54	.02	.64
21.	L-L Comprehension	.19	.19	.19	−.05	.29	.68	.10	.66
22.	L-L Similarities	.38	.03	.28	−.05	.35	.11	.04	.37
23.	L-L Information	.21	−.01	.30	.18	.08	.74	−.09	.73

TABLE 5—continued
Rotated Factor Matrix for Monolinguals

Variable	I	II	III	IV	V	VI	VII	h^2
24. Achievement in general	.26	.88	−.02	.14	.07	−.05	.08	.88
25. Achievement in French	.15	.87	.03	.09	.01	.12	.15	.82
26. Achievement in English	.11	.48	.08	.13	.79	.06	.32	.99
27. Marks in French <u>dictée</u>	.08	.85	.12	.01	.09	.14	.12	.78
28. Marks in French <u>lecture</u>	.15	.67	.03	−.07	.38	−.07	−.13	.65
29. Marks in French <u>composition</u>	.10	.74	−.15	−.28	.36	.11	.00	.80
30. French skills of parents	.12	.22	.25	.10	−.11	.09	.30	.24
31. English skills of parents	.12	−.04	.76	.15	.03	−.02	.21	.66
33. Attitude-to-English scale	−.03	.03	.42	−.35	.21	.17	.30	.47
34. Attitude-to-French scale	.10	−.08	.03	.52	.02	.13	−.04	.31
38. Parents' attitude to English Canadians (EC)	.09	.01	.34	−.05	.13	.07	−.02	.14
39. Parents' attitude to French Canadians (FC)	−.04	.09	.22	−.02	.24	.16	−.07	.14
43. Identification of FC and Me	−.00	−.14	−.12	−.63	−.19	−.03	−.19	.50
45. Identification of Me and EC	−.01	−.11	.02	−.14	−.58	−.10	−.12	.39
46. Voice Study	−.04	−.06	−.36	.04	.12	−.01	.19	.19

TABLE 6
Rotated Factor Matrix for Bilinguals

Variable	I	II	III	IV	V	VI	VII	h^2
3. Socioeconomic class	-.05	.07	.07	-.06	-.05	.06	.47	.24
4. School grade	.14	.19	-.26	.58	.26	-.11	.08	.54
10. Raven Matrices	.32	.16	.54	.14	-.08	.39	.11	.61
11. Primary Mental Abilities (PMA) Verbal Meaning	.27	.03	.18	.75	.13	.09	-.01	.69
12. PMA Space	.09	.02	.24	.26	.41	.29	.40	.54
13. PMA Figure-Grouping	.18	.14	.41	.15	.06	.50	-.02	.50
14. PMA Perception	-.05	-.20	.11	.22	.56	.21	.02	.47
15. PMA Number	.22	.05	-.11	.07	.48	-.11	-.02	.32
16. Lavoie-Laurendeau (L-L) Picture Arrangement	.03	.12	.49	.31	.12	.06	.15	.40
17. L-L Figure Manipulation	.29	-.08	.32	.16	.10	.38	.32	.47
18. L-L Dissimilarities	.03	.08	-.02	-.05	.04	.60	.08	.38
19. L-L Picture Completion	-.17	-.14	.32	.43	.17	-.09	.15	.40
20. L-L Vocabulary	.21	-.20	.10	.68	.04	.11	.05	.58
21. L-L Comprehension	.11	-.08	.08	.41	-.02	.08	-.13	.22
22. L-L Similarities	-.02	-.05	.15	.36	-.02	.40	-.22	.37
23. L-L Information	.42	-.22	.07	.44	.22	-.08	.15	.50
24. Achievement in general	.78	.02	.07	.15	.10	.25	.15	.74
25. Achievement in French	.83	-.07	.10	.20	.09	.16	.00	.78

TABLE 6—continued
Rotated Factor Matrix for Bilinguals

Variable	I	II	III	IV	V	VI	VII	h^2
26. Achievement in English	.19	.26	.13	.12	.62	.05	−.08	.53
27. Marks in French *dictée*	.75	−.05	.01	.19	−.09	−.03	.02	.61
28. Marks in French *lecture*	.62	−.34	.06	.08	.42	−.05	−.20	.73
29. Marks in French *composition*	.71	−.04	.06	.07	.19	.21	−.27	.67
30. French skills of parents	−.13	−.42	−.16	.27	−.22	−.54	.11	.64
31. English skills of parents	−.38	.34	.11	.06	−.07	.14	−.06	.30
33. Attitude-to-English scale	−.10	.69	.02	−.13	.14	.21	.13	.58
34. Attitude-to-French scale	−.01	−.73	.09	.05	−.09	−.04	.01	.55
38. Parents' attitude to English Canadians (EC)	−.13	.67	.04	.09	−.19	.12	.11	.54
39. Parents' attitude to French Canadians (FC)	.03	−.49	−.33	.14	−.32	.10	−.09	.49
43. Identification of FC and Me	−.28	.35	.09	−.09	.36	−.36	−.19	.51
45. Identification of Me and EC	−.06	−.03	−.07	−.13	.13	−.42	−.29	.30
46. Voice Study	−.10	.38	.15	−.13	−.04	−.26	−.06	.27

and bilinguals, including a greater number of different types of measures of intelligence, might prove extremely useful in current attempts to define the nature of intelligence. It would also be interesting to investigate whether the monolinguals eventually develop similar factors, or whether the basic structure remains different.

It is important to realize that it is not possible to ascertain from the present study whether the more diversified structure of intelligence of the bilinguals is attributable to their bilinguality or simply to the fact that they are more intelligent. Perhaps a higher degree of intelligence means more diversified abilities and aptitudes.

Attitudes to English and French

For all the measures of attitudes used, the means for the bilingual group were in the direction of being more favorable to English Canadians, while the means for the monolingual group were more favorable to the French Canadians. A comparison of Tables 1 and 2 shows that the differences between means reached significance on more of the relevant attitude variables for the large sample than for the small sample. These results present a clear picture of the bilingual group being more favorably disposed to English Canadians, and less to French Canadians than the monolingual group.

Several possible explanations of these findings come to mind. The greater contact which the bilinguals have with English Canadians and English culture may account in part for their more favorable attitudes. The very fact that they have succeeded in becoming bilingual indicates that getting to know the English and their language must have been a goal or value for them. This goal, which may have been engendered by parents (Gardner, 1960), led them to seek more contact with the English community. These contacts may well have been positively reinforcing thereby increasing the desire for further interactions. Support for the notion of the influence of the parents comes from our data. The bilingual children report that their parents' attitudes toward English Canadians are favorable. Their parents' skill in English is also significantly higher than that of the monolinguals' parents. The correlation (.48) between the bilinguals' attitudes to EC and the attitudes they reported that their parents held may indicate that the Parents' Attitude-to-English scale was just a reflection of how the children themselves feel. This in no way diminishes the importance of it as a measure. It is a child's perception of the attitudes his parents hold that to a great extent influences his behavior and thinking, whether or not this perception is in line with reality. For the monolinguals, the correlation between Attitude-to-English scale and the Parents' Attitude-to-English is lower (.27). Attitudes toward the English may not be salient for monolingual families and therefore less frequently discussed.

Because the bilinguals held more favorable attitudes toward English Canadians, does this necessarily mean they had to hold less favorable attitudes to French Canadians? The scales devised to measure these two attitudes were composed from the same questionnaire and had some overlapping items (e.g., My best friend is English Canadian? French Canadian? or other?) which might suggest that there is a built-in negative relation between the Attitude-to-English scale and the Attitude-to-French scale. If we examine the correlations between these two scales (Variables 33 and 34), we find that for the monolinguals the $\underline{r}$ is only -.11 which clearly suggests that the relation between attitudes to French and attitudes to English is not inherent in the nature of the scales. The correlation of -.48 for the bilinguals therefore needs some explanation. The fact that they have learned English indicates that they must have identified, to some extent at least, with the English Canadians. This tendency is reflected in the measure of Identification with English Canadians (Variable 45) on which the bilinguals identify with English Canadians more closely than do the monolinguals. It is psychologically difficult to belong to two communities at once, to identify to the same extent with two groups which are culturally different. It appears that the bilinguals have resolved this "conflict" by clearly identifying with the English Canadians rather than with the French Canadians. The closer identification with English Canadians is supported by the higher means for bilinguals on the Differential Evaluation measures where a higher score indicates that the second concept is evaluated more favorably than the first. This strong identification with the English seems to require the bilinguals to identify less with the French Canadians.

On the reactions to spoken language (Variable 46), the mean score for the bilinguals was 4.98, which suggests that the stereotypes they hold of French Canadians and English Canadians are of a similar degree of favorableness. This variable measures stereotypes and does not correlate with the attitude scores. The monolinguals' evaluations indicate that they hold more favorable stereotypes of the French Canadians than of the English Canadians.

Many of the monolinguals and bilinguals in our sample live in the same districts and have approximately the same opportunities to learn English. Why did the one group take advantage of these occasions for interaction while the other group did not? One could suggest that the less favorable attitudes of the monolinguals toward English Canadians and the lack of encouragement from their parents on this matter have had a powerful negative effect. This will be dealt with more fully in the following discussion of the relation between attitudes to English and achievement in English.

Attitude and English Achievement

If we examine the correlation and factor tables to determine which variables are related to achievement in English, we discover that the attitude variables are important for the monolinguals, but not for the bilinguals. The bilinguals as a group appear to have more clearly defined attitudes which are favorable to the English, and which have ceased to present a problem for them. To the extent that there is consensus among the bilinguals there would be less variance and less chance for correlation. For the bilinguals, Achievement in English is related more to intelligence than to attitude. The only significant relation for them between attitude and achievement is the negative relation between Achievement in English and Attitude-to-French scale (-.42) which indicates that the more unfavorable attitudes to French the bilingual holds, the better he does in English. For the monolinguals on the other hand, attitudes play as important a role as intelligence. Factor V obtains its highest loadings from achievement in English. The high loading of the Identification of moi and English Canadians on this factor (-.58) indicates the importance of attitudes for English achievement for monolinguals. Correlations of -.51, -.52, and -.54 between Achievement in English and Identification of Me and English Canadians, of French Canadians and Me, and of French Canadians and English Canadians, respectively, suggest that a monolingual does better in English if he sees all these three as being similar, that is, French Canadians, English Canadians, and himself. Apparently it is necessary for him to identify with both groups in order to do well in English. This attempt at dual identification may well constitute a conflict for him and possibly hinder him from becoming bilingual. If he fails to identify with both, he does poorly in English.

It appears, then, that the attitude an individual holds toward the other language community plays a vitally important role in his learning the other group's language in school, as is particularly the case with our monolingual sample. If he views the other community with favor, he is more likely to do well in his attempts to learn the language, and vice versa. It also becomes evident that for those who have already practically mastered a second language, (e.g., our bilinguals) their attitudes to the second language community, of which they are in some way now a part, no longer play as important a role in their continued achievement in that language as do factors such as intelligence. The hypothesis that those with more favorable attitudes toward the English community would do better in learning English has received substantial support.

Bilingualism and School Grade

Previous studies had pointed out that bilinguals suffered from a language handicap and possibly because of it were behind in school. In the present study, where no handicap became evident, one should not expect bilinguals to be retarded in school. Indeed, the bilinguals as a group were significantly more advanced in school grade than were the monolinguals, and this, undoubtedly, can be attributed to their higher intelligence. For the bilinguals, school grade loads on the intelligence factors, especially the verbal intelligence factor (IV), suggesting that it is the verbal skills of the bilinguals that help them do well in school. Their bilingualism apparently gives them an advantage in those skills which depend on verbal fluency. For the monolinguals the picture is somewhat different. Grade in school loads about equally on Factor VI (intelligence) and Factor III (essentially an attitude factor). It is related to such variables as Space, Perception, Figure Manipulation, but not to Verbal Meaning or Vocabulary. Thus the monolinguals draw more on nonverbal than verbal abilities for their advancement in school grade, in contrast to the bilinguals. Socioeconomic class also seems to be a powerful determinant of how well monolinguals will do in school ($r = .46$). The implications of the correlates of achievement in school such as the contribution of socioeconomic class to school grade advancement for the monolinguals but not for the bilinguals, will not be fully considered in this thesis. In fact, many of the ramifications of the factor structures in general have not been fully explored. They constitute the start of the next phase of this research.

CONCLUSION

This study has found that bilinguals performed better than monolinguals on verbal and nonverbal intelligence tests. These results were not expected because they constitute a clear reversal of previously reported findings. How can we account for this difference in intelligence between the two groups? An attempt will be made here to integrate the explanations presented above into a description of the differences between the groups which may partially account for their differences in intellectual functioning.

The picture that emerges of the French-English bilingual in Montreal is that of a youngster whose wider experiences in two cultures have given him advantages which a monolingual does not enjoy. Intellectually his experience with two language systems seems to have left him with a mental flexibility, a superiority in concept formation, and a more diversified set of mental abilities, in the sense that the patterns of abilities developed by bilinguals were more heterogeneous. It is not possible to state from the present study whether the more intelligent child became bilingual or whether bilingualism aided his intellectual development, but there is no question about the fact that he is superior intellectually. In contrast, the monolingual appears to have a more unitary structure of intelligence which he must use for all types of intellectual tasks.

Because of superior intelligence, these bilingual children are also further ahead in school than the monolinguals and they achieve significantly better than their classmates in English study, as would be expected, and in school work in general. Their superior achievement in school seems to be dependent on a verbal facility. Those monolinguals who do poorly in their English study apparently fail to identify either with the English or the French cultural groups. In contrast, those monolinguals who do well in English, have closely identified themselves with both communities. Their failure to become bilingual may be attributed in part to the difficulties they may encounter in making a dual identification with both cultural groups, coupled with their acceptance of their own group (i. e., French Canadians) as being superior. The attitudes of the bilinguals are quite different. They hold more favorable attitudes towards the English than toward the French. Their clear identification with one group may contribute to their mastery of English. It is interesting to note that in the Voice Study, which attempts to tap stereotypes, the bilinguals evaluate the personalities of French and English speakers in a similar manner while the monolinguals evaluate the French more favorably than the English.

The pattern of attitudes that emerges for the two groups is distinctively different and these attitude differences might be expected to influence performance on intelligence tests, but this is not the case. There are no significant correlations between attitude and intelligence for either group. Nevertheless it is worthwhile examining the group differences in attitude patterns since they throw light on the possible reasons why some students become bilingual while others remain monolingual. This can best be done by comparing Factor III for the monolinguals with Factor II for the bilinguals. Factor III, for the monolinguals reflects a family-wide attitude to English Canadians, while Factor II for the bilinguals reflects a family-wide attitude to English Canadians versus French Canadians. The bilingual factor is bipolar in the sense that it has positive loadings of attitude variables favorable to English as well as negative loadings of attitude variables favorable to French. That is, the bilinguals, very likely through parental influence, are favorable toward the English community and at the same time unfavorable to the French.

Factor III for the monolinguals is a unitary factor. It indicates that the monolingual children of higher socioeconomic class, even though they hold positive attitudes to the English as do their parents, still have more favorable stereotypes of the French than of the English. This tendency to see the French as better may partly explain why the children have remained monolingual. Possibly children from these families of higher social class have developed positive attitudes to the English and yet feel a pressure to remain French. It is possible that some conservative nationalistic sentiment for the retaining of the French language exists among these children and prevents them from identifying sufficiently with the English community to be psychologically set to learn the language and thus they remain monolingual. And yet the higher social class families may admire and emulate the English Canadians as instrumentally valuable models in spheres of activity which contribute to maintaining higher social class standing, such as economic and social situations. Factor III also affords a second description of the monolingual family. In this case, the lower social class monolingual family has the following characteristics: the parents have little skill in English and hold negative attitudes to the English, although they do endorse favorable stereotypes of the English. The children are comparatively retarded in school grade. This pattern suggests that those French-Canadian families of lower socioeconomic class may become envious of the English Canadians and, perhaps through places of residence and type of work, culturally isolated and remain monolingual.

Thus a picture emerges of monolingual and bilingual children as representatives of two distinct groups, differing in intellectual structure, attitude patterns, achievement in school, and achievement in languages. The results of this study indicate the value of shifting emphasis from looking for favorable or unfavorable effects of bilingualism on intelligence to an inquiry into the basic nature of these effects. Perhaps further research may profit from this different emphasis.

SUMMARY

The effects of bilingualism on intellectual functioning are explored in this study. A group of monolingual and a group of bilingual 10-year-old children from six Montreal French schools were administered verbal and nonverbal intelligence tests, and measures of attitudes to the English and French communities. Contrary to previous findings this study found that bilinguals performed significantly better than monolinguals on both verbal and nonverbal intelligence tests.

Several explanations are suggested as to why bilinguals have this general intellectual advantage. It is argued that they have a language asset, are more facile at concept formation, and have a greater mental flexibility. The results of factor analyses applied to the data supported the hypothesis that the structure of intellect for the two groups differ. The bilinguals appear to have a more diversified set of mental abilities than the monolinguals. The correlations of the attitude measures with other variables are also discussed.

NOTES

This research was carried out with the financial support of the Carnegie Corporation of New York, through a subvention to W. E. Lambert. The authors are grateful to G. Barbeau and T. Boulanger of the Catholic School Commission of Montreal and to the principals and teachers of the six schools used in this study for their assistance and cooperation during the testing programs in their schools. Special thanks are expressed to Irene Vachon-Spilka for her assistance in translation and administration of the tests. The writer is indebted to R. C. Gardner (McGill) and R. M. Olton (McGill) for writing the necessary programs for the IBM 650 computer, without which the statistical analysis would not have been possible. Thanks are also due to G. A. Ferguson (McGill) for his advice on statistical matters.

[1] Several studies (Arthur, 1937; Bere, 1924; Feingold, 1924; Hirsch, 1926) which have reported that bilingualism has no effect on intelligence lack too many important controls to be worth considering in detail here.

[2] From *Speech development of a bilingual child*, Vol. 3, by W. F. Leopold. Copyright 1949, Northwestern University Press. Used by permission.

[3] Appendices A-D have been deposited with the American Documentation Institute. Order Document No. 7308, from ADI Auxiliary Publications Project, Photoduplication Service, Library of Congress; Washington 25, D. C., remitting in advance $2.25 for microfilm or $5.00 for photocopies. Make checks payable to: Chief, Photoduplication Service, Library of Congress.

[4] The numbering in the following sections refers to the number assigned to that variable for the analysis and is consistent throughout the rest of the paper. For names and numbering of subtests of intelligence, see Appendix B.

[5] From Psychological testing, by Anne Anastasi. Copyright 1961, Macmillan Company. Used by permission.

REFERENCES

Ahmed, M. A.-S. Mental manipulation. Egypt. Yearbk. Psychol., 1954, 1, 23-88.

Altus, Grace T. WISC patterns of a selective sample of bilingual school children. J. genet. Psychol., 1953, 83, 241-248.

Anastasi, Anne. Psychological testing. (2nd ed.). New York: Macmillan, 1961.

Anisfeld, M., Beese, N., and Lambert, W. E. Evaluational reactions to accented English-speech. McGill University, 1961. (mimeo)

Arsenian, S. Bilingualism and mental development. Teach. Coll. Contr. Educ., 1937, No. 712.

Arthur, G. The predictive value of the Kuhlmann-Binet Scale for a partially Americanized school population. J. appl. Psychol., 1937, 21, 359-364.

Bere, M. A comparative study of mental capacity of children of foreign parentage. New York: Teachers College, Columbia University, 1924.

Central Advisory Council for Education (Wales). The place of Welsh and English in the schools of Wales. London: Her Majesty's Stationery Office, 1953.

Christophersen, P. Bilingualism. London: Methuen, 1948.

Darcy, Natalie T. The effect of bilingualism upon the measurement of the intelligence of children of preschool age. J. educ. Psychol., 1946, 37, 21-44.

__________ A review of the literature on the effects of bilingualism upon the measurement of intelligence. J. genet. Psychol., 1953, 82, 21-57.

Darsie, M. L. The mental capacity of American-born Japanese children. Comp. Psychol. Monogr., 1926, 3, 1-18.

Davies, M., and Hughes, A. G. An investigation into the comparative intelligence and attainments of Jewish and non-Jewish school children. Brit. J. Psychol., 1927, 18, 134-146.

Dunn, L. M. Peabody Picture Vocabulary Test. Tennessee: American Guidance Service, 1959.

Evans, S. J. Address of the Conference of Headmasters of Grammar Schools, Wales, 1902. In Central Advisory Council for Education (Wales), *The place of Welsh and English in the schools of Wales*. London: Her Majesty's Stationery Office, 1953.

Feingold, G. A. Intelligence of the first generation immigrant groups. *J. educ. Psychol.*, 1924, 15, 65-82.

Ferguson, G. A. On learning and human ability. *Canad. J. Psychol.*, 1954, 8, 95-112.

Gardner, R. C. Motivational variables in second-language acquisition. Unpublished doctoral dissertation, McGill University, 1960.

Gardner, R. C., and Lambert, W. E. Motivational variables in second-language acquisition. *Canad. J. Psychol.*, 1959, 13, 266-272.

Graham, V. T. The intelligence of Italian and Jewish children. *J. abnorm. soc. Psychol.*, 1925, 20, 371-376.

Guilford, J. P. The structure of intellect. *Psychol. Bull.* 1956, 53, 267-293.

Hill, H. S. The effects of bilingualism on the measured intelligence of elementary school children of Italian parentage. *J. exp. Educ.*, 1936, 5, 75-79.

Hirsch, N. D. A study of natio-racial mental differences. *Genet. Psychol. Monogr.*, 1926, 1, 231-407.

James, C. B. E. Bilingualism in Wales: An aspect of semantic organization. *Educ. Res.*, 1960, 2, 123-136.

Johnson, G. B. Bilingualism as measured by a reaction-time technique and the relationship between a language and a non-language intelligence quotient. *J. genet. Psychol.*, 1953, 82, 3-9.

Jones, W. R. A critical study of bilingualism and nonverbal intelligence. *Brit. J. educ. Psychol.*, 1960, 30, 71-76.

Jones, W. R., and Stewart, W. A. Bilingualism and verbal intelligence. *Brit. J. Psychol.*, 1951, 4, 3-8.

Lambert, W. E. Developmental aspects of second-language acquisition: I. Associational fluency, stimulus provocativeness, and word-order influence. *J. soc. Psychol.*, 1956, 43, 83-89. [In this volume, pp. 9-16.]

Lambert, W. E., Havelka, J., and Crosby, C. The influence of language-acquisition contexts on bilingualism. *J. abnorm. soc. Psychol.*, 1958, 56, 239-244. [In this volume, pp. 51-62.]

Lambert, W. E., Havelka, J., and Gardner, R. C. Linguistic manifestations of bilingualism. *Amer. J. Psychol.*, 1959, 72, 77-82. [In this volume, pp. 63-71.]

Lambert, W.E., Hodgson, R.C., Gardner, R.C., and Fillenbaum, S. Evaluational reactions to spoken languages. J. abnorm. soc. Psychol., 1960, 60, 44-51. [In this volume, pp. 80-96.]

Langer, Susanne. Philosophy in a new key. Cambridge: Harvard Univer. Press, 1942.

Lavoie, G., and Laurendeau, Monique. Tests collectifs d'intélligence générale. Montreal, Canada: Institut de Recherches Psychologiques, 1960.

Lazowick, L.M. On the nature of identification. J. abnorm. soc. Psychol., 1955, 51, 175-183.

Leopold, W.F. Speech development of a bilingual child. Vol. 3. Evanston: Northwestern Univer. Press, 1949.

Levinson, B.M. A comparison of the performance of bilingual and monolingual native born Jewish preschool children of traditional parentage on four intelligence tests. J. clin. Psychol., 1959, 15, 74-76.

Lewis, D.G. Bilingualism and non-verbal intelligence: A further study of test results. Brit. J. educ. Psychol., 1959, 29, 17-22.

McCarthy, Dorothea. Language development in children. In L. Carmichael (Ed.), Manual of child psychology. New York: Wiley, 1954.

Mead, M. Group intelligence and linguistic disability among Italian children. Sch. Soc., 1927, 25, 465-468.

Morrison, J.R. Bilingualism: Some psychological aspects. Advanc. Sci., 1958, 56, 287-290.

O'Doherty, E.F. Bilingualism: Educational aspects. Advanc. Sci., 1958, 56, 282-286.

Osgood, C.E., Suci, G.J., and Tannenbaum, P.H. The measurement of meaning. Urbana: Univer. Illinois Press, 1957.

Pintner, R. The influence of language background on intelligence tests. J. soc. Psychol., 1932, 3, 235-240.

Pintner, R., and Arsenian, S. The relation of bilingualism to verbal intelligence and school adjustment. J. educ. Res., 1937, 31, 255-263.

Pintner, R., and Keller, R. Intelligence tests of foreign children. J. educ. Psychol., 1922, 13, 214-222.

Raven, J.C. Coloured Progressive Matrices: Sets A, Ab, B. London: Lewis, 1956.

Rigg, M. Some further data on the language handicap. J. educ. Psychol., 1928, 19, 252-257.

Saer, D. J. The effects of bilingualism on intelligence. *Brit. J. Psychol.*, 1923, 14, 25-38.

Saer, Hywela. Experimental inquiry into the education of bilingual peoples. In, *Education in a changing commonwealth.* London. New Education Fellowship, 1931. Pp. 116-121.

Seidl, J. C. G. The effect of bilingualism on the measurement of intelligence. Unpublished doctoral dissertation, Fordham University, 1937.

Smith, F. Bilingualism and mental development. *Brit. J. Psychol.*, 1923, 13, 270-282.

Spoerl, Dorothy, T. The academic and verbal adjustment of college-age bilingual students. *J. genet. Psychol.*, 1944, 64, 139-157.

Stark, W. A. The effect of bilingualism on general intelligence: An investigation carried out in certain Dublin primary schools. *Brit. J. educ. Psychol.*, 1940, 10, 78-79.

Thurstone, L. L. *Multiple factor analysis.* Chicago: Univer. Chicago Press, 1947.

Thurstone, L. L., and Thurstone, Thelma G. *Primary Mental Abilities: Ages 7 to 11.* Chicago: Science Research Associates, 1954.

Wang, S. L. A demonstration of the language difficulty involved in comparing racial groups by means of verbal intelligence tests. *J. appl. Psychol.*, 1926, 10, 102-106.

Warner, W. L., Meeker, Marchia, and Eells, K. *Social class in America.* Chicago: Science Research Associates, 1949.

Weinreich, U. *Languages in contact.* New York: Linguistic Circle of New York, 1953.

Wittenborn, J. R., and Larsen, R. P. A factorial study of achievement in college German. *J. educ. Psychol.*, 1944, 35, 39-48.

11 Psychological Approaches to the Study of Language

I: ON LEARNING, THINKING AND HUMAN ABILITIES

My assignment was to set forth and explain certain subject matter and research from the field of psychology that, if included in the training of language specialists, would enrich their understanding of the phenomena of language and increase their efficiency as teachers of foreign languages. Accordingly, I have selected various psychological approaches to language that seem to me to be of instructive value and practical use to language teachers. These particular approaches were selected because they promise to be of permanent value both in explaining the known facts about language and in orienting future research. To limit the scope of this paper, no consideration will be given to other psychological developments that could be of value to language teachers even though they do not deal with language specifically. For example, language teachers and their trainers could profit from a careful study of current research in the psychology of personality and the problem of attitude changes. Psychological work on these matters suggests means of selecting those who would be most effective as language teachers, and indicates effective ways of forming favorable attitudes towards other cultural groups—matters as important as they are neglected in educational research.

My aim is to introduce briefly the basic ideas and implications of each approach, as I see them, with a view of enticing foreign language specialists to turn to the more complete accounts which are referred to in the references.

1. Theories of Learning of Relevance for Language Specialists

Since its beginning as an independent discipline, psychology has considered the phenomena of language and the language learning process as important matters falling within its field of specialization. But since World War II, a surge of interest in the cognitive aspects of behavior and the development of new methodologies have generated a widely-felt hope that perhaps now psychologists can systematically study the phenomena of language rather than speculate about them. Today many psychologists are starting to teach courses and conduct research on "verbal behavior," "psycholinguistics," and "language and thought." This new attitude stems from advances, perhaps normal ones, in many fields of specialization that feed into psychology, for example, advances in the neurology of brain functioning, in statiscal and experimental procedures, in the design and operation of computers, and in methods of language teaching. As a response to these developments, psychologists are beginning to extend their principles and theories beyond the level of animal research (so very necessary for the establishment of basic principles in the first place) to the more complex behavior of man. Currently, all major theories of learning concern themselves with language and the growing body of empirical data on the subject. The following discussion of two contemporary learning theories is needed to understand the current psychological interest in two basic processes: meaning, the symbol-referent problem, and verbal behavior, how words are used in communication, either as units or as elements in larger response sequences. What follows is a very brief sketch of two contrasting learning theories, one dealing with meaning, the other with verbal behavior. There is nothing necessarily inconsistent in a discipline having more than one scheme of analysis to integrate facts and explain events, especially when these are as complex as learning and human cognitive behavior. As more data becomes available, two or more theories of learning may prove to be necessary, or as others very convincingly argue[1] a single set of principles may ultimately draw the two schemes together.

The contrast here is between what are called "classical" and "instrumental" forms of conditioning or learning. "Classical" refers to Pavlov's notions about the response conditioned to an unnatural stimulus. In this case, a stimulus with some "natural" or built-in evocative tendency (such as a hammer tap on the patellar tendon of the knee which evokes an involuntary muscular kicking response) can be replaced by a stimulus that is "unnatural" for such a response (such as the sound of a bell). The unnatural stimulus takes over the evocative capacity of the natural stimulus when the two stimuli are repeatedly paired in the order bell—hammer tap, bell—hammer tap, etc. for a long series of presentations. Several notions are of importance in this statement. A stimulus which has a natural response sequel is a required ingredient; this is the "unconditioned" or uncontaminated element. The knee jerk is not a natural sequel to the hearing of a bell, and when a bell—knee jerk connection is finally made, the kick response is referred to as a "conditioned" response and the bell is called a "conditioned" stimulus. The time separating the conditioned and unconditioned stimuli is of major importance. The two stimuli must be nearly simultaneously presented, the conditioned stimulus (the bell) coming a fraction of a second earlier than the unconditioned stimulus. It is not known how this transfer of evocative capacity takes place; psychology and neurology have had and will continue to have fun trying to understand the process. But the empirical facts are very dependable. Pavlov's dogs salivated (a conditioned response) to the sound of a bell (a conditioned stimulus) when bell and food were repeatedly paired. And Pavlov's dogs were not special in this respect. Literally thousands of experiments have demonstrated the phenomenon with organisms at nearly every level of the phylogenetic scale.

The evocative capacity of the conditioned stimulus, when on its own, is ephemeral; it must be "re-charged" by being periodically paired with the unconditioned stimulus. The repeated association of the two stimuli permits the transfer of evocative capacity and there must be periodical re-association of the two if the transferred capacity is to be maintained. When fully charged the conditioned stimulus itself can be repeatedly paired with a second unnatural stimulus (for example, the flash of a light) permitting the second conditioned stimulus to pick up the charge in the sense that it, too, can evoke the "conditioned" response. This chain of events is referred to as "second-order" conditioning. If a second conditioned stimulus which is similar in some sense to the first is introduced for the first time, it will also have an evocative capacity to call out the conditioned response. The conditioning is said to "generalize" to related stimuli, the degree of generalization depending on the degree of similarity between the original conditioned stimulus and the "similar" stimulus. If the original bell had a tone quality of 300 cycles per second, generalization would likely take place to a tone of 325 or 275 cycles per second.

Note in this argument that the conditioned stimulus (the hearing of a bell) functions as a signal or sign that something is to come, somewhat analogous to a symbol relating to its referent. The organism comprehends that the bell "stands for" the hammer tap and it is likely that a mental image of the hammer tap eventually occurs when the signal is received, as though some mental replica of the actual referent is evoked by the symbol because of changes within the nervous system introduced by the continual pairing of stimuli. Here, in compressed form, is the psychological basis for the relation of symbols to referents. Charles E. Osgood[2] has made this extension of the theory especially clear. For Osgood, the meaning of a sign or symbol _is_ the mental or neurological counterpart, in attenuated form, of the actual emotional and behavioral responses that have habitually been made to the referent for which the symbol stands. That is, linguistic symbols are originally learned in a context where they are repeatedly paired with their appropriate referents. An infant hears the word "dog" repeated several times while in the presence of an actual dog and in time whatever emotional and behavioral reactions are elicited by the presence of the actual dog are transferred to the symbol "dog." Symbols then come to evoke some miniature replica of the actual responses made to the referent, and these responses, referred to as "representational mediational responses," constitute the meaning of the symbol. They _represent_ or stand for the full-pattern of responses made to the referent, they _mediate_ or link the responses made to the referent with those made to the symbol, and they are some form of nervous system _response_, hence their label, "representational mediational responses."

Osgood uses this scheme to explain how meanings are developed directly through classical learning principles or how meanings are "assigned" to us, ready-made so to speak, by "teachers" in our social environment. Because Osgood's conceptualization of meaning has the advantage of integrating a wide range of empirical facts, and because it has stimulated so much current research,[3] it should be of particular value in the teaching of languages. It offers a new and instructive orientation to meaning and it will suggest methods of studying the development, assignment and modification of meanings —matters of everyday concern to language teachers. Comparisons can be made of methods of teaching languages and their effectiveness in developing vivid and persistent meanings. The work of Staats and

Staats indicates how favorable (or, inadvertently, unfavorable) emotional components of meaning can be assigned to foreign language vocabularies as they are being learned. The work of Lambert and Jakobovits shows how meanings can be dissipated or "satiated" when continuous repetition of words takes place, as in vocabulary drill.

Other psychologists are interested in "associative meaning," that is, the organized interrelations of verbal associations.[4] Verbal associations are determined by asking subjects to give the first word that comes to mind after they think about a particular word given them. For example, *night* popularly leads to *day* and *day* to *break* or back to *night*, etc. Verbal linkages of this sort are learned according to principles or "laws" of association, in particular the laws of contiguity, similarity and frequency. One association leads to another apparently because they have freqeuntly occurred in sequence in the past, in much the same way as contiguous elements become linked in classical conditioning.

This group of researchers is less concerned with the symbol-referent problem than with the reliable or common patterns of verbal associations themselves. They have been able to determine the similarity of associative meanings of words by their associative overlap. For example, Deese noted that *piano* and *symphony* do not associate directly with one another but they both elicit a common set of associations among college students: *note*, *song*, *sound*, *noise*, *music* and *orchestra*. Sub-groups of individuals of similar age and educational background have very similar associative networks. (There are some interesting exceptions. For example, some have closed associative networks, where *night* leads to *day* and *day* to *night*, whereas others, with quite different personalities, have wide open networks with little or no circular units.)

Foreign language teachers could utilize these common associative structures to advantage in their teaching procedures. For instance, vocabulary training might be patterned on the common networks of native speakers of the language. As students become skilled in their second language, fascinating studies of the networks in the two languages could be conducted. Certain associative networks might be found to be similar in the two languages while others are dissimilar. If so, one might then examine the dissimilar networks as sources of semantic interference between languages. Furthermore, grammatical or syntactical structures in two contrasting languages could be studied with this procedure. For example, Lambert[5] noted that the French noun-adjective word order affected associative networks in a quite different fashion from the English adjective-noun word order.

None of the richness of language is lost in the treatment given it by these psychologists. In fact, they contribute to its richness by highlighting its complexity. They do not claim to have made much more than a start, but few will disagree that they have started a promising movement of language research. The excitement of the psychologist in the study of meaning, noted especially in the work of Osgood and Mowrer, contrasts with the uninterested treatment given the problem by most linguists.

B. F. Skinner of Harvard is the best known modern exponent of a contrasting form of learning known as instrumental (operant) conditioning.[6] The distinctive characteristic of instrumental learning is the importance attributed to the consequences of responses (reinforcers) in influencing the strength of these responses. Consider the case of an animal that, presumably in his exploration and random activity in a puzzle box, accidentally depresses a lever situated at one end of the box. The box is typically rigged so that on depression of the lever the animal immediately receives some desired outcome. For a cat in a puzzle box, the lever depression can open a door and release the animal; for a hungry white rat or pigeon, the lever pressing may deliver a pellet of wanted food. Getting out or getting wanted food are examples of "reinforcements" or rewards. Timing is crucial in this form of learning, especially the interval separating the organism's <u>response</u> (lever pushing) and the reception of <u>reinforcement</u> (food pellet). Note that in this case there is no close temporal pairing of an unnatural stimulus with a natural one as was the case in classical conditioning. Instead, attention is given to the development of a brand new response that is brought under the management of other people in the environment (in this case the experimenter who controls the food-delivery mechanism) who control the doling out of reinforcements when the appropriate response is made. Once the reinforcement has been received, the response potential is raised and it will be noted that on further trials the organism will more quickly move closer to the lever and, with consistent reinforcement, will execute the new act with polished efficiency. When reinforcements are withheld, the lever-depression habit will gradually be "extinguished," that is, the animal will refrain from pressing the lever. Signals can be introduced to inform the animal when it is appropriate to respond. For example, a light can be flashed to indicate that the lever-pressing will now lead to reinforcement. After practice, the animal will differentiate when it is worthwhile responding and when not. The basic plan can be complicated when two animals learn to cooperate. Skinner describes how two pigeons can be taught to respond in coordination if food reinforcement is given both for a coordinated set of responses. With this example, Skinner moves his attention up to the intricate level of cooperative behavior and his experimentation suggests that simple forms of animals are docile enough to learn at least the rudiments of cooperative behavior.

Food is only one type of reinforcement which proves effective. Animals will also learn complicated patterns of response to escape from confinement or from fearful settings, or they will learn how to turn on a light when subjected to darkness. If the reinforcement is given with care, the animal will learn precise response sequences, but if the reinforcements are administered haphazardly, the nature of the habit learned will also be vague and over-generalized. The reinforcements need not be regular, however. If the reinforcements are presented only a certain proportion of times (some responses reinforced and others not) the habit is often more rapidly learned and better retained than when reinforcements are given consistently. When they are given, however, the reinforcements must be precisely timed. Animals will often learn "superstitions" or unnecessary elements of responding. For example, a pigeon may have stretched its neck just before pecking an electronically-active button. The pecking response leads to food reinforcement, but for the animal the total sequence (neck stretch and then peck) is learned, so that neck-stretching regularly precedes the pecking response, in much the same way as a baseball batter will spit in his hands, knock the dirt from his cleats, and twist his cap as he waits for a pitch.

In his major work on "verbal behavior," Skinner[7] views the learning of language in essentially the same terms he uses to analyze the development of simple habits. Drawing on certain descriptive facts about the infant's extensive repertoire of sounds, Skinner argues that others in the baby's environment give reinforcements for the production of certain sound patterns and thereby restrict his range of sounds and make more probable certain oral productions. The parents or siblings must wait for the child to produce (presumably in his random verbalizations) something which is close enough to "belonging" so that they can realistically reinforce the attempt. For example, an infant's "baba" may be close enough to "mama" to surprise and please a new mother, and her excitement may be transmitted to the infant in the form of affectionate and spirited attention. This attention is an example of reinforcement, and in this sense the child should be launched on a word-learning program. The reinforcements used are more social in nature than was the case with the animal studies mentioned above. It is argued that the infant and child will learn symbols for objects in his environment because he thereby gains a control over people and things. Saying "milk" or something close enough to be understood as "milk" gets him something he wants. If his attempt is not recognizable, he suffers a frustrating delay in getting things which prompts him to be more exact. Following the pattern of instrumental learning, the word learner also learns to be a "demander" if he consistently gets what he asks for, i.e., if he is reinforced for demanding.

If the child's socializers hold off reinforcement until the verbal response is clear and appropriate, his use of words will be precise. However, others are often unable to check on the appropriateness of a response. When a child says he has a "stomach ache" (a very private feeling) he may actually have a pain in the intestinal region. The child may receive sympathy and some general pain reliever and thereby incidentally be reinforced for the idea that "stomach" runs from the throat region to the groin, with no differentiation being called for. On the other hand, the skill of the literary artist who can precisely describe very private emotional states is likely attributable to his having received appropriate reinforcements. Thus, infants, children and adults may be precise or sloppy in their use of words depending upon the exactitude with which reinforcements have been administered to them for their verbal attempts.

It is characteristic of Skinner to leave matters such as semantics to others. His writings are marked by his zeal to be a "descriptive behaviorist," meaning that he wants to keep his attention on observable behavioral responses and to relate them to such observable environmental events as reinforcements. Any theorizing about internal mental or neurological processes is scorned by him and his large host of followers. Meaning is considered as a mentalistic concept and he tries to explain language without reference to it. He is hampered in this attempt because his theory is limited.[8] Consequently it may appear that he approaches psychological matters much as an engineer might, given the two notions that simple responses can be quantified and that certain reinforcements are effective when properly administered. It is difficult for those not aware of Skinner's desire to help psychology become a "science" to understand his hard-headed position. However, in view of recent developments in cognitive and neurophysiological psychology, an imaginative person like Skinner must feel that being forced to be consistently the descriptive behaviorist is really being left with a very sticky wicket.

But the practical implications of this movement should be well understood by language specialists. Much important research has issued from his basic notions, much of it of direct relevance to the language learning of human subjects. For example, it has been clearly demonstrated that well-established verbal habits (some simple,[9] and others more complex[10]) can be modified under certain schedules of reinforcement. In these studies, subjects are typically reinforced by the experimenter's saying "good" or "uh-uh" when, for example, the plural forms of nouns or particular pronouns are used in sentence constructions. Because of the reinforcement, the tendency to use the reinforced forms is markedly increased. Barik and Lambert found that complex structures can also be modified by verbal reinforcement. For example, a person who habitually forms his sentences in the fashion: "This is the (house) that (burned) last night" can be trained to shift to the form "This is the (house) that (I saw) burning last night." Apparently these modifications take place without the subject becoming aware of any relation between the experimenter's saying "good" and his own behavior, although this point is not certain as yet.[11] These developments can be of immediate importance for language teachers who can be either effective or ineffective as social reinforcers of their students' attempts to develop appropriate verbal habits.

The most recent development in Skinner's thinking is evident in his interest in programmed learning and teaching machines.[12]

Mechanical modes of instruction are old ideas in psychology. They didn't catch on in the 1930's but are being enthusiastically entertained today, perhaps because Skinner is such a convincing proponent and because there has been a value shift toward mechanized instrumentation (gadgets) in this era. Skinner argues that teaching machines in certain respects are more effective than are teachers. The machines escape the problems of developing potentially unhealthy interpersonal dependencies between pupils and teachers. Furthermore, programmed machine instruction is tailor-made to each student's learning pace. The machines also control the timing between the pupil's response and his reinforcement (in this case, reinforcement is the realization that he was correct and that he may now move on to the next step). Furthermore, since the machine teaches so effectively, the student feels he is clearly progressing in his task and is much better motivated than is the case in most classrooms. Experienced teachers who are not psychologists should study this new development, comprehending its origins. And they should study it soon before it's too late, since so much money will be invested in these potentially useful procedures that educationists will be unable to evaluate objectively their long-term effectiveness in teaching. For this purpose experimentation should be started soon. They may have a strong initial or novelty effect with teen-agers that diminishes rapidly. The programmed materials should be tested in classroom settings <u>without</u> the machines themselves. The creation of good programs depends on a personal skill. Programs can be of great help for teachers who do not have the time or ability to analyze course content into its most logical steps. On the other hand, programs should be carefully examined by specialists in human abilities (see section 3 below) to be more certain that the sequencing of steps is actually psychologically appropriate and maximally beneficial.

2. Neurophysiological Bases of Thought and Language

As we have seen, Skinner focuses attention on observable responses, including speech, and, in the manner of a skilled technician, indicates how response patterns can be developed, manipulated and modified. The empirical research of those adopting this approach is impressive and usually of great practical value. Because the proponents of the approach reject the use of theory, they also contribute little to psychological theory and this bias may eventually limit the movement's contribution to psychology. An important counter-movement, developed particularly during the past fifteen years, is probing much deeper into the organism than those interested only in response patterns care to. This group is interested in inside mechanisms, those processes going on within the nervous system of people when they speak and comprehend others speaking. These processes have been alluded to by Osgood in his description of meaning, likely because Osgood's own thinking has been guided by this movement. In fact, neurophysiological psychology is becoming one of the most popular areas of specialization for academically trained psychologists. The theories and research findings of this group should be of interest for teachers of language, at least for those who have seriously pondered the magical complexity and beauty of language, and for those who may be discouraged about psychology's role in the study of language because they have primarily encountered technician-type psychologists.

One of the chief catalysts in this new movement is Donald O. Hebb.[13] His aim in psychology has been to extend the significance of psychological concepts, especially those concerned with complex cognitive processes, by relating them to what is known about the neurology of the central nervous system. As a consequence of attempting to make this integration, he has liberalized some neurophysiological concepts and theories far beyond the known facts, and, at the same time, he has forced most psychologists to become interested in the workings of man's nervous system and brain, stimulating many of them to search for neurophysiological correlates of psychological phenomena.

What are his basic ideas? First of all, he feels that the study of thinking should be psychology's major concern, and thought processes are the central theme of his own work. He is interested in how contacts with the environment leave their residues or traces within the nervous system, how, in other words, the nervous system stores up images and memories which can later be called into play often without the intervention of environmental stimulation. All the evidence in neurology and physiology made it clear that the brain is in a continuous state of activity, slowing down only in deep sleep. Other evidence suggested that nerve cells were so distributed that one cell could activate neighboring cells. When an appropriately interconnected family of cells received one unit of stimulation, it would be passed on to the whole family. If, as seems to be the case in certain centers of the brain, the family unit of cells were appropriately intermeshed, a stimulation from one cell would lead on to another and, in a chain-like fashion, the stimulation would ultimately come back onto the _first_ cell again. In such a fashion a stimulated network could store the input signal and maintain its fidelity long after the environmental stimulation had ceased. Not only were there networks of cells found in the brain which might become reverberatory circuits of this sort, but it was also noted that the transition points from one cell to the next often involve a physical enlargement, a "terminal end bulb." These bulbs it is argued might facilitate transmission within a circuit; in fact it may be that the bulbs develop from regular and continuous contact between certain nerve cells. Once a circuit unit has become established it would be possible either for outside stimulation to activate the whole unit or for some other _inside_ stimulation coming from another point in the continuously active nervous system to activate it.

These reverberatory circuits Hebb calls "cell assemblies." It is apparent that such systems as these could[14] well be the neural centers underlying the mediating processes described by Osgood. Representational mediation processes, considered by Osgood to constitute meaning, could have the biological form of assemblies of cells. Cell assemblies could become conditioned responses to verbal symbols so that they are activated when a symbol is recognized in either its auditory or visual forms. The activation of assemblies could revoke the complex of responses formerly made to the referent for which the symbol stands as Osgood's theory demands.

Cell assemblies, according to Hebb, can have elements in common with other functionally distinct assemblies. For example, in a series such as ABCDX and ABCDY (where each letter stands for a cell assembly and the whole series makes up what he refers to as a "sequence" of assemblies) two different sequences can have certain assemblies in common. This postulate of the theory suggests that there may be a neural mechanism whereby root words can take on various endings and yet be recognized as derived from a common core. Synonyms, too, can be thought of as having certain assembly elements in common. Hebb argues that two originally distinct assemblies of cells which habitually play functionally similar roles can become fused into a single neural system if no new element is introduced to reinstate their distinctiveness. Furthermore, two very similar networks of cell assemblies can develop more permanent distinctiveness if some elements are regularly found to play discriminable roles. In this fashion, Hebb describes how either fused or separated neural systems could develop. Such systems could, in turn, help explain how we can be precise in our use of synonyms and antonyms in language and how bilinguals manage to keep second-language equivalents functionally distinctive from first-language concepts. Recent theorizing about coordinate and compound bilingual systems have profited from Hebb's perspective.[15] A recent paper by P. Milner,[16] a colleague of Hebb, discusses a mechanism of neural inhibition which helps account for the bilingual's control over inter-lingual interference. Milner indicates that certain adjacent neural structures function in a reciprocal manner so that when structure X is activated the adjacent structure Y is automatically made inactive and unable to be stimulated. This mechanism may turn out to be an explanation of how bilinguals can keep their languages functionally segregated in usage, especially in the case of "coordinate" bilinguals (see Section 4 below). That is, when the sequence of cell assemblies underlying the concept "house" is activated, the correlated neural assemblies underlying the concept "maison" may automatically be made inactive. Or when the neural mechanisms underlying a total language system, such as English, is activated, it may make the potentially competing system inactive.

Hebb is interested, as was K. S. Lashley before him,[17] in how complex sequences of responses can be so perfectly coordinated as is the case with the arpeggios of a skilled violinist or the rapid speech of native speakers of a language. Hebb argues that the appropriate serial ordering of such sequences is determined both by the "sensory feed-back" received when a single response is completed and by the action of mediating processes or cell assemblies within the central nervous system. A sequence of cell assemblies could have some order built into it during the course of its development into a sequence. But Hebb feels this would not likely be sufficient. Take the case of the arpeggio.. A violinist can perform up to 16 finger movements a second. The precise timing of the different responses cannot be determined by feedback from each preceding movement because there is insufficient time. There are only about 50-60 milliseconds available before the next response, and the established reaction time for tactual stimulation is much slower, taking 140 milliseconds. But Hebb believes that possibly the feedback from the first response to the brain could regulate the fourth or fifth output in the long sequence, so that precise ordering could be achieved. In a similar fashion, Hebb argues that a speaker's sentence construction cannot be explained "as a series of CR's (conditioned responses) linked together by feedback alone," or as entirely controlled by cell assemblies, since there are strong indications that his thought processes (controlled by cell assemblies) run well ahead of his actual articulations. Apparently some word ordering and grammatical sequencing must first be decided on, then rapidly scanned and found appropriate, and finally set in motion while active thought moves on ahead to the next phase. This whole chain of processes is remarkably fast and "automatic" in the native speaker, making a sharp contrast with the novice in a language who slows the process way down and makes evident to listeners that his thought and speech are running nearly in parallel.

For Hebb, both the mediating processes in the form of cell assemblies and sensory feedback must be necessary for the precise temporal sequencing required for normal speech. The background accompaniment of one's own speech testifies to the role of sensory feedback in speech. When the feedback of one's own speech is very slightly slowed down mechanically[18] one hesitates and is often unable to continue his normal speaking. Because of the inquisitiveness of men like Hebb and Lashley, we can look forward to continued research directed toward an understanding of how speech sequences occur.

Concepts, too, apparently have a neurological sub-structure. Hebb discusses how the concept of triangularity, for example, develops. As a consequence of the interplay between visual stimulation of triangular figures and ocular-motor adjustments made to them, a sequence of cell assemblies is activated in those areas of the brain sensitive to visual stimulation (referred to technically as cortex region #17). Neurological findings have established that other areas of the cortex are concurrently active when cells are activated in area 17. For example, area 18 cells are concurrently made active when the cells in area 17 are stimulated by direct neural routes from the retina of the eye. It is argued that cell assemblies may be formed in area 18 and these may become electro-chemically active whenever various different sequences fire in area 17, each area 17 response corresponding to a particular type of stimulation. Thus the co-related activity in area 18 is conceived of as the neural basis of a generalized concept, for example, of triangularity. Area 18 received impulses from different assemblies in area 17 and also sends neural impulses to area 17 whenever a particular activity takes place in area 17, as though the conceptual system could indicate to the sensory receiving area that the new instance of stimulation belongs to a concept already established! Just as the visual system has its theoretically possible "conceptual" neural centers, so other regions in the cortex very likely have a similar capacity for the conceptual development of other than visual information. These hypothetical centers concerned with the more generalized functions hold out a fascinating promise. They suggest that some day we will be able to understand more comprehensively the mechanisms which make possible the development and use of thought and language.

3. Language Aptitude and the Theory of Human Abilities

Psychology as a discipline offers a specialization in the study of "individual differences." Practitioners of this specialty, often referred to as psychometricians, make use of a number of skills, including competence in statistical procedures and their application to the theory, construction and evaluation of psychological tests. Psychometricians have historically been called on to answer questions about the nature of intelligence and human abilities and they have developed some of psychology's most comprehensive conceptualizations of human capacities and behavior. Because of their training and interests, psychometricians have been concerned with the selection and placement of personnel in academic and applied settings. Several, through personal interest in the nature of language, have studied the nature of language aptitude, carefully constructing batteries of ingenious tests designed to measure individual differences in such a capacity. Their products usually are about the closest to good science one can find in the social or biological sciences. Their contributions are often not fully appreciated because of naïveté on the part of those who ultimately use their theories and tests. It is not often understood, for example, that each of the tests in a battery usually has a long and interesting history, and any test finally used must add its special predictive power to the total battery of tests. From the patterning of subjects' responses to the items of reliable and distinctive tests come theories of intelligence and aptitude.

We will be concerned here with the current work of one of these specialists, Dr. John B. Carroll of Harvard University who, with Stanley Sapon, developed an instrument of obvious value for those in the field of language—the Modern Language Aptitude Test.[19] In the following paragraphs, we will describe the test, indicating its usefulness in educational research and placement, and then discuss how this test is related to a theory of human abilities developed by George A. Ferguson of McGill University. Certain papers by Carroll[20] and Ferguson[21] are suggested as important summaries of the relevant features of their thinking.

The learning of a foreign language is one of the most difficult of human skills to develop. Furthermore, language training is expensive. One could argue from these two facts alone that military, governmental and educational institutions must select those who can most certainly profit from prolonged training, just as piano teachers and parents must select; to the majority of piano students, they communicate the fact that they have little chance for excellence. But just as a thorough introduction to piano can have important personal and educational value, so too can a series of well-taught introductory courses in foreign languages. Carroll turns his attention to the selection of those with great potential for languages, and in doing so his study of the components of language aptitude reveal for us the component skills that must be taught by teachers and learned by students. Future research will certainly reveal other components, and, of equal significance, it may also lead to a better understanding of the sequence or order in which these component skills should be learned and how best they can, if possible, be developed.

What are some of these components of language aptitude? The following extensive quotation gives a summary of Carroll's answer.

> "Our current thinking tends to consider language aptitude under the following headings:

(1) One of the most important variables in learning a foreign language is phonetic coding, the ability to "code" auditory phonetic material in such a way that this material can be recognized, identified and remembered over something longer than a few seconds. . . . Thus, this ability is not the ability to make an echoic response to phonetic material, but the ability somehow to "code" or represent it in imagery so that it can be recognized or reproduced after an intervening period filled with other activity. This ability, it would seem, is measured chiefly by the Phonetic Script test, in which the individual has to learn how a series of speech sounds are represented by alphabetic characters; . . . .

In learning a foreign language, a person low in this ability will have trouble not only in remembering phonetic materials (words, forms, etc.) but also in mimicking speech sounds.

(2) A second important variable in language aptitude is the ability to handle "grammar," i.e. the forms of language and their arrangements in natural utterances. This implies that the individual is sensitive to the functions of words in a variety of contexts. . . . It is postulated that this trait is particularly well measured by the Words and Sentences subtest of the Modern Language Aptitude Test battery.

(3) A third important variable is that of rote memorization ability for foreign language materials. This ability. . . has to do with the capacity to learn a large number of these associations in a relatively short time. . . . We may postulate that the Paired Associates test measures this ability fairly accurately; it is also tapped by the Number Learning test.

(4) A fourth variable. . . is the ability to infer linguistic forms, rules and patterns from new linguistic content itself with a minimum of supervision or guidance. It is not measured to any appreciable degree by the tests of the present final MLAT battery, but it had turned up in certain earlier studies.

The above four factors do not include what is ordinarily called the verbal or verbal knowledge factor, which according to our results is not very important in predicting success. Vocabulary tests do not serve as particularly good predictors, at least in situations where other tests serve well, since the first stages of learning a language do not require one to acquire a large vocabulary. On the other hand, the present Spelling Clues test functions in part as a vocabulary test."

Carroll's evaluation of the test (summarized in his 1960 paper) indicates its great potential in selection and in educational research. The fact that the test is more valid in some settings than in others suggests that variables other than aptitude itself must also be involved in language learning efficiency. Carroll mentions that variables such as adequacy of presentation of the material, adequate opportunity to learn, individual differences in general intelligence, and motivation to learn may vary from situation to situation. In fact, in the final section of this paper we will discuss the role of certain other variables. It should be realized that Carroll expects that there will be modifications and improvements in the analysis of language aptitude.

What does Carroll mean by "aptitude?" He views aptitude as a "relatively invariant characteristic of the individual, not subject to easy modification by learning." This stable personal characteristic manifests itself in the rapidity of progress or advancement made in language learning when the language is well taught, particularly when the teaching is geared to the basic intelligence of the learner.

Carroll, therefore, views language aptitude as a relatively stable personal characteristic, one which is made up of various component skills or "abilities." It will be instructive to consider what is meant by "abilities" since they play such a fundamental role in more complex aptitudes.

Ferguson views abilities as relatively invariant aspects of behavior that manifest themselves in modes of responding to particular psychological tests. Thus one's "intelligence" is his peculiar pattern of abilities that have become stabilized for him at his particular age level. Abilities are developed through over-learning. The stability of behavior that characterizes an ability reflects the fact that little change in behavior occurs as learning is continued. Basically, then, individuals vary in terms of the speed with which they reach this point of behavioral stability, and also in terms of the level of skill attained before the stability manifests itself. These individual differences, Ferguson argues, can be attributed to some complex by-product of biologically transmitted capacity and the type and amount of "learning which occurs at particular stages of life." Ferguson agrees with Hebb that the sequencing of what is taught (and learned) at particular stages of the organism's development is of prime importance. "Early learning or its lack may have a permanent and generalized effect in the adult." Ferguson develops the important notion that "a slow learner under given learning conditions may have a capacity for ultimate performance in excess of the fast learner under the same training conditions." Likewise, people may have the abilities to learn rapidly in the earlier stages of learning, then perform so well, in relation to others, that they might not be prompted to acquire the necessary next-level abilities needed for later stages of learning. As a consequence, they might find themselves showing a stability of performance in the face of further training. This deceleration would not be due so much to a capacity difference as to poor sequencing of the learning of abilities; the point here is that there is proper and necessary order for the acquiring of abilities.

The sequencing problem may be crucial; Ferguson argues that "an individual will learn more readily activities which are facilitated by prior acquisitions, and will learn less readily those activities which are not facilitated or are perhaps inhibited by prior learning." He also notes the likelihood that the transfer effects from previously acquired abilities are of greatest importance in the early stages of learning new activities. Ultimately, learning for the adult involves in large part a transfer and integration of appropriate components from previously acquired abilities. Future research, following from such a theory as Ferguson's, may indicate how this integration of abilities may be properly taught and properly learned.

Perhaps the most important notion which emerges from this approach is a novel one for most people: man's abilities are not permanently fixed by hereditary background. "This position is no longer tenable. Although it is conceded that biological factors fix certain boundaries, all the evidence seems to suggest that the range of variation that results from learning is, indeed, very great. It this is so, it immediately raises questions of value and social responsibility. It means that a society, through control of the environment and the educative process, can in some considerable degree determine the patterns of ability which emerge in its members."

The implications of this view of abilities for language teachers are immense. Over and above its value as a general theory, it offers various practical guides: that the learning of languages should be shifted to early age levels, and that experimentation on such a shift should be undertaken with very careful consideration given to ability requirements and their sequencing. It suggests that modern movements should be carefully studied to determine which students, according to their patterns of abilities, will profit from such new approaches. For example, the generalized plan of commencing second languages audio-lingually at all age levels probably has not taken into consideration age level changes in ability structures, nor individual differences in visual and auditory preferences at any age level.[22] It may well be that the audio-lingual method is appropriate for second language learning at very early levels for certain children, but it may, for older subjects, run counter to ability patterns developed over many years.

The theory also suggests that the next steps in language aptitude research might profit from a consideration of which abilities, such as those isolated by Carroll, typically show themselves at specific age levels. The sequencing of training in different skills could capitalize on normal age-level emergences of particular ability patterns. As a first step in this direction, those ability patterns that are considered basic to language aptitude could be isolated for children and adolescents at various age levels.

II: ON SECOND-LANGUAGE LEARNING AND BILINGUALISM

4. A Social Psychology of Second-Language Learning

When viewed from a social-psychological perspective, the process of learning a second language takes on a special significance. From this viewpoint, one anticipates that if the learner is appropriately oriented, he may find that by learning another social group's language he has made the crucial step in becoming an acculturated part of a second linguistic-cultural community. Advancing toward biculturality in this sense may be viewed as a broadening experience in some cases, or it can engender "anomie," a feeling of not comfortably belonging in one social group or the other. With a different orientation, a language learner may look on his learning task as making him better educated or more cultured, or as equipping him with a useful skill for his future occupation, with little regard for the culture or the people represented by the other language. In other circumstances, one might consider learning another group's language as a means of getting on the "inside" of a cultural community in order to exploit, manipulate or control, with clearly personal ends in mind.

A series of studies carried out at McGill University has been concerned with such topics, and various findings have increased our confidence in a social-psychological theory of language learning. This theory, in brief, holds that an individual successfully acquiring a second language gradually adopts various aspects of behavior which characterize members of another linguistic-cultural group. The learner's ethnocentric tendencies and his attitudes toward the other group are believed to determine his success in learning the new language. His motivation to learn is thought to be determined by his attitudes and by his orientation toward learning a second language. The orientation is "instrumental" in form if the purposes of language study reflect the more utilitarian value of linguistic achievement, such as getting ahead in one's occupation, and is "integrative" if the student is oriented to learn more about the other cultural community as if he desired to become a potential member of the other group. It is also argued that some may be anxious to learn another language as a means of being accepted in another cultural group because of dissatisfactions experienced in their own culture while other individuals may be equally as interested in another culture as they are in their own. However, the more proficient one becomes in a second language the more he may find that his place in his original membership group is modified at the same time as the other linguistic-cultural group becomes something more than a reference group for him. It may, in fact, become a second membership group for him. Depending upon the compatibility of the two cultures, he may experience feelings of chagrin or regret as he loses ties in one group, mixed with the fearful anticipation of entering a relatively new group. The concept "anomie," first proposed by Durkheim[23] and more recently extended by Srole[24] and Williams,[25] refers to the feelings of social uncertainty or dissatisfaction which sometimes characterize not only the bilingual but also the serious student of a second language.

We are viewing the learning of a second language in much the same way as Mowrer interprets the child's learning of his first language. Mowrer's fascinating "autistic" theory[26] differs in an essential manner from Skinner's approach to the matter. For Mowrer, word learning in talking birds and children takes place when the sounds of words have come to carry a reinforcement power in themselves so that the learner wants to produce words. The sounds become reinforcing agents through association with the users of words who are held in affection by the learner. Language learning is motivated by a basic desire to be like valued people in one's environment, first family members and then others in the linguistic community. A successful learner has to identify with language users to the extent that he wants to be like them linguistically, and undoubtedly in many other ways. It is not the case, as Skinner would require it, that the learner must emit words and have them immediately reinforced. All that is necessary, Mowrer makes clear, is for the word to be said by the bird trainer or the child's mother and have this sound followed by a reinforcing state for the learner (in the form of reception of food for the bird or affectionate handling for the child). "The secondary (autistic) reinforcement provided by the sound of the word is alone sufficient to bring it (the word) into existence." In similar fashion we argue that the learner must want to identify with members of the other linguistic-cultural group and be willing to take on very subtle aspects of their behavior such as their language or even their style of speech. We also feel that there are various types of motivation which can underlie his willingness to be like the other group's members and we are interested in explicating each of these.

The first studies[27] were carried out with English-speaking Montreal high school students studying French who were examined for language learning aptitude, verbal intelligence, attitudes toward the French community and intensity of motivation to learn French. Our measure of motivation is conceptually similar to the index of interest in learning a language that Jones[28] found to be important for successful learning among Welsh students. A factor analysis indicated that aptitude and intelligence formed a factor that was independent of a second comprising indices of motivation, type of orientation toward language and social attitudes toward French-Canadians. A measure of achievement in French was reflected with equal prominence in both factors. In this case, then, French achievement was dependent upon both aptitude and intelligence as well as a sympathetic orientation toward the other group. This orientation apparently sustained a strong motivation to learn the other group's language. In the Montreal setting, it was clear that students with an integrative orientation were the more successful in language learning in contrast to those instrumentally oriented. (We have not concentrated on the manipulative orientation mentioned earlier and we are aware that a certain degree of error in classifying students may occur until attention is given to this form of orientation.)

Gardner's 1960 study confirmed and extended these findings. Using a larger sample of English-Canadians and incorporating various measures of French achievement, the same two independent factors were revealed, and again both were related to French achievement. But whereas aptitude and achievement were especially important for those French skills stressed in school training, the acquisition of French skills, whose development depends on the active use of the language in communicational settings, was determined solely by measures of an integrative motivation to learn French. Further evidence indicated that this integrative motive was the converse of an authoritarian ideological syndrome, opening the possibility that basic personality dispositions may be involved in language learning efficiency.

Information had been gathered from parents about their orientation toward the French community. These data supported the notion that the proper orientation toward the other group is developed within the family: students with an integrative disposition to learn French had parents who also were integrative and sympathetic to the French community. The students' orientations were not related to parents' skill in French nor to the number of French acquaintances the parents had, indicating that the integrative motive is not due to having more experience with French at home but more likely stems from a family-wide attitudinal disposition.

A study by Anisfeld and Lambert[29] extended the experimental procedure to samples of Jewish high school students studying Hebrew at parochial schools in Montreal. They were administered tests measuring their orientation toward learning Hebrew and their attitudes toward the Jewish culture and community, as well as tests of verbal intelligence and language aptitude. These tests were correlated with measures of achievement in the Hebrew language at the school year's end. The results support the generalization that both intellectual capacity and attitudinal orientation affect success in learning Hebrew. However, whereas intelligence and linguistic aptitude are relatively stable predictors of success, the attitudinal measures vary from one social class school district to another. The measure of a Jewish student's desire to become more acculturated into the Jewish tradition and culture was sensitive for children in a district of Montreal where socio-psychological analysis of the nature of the Jewish population's adjustment to the American Gentile culture suggested that these particular Jews were concerned with problems of integrating into the Jewish culture. In another district, made up of Jews more recently arrived in North America who were clearly of a lower socio-economic class level, the measure of desire for Jewish acculturation did not correlate with achievement in Hebrew whereas measures of pro-Semitic attitudes or pride in being Jewish did.

More recently, students undergoing an intensive course in French at the French Summer School of McGill University were examined for changes in attitude during the study period.[30] Most were American university students or secondary school language teachers who referred themselves more to the European-French than the American-French community in their orientations to language learning. In this study, it became apparent that feelings of anomie were markedly increased during the course of study. As students progressed to the point that they "thought" in French, it was noted that their feelings of anomie also increased. At the same time, they tried to find means of using English even though they had pledged to use only French for the six-week period. The pattern suggests that American students experience anomie when they concentrate on and commence to master a second language and, as a consequence, develop stratagems to control or minimize such feelings.

The most recent study[31] compare 10-year old monolingual and bilingual students on measures of intelligence. Of relevance here is the very clear pattern that bilingual children have markedly more favorable attitudes towards the "other" language community in contrast to the monolingual children. Furthermore, the parents of bilingual children are believed by their children to hold the same strongly sympathetic attitudes in contrast to the parents of monolingual children, as though the linguistic skills in a second language, extending to the point of bilingualism, are controlled by family-shared attitudes toward the other linguistic-cultural community.

These findings are consistent and reliable enough to be of more general interest. For example methods of language training may be modified and strengthened by giving consideration to the social-psychological implications of language learning. Important recent work by Paul Pimsleur and his associates lends support to our findings and the general theory.[32] Because of the possible practical as well as theoretical significance of this approach, it seemed appropriate to test its applicability in a cultural setting other than the bicultural Quebec scene. Our most recent study[33] was therefore conducted in various regional settings in the United States, two of them also bicultural and a third more representative of "typical" urban American cities. The bicultural settings permitted an examination of attitudes working two ways: attitudinal dispositions of American students toward linguistic minority groups in their immediate environment and the general attitudes of members of the cultural minority group toward the general American culture about them. In this study, we were interested in comparing the importance, in the language learning process, of intellectual ability and language learning aptitude on the one hand, and social attitudes toward the "other" language group and motivation to learn the language, on the other hand. Our attention was first directed to an examination of how these variables affect the language learning of American students who come from homes where only English is spoken. In order to compare the results of the United States investigation with earlier studies carried out with English-speaking students learning French in Montreal, we chose two samples of students from bicultural American communities in Louisiana and Maine. A third sample of American students was drawn from the public school system of Hartford, Connecticut, considered representative of most large city school systems along the Eastern coast of America. The Connecticut setting did not have a distinctive sub-community of Franco-Americans in its immediate environment comparable to those in the Louisiana and Maine districts studied. Thus, the Hartford students would not be expected to have a clear linguistic cultural group in their immediate experience toward which favorable or unfavorable attitudes would have developed through direct contact.

A large battery of tests was administered to these students early in the year, and near the end of the year, tests of achievement in French were given, and grades in French were obtained from teachers. The tests were intercorrelated and factor analyzed. The resulting patterns of interrelations were studied and interpreted. The results indicate that, similar to the Montreal studies, two independent factors underlie the development of skill in learning a second language: an intellectual capacity and an appropriate attitudinal orientation toward the other language group coupled with a determined motivation to learn the language.

The second phase of the investigation was concerned with the role of aptitudinal, attitudinal and motivational variables in the linguistic development of potentially bilingual Franco-American students —those coming from homes in which primarily French was spoken. Two samples of Franco-American high school students were chosen from the Louisiana and Maine settings. The analysis indicated the manner in which social attitudes toward their own linguistic group and the American culture around them influence their (a) progress in becoming bilingual, (b) retaining the dominance of French, or (c) developing dominance of English. The manner in which the Franco-American student faces and resolves the cultural conflict he is likely to encounter in the American society was found to determine his linguistic development in French and English.

The third phase of the study focused on a comparison of Franco-American students from the Louisiana and Maine settings. The results make it very clear that whereas the Louisiana French culture is rapidly merging into the general American culture, the Maine community of Franco-Americans enjoys a comparatively dynamic and distinctive existence.

The fourth phase compared the Franco-American and American students in their various competences in French and in their attitudinal dispositions. The results reinforce the finding mentioned above of the cultural conflicts faced by Franco-American students. Furthermore, the Maine Franco-Americans show a decided superiority over the American students in their French skills whereas the Louisiana Franco-Americans show little or no advantage in French over American students.

The fifth phase of the study examined the stereotype both American and Franco-American groups of students hold toward French people. The analysis indicates that all groups except the Maine Franco-Americans hold unfavorable stereotypes of French people. The Maine Franco-Americans give evidence of a basic pride in their French heritage. The consequences of holding negative stereotypes toward the very people whose language one is supposed to learn become apparent in this analysis.

The sixth and final phase deals with the role of students' values in the language-learning process. The results indicate that achievement in foreign language training is not a central goal for American students. Rather it is apparently incidental to the more challenging goal of trying to find and prepare one's way for the future. Intelligence coupled with a value placed on achievement are major determiners of success in most school work, including the study of language.

These findings not only supply needed information about the student learning languages, they also point the way to a large number of next steps to be taken in the fascinating study of language learning and bilingualism.

5. A Psychology of Bilingualism

Psychologists are now becoming interested in systematically studying how one acquires a second language and how certain individuals are able to make efficient use of two or several languages. A group of us at McGill University have found the Montreal bicultural setting to be an outstanding field station for research on bilingualism. But we have also noted that the linguistic backgrounds of actual bilinguals are often too complex for experimental studies. As a consequence, we have been forced often to restate certain bilingual problems in a more general form so that they can be investigated with experimental methods that only approximate the real bilingual case.

Our first step was to develop means of measuring individual variations in bilingual skill.[34] This work assumed that linguistic habits should be revealed in tests calling for speed of response, a commonly accepted measure of habit strength. It was hypothesized that students with different amounts of study experience in a second language should show a corresponding facility in responding with the second language when required to. It was found that students at three progressively more advanced stages of experience with French showed progressively greater speed of responding to directions given them in French. This speed of response measure correlated highly with active vocabulary in French.

In a second study[35] a large number of tests were administered to students at various levels of skill in a second language, ranging from undergraduate experience to native-like competence. The pattern of results on these tests suggested that one's degree of bilingualism is reflected in his ability to perceive and to make efficient use of the words in either language. These studies made it evident that an adequate conceptualization of bilingualism should account for individual differences. That is, one person can show equal facility in his two languages and yet be comparatively a limited person in both languages. Another person can be intellectually brilliant in both his languages and equally skilled in both. Thus, we introduced the concepts of "bilingual balance," where a person shows essentially similar skills in both languages, and "linguistic dominance," where there is a measurably greater facility in one of the individual's two languages. Questions then arise as to how bilingual balance is best nurtured and what the psychological concomitants of balance are. Also, it has been intriguing to search out the motives and learning settings that promote dominance, especially cases where the *acquired* language becomes dominant over the first-learned language.

The next step was to study the "route" which leads to bilingualism.[36] Students at various levels of experience with a second language were given a series of tests differing in the complexity of their content. The results indicated that students have to surmount progressively more difficult levels of skill in order to approach native-like performance in their second language. The easiest level to master involved the acquisition of vocabulary and grammatical skills. Then the student must become experienced to the extent that he can react automatically in the second language. Then he faces the problem of surmounting a "cultural" barrier where, for example, he thinks in terms of culturally appropriate concepts, such as those revealed in the type and form of free associations given in the second language. We have become interested in how the perfect accent is learned and we use a theory of "identification" with members of the other linguistic group to explain this process.

It is of psychological interest to understand how bilinguals can learn two symbols for each referent and yet manage to use each language system with a minimum of inter-lingual interferences. Consideration of this problem led us to examine the implications of theories of "coordinate" and "compound" bilingualism, proposed by linguists,[37] and recently examined by psychologists.[38] This theory states that bilinguals who have learned their two languages within one context will develop a "compound" bilingual system wherein the symbols of both languages function as interchangeable alternatives with essentially the same meanings. A "coordinate" system would be developed when the language-acquisition contexts were culturally, temporally or functionally segregated. This form of learning would promote bilinguals whose two sets of symbols would correspondingly be functionally more distinct and independent. We have tested these notions and have found that the learning contexts are apparently critical in determining the form of bilingualism which ultimately develops. Behavioral differences are measurable in terms of inter-lingual independence and degrees of similarity between meanings.[39] Coordinate bilinguals in contrast to compounds apparently can keep their two languages more functionally separated. They may be aided in this respect by the fact that they have distinctive connotative meanings for translated equivalents in their two languages. Furthermore, when the meaning of a symbol in one language is reduced through overuse, the other-language equivalent is <u>not</u> co-reduced as is the case for compound bilinguals.[40] We have also examined the implications of coordinate and compound systems among bilinguals who become aphasic.[41] Bilingual aphasics who learned their languages in a coordinate fashion are more likely to lose the use of only one of their two languages if they become aphasic whereas compound bilinguals show a more general language deficit affecting their two languages when they become aphasic.

This line of research suggests that inter-lingual interference is reduced for coordinate bilinguals by the intrinsic distinctiveness of their two languages while compound bilinguals may have to rely more on cues emanating from the language-usage contexts in order to minimize the potential interference. That is, compound bilinguals may be more prone to switch from one language to another if the context, in which communication takes place, prompts them to switch. For example, another communicator's use of a word or phrase from language X might prompt the compound bilingual to switch to language X; or the physical features of one member of a group might suggest that this person belongs to a particular linguistic group and be a sufficient cue for a compound to use a particular language. If the context provides various conflicting cues, the compound bilingual would be more likely to encounter inter-lingual confusions. The point here is that the coordinate bilingual would be less dependent on the cues stemming from the language-usage context because of the "built-in" distinctiveness of his two language systems. Future research will examine the validity of such notions as these.

Methods of teaching a second language take into account this matter of inter-lingual interference. For example, the "direct" methods require students to relate a symbol directly with an environmental event rather than indirectly through the association of the equivalent symbol of the first language. The direct method, therefore, is analogous to coordinate training as the indirect method is to compound training. It was at this point we felt it wise to use closely controlled experimental methods to study the comparative merits of direct and indirect methods of training.[42] For this purpose, we followed the tradition of experimental research on verbal learning, as covered in such work as McGeoch,[43] and Underwood and Schulz.[44] Actually, the problem of direct and indirect methods is an old one and has been examined many times in the early 1900's by psychologists and educators. We improved on their procedures, we believed, and found that the direct method was relatively more efficient, at least for vocabulary learning, primarily because the task of associating new language words with referents (the direct procedure) afforded greater distinctiveness of elements to be learned than did the task of associating new language words with their equivalents in the first language. However, in a recent investigation of advanced students of a second language studying the language for a concentrated six-week period in a setting that was as "direct" as one could hope for, it was found that those students who kept their two languages functionally separated throughout the course did poorer in their course work than did those who permitted the semantic features of their two languages to interact.[45] Thus this study indicates that students studying under a direct method utilize the semantic features of both their languages and permit the two to interact and that this tendency toward linguistic interdependency apparently assists students in acquiring their second language. This finding may well prompt further research on the question of direct methods of training.

A current study is examining the merits of learning two languages concurrently from an early age, in contrast to learning one language well before the second is attempted, i.e. learning two languages consecutively.[46] This problem is often faced by educators and parents who fear that confusion will accompany the early introduction of a second language before competence is developed in the first. Lack of information on this point makes most parents cautious and children are often kept away from a second language until, inadvertently, it may be too late to learn it well. Our approach in this study is to approximate the real-life situation using artificial languages and restricting ourselves to the vocabulary acquisition phase of the process. The study will be completed during the year.

Finally, we have examined the question of the intellectual deficit which is supposed to plague bilinguals. Many studies in the educational and psychological literature have concluded that bilingual children show a lower average score on tests of intelligence when compared with monolingual children who are supposedly matched on all pertinent characteristics except bilingual experience. The findings are not convincing when one surveys the total range of studies undertaken. Elizabeth Peal and I carried out a large study on this question last year with ten-year olds in Montreal.[47] We attempted to match very carefully the students who finally were categorized as bilingual or monolingual. For example, we painstakingly checked on the socio-economic background of the two groups of students and made sure the bilinguals were really competent in both languages. Our results clearly show that the bilingual students are far superior to monolinguals on both verbal and non-verbal tests of intelligence. We concluded that the bilinguals may have an advantage in tests requiring "cognitive flexibility" due, perhaps, to their being bilingual. Miss Peal is presently examining this possibility more carefully. Because our results are in conflict with so many others on this point (although we have no doubt at all about the differences in intelligence just mentioned) we are not yet sure that this bilingual advantage is peculiar to bilinguals in Canada or to those who are actually "good" bilinguals. Our confidence in the generalizability of these findings for different settings will depend on more careful re-examinations in those settings where a bilingual deficit has been reported in the literature.

McGill University is but one of the centers studying bilingualism. The extremely important work of Susan Ervin at the University of California, Berkeley would be of particular value to language teachers.[48] Her intriguing analysis of personality and value changes taking place when bilinguals switch from one language context to another makes evident the important role second-language learning can have in the lives of students.

NOTES

A work paper prepared for a Seminar on Language Teacher Training, initiated by the Department of Romance Languages and Literature of the University of Washington, and held at the University of Washington, September 1962.

[1] See O. H. Mowrer, Learning theory and the symbolic processes. New York: Wiley, 1960. Chaps. 3 and 4.

[2] C. E. Osgood, Method and theory in experimental psychology. New York: Oxford University Press, 1953.

[3] C. E. Osgood, G. J. Suci, and P. H. Tannenbaum, The measurement of meaning. Urbana: University of Illinois Press, 1957.

Carolyn K. Staats, and W. W. Staats, "Meaning established by classical conditioning." Journal of Experimental Psychology, 1957, 54, 74-80.

W. E. Lambert, and L. Jakobovits, "Verbal satiation and changes in the intensity of meaning." Journal of Experimental Psychology, 1960, 60, 376-383. [In this volume, pp. 97-110.]

[4] W. A. Bousfield, "The occurrence of clustering in the recall of randomly arranged associates." Journal of General Psychology, 1953, 49, 229-240.

J. J. Jenkins, and W. A. Russell, "Associative clustering during recall." Journal of Abnormal and Social Psychology, 1952, 47, 818-821.

J. Deese, "On the structure of associative meaning." Psychological Review, 1962, 69, 161-175.

[5] W. E. Lambert, "Developmental aspects of second-language acquisition." (Parts I, II, & III.) Journal of Social Psychology, 1956, 43, 83-104. [In this volume, pp. 9-31.]

[6] B. F. Skinner, The behavior of organisms. New York: Appleton, 1938.

B. F. Skinner, Science and human behavior. New York: Macmillan, 1953.

[7] B. F. Skinner, Verbal behavior. New York: Appleton, 1957.

[8] C. E. Osgood, "Language in the objective mode: The question of sufficiency." Contemporary Psychology, 1958, 3, 209-212.

[9] J. Greenspoon, referred to in L. Krasner, "Studies of the conditioning of verbal behavior." Psychological Bulletin, 1958, 55, 148-170.

[10] H. C. Barik, and W. E. Lambert, "Conditioning of complex verbal sequences." Canadian Journal of Psychology, 1960, 14, 87-95.

[11] D. E. Dulany, "Hypotheses and habits in verbal 'operant conditioning.'" Journal of Abnormal and Social Psychology, 1961, 63, 251-263.

[12] B. F. Skinner, "Teaching machines." Science, 1958, 128, 969-977.

[13] D. O. Hebb, Organization of behavior. New York: Wiley, 1949.

D. O. Hebb, A textbook of psychology. Philadelphia: Saunders, 1958.

[14] The word "could" is used here because the cell assembly is not a verified entity; it is a theoretical construction. Neurophysiology has not yet advanced to the point where on-going processes can be precisely studied and defined. Hebb has used evidence of a static sort, such as histological diagrams of interconnected nerve cells and end bulbs, and hypothesized about active states of nervous integration, keeping his theory in line with the facts known about active states derived from external manifestations of brain activity, such as electro-encephalographic recordings.

[15] Susan Ervin, and C. E. Osgood, "Second language learning and bilingualism." In C. E. Osgood and T. A. Sebeok (Eds.), "Psycholinguistics." Journal of Abnormal and Social Psychology, Supplement, 1954, 49, 139-146.

W. E. Lambert, J. Havelka, and Cynthia Crosby, "The influence of language-acquisition contexts on bilingualism." Journal of Abnormal and Social Psychology, 1958, 56, 239-244. [In this volume, pp. 51-62.]

W. E. Lambert, and S. Fillenbaum, "A pilot study of aphasia among bilinguals." Canadian Journal of Psychology, 1959, 13, 28-34. [In this volume, pp. 72-79.]

[16] P. M. Milner, "The cell assembly: Mark II." Psychological Review, 1957, 64, 242-252.

[17] K. S. Lashley, "The problem of serial order in behavior." In L. A. Jeffress (Ed.), Cerebral mechanisms in behavior. New York: Wiley, 1951, pp. 112-136.

[18] B. S. Lee, "On delayed auditory feedback." Journal of the Acoustical Society of America, 1950, 22, 639.

[19] J. B. Carroll, and S. M. Sapon, Modern language aptitude test. New York: Psychological Corporation, 1958.

[20] J. B. Carroll, "A factor analysis of two foreign language aptitude batteries." The Journal of General Psychology, 1958, 59, 3-19.

J. B. Carroll, The prediction of success in intensive foreign language training. Cambridge: Graduate School of Education, Harvard University, 1960 (Mimeo.).

[21] G. A. Ferguson, "On learning and human ability." Canadial Journal of Psychology, 1954, 8, 95-112.

G. A. Ferguson, "On transfer and the abilities of man." Canadian Journal of Psychology, 1956, 10, 121-131.

[22] UNESCO, L'enseignement des langues vivantes. Paris, 1955, pp. 77 ff.

[23] E. Durkheim, Le suicide. Paris: F. Alcan, 1897.

[24] L. Srole, Social dysfunction, personality and social distance attitudes. (Paper read before the American Sociological Society, 1951, Chicago, Illinois.)

[25] R. M. Williams, American society. New York: Knopf, 1952.

[26] O. H. Mowrer, Learning theory and the symbolic processes. New York: Wiley, 1960. (See especially chapters 3 and 4.)

[27] R. C. Gardner and W. E. Lambert, "Motivational variables in second-language acquisition." Canadian Journal of Psychology, 1959, 13, 266-272.

R. C. Gardner, Motivational variables in second-language acquisition. Unpublished Ph.D. thesis, McGill University, Redpath Library, 1960.

[28] W. R. Jones, "Attitude towards Welsh as a second language. A preliminary investigation." British Journal of Educational Psychology, 1949, 19, 44-52.

W. R. Jones, "Attitude towards Welsh as a second language. A further investigation." British Journal of Educational Psychology, 1950, 10, 117-132.

[29] M. Anisfeld and W. E. Lambert, "Social and psychological variables in learning Hebrew." Journal of Abnormal and Social Psychology, 1961, 63, 524-529.

[30] W. E. Lambert, R. C. Gardner, H. C. Barik, and K. Tunstall, "Attitudinal and cognitive aspects of intensive study of a second language." J. abnorm. soc. Psychol., 1963, 66, 358-368.

[31] Elizabeth Peal and W. E. Lambert, The relation of bilingualism to intelligence. Psychological Monographs, 1962, 76, 27. Whole No. 546. [In this volume, pp. 111-59.]

[32] P. Pimsleur, L. Mosberg, and A. V. Morrison, "Student Factors in Foreign Language Learning." Modern Language Journal, 1962, 46, 160-170.

P. Pimsleur, R. P. Stockwell, and A. L. Comrey, "Foreign language learning ability." Journal of Educational Psychology, 1962, 53, 15-26.

[33] W. E. Lambert, R. C. Gardner, R. Olton, and K. Tunstall, A study of the roles of attitudes and motivation in second-language learning. Mimeographed, McGill University, 1962.

[34] W. E. Lambert, "Measurement of the linguistic dominance of bilinguals." Journal of Abnormal and Social Psychology, 1955, 50, 197-200. [In this volume, pp. 1-8.]

[35] W. E. Lambert, J. Havelka, and R. C. Gardner, "Linguistic manifestations of bilingualism." American Journal of Psychology, 1959, 72, 77-82.

[36] W. E. Lambert, "Developmental aspects of second-language acquisition." (Parts I, II and III.) Journal of Social Psychology, 1956, 43, 83-104. [In this volume, pp. 9-31.]

[37] U. Weinreich, Languages in contact. New York: Linguistic Circle of New York, 1953.

[38]Susan Ervin and C. E. Osgood, "Second language learning and bilingualism." In C. E. Osgood and F. Sebeok (Eds.), "Psycholinguistics." *Journal of Abnormal and Social Psychology*, Supplement, 1954, 49, 139-146.

[39]W. E. Lambert, J. Havelka, and Cynthia Crosby, "The influence of language-acquisition contexts on bilingualism." *Journal of Abnormal and Social Psychology*, 1958, 56, 239-244. [In this volume, pp. 51-62.]

W. E. Lambert, Behavioral evidence for contrasting forms of bilingualism. *Georgetown University Monograph Series on Languages and linguistics*, 1962, 14, 73-80.

[40]L. Jakobovits and W. E. Lambert, "Semantic satiation among bilinguals." *Journal of Experimental Psychology*, 1961, 62, 576-582.

[41]W. E. Lambert and S. Fillenbaum, "A pilot study of aphasia among bilinguals." *Canadian Journal of Psychology*, 1959, 13, 28-34. [In this volume, pp. 72-79.]

[42]Cynthia Wimer and W. E. Lambert, "The differential effects of word and object stimuli on the learning of paired associates." *Journal of Experimental Psychology*, 1959, 57, 31-36.

[43]J. A. McGeoch, *The psychology of human learning*. New York: Longmans, 1942.

[44]B. J. Underwood and R. W. Schulz, *Meaningfulness and verbal learning*. New York: Lippincott, 1960.

[45]W. E. Lambert, R. C. Gardner, H. C. Barik, and K. Tunstall, "Attitudinal and cognitive aspects of intensive study of a second language." *Journal of Abnormal and Social Psychology*, 1963, 66, 4, 358-368.

[46] W. E. Lambert and Grace Yeni-Komshian, "Concurrent and consecutive modes of learning two languages." Research in progress, McGill University.

[47]Elizabeth Peal and W. E. Lambert, "The relation of bilingualism to intelligence." *Psychological Monographs*, 1962, 76, 27. Whole No. 546. [In this volume, pp. 111-59.]

[48]Susan Ervin, "The verbal behavior of bilinguals: the effects of language of response upon the T. A. T. stories of adult French bilinguals." *American Psychologist*, 1955, 10, 391. See also "Language and T. A. T. content in bilinguals," *Journal of Abnormal and Social Psychology*, 1964, 68, 500-507.

Susan Ervin and C. E. Osgood, "Second language learning and bilingualism." In C. E. Osgood and T. A. Sebeok (Eds.), "Psycholinguistics." _Journal of Abnormal and Social Psychology_, Supplement, 1954, 49, 139-146.

Susan Ervin, "Language and recall in bilinguals." _American Journal of Psychology_, 1961, 74, 445-451.

Susan Ervin, "Semantic shift in bilingualism." _American Journal of Psychology_, 1961, 74, 233-241.

12 Word-Association Responses: Comparisons of American and French Monolinguals with Canadian Monolinguals and Bilinguals

In Collaboration with Nancy Moore

As more word-association norms from different parts of the world become available, it is possible to make comparisons, both within and between language communities, that lead to intriguing questions about changes through time and cultural differences in associational responses. For example, a standard list of stimulus words (the Kent-Rosanoff list) has been used with samples of English-speaking Americans since 1910. Jenkins and Russell (1960) noted that Americans increased the use of common or popular responses between 1910 and 1952 and changed in certain respects the content of their associational responses, although differentially since the less popular ones were those that changed most. Furthermore, during the time period there was a decrease in the use of superordinate responses (e.g., table-furniture). Jenkins and Russell argued that both the increase in the use of popular responses and the decrease in superordination over 40 years were likely due to an increased sophistication with short-answer-type questions. They chose this over an alternative interpretation: that American language habits may have become more standardized because of the growth of mass communications.

In 1918, Esper (1918) translated a list of German stimulus words into English and found many similarities between the responses of German and English subjects with regard to reaction time and types of responses given. More recently, Rosenzweig (1957) compared the associational responses of groups of American and French students and noted that the French group gave more diversified responses than the Americans did and that the two groups had equivalent primaries (most popular responses) in only about 50% of the possible cases. It is of interest that the French students gave many less superordinate responses than did the Americans, indicating that the frequency of use of popular responses is not systematically related to superordination, as one might have inferred from changes over time mentioned in the Jenkins-Russell study. Rosenzweig attributed the French tendency toward associational diversity to the greater stress placed on individuality in French education. He did not speculate about the comparatively infrequent use of superordinates among the French.

Later, Rosenzweig (1961) examined the primary responses of comparable groups of French, Italian, German, and American subjects and found that even in this case the American group was distinctive in its marked tendency to use common responses. All four groups gave the same primary responses to only 21 out of the 89 possible cases, and the American, French, and German primaries agreed in only 36 out of 100 cases. Variations in the degree of overlap of primary responses have also been noted among subgroups from the same linguistic community by Rosenzweig (1964). He compared French students and workers with comparable groups of Americans and found that the worker-student response differences were greater for the French sub-samples, suggesting that education and social-class differences may affect modes of associating or types of associations given in certain cultures more so than in others.

In the present study, comparisons of associational responses are extended to include three distinctive social groups living in one geographical community, two of them monolingual and one bilingual. The setting is the Province of Quebec and the groups are English-Canadian and French-Canadian monolinguals and Canadian English-French bilinguals. The purpose of the investigation is to compare the associational responses of English-Canadians and Americans, making it possible to examine critically the belief some English-Canadians hold that they have a distinctive language and culture; to compare the responses of French-Canadians, Americans, English-Canadians, and French students from France in order to evaluate the conflicting claims that Canadian French is largely Americanized, that French-Canadians are a linguistically and culturally isolated group, or that they are North American representatives of European French language and culture; and to examine the responses of English-French bilinguals from Quebec who may or may not be linguistically dependent on the English and French monolingual groups and who may or may not be effective when acting as communicational liaisons between them.

Attention will be given to three features of the various groups' responses: their distribution, that is, the degree of group stereotypy or dispersion of responses; their content, that is, the degrees of equivalence of specific responses to the same or translated equivalent stimulus, including analyses of all responses given as well as the primaries; and one aspect of the form of the responses, namely, variations in the use of superordinates.

METHOD

The Kent-Rosanoff stimulus-word list was translated for French-Canadians by a panel of Canadian French-English bilinguals, working from both the English and French versions. The final form was different for 8 of the 100 stimuli from Rosenzweig's (1957) version used for French students. These changes make the stimuli, even when translated, as equivalent as possible for all groups. Comparisons are based on the 100 stimuli except when otherwise noted. According to the bilingual translators, the stimuli appeared to be as appropriate, that is, as common and unemotional in meaning, in their French as in their English versions.

The subjects were 136 male French-Canadian monolingual students from a collège (the equivalent of a French lycée or an American junior college) in Quebec City; 206 male and female English-Canadian monolingual advanced students in Montreal high schools; and 88 English-French bilinguals, males and females, from one high school and two collèges in Montreal. Approximately half the bilinguals received the English version first and the Canadian French version about 3 weeks later; the other half started with the French version. Responses of males and females were tabulated together.

The criteria for bilinguality included a self-evaluation indicating a fairly good or good degree of skill in speaking, reading, writing, and understanding the second language, and completion of at least 90 of the 100 responses in both languages. Monolinguals were those who had very little or no skill in the second language as reflected in the same measures. Response frequencies were computed with a varying number of subjects due to incomplete or illegible answers.

The list of 100 words was given as a group test, and subjects were asked to write down immediately the first word that came to mind as they read each stimulus word. They were also instructed to work rapidly through the list.

RESULTS

Associational Response Distributions

In Table 1 the four Canadian groups are compared with the American and French-French student norms in terms of the mean percentages (over the 100 stimulus words) of subjects who contribute to the primary, secondary, tertiary responses, and the average of these three most popular responses combined.[1]

It is apparent that the American group shows the most stereotypy in responding and the French-French group least, with the

TABLE 1

Response Stereotypy of Various Groups of Students, in Mean Percentages

	American 1952[a]	English-Canadian 1964	Bilinguals in English 1964	French-Canadian 1964	Bilinguals in French 1964	French-French 1955[b]
Primaries	37.5	33.3	25.9	23.7	23.0	20.4
Secondaries	13.6	11.5	11.7	11.2	10.3	9.8
Tertiaries	8.0	7.4	7.2	7.5	6.9	6.9
Total	59.1	52.2	44.8	42.4	40.2	37.1
Median percentage of primaries	.34	.30	.23	.20	.19	.18
Rank-frequency slopes	−1.4	−1.3	−1.1	−1.0	−1.1	−1.0

[a] From Russell and Jenkins (1954).
[b] From Rosenzweig (1959).

English-Canadians being notably like the Americans and the other three groups placing progressively closer to the French-French. The bilingual group presents different distributions when using the two languages, behaving like the English-Canadians when responding in English and more like the French-Canadians and French-French when responding in French. The same pattern is reflected in the "median percentage" of primaries presented in Table 1.

Rosenzweig (1959) used a "rank-frequency function" to express differences in the tendency to diversify associational responses in another fashion. For this measure, the mean frequency of all primaries becomes the frequency for Rank 1, the mean frequency of all secondaries becomes the frequency for Rank 2, and so on, and these values are plotted on the abscissa of log-log coordinates with the frequencies of response distributed on the ordinate. These curves are approximately linear for sizable samples; the steeper the slope, the more stereotyped the response pattern is. Rosenzweig found that the American slope was −1.4 and the French-French slope −1.0. It will be noticed in Table 1 that the slope for the English-Canadian responses approximates closely that of the Americans while those of the other three groups are essentially alike and similar to that of the French-French.

Equivalence of Associational Responses

For 20 of the stimulus words, all six of the norm groups produce the same (or translated equivalent) response as a primary. In 15 of these instances, the primaries are above the median percentage of all primaries for the group, showing a tendency for responses with a high probability of occurring to make up a core, albeit small, of common associational responses for these language groups. The stimuli (in capitals) and responses in question are: TABLE-chair, MAN-woman, BLACK-white, FRUIT-apple, CHAIR-table, WOMAN-man, SPIDER-web, NEEDLE-thread, GIRL-boy, EAGLE-bird, STEM-flower, LAMP-light, DREAM-sleep, BOY-girl, BLUE-sky, HEAD-hair, LONG-short, SQUARE-round, SCISSORS-cut, and KING-queen.

Table 2 shows the degree of equivalence of primary responses between pairs of language groups. The equivalence for the English-Canadian and American student groups is striking (.78) especially in

TABLE 2

Group Comparisons of Equivalent Primary Responses

	French-Canadian	English-Canadian	American	French-French	Bilinguals in English	Bilinguals in French
French-Canadian		.51	.45	.44	.57	.68
English-Canadian			.78	.46	.61	.56
American				.46	.52	.50
French-French					.33	.45
Bilinguals in English						.59
Bilinguals in French						

Note.—In proportions, since translated equivalents of stimuli in certain comparisons were not equivalent in others. This variance affected three or four stimuli in various cases.

view of Rosenzweig's finding that two halves of the same French-French student group agreed in 75% of the cases only. In contrast, the English-Canadian group shows only 51% agreement with the French-Canadian which in turn has only 44% agreement with the French-French. The relationship of the bilinguals to the two Canadian monolingual groups is also relatively strong and generally much stronger than the relation of the two monolingual groups with one another. It is also evident that the content of the bilinguals' associations change when they use their other language for responding, the closeness of overlap shifting from the English-Canadian to the French-Canadian groups as they change from English to French.

Our next step was to determine if these same trends are apparent when consideration is given to all the responses obtained, not only the primaries. Table 3 presents "group overlap coefficients" of all possible comparisons with the exception of the French-French

TABLE 3

Group Overlap Coefficients and Significance Tests for Various Group Comparisons

Groups Compared	Overlap coefficient
1. English Canadian-American	.69
2. French Canadian-Bilinguals, French	.54
3. American-Bilinguals, English	.52
4. English Canadian-Bilinguals, English	.45
5. English Canadian-French Canadian	.43
6. French Canadian-American	.42
7. American-Bilinguals, French	.40
8. English Canadian-Bilinguals, French	.40
9. Bilinguals, English-Bilinguals, French	.39
10. French Canadian-Bilinguals, English	.36

Note.—Using the Duncan range test values, any coefficients that differ by .09 and .11 are significant at the .05 and .01 levels, respectively. Thus, the English Canadian-American overlap (1) is significantly greater than any other (2-10) whereas there are no significant differences in degrees of overlap among Comparisons 5-10.

group because these norms have not been published. The overlap coefficient was developed by Rosenzweig as a means of using all of the responses, not just the primaries, in estimating the similarities and differences of any pair of subgroups in their modes of associating to the same set of stimulus words. The coefficient (given in detail by Rosenzweig, 1964, pp. 60 ff.) determines for any stimulus how much overlap there is, considering all the responses given by any two groups. For example, if .75 of one group gave the response chair to TABLE and .50 of the comparison group gave the same response to TABLE, then .50 is taken as the "common fraction" of overlap. This procedure is followed for all the different responses given by both groups to any particular stimulus word and the sum of the common fractions is the overlap coefficient. In the present case, coefficients were determined for the first and every fifth word of the 100 stimuli for each group. The mean coefficients are given in Table 3. The reliability of the differences among means was tested by analysis of variance and it was apparent that both the differences among comparison group pairs ($F = 28.10$, $df = 9/180$) and among stimulus words ($F = 13.70$, $df = 20/180$) were significant beyond the .01 level.

The Duncan range test, a multiple group comparison statistic, was used to isolate the group comparisons which contribute to the overall significance. Reading from Table 3, it is evident that the Americans are more like the English-Canadians and the bilinguals in English than they are like the French-Canadians or the bilinguals in French. The English-Canadians, in turn, are more like the Americans than they are like any of the other three Canadian groups. The French-Canadians are more like the bilinguals in French than they are to any of the other three groups. In fact, they are equally distant in response overlap from the Americans and the English-Canadians. The bilinguals in English are equally distant from English- and French-Canadians. They are even more like Americans than French-Canadians and slightly more like Americans than English-Canadians (*ns*) suggesting that they may model on American speakers of English as much or more than on English-Canadians. On the other hand, the bilinguals in French are more similar to the French-Canadians than to the English-Canadians, the Americans, or the bilinguals in English. This pattern of findings is essentially similar to that produced by the analysis of primaries only, except that no statements can be made about the relations with the French-French. In general both analyses indicate that: (a) The major difference in the content of associational responses uncovered in these comparisons is that between the American and the French monolingual groups. The similarity of the English-Canadian monolinguals and American responses suggests that the English-Canadian may model on American speech habits to a marked degree. (b) The English- and French-Canadian monolinguals are relatively dissimilar in their response content. (c) The bilinguals have quite distinctive associations in their two languages, especially noticeable when all responses are considered. However, because of these language discrepancies, the bilinguals become very much like the two Canadian monolingual groups as they switch from one language to the other indicating their presumed dependence on the monolingual groups for their skill in both languages and their potential role as linguistic mediators for the two monolingual groups. This point will be taken up in the discussion to follow.

Superordinate Responses

Jenkins and Russell (1960) devised an objective means of determining which responses given to the Kent-Rosanoff stimuli were superordinates and found that 39 of the 100 stimuli could call out unambiguous superordinates. For the French version of the list, two of these had to be eliminated (BLOSSOM and MUTTON) for the reasons given by Rosenzweig (1964, p. 65); the stimulus ANGER was also eliminated because our bilingual judges felt that its superordinate ("emotion") was somewhat ambiguous in both French and English. Thus, the proportions given below are based on 36 words for the French-Canadians and the bilinguals in French and on 38 words for the English-Canadians and the bilinguals in English.

The superordinates accounted for the following percentage of responses: for French-Canadians, 8.58; for English-Canadians, 8.12; for bilinguals in English, 7.20; and for bilinguals in French, 6.45. All four of these are substantially like the 8% found for the Americans and they all contrast with the 3.3% for the French-French students.

DISCUSSION

Associational Response Diversity

It was found that the group of American students was the most stereotyped in their associational responses and the French-French students least so, with the English-Canadians very similar to the Americans and the French-Canadians very similar to the French-French. The bilinguals placed between the English- and French-Canadian monolingual groups when responding in English and between the French-Canadians and French-French when using French. These findings not only support those of Rosenzweig (1961) on European and American group differences, but they also extend the contrasts with Americans to include French-Canadians (i.e., North Americans) who show as much response diversity as the European groups do.

One can only speculate about the reasons for these differences. There is likely not much difference between the English- and French-Canadian monolingual groups with respect to their selection for schooling, one possibility given by Rosenzweig to account for French-French and American student differences. Although the French-Canadian students were at *lycées*, they would not likely be more carefully selected than the English-Canadian high school students, most of whom were from middle or upper-middle class districts and preparing for university study. It is more likely that differences in educational experiences play an important role. Compared to the Americans and English-Canadians, the French-Canadians, like the French-French, follow a so-called classical program of instruction where much less use is made of short-answer-type questioning than of composition writing which stresses the development of ideas. There may be, however, a more general cultural contrast reflected here between French people, both in France and Canada, who may place more value on verbal brilliance and linguistic wittiness than Americans who in turn may value more the ability to talk the other fellow's language. The present findings are consonant with an earlier study by Lambert (1956) who noted that English-French bilinguals from France were less stereotyped than American monolinguals in both their French and English associations, suggesting that some cultural factor affects associational stereotypy. However, various lines of research are clearly needed to actually account for these cultural differences, and to determine whether these differences hold for other than student groups in the countries being compared.

The modifications of response stereotypy noted as bilinguals change their language of response is of interest, first because it indicates that, in becoming bilingual, they are able to incorporate such relatively subtle features of the two languages, and second because it suggests that associational response diversity may be one of the features of the languages learned that assist bilinguals in keeping their two languages functionally separated, a matter of theoretical concern (see Lambert, 1963; Lambert, Havelka, and Crosby, 1958). It is also of interest that not all bilinguals are able to modify their responses to accord with those typical of the two languages they have learned. The French-French bilinguals referred to above (Lambert, 1956) were as diversified in their English as in their French responses. In contrast to the bilinguals examined here, they were adult French natives, many of them teachers of French in the United States, who had learned English at school and in American communities later in life. In other words, their English skill, although brought up to a high level, was apparently a recent overlay on a basic French language system.

Equivalence of Associational Content

When comparing the equivalence of response content from group to group, we found some pairs agreeing on primaries in 78% of the possible cases and others, only 33%. In Rosenzweig's (1961) study, he found agreement of primaries between American and European groups ranging from 35 to 48%. He felt these percentages of equivalence were artificially low because: he was dealing only with primaries, thereby missing equivalences in the rest of the responses given; because the translations of stimulus words were often not equivalents; and because the methods of collecting the responses were not standardized. Rosenzweig, in fact, believed that the agreements were strong enough to indicate a "cross-cultural community which shares verbal associations and meanings [p. 357]." In the present case, we can have somewhat more confidence in the percentages of equivalence not only because the range is greater but also because all responses (except for comparisons with the French-French group) as well as primaries can be compared, the translations have been more exactly matched, and the procedures used for collecting the responses were standardized.

Because we are as interested in group dissimilarities of associational content as in the similarities, it is necessary to explain briefly how we interpret associational responses. We view them as particular connotative meaning networks, parts of which may be activated whenever their appropriate stimulus words are either decoded or are about to be encoded. The networks not only convey emotional connotations but also direct the train of thought as particular stimulus words are encountered. This view is similar to that of Carroll (1964) who interprets word-association responses as "some part of an assemblage of mediating processes [p. 100]" reflecting "the variety of experiences represented in a concept [p. 101]." The present view is also basically related to Deese's (1962) notion of "associative meaning." Deese noted that two words often do not elicit one another as associational responses yet they do have a great many associations in common. For example, samples of undergraduates gave the associations note, song, sound, noise, music, and orchestra to both PIANO and SYMPHONY. Such words, he argues, have much associative meaning in common and are thus linked within some general concept. In the present case, the same or translated equivalent stimulus word may have the same or different associational meanings for different groups and when the associational systems are discordant, the social communication may be disrupted. For example, the English-Canadian and bilinguals in English gave the primary response God to the stimulus word BIBLE whereas the French-Canadians and the bilinguals in French gave livre (book) as their primary responses. In communication, the two monolingual groups could easily miss the full significance of one another's messages because such associational discordances color the meaning and shunt the line of associations off on quite different routes. In this example, the bilinguals would likely transmit the discrepancy with fidelity from one monolingual group to another, switching from one associational network to another as they change languages. The discordance would accumulate when sequences of ideas, as in sentences, are socially transmitted. For instance, one might want to relate the concepts CHILD, SICKNESS, and DOCTOR. The primary associates to these words are: mother, health, and nurse for our English-Canadian subjects and baby, hospital, sickness for the French-Canadians. If bilinguals are used to transmit this message, additional distortion is likely since the primaries are mother, bed, sick for the bilinguals in English and baby, bed, sickness for the bilinguals in French.

Assuming then that these group differences in associational correspondence determine in part the difficulty or ease of communication both across and within linguistic groups, we can profit from a reexamination of Table 2. In view of the long-term tensions between French- and English-Canadians in Quebec, attention is first drawn to the relatively low correspondence between their associational networks (.51), much lower than that between English-Canadians and Americans (.78). The communication of connotative significance between members of these groups might be improved through the bilinguals who have somewhat more associational similarity with themselves in their other language (.59) and who make better contact with each of the monolingual groups, especially when using the same language as the monolinguals (bilinguals in English and English-Canadians = .61, bilinguals in French and French-Canadians = .68) but also when using the other language (bilinguals in English and French-Canadians = .57, bilinguals in French and English-Canadians = .56). The bilinguals are potential sources of rapprochement between these two relatively discordant monolingual groups and they might be used as linguistic mediators to help prepare, transmit, and receive messages from one group to the other.

The discordance in the networks of the English- and French-Canadian monolingual groups might also be improved on if the French-Canadians were to move toward the American pattern (equivalence of primaries for the French-Canadian and Americans is .45 compared to the .78 for the English-Canadian and American groups). Since the associational pattern of the French-Canadian group is relatively isolated from all of the others, French-Canadians may realize their difficulty in expressing the full meaning of their ideas and thereby sense a certain pressure to adjust to either the English-Canadian and American pattern, or at least the French-French pattern.

Finally, English-Canadian associational contact with the French-French (.46) could be made worse by the use of bilinguals in English who have relatively low equivalence of primaries with the French-French (.33). The distortions would come mainly from transmitting messages from the English-Canadian monolinguals to the bilinguals in English, but even then the relay of the message through the bilinguals' French would not likely be good (bilinguals in French and French-French = .45). Possibly English-French bilinguals from France might be better mediators in this case.

These notions need the support of further normative studies with more careful selection of bilinguals who have demonstrable skill of equal power in both languages. If these norms are reliable, then laboratory investigations of bilinguals transmitting and receiving messages in each of their languages could be attempted as a means of studying ease and difficulty of communication.

Superordinate Responses

The fact that the French-French students, but not the French-Canadians, gave so few superordinates eliminates the possibility that the French language limits superordination in some way—an inference one might draw from Rosenzweig's (1964) study. The analysis of superordination also makes it clear that the French-Canadian students are similar to the French-French only in their relative diversity of responses, but are as different from the French-French as the Americans are with regard both to the content of their responses and their use of superordinates. The English-Canadian norms, however, are very similar to those of the Americans on all three counts.

NOTES

This research was supported by a subvention from the Carnegie Corporation of New York and by Research Grant D77-94-01-10 from the Defense Research Board of Canada. The authors are very grateful for suggestions given them by James Jenkins, Lyle Jones, and Sol Saporta.

[1] Tables giving the primary responses and percentage of students for each of the Canadian groups have been deposited with the American Documentation Institute. Order Document No. 8734 from ADI Auxiliary Publications Project, Photoduplication Service, Library of Congress, Washington, D. C. 20540. Remit in advance $1.25 for microfilm or $1.25 for photocopies and make checks payable to: Chief, Photoduplication Service, Library of Congress.

REFERENCES

Carroll, J.B. Language and thought. Englewood Cliffs, N.J.: Prentice-Hall, 1964.

Deese, J. On the structure of associative meaning. Psychological Review, 1962, 69, 161-175.

Esper, E.A. A contribution to the experimental study of analogy. Psychological Review, 1918, 25, 468-487.

Jenkins, J.J., and Russell, W.A. Systematic changes in word association norms: 1910-1952. Journal of Abnormal and Social Psychology, 1960, 60, 293-304.

Lambert, W.E. Developmental aspects of second-language acquisition. Journal of Social Psychology, 1956, 43, 83-104.

Lambert, W.E. Psychological approaches to the study of language: II. On second-language learning and bilingualism. Modern Language Journal, 1963, 47, 114-121.

Lambert, W.E., Havelka, J., and Crosby, C. The influence of language-acquisition contexts on bilingualism. Journal of Abnormal and Social Psychology, 1958, 56, 239-244.

Rosenzweig, M.R. Etudes sur l'association des mots. L'Année Psychologique, 1957, 57, 23-32.

Rosenzweig, M.R. Comparisons between French and English word association norms. American Psychologist, 1959, 14, 363. (Abstract).

Rosenzweig, M.R. Comparisons among word association responses in English, French, German and Italian. American Journal of Psychology, 1961, 74, 347-360.

Rosenzweig, M.R. Word associations of French workmen: Comparisons with associations of French students and American workers and students. Journal of Verbal Learning and Verbal Behavior, 1964, 3, 57-69.

Russell, W.A., and Jenkins, J.J. The complete Minnesota norms for responses to 100 words from the Kent-Rosanoff Word Association Test. Technical Report No. 11, 1954, University of Minnesota, Contract N8 onr 66216, Office of Naval Research.

13 A Social Psychology of Bilingualism

Other contributions in this series* have drawn attention to various aspects of bilingualism, each of great importance for behavioral scientists. For instance, we have been introduced to the psychologist's interest in the bilingual switching process with its attendant mental and neurological implications, and his interest in the development of bilingual skill; to the linguist's interest in the bilingual's competence with his two linguistic systems and the way the systems interact; and to the social-anthropologist's concern with the sociocultural settings of bilingualism and the role expectations involved. The purpose of the present paper is to extend and integrate certain of these interests by approaching bilingualism from a social-psychological perspective, one characterized not only by its interest in the reactions of the bilingual as an individual but also by the attention given to the social influences that affect the bilingual's behavior and to the social repercussions that follow from his behavior. From this perspective, a process such as language switching takes on a broader significance when its likely social and psychological consequences are contemplated, as, for example, when a language switch brings into play contrasting sets of stereotyped images of people who habitually use each of the languages involved in the switch. Similarly, the development of bilingual skill very likely involves something more than a special set of aptitudes because one would expect that various social attitudes and motives are intimately involved in learning a foreign language. Furthermore, the whole process of becoming bilingual can be expected to involve major conflicts of values and allegiances, and bilinguals could make various types of adjustments to the bicultural demands made on them. It is to these matters that I would like to direct attention.

---

*Chapters in Problems in bilingualism, ed. by John Macnamara. Special issue of The Journal of Social Issues 23:2 (1967).

Linguistic Style and Intergroup Impressions

What are some of the social psychological consequences of language switching? Certain bilinguals have an amazing capacity to pass smoothly and automatically from one linguistic community to another as they change languages of discourse or as they turn from one conversational group to another at multilingual gatherings. The capacity is something more than Charles Boyer's ability to switch from Franco-American speech to Continental-style French when he turns from the eyes of a woman to those of a waiter who wants to know if the wine is of the expected vintage. In a sense, Boyer seems to be always almost speaking French. Nor is it the tourist guide's ability to use different languages to explain certain events in different languages. In most cases they are not fluent enough to pass and even when their command is good, their recitals seem to be memorized. Here is an example of what I do mean: a friend of mine, the American linguist, John Martin, is so talented in his command of various regional dialects of Spanish, I am told, that he can fool most Puerto Ricans into taking him for a Puerto Rican and most Columbians into taking him for a native of Bogota. His skill can be disturbing to the natives in these different settings because he is a potential linguistic spy in the sense that he can get along too well with the intimacies and subtleties of their dialects.

The social psychologist wants to know how this degree of bilingual skill is developed, what reactions a man like Martin has as he switches languages, and what social effects the switching initiates, not only the suspicion or respect generated by an unexpected switch but also the intricate role adjustments that usually accompany such changes. Research has not yet gone far enough to answer satisfactorily all the questions the social psychologist might ask, but a start has been made, and judging from the general confidence of psycholinguists and sociolinguists, comprehensive answers to such questions can be expected in a short time.

I will draw on work conducted by a rotating group of students and myself at McGill University in Montreal, a fascinating city where two major ethnic-linguistic groups are constantly struggling to maintain their separate identities and where bilinguals as skilled as John Martin are not at all uncommon. Two incidents will provide an appropriate introduction to our work. One involves a bus ride where I was seated behind two English Canadian ladies and in front of two French Canadian ladies as the bus moved through an English-Canadian region of the city. My attention was suddenly drawn to the conversation in front wherein one lady said something like: "If I couldn't speak English I certainly wouldn't shout about it", referring to the French conversation going on behind them. Her friend replied: "Oh, well, you can't expect much else from them". Then one of the ladies mentioned that she was bothered when French people laughed among themselves in her presence because she felt they might be making fun of her. This was followed by a nasty interchange of pejorative stereotypes about French Canadians, the whole discussion prompted, it seemed, by what struck me as a humorous conversation of the two attractive, middle class French Canadian women seated behind them. The English ladies couldn't understand the French conversation, nor did they look back to see what the people they seemed to know so much about even looked like.

The second incident involved my daughter when she was about 12 years old. She, too, has amazing skill with English and two dialects of French, the Canadian style and the European style. One day while driving her to school, a lycée run by teachers from France, I stopped to pick up one of her friends and they were immediately involved in conversation, French-Canadian French style. A block or two farther I slowed down to pick up a second girlfriend when my daughter excitedly told me, in English, to drive on. At school I asked what the trouble was and she explained that there actually was no trouble although there might have been if the second girl, who was from France, and who spoke another dialect of French, had got in the car because then my daughter would have been forced to show a linguistic preference for one girl or the other. Normally she could escape this conflict by interacting with each girl separately, and, inadvertently, I had almost put her on the spot. Incidents of this sort prompted us to commence a systematic analysis of the effects of language and dialect changes on impression formation and social interaction.

Dialect Variations Elicit Stereotyped Impressions

Over the past eight years, we have developed a research technique that makes use of language and dialect variations to elicit the stereotyped impressions or biased views which members of one social group hold of representative members of a contrasting group. Briefly, the procedure involves the reactions of listeners (referred to as judges) to the taped recordings of a number of perfectly bilingual speakers reading a two-minute passage at one time in one of their languages (e.g., French) and, later a translation equivalent of the same passage in their second language (e.g., English). Groups of judges are asked to listen to this series of recordings and evaluate the personality characteristics of each speaker as well as possible, using voice cues only. They are reminded of the common tendency to attempt to gauge the personalities of unfamiliar speakers heard over the phone or radio. Thus they are kept unaware that they will actually hear two readings by each of several bilinguals. In our experience no subjects have become aware of this fact. The judges are given practice trials, making them well acquainted with both versions of the message, copies of which are supplied in advance. They usually find the enterprise interesting, especially if they are promised, and receive, some feedback on how well they have done, for example, if the profiles for one or two speakers, based on the ratings of friends who know them well, are presented at the end of the series.

This procedure, referred to as the _matched-guise_ technique, appears to reveal judges' more private reactions to the contrasting group than direct attitude questionnaires do (see Lambert, Anisfeld and Yeni-Komshian, 1965), but much more research is needed to adequately assess its power in this regard. The technique is particularly valuable as a measure of _group_ biases in evaluative reactions; it has very good reliability in the sense that essentially the same profile of traits for a particular group appear when different samples of judges, drawn from a particular subpopulation, are used. Differences between subpopulations are very marked, however, as will become apparent. On the other hand, the technique apparently has little reliability when measured by test-retest ratings produced by the same group of judges; we believe this type of unreliability is due in large part to the main statistic used, the difference between an individual's rating of a pair of guises on a single trait. Difference scores give notoriously low test-retest reliability coefficients although their use for comparing means is perfectly appropriate (Bereiter, 1963; and Ferguson, 1959, 285f).

Several of our studies have been conducted since 1958 in greater Montreal, a setting that has a long history of tensions between English- and French-speaking Canadians. The conflict is currently so sharp that some French-Canadian (FC) political leaders in the Province of Quebec talk seriously about separating the Province from the rest of Canada, comprising a majority of English-Canadians (ECs). In 1958-59, (Lambert, Hodgson, Gardner and Fillenbaum, 1960) we asked a sizeable group of EC university students to evaluate the personalities of a series of speakers, actually the matched guises of male bilinguals speaking in Canadian style French and English. When their judgements were analyzed it was found that their evaluations were strongly biased against the FC and in favor of the matched EC guises. They rated the speakers in their EC guises as being better looking, taller, more intelligent, more dependable, kinder, more ambitious and as having more character. This evaluational bias was just as apparent among judges who were bilingual as among monolinguals.

We presented the same set of taped voices to a group of FC students of equivalent age, social class and educational level. Here we were in for a surprise for they showed the same bias, evaluating the EC guises significantly *more* favorably than the FC guises on a whole series of traits, indicating, for example, that they viewed the EC guises as being more intelligent, dependable, likeable and as having more character! Only on two traits did they rate the FC guises more favorably, namely kindness and religiousness, and, considering the whole pattern of ratings, it could be that they interpreted too much religion as a questionable quality. Not only did the FC judges generally downgrade representatives of their own ethnic-linguistic group, they also rated the FC guises much more negatively than the EC judges had. We consider this pattern of results as a reflection of a community-wide stereotype of FCs as being relatively second-rate people, a view apparently fully shared by certain subgroups of FCs. Similar tendencies to downgrade one's own group have been reported in research with minority groups conducted in other parts of North America.

Extentions of the Basic Study

The Follow-up Study. Some of the questions left unanswered in the first study have been examined recently by Malcolm Preston

(Preston, 1963). Using the same basic techniques, the following questions were asked: (a) Will female and male judges react similarly to language and accent variations of speakers? (b) Will judges react similarly to male and female speakers who change their pronunciation style or the language they speak? (c) Will there be systematic differences in reactions to FC and Continental French (CF) speakers?

For this study, 80 English Canadian and 92 French Canadian first year college age students from Montreal served as judges. The EC judges in this study were all Catholics since we wanted to determine if EC Catholics would be less biased in their views of FCs than the non-Catholic EC judges had been in the original study. Approximately the same number of males and females from both language groups were tested, making four groups of judges in all: an EC male group, an EC female, a FC male and a FC female group.

The 18 personality traits used by the judges for expressing their reactions were grouped, for the purposes of interpretation, into three logically distinct categories of personality: (a) competence which included intelligence, ambition, self-confidence, leadership and courage; (b) personal integrity which included dependability, sincerity, character, conscientiousness and kindness; (c) social attractiveness which included sociability, likeability, entertainingness, sense of humor and affectionateness. Religiousness, good looks and height were not included in the above categories since they did not logically fit.

Results: Evaluative Reactions of English-Canadian Listeners. In general it was found that the EC listeners viewed the female speakers more favorably in the French guises while they viewed the male speakers more favorably in their English guises. In particular, the EC men saw the FC lady speakers as more intelligent, ambitious, self-confident, dependable, courageous and sincere than their English counterparts. The EC ladies were not quite so gracious although they, too, rated the FC ladies as more intelligent, ambitious, self-confident (but shorter) than the EC women guises. Thus, ECs generally view FC females as more competent and the EC men see them as possessing more integrity and competence.

Several notions came to mind at this point. It may be that the increased attractiveness of the FC woman in the eyes of the EC male is partly a result of her inaccessibility. Perhaps also the EC women are cognizant of the EC men's latent preference for FC women and accordingly are themselves prompted to upgrade the FC female, even to the point of adopting the FC woman as a model of what a woman should be.

However, the thought that another group is better than their own should not be a comfortable one for members of any group, especially a group of young ladies! The realization, however latent, that men of their own cultural group prefer another type of women might well be a very tender issue for the EC woman, one that could be easily exacerbated.

To examine this idea, we carried out a separate experiment. The *S*s for the experiment were two groups of EC young women, one group serving as controls, the other as an experimental group. Both groups were asked to give their impressions of the personalities of a group of speakers, some using English, some Canadian style French. They were, of course, actually presented with female bilingual speakers using Canadian French and English guises. Just before they evaluated the speakers, the experimental group was given false information about FC women, information that was designed to upset them. They heard a tape recording of a man reading supposedly authentic statistical information about the increase in marriages between FC women and EC men. They were asked to listen to this loaded passage twice, for practice only, disregarding the content of the message and attending only to the personality of the speaker. We presumed, however, that they would not likely be able to disregard the content since it dealt with a matter that might well bother them—FC women, they were told, were competing for EC men, men who already had a tendency to prefer FC women, a preference that they possibly shared themselves. In contrast, the control group received quite neutral information which would not affect their ratings of FCs in any way. The results supported the prediction: The experimental *S*s judged the FC women to be reliably more attractive but reliably less dependable and sincere than did the control *S*s. That is, the favorable reactions toward FC women found previously were evident in the judgments of the control group, while the experimental *S*s, who had been given false information designed to highlight the threat posed by the presumed greater competence and integrity of FC women, saw the

FC women as men stealers—attractive but undependable and insincere. These findings support the general hypothesis we had developed and they serve as a first step in a series of experiments we are now planning to determine how judgments of personalities affect various types of social interaction.

Let us return again to the main investigation. It was found that FC men were not as favorably received as the women were by their EC judges. EC ladies liked EC men, rating them as taller, more likeable, affectionate, sincere, and conscientious, and as possessing more character and a greater sense of humor than the FC versions of the same speakers. Furthermore, the EC male judges also favored EC male speakers, rating them as taller, more kind, dependable and entertaining. Thus, FC male speakers are viewed as lacking integrity and as being less socially attractive by both EC female, and, to a less marked extent, EC male judges. This tendency to downgrade the FC male, already noted in the basic study, may well be the expression of an unfavorable stereotyped and prejudiced attitude toward FCs, but, apparently, this prejudice is selectively directed toward FC males, possibly because they are better known than females as power figures who control local and regional governments and who thereby can be viewed as sources of threat or frustration, (or as the guardians of FC women, keeping them all to themselves).

The reactions to Continental French (CF) speakers are generally more favorable although less marked. The EC male listeners viewed CF women as slightly more competent and CF men as equivalent to their EC controls except for height and religiousness. The EC female listeners upgraded CF women on sociability and self-confidence, but downgraded CF men on height, likeability and sincerity. Thus, EC judges appear to be less concerned about European French people in general than they are about the local French people; the European French are neither downgraded nor taken as potential social models to any great extent.

Evaluative Reactions of French-Canadian Listeners. Summarizing briefly, the FC listeners showed more significant guise differences than did their EC counterparts. FCs generally rated European French guises more favorably and Canadian French guises less favorably than they did their matched EC guises. One important exception was the *FC* women who viewed *FC* men as more competent and as more socially attractive than *EC* men.

The general pattern of evaluations presented by the *FC* judges, however, indicates that they view their own linguistic cultural group as *inferior* to both the English Canadian and the European French groups, suggesting that *FC*s are prone to take either of these other groups as models for changes in their own manners of behaving (including speech) and possibly in basic values. This tendency is more marked among *FC* men who definitely prefered male and female representatives of the *EC* and *CF* groups to those of their own group. The *FC* women, in contrast, appear to be guardians of *FC* culture at least in the sense that they favored male representatives of their own cultural group. We presume this reaction reflects something more than a preference for *FC* marriage partners. *FC* women may be particularly anxious to preserve *FC* values and to pass these on in their own families through language, religion and tradition.

Nevertheless, *FC* women apparently face a conflict of their own in that they favor characteristics of both *CF* and *EC* women. Thus, the *FC* female may be safe-guarding the *FC* culture through a preference for *FC* values seen in *FC* men, at the same time as she is prone to change her own behavior and values in the direction of one of two foreign cultural models, those that the men in her group apparently favor. It is of interest that *EC* women are confronted with a similar conflict since they appear envious of *FC* women.

The Developmental Studies. Recently, we have been looking into the background of the inferiority reaction among *FC* youngsters, trying to determine at what age it starts and how it develops through the years. Elizabeth Anisfeld and I (1964) started by studying the reactions of ten year old *FC* children to the matched guises of bilingual youngsters of their own age reading French and English versions of *Little Red Riding Hood*, once in Canadian style French and once in standard English. In this instance, half of the judges were bilingual in English and half were essentially monolingual in French. Stated briefly, it was found that *FC* guises were rated significantly *more* favorable on nearly all traits. (One exception was height; the *EC* speakers were judged as taller.) However, these favorable evaluations of the *FC* in contrast to the *EC* guises were due almost entirely to the reactions of the monolingual children. The bilingual children saw very little difference between the two sets of guises, that is, on nearly all traits their ratings of the FC guises were essentially the same as their ratings of EC guises. The results, therefore, made it clear that, unlike college-age judges, FC children at the ten year age level do not have a negative bias against their own group.

The question then arises as to where the bias starts after age ten. A recent study (Lambert, Frankel and Tucker, 1966) was addressed to solving this puzzle. The investigation was conducted with 375 FC girls ranging in age from 9 to 18, who gave their evaluations of three groups of matched guises, (a) of some girls about their own age, (b) of some adult women, and (c) of some adult men. Passages that were appropriate for each age level were read by the bilingual speakers once in English and once in Canadian style French. In this study attention was given to the social class background of the judges (some were chosen from private schools, some from public schools) and to their knowledge of English (some were bilingual and some monolingual in French). It was found that definite preferences for EC guises appeared at about age twelve and were maintained through the late teen years. There was, however, a marked difference between the private and public school judges: the upper middle class girls were especially biased after age 12, whereas the pattern for the working class girls was less pronounced and less durable, suggesting that for them the bias is shortlived and fades out by the late teens. Note that we probably did not encounter girls from lower class homes in our earlier studies using girls at FC collèges or universités.

The major implication of these findings is that the tendency for certain subgroups of college-age FCs to downgrade representatives of their own ethnic-linguistic group, noted in our earlier studies, seems to have its origin, at least with girls, at about age 12, but the ultimate fate of this attitude depends to a great extent on social-class background. Girls who come from upper middle class FC homes, and especially those who have become bilingual in English, are particularly likely to maintain this view, at least into the young adult years.

The pattern of results of these developmental studies can also be examined from a more psychodynamic perspective. If we assume that the adult female and male speakers in their FC guises represent parents or people like their own parents to the FC adolescent judges, just as the same-age speakers represent someone like themselves, then the findings suggest several possibilities that could be studied in more detail. First, the results are consistent with the notion that teen-age girls have a closer psychological relation with their fathers than with their mothers in the sense that the girls in the study rated FC female guises markedly inferior to EC ones, but generally favored or at least showed much less disfavor for the FC guises of male speakers. Considered in this light, social-class differences and bilingual skill apparently influence the degree of same-sex rejection and cross-sex identification: by the mid-teens the public school girls, both monolinguals and bilinguals, show essentially no rejection of either the FC female or male guises, whereas the private school girls, especially the bilinguals, show a rejection of both female and male FC guises through the late teens. These bilinguals might, because of their skill in English and their possible encouragement from home, be able to come in contact with the mothers of their EC associates and therefore may have developed stronger reasons to be envious of EC mothers and fathers than the monolingual girls would have.

Similarly, the reactions to "same-age" speakers might reflect a tendency to accept or reject one's peer-group or one's self, at least for the monolinguals. From this point of view, the findings suggest that the public school monolinguals are generally satisfied with their FC image since they favor the FC guises of the same-age speakers at the 16 year level. In contrast, the private school monolinguals may be expressing a marked rejection of themselves in the sense that they favor the EC guises. The bilinguals, of course, can consider themselves as being potential or actual members of both ethnic-linguistic groups represented by the guises. It is of interest, therefore, to note that both the public and particularly the private school bilinguals apparently favor the EC versions of themselves.

Two Generalizations

This program of research, still far from complete, does permit us to make two important generalizations, both relevant to the main argument of this paper. First, a technique has been developed that rather effectively calls out the stereotyped impressions that members of one ethnic-linguistic group hold of another contrasting group. The type and strength of impression depends on characteristics of the speakers—their sex, age, the dialect they use, and, very likely, the social-class background as this is revealed in speech style. The impression also seems to depend on characteristics of the audience of judges—their age, sex, socio-economic background, their bilinguality and their own speech style. The type of reactions and adjustments listeners must make to those who reveal, through their speech style, their likely ethnic group allegiance is suggested by the traits that listeners use to indicate their impressions. Thus, EC male and female college students tend to look down on the FC male speaker, seeing him as less intelligent, less dependable and less interesting than he would be seen if he had presented himself in an EC guise. Imagine the types of role adjustment that would follow if the same person were first seen in the FC guise and then suddenly switched to a perfect EC guise. A group of EC listeners would probably be forced to perk up their ears, reconsider their original classification of the person and then either view him as becoming too intimate in "their" language or decide otherwise and be pleasantly amazed that one of their own could manage the other group's language so well. Furthermore, since these comparative impressions are widespread throughout certain strata of each ethnic-linguistic community, they will probably have an enormous impact on young people who are either forced to learn the other group's language or who choose to do so.

The research findings outlined here have a second important message about the reactions of the bilingual who is able to convincingly switch languages or dialects. The bilingual can study the reactions of his audiences as he adopts one guise in certain settings and another in different settings, and receive a good deal of social feedback, permitting him to realize that he can be perceived in quite different ways, depending on how he presents himself. It could well be that his own self-concept takes two distinctive forms in the light of such feedback. He may also observe, with amusement or alarm, the role adjustments that follow when he suddenly switches guises with the same group of interlocutors. However, research is needed to document and examine these likely consequences of language or dialect switching from the perspective of the bilingual making the switches.

Although we have concentrated on a Canadian setting in these investigations, there is really nothing special about the Canadian scene with regard to the social effects of language or dialect switching. Equally instructive effects have been noted when the switch involves a change from standard American English to Jewish-accented English (Anisfeld, Bogo and Lambert, 1962); when the switch involves changing from Hebrew to Arabic for Israeli and Arab judges, or when the change is from Sephardic to Ashkenazic style Hebrew for Jewish listeners in Israel (Lambert, Anisfeld and Yeni-Komshian, 1965). Our most recent research, using a modified approach, has been conducted with American Negro speakers and listeners (Tucker and Lambert, 1967). The same type of social effects are inherent in this instance, too: Southern Negroes have more favorable impressions of people who use what the linguists call *Standard Network Style* English than they do of those who speak with their own style, but they are more impressed with their own style than they are with the speech of educated, Southern whites, or of Negroes who become too "white" in their speech by exaggerating the non-Negro features and over-correcting their verbal output.

Social-Psychological Aspects of Second-Language Learning

How might these intergroup impressions and feelings affect young people living in the Montreal area who are expected by educators to learn the other group's language? One would expect that both French-Canadian youngsters and their parents would be more willing, for purely social psychological reasons, to learn English than *EC*s to learn French. Although we haven't investigated the French-Canadians' attitudes toward the learning of English, still it is very apparent that bilingualism in Canada and in Quebec has long been a one-way affair, with *FC*s much more likely to learn English than the converse. Typically, this trend to English is explained on economic grounds and on the attraction of the United States, but I would like to suggest another possible reason for equally serious consideration. *FC*s may be drawn away from Canadian style French to English, or to bilingualism, or to European style French, as a psychological reaction to the contrast in stereotyped images which English and French Canadians have of one another. On the other hand, we would expect *EC* students and their parents in Quebec, at least, to be drawn away from French for the same basic reasons. It is, of course, short-sighted to talk about groups in this way because there are certain to be wide individual differences of reaction, as was the case in the impression studies, and as will be apparent in the research to be discussed, but one fact turned up in an unpublished study Robert Gardner and I conducted that looks like a group-wide difference. Several samples of Montreal _EC_, high school students who had studied French for periods of up to seven years scored no better on standard tests of French achievement than did Connecticut high schoolers who had only two or three years of French training.

Instrumental and Integrative Motivation

When viewed from a social-psychological perspective, the process of learning a second language itself also takes on a special significance. From this viewpoint, one would expect that if the student is to be successful in his attempts to learn another social group's language he must be both able and willing to adopt various aspects of behavior, including verbal behavior, which characterize members of the other linguistic-cultural group. The learner's ethnocentric tendencies and his attitudes toward the other group are believed to determine his success in learning the new language. His motivation to learn is thought to be determined by both his attitudes and by the type of orientation he has toward learning a second language. The orientation is _instrumental_ in form if, for example, the purposes of language study reflect the more utilitarian value of linguistic achievement, such as getting ahead in one's occupation, and is _integrative_ if, for example, the student is oriented to learn more about the other cultural community, as if he desired to become a potential member of the other group. It is also argued that some may be anxious to learn another language as a means of being accepted in another cultural group because of dissatisfactions experienced in their own culture while other individuals may be as much interested in another culture as they are in their own. In either case, the more proficient one becomes in a second language the more he may find that his place in his original membership group is modified at the same time as the other linguistic-cultural group becomes something more than a reference group for him. It may, in fact, become a second membership group for him. Depending upon the compatibility of the two cultures, he may experience feelings of chagrin or regret as he loses ties in one group, mixed with the fearful anticipation of entering a relatively new group. The concept of _anomie_ first proposed by Durkheim

(1897) and more recently extended by Srole (1951) and Williams (1952), refers to such feelings of social uncertainty or dissatisfaction.

My studies with Gardner (1959) were carried out with English-speaking Montreal high school students studying French who were evaluated for their language learning aptitude and verbal intelligence, as well as their attitudes and stereotypes toward members of the French community, and the intensity of their motivation to learn French. Our measure of motivation is conceptually similar to Jones' (1949 and 1950) index of interest in learning a language which he found to be important for successful learning among Welsh students. A factor analysis of scores on these various measures indicated that aptitude and intelligence formed a common factor which was independent of a second one comprising indices of motivation, type of orientation toward language and social attitudes toward FCs. Furthermore, a measure of achievement in French taken at the end of a year's study was reflected equally prominently in both factors. This statistical pattern meant that French achievement was dependent upon both aptitude and verbal intelligence as well as a sympathetic orientation toward the other group. This orientation was much less common among these students than was the instrumental one, as would be expected from the results of the matched-guise experiments. However, when sympathetic orientation was present it apparently sustained a strong motivation to learn the other group's language. Furthermore, it was clear that students with an integrative orientation were more successful in learning French than were those with instrumental orientations.

A follow-up study (Gardner, 1960) confirmed and extended these findings. Using a larger sample of EC students and incorporating various measures of French achievement, the same two independent factors were revealed, and again both were related to French achievement. But whereas aptitude and achievement were especially important for those French skills stressed in school training, such as grammar, the development of such skills, skills that call for the active use of the language in communicational settings, such as pronunciation accuracy and auditory comprehension, was determined in major part by measures of an integrative motivation to learn French. The aptitude variables were insignificant in this case. Further evidence from the intercorrelations indicated that this integrative motive was the converse of an authoritarian ideological syndrome, opening the possibility that basic personality dispositions may be involved in language learning efficiency.

In this same study information had been gathered from the parents of the students about their own orientations toward the French community. These data suggested that integrative or instrumental orientations toward the other group are developed within the family. That is, the minority of students with an integrative disposition to learn French had parents who also were integrative and sympathetic to the French community. However, students' orientations were not related to parents' skill in French nor to the number of French acquaintances the parents had, indicating that the integrative motive is not due to having more experience with French at home. Instead the integrative outlook more likely stems from a family-wide attitudinal disposition.

Language Learning and Anomie

Another feature of the language learning process came to light in an investigation of college and postgraduate students undergoing an intensive course in advanced French at McGill's French Summer School. We were interested here, among other matters, in changes in attitudes and feelings that might take place during the six-week study period (Lambert, Gardner, Barik and Tunstall, 1961). The majority of the students were Americans who oriented themselves mainly to the European-French rather than the American-French community. We adjusted our attitude scales to make them appropriate for those learning European French. Certain results were of special interest. As the students progressed in French skill to the point that they said they "thought" in French, and even dreamed in French, their feelings of anomie also increased markedly. At the same time, they began to seek out occasions to use English even though they had solemnly pledged to use only French for the six-week period. This pattern of results suggests to us that these already advanced students experienced a strong dose of anomie when they commenced to *really* master a second language. That is, when advanced students became so skilled that they begin to think and feel like Frenchmen, they then became so annoyed with feelings of anomie that they were prompted to develop strategies to minimize or control the annoyance. Reverting to English could be such a strategy. It should be emphasized however, that the chain of events just listed needs to be much more carefully explored.

Elizabeth Anisfeld and I took another look at this problem, experimenting with 10-year old monolingual and bilingual students (Peal and Lambert, 1962). We found that the bilingual children (attending French schools in Montreal) were markedly more favorable towards the "other" language group (i.e., the ECs) than the monolingual children were. Furthermore, the bilingual children reported that their parents held the same strongly sympathetic attitudes toward ECs, in contrast to the pro-FC attitudes reported for the parents of the monolingual children. Apparently, then, the development of second language skill to the point of balanced bilingualism is conditioned by family-shared attitudes toward the other linguistic-cultural group.

These findings are consistent and reliable enough to be of general interest. For example methods of language training could possibly be modified and strengthened by giving consideration to the social-psychological implications of language learning. Because of the possible practical as well as theoretical significance of this approach, it seemed appropriate to test its applicability in a cultural setting other than the bicultural Quebec scene. With measures of attitude and motivation modified for American students learning French, a large scale study, very similar in nature to those conducted in Montreal, was carried out in various settings in the United States with very similiar general outcomes (Lambert and Gardner, 1962).

One further investigation indicated that these suggested social psychological principles are not restricted to English and French speakers in Canada. Moshe Anisfeld and I (1961) extended the same experimental procedure to samples of Jewish high school students studying Hebrew at various parochial schools in different sectors of Montreal. They were questioned about their orientations toward learning Hebrew and their attitudes toward the Jewish culture and community, and tested for their verbal intelligence, language aptitude and achievement in the Hebrew language at the end of the school year. The results support the generalization that both intellectual capacity and attitudinal orientation affect success in learning Hebrew. However, whereas intelligence and linguistic aptitude were relatively stable predictors of success, the attitudinal measures varied from one

Jewish community to another. For instance, the measure of a Jewish student's desire to become more acculturated in the Jewish tradition and culture was a sensitive indicator of progress in Hebrew for children from a particular district of Montreal, one where members of the Jewish sub-community were actually concerned with the problems of integrating into the Jewish culture. In another district, made up mainly of Jews who recently arrived from central Europe and who were clearly of a lower socio-economic level, the measure of desire for Jewish acculturation did not correlate with achievement in Hebrew, whereas measures of pro-Semitic attitudes or pride in being Jewish did.

Bilingual Adjustments to Conflicting Demands

The final issue I want to discuss concerns the socio-cultural tugs and pulls that the bilingual or potential bilingual encounters and how he adjusts to these often conflicting demands made on him. We have seen how particular social atmospheres can affect the bilingual. For example, the French-English bilingual in the Montreal setting may be pulled toward greater use of English, and yet be urged by certain others in the FC community not to move too far in that direction, just as EC's may be discouraged from moving toward the French community. [In a similar fashion, dialects would be expected to change because of the social consequences they engender, so that Jewish accented speech should drop away, especially with those of the younger generation in American settings, as should Sephardic forms of Hebrew in Israel or certain forms of Negro speech in America.] In other words, the bilingual encounters social pressure of various sorts: he can enjoy the fun of linguistic spying but must pay the price of suspicion from those who don't want him to enter too intimately into their cultural domains and from others who don't want him to leave his "own" domain. He also comes to realize that most people are suspicious of a person who is in any sense two-faced. If he is progressing toward bilingualism, he encounters similar pressures that may affect his self-concept, his sense of belonging and his relations to two cultural-linguistic groups, the one he is slowly *leaving*, and the one he is *entering*. The conflict exists because so many of us think in terms of in-groups and out-groups, or of the need of showing an allegiance to one group or another, so that terms such as own language, other's language, leaving and entering one cultural group for another seem to be appropriate, even natural, descriptive choices.

Bilinguals and Ethnocentrism

Although this type of thought may characterize most people in our world, it is nonetheless a subtle form of group cleavage and ethnocentrism, and in time it may be challenged by bilinguals who, I feel, are in an excellent position to develop a totally new outlook on the social world. My argument is that bilinguals, especially those with bicultural experiences, enjoy certain fundamental advantages which, if capitalized on, can easily offset the annoying social tugs and pulls they are normally prone to. Let me mention one of these advantages that I feel is a tremendous asset.[1] Recently, Otto Klineberg and I conducted a rather comprehensive international study of the development of stereotyped thinking in children (Lambert and Klineberg, 1967). We found that rigid and stereotyped thinking about in-groups and out-groups, or about own groups in contrast to foreigners, starts during the pre-school period when children are trying to form a conception of themselves and their place in the world. Parents and other socializers attempt to help the child at this stage by highlighting differences and contrasts among the groups, thereby making his own group as distinctive as possible. This tendency, incidentally, was noted among parents from various parts of the world. Rather than helping, however, they may actually be setting the stage for ethnocentrism with permanent consequences. The more contrasts are stressed, the more deep-seated the stereotyping process and its impact on ethnocentric thought appear to be. Of relevance here is the notion that the child brought up bilingually and biculturally will be less likely to have good versus bad contrasts impressed on him when he starts wondering about himself, his own group and others. Instead he will probably be taught something more truthful, although more complex: that differences among national or cultural groups of peoples are actually not clear-cut and that basic similarities among peoples are more prominent than differences. The bilingual child in other words may well start life with the enormous advantage of having a more open, receptive mind about himself and other people. Furthermore, as he matures, the bilingual has many opportunities to learn, from observing changes in other people's reactions to him, how two-faced and ethnocentric others can be. That is, he is likely to become especially sensitive to and leery of ethnocentrism.

Bilinguals and Social Conflicts

This is not to say that bilinguals have an easy time of it. In fact, the final investigation I want to present demonstrates the social conflicts bilinguals typically face, but, and this is the major point, it also demonstrates one particular type of adjustment that is particularly encouraging.

In 1943, Irving Child (1943) investigated a matter that disturbed many second-generation Italians living in New England: what were they, Italian or American? Through early experiences they had learned that their relations with certain other youngsters in their community were strained whenever they displayed signs of their Italian background, that is, whenever they behaved as their parents wanted them to. In contrast, if they rejected their Italian background, they realized they could be deprived of many satisfactions stemming from belonging to an Italian family and an Italian community. Child uncovered three contrasting modes of adjusting to these presssures. One subgroup rebelled against their Italian background, making themselves as American as possible. Another subgroup rebelled the other way, rejecting things American as much as possible while proudly associating themselves with things Italian. The third form of adjustment was an apathetic withdrawal and a refusal of think of themselves in ethnic terms at all. This group tried, unsuccessfully, to escape the conflict by avoiding situations where the matter of cultural background might come up. Stated in other terms, some tried to belong to one of their own groups or the other, and some, because of strong pulls from both sides, were unable to belong to either.

Child's study illustrates nicely the difficulties faced by people with dual allegiances, but there is no evidence presented of second-generation Italians who actually feel themselves as belonging to both groups. When in 1962, Robert Gardner and I (1962) studied another ethnic minority group in New England, the French-Americans, we observed the same types of reactions as Child had noted among Italian-Americans. But in our study there was an important difference.

We used a series of attitude scales to assess the allegiances of French-American adolescents to both their French and American heritages. Their relative degree of skill in French and in English were used as an index of their mode of adjustment to the bicultural conflict they faced. In their homes, schools and community, they all had ample opportunities to learn both languages well, but subgroups turned up who had quite different patterns of linguistic skill, and each pattern was consonant with each subgroup's allegiances. Those who expressed a definite preference for the American over the French culture and who negated the value of knowing French were more proficient in English than French. They also expressed anxiety about how well they actually knew English. This subgroup, characterized by a general rejection of their French background, resembles in many respects the rebel reaction noted by Child. A second subgroup expressed a strong desire to be identified as French, and they showed a greater skill in French than English, especially in comprehension of spoken French. A third group apparently faced a conflict of cultural allegiances since they were ambivalent about their identity, favoring certain features of the French and other features of the American culture. Presumably because they had not resolved the conflict, they were retarded in their command of both languages when compared to the other groups. This relatively unsuccessful mode of adjustment is very similar to the apathetic reaction noted in one subgroup of Italian-Americans.

A fourth subgroup is of special interest. French-American youngsters who have an open-minded, nonethnocentric view of people in general, coupled with a strong aptitude for language learning are the ones who profited fully from their language learning opportunities and became skilled in *both* languages. These young people had apparently circumvented the conflicts and developed means of becoming members of both cultural groups. They had, in other terms, achieved a comfortable bicultural identity.

It is not clear why this type of adjustment did not appear in Child's study. There could, for example, be important differences in the social pressures encountered by second-generation Italians and French in New England. My guess, however, is that the difference in findings reflects a new social movement that has started in America in the interval between 1943 and 1962, a movement which the American linguist Charles Hockett humorously refers to as a "reduction of the heat under the American melting pot". I believe that bicultural bilinguals will be particularly helpful in perpetuating this movement. They and their children are also the ones most likely to work out a new, nonethnocentric mode of social intercourse which could be of universal significance.

NOTE

[1] For present purposes, discussion is limited to a more social advantage associated with bilingualism. In other writings there has been a stress on potential intellectual and cognitive advantages, see Peal and Lambert (1962) and Anisfeld (1964); see also Macnamara (1964) as well as Lambert and Anisfeld (1966). The bilingual's potential utility has also been discussed as a linguistic mediator between monolingual groups because of his comprehension of the subtle meaning differences characterizing each of the languages involved, see Lambert and Moore (1966).

REFERENCES

Anisfeld, Elizabeth. A comparison of the cognitive functioning of monolinguals and bilinguals. Unpublished Ph.D. thesis, Redpath Library, McGill University, 1964.

Anisfeld, Elizabeth, and Lambert, W.E. Evaluational reactions of bilingual and monolingual children to spoken language. Journal of Abnormal and Social Psychology, 1964, 69, 89-97.

Anisfeld, M., Boco, N., and Lambert, W.E. Evaluational reactions to accented English speech. Journal of Abnormal and Social Psychology, 1962, 65, 223-231.

Anisfeld, M., and Lambert, W.E. Social and psychological variables in learning Hebrew. Journal of Abnormal and Social Psychology, 1961, 63, 524-529.

Bereiter, C. Some persisting dilemmas in the measurement of change. In Harris, C.W. (Ed.), Problems in measuring change. Madison: The University of Wisconsin Press, 1963.

Child, I.L., Italian or American? The second generation in conflict. New Haven: Yale University Press, 1943.

Durkheim, E. Le suicide. Paris: F. Alcan, 1897.

Ferguson, G. A. Statistical analysis in psychology and education. New York: McGraw-Hill, 1959.

Gardner, R. C. and Lambert, W. E. Motivational variables in second-language acquisition. Canadian Journal of Psychology, 1959, 13, 266-272.

Gardner, R. C. Motivational variables in second-language acquisition. Unpublished Ph. D. thesis, McGill University, 1960.

Jones, W. R. Attitude towards Welsh as a second language. A preliminary investigation. British Journal of Educational Psychology, 1949, 19, 44-52.

Jones, W. R. Attitude towards Welsh as a second language, a further investigation. British Journal of Educational Psychology, 1950, 20, 117-132.

Labov, W. Hypercorrection by the lower middle class as a factor in linguistic change. Columbia University, 1964. (Mimeo)

Lambert, W. E., Hodgson, R. C., Gardner, R. C., and Fillenbaum, S. Evaluational reactions to spoken languages. Journal of Abnormal and Social Psychology, 1960, 60, 44-51.

Lambert, W. E., Gardner, R. C., Olton, R., and Tunstall, K. A study of the roles of attitudes and motivation in second-language learning. McGill University, 1962. (Mimeo)

Lambert, W. E., Gardner, R. C., Barik, H. C., and Tunstall, K. Attitudinal and cognitive aspects of intensive study of a second language. Journal of Abnormal and Social Psychology, 1963, 66, 358-368.

Lambert, W. E., Anisfeld, M., and Yeni-Komshian, Grace. Evaluational reactions of Jewish and Arab adolescents to dialect and language variations. Journal of Personality and Social Psychology, 1965, 2, 84-90.

Lambert, W. E., Frankel, Hannah, and Tucker, G. R. Judging personality through speech: A French-Canadian example. The Journal of Communication, 1966, 16, 305-321.

Lambert, W. E., and Anisfeld, Elizabeth. A note on the relationship of bilingualism and intelligence. Canad. J. Behav. Sci., 1969, 1, 123-128.

Lambert, W. E., and Moore, Nancy. Word-association responses: Comparison of American and French monolinguals with Canadian monolinguals and bilinguals. Journal of Personality and Social Psychology, 1966, 3, 313-320.

Lambert, W.E., and Klineberg, O. *Children's views of foreign peoples: A cross-national study*. New York: Appleton, 1967.

Macnamara, J. The Commission on Irish: Psychological aspects. *Studies*, 1964, 164-173.

McDavid, R.I. The dialects of American English. In Francis, W.N. (Ed.), *The structure of American English*, New York: Ronald, 1958.

Peal, Elizabeth, and Lambert, W.E. The relation of bilingualism to intelligence. *Psychological Monographs*, 1962, 76, Whole No. 546.

Preston, M.S. Evaluational reactions to English, Canadian French and European French voices. Unpublished M.A. thesis, McGill University, Redpath Library, 1963.

Srole, L. Social dysfunction, personality and social distance attitudes. Paper read before American Sociological Society, 1951, National Meeting, Chicago, Ill. (Mimeo)

Tucker, G.R., and Lambert, W.E., White and Negro listeners' reactions to various American-English dialects. *Social Forces*, 1969, 47, 463-68.

Williams, R.N. *American society*. New York: Knopf, 1952.

14 The Use of 'Tu' and 'Vous' as Forms of Address in French Canada: A Pilot Study

Depending on how we choose to address others, we can very clearly, although subtly, indicate whether we consider them as close associates or whether we want to keep them at a certain social distance, either because they are not yet perceived as friends or because we are never likely to become that intimate with them. Thus in English, for example, we may keep a proper social distance by using titles (Mr. or Mrs.) and last names rather than first names, or we may indicate a status difference by using first names only with hired help. Other languages, for example French, German, Spanish, and Italian, afford greater precision and flexibility in expressing the desired intimacy of social interaction because the languages themselves have recognized provisions—namely, the use of _tu_ and _vous_ or their equivalents—for indicating differences in solidarity and/or social status.

Brown and Gilman (1960) have recently traced out the fascinating story of how the use of _tu_ and _vous_ (or their equivalents) developed in various countries and how this usage has changed through time. For example, it has only been within the past decade that French army officers have been told to refrain from the practice of using _tu_ when addressing their men while expecting them to use _vous_ in return. Likewise, European residents in French Africa have been advised only since 1957 that it is no longer appropriate (or safe) to use nonreciprocal address forms when conversing with native Africans. During the same time span, it apparently has become socially uncomfortable for a Frenchman patronizing the very best restaurants to use _tu_ with his waiter and expect the _vous_ form in return.

From a wide array of evidence, including interviews with samples of informants from France, Germany, and Italy, Brown and

Gilman (1960; Brown, 1965) have drawn several important conclusions about this trend. They argue that the nonreciprocal use of address forms has given way, through time, to a symmetrical use of the same form by both interlocutors, tu being used by both to indicate solidarity and vous being used to indicate social distance. This trend suggests that the importance of expressing status differences in this manner has diminished in recent times relative to the importance of expressing degree of solidarity, reflecting, it is presumed, basic changes in the value systems. At the same time, Brown and Ford (1961) have found that other more subtle ways of expressing status differences are still frequently used. For instance, one person may use the first name of another and expect a title plus last name in return as is evident in such an exchange as: "Is that you, Max?" "Yes, Mr. Adams." However, the central idea of interest here is that nowadays there is very little expression of status differences through the nonreciprocal use of tu and vous as forms of address.

A question about the generality and universality of these conclusions arises for those who live in French Canada where it is not uncommon either to encounter directly or to hear about parents who use tu with their children and receive vous in return. This pilot study was undertaken to examine how French Canadians actually address various others in their social environments.

METHOD

The informants were 136 French-Canadian boys, 16-19 years of age, who were attending a collège (similar to an American junior college) in Quebec City. They were asked by their teachers to complete a questionnaire concerning both their own use of tu and vous when speaking with others and the form of address others typically use when speaking with them. First they were asked: "When the following people speak with you, do they use tu or vous?" The list of people is presented in Table 1. Then: "When you speak with each one of the following people individually, do you use tu or vous?" Finally, they were asked to describe their father's occupation in as much detail as possible.

TABLE 1

Form of Address Between French-Canadian Boys and Others[a]

Interaction with	Tu Rec'd	Vous Rec'd	It depends; no answer	Tu Sent	Vous Sent	It depends; no answer
Mother	129	6	1	67	65	4
Parents	129	7	—	68	66	2
Grandparents	112	13	11	16	108	12
Uncles, Aunts	119	13	4	24	105	7
Boy Friends	133	3	—	133	—	3
Girl Friends	120	9	7	122	8	6
Teachers	2	129	5	1	133	2
Priests	27	95	14	1	133	2
Nuns	15	115	6	5	125	6
Older People	88	34	14	7	118	11
Strangers	15	110	11	1	132	3

[a]Entries are actual frequencies based on the replies of 136 boys, distributed according to the form of address received from others and the form used (sent) in discourse with others.

RESULTS AND DISCUSSION

It is apparent in Table 1 that there are noteworthy instances of nonsymmetrical usage of address forms, two of particular significance. First, most of these boys receive the tu form from their grandparents at the same time as they use the vous form in addressing their grandparents. Second, the vast majority receive tu from their parents (and from "mother") at the same time as half of them use vous in addressing their parents. (In over 97% of the cases, the same boys gave exactly the same responses to "mother" as to "parents.")

What does the first finding suggest about children's relations with grandparents in French Canada? There appears to be a widely accepted standard of nonreciprocal usage here, much more general than that found with parents. On the grandparent's part, it may reflect the accepted standard for expressing respect toward elders, while from the perspective of the boys it may be (or become) an index of social distance from grandparents. The difference between the two older generations may in turn be a symptom of a value change which could in time dictate a more general use of the address pattern for solidarity. And what might underlie the two different manners of responding to parents, when nearly all are receiving the tu form from their parents? It was anticipated that social-class differences would play an important role, but it was not clear what form the relation might take. The middle- and upper-class parents might be more traditional in this sense and expect their children to show respect for parents by using the more formal vous. On the other hand, it is just as reasonable to argue that the "working" or comparatively lower-class parents might have reason, because of their lower status in society, to expect or even demand that their own children, at least, show them respect by using the vous form of address. Of course, the use of vous and tu may have some other and specific meanings in French Canada. For example, it may not indicate formality or demand for respect as much as social distance or lack of intimacy between children and parents. None of these issues will be settled with a pilot study, but the following analysis is statistically strong enough to indicate that social-class differences should be examined more carefully in future studies of this aspect of French-Canadian social interaction.

By use of the descriptions each boy gave of his father's occupation, it was possible to classify 113 of the 136 boys into one of three socioeconomic categories: *professional*, if the father was, for example, a doctor, lawyer, engineer, dentist, or college professor; *white-collar*, if the father was, for example, a bank manager, a journalist, a salesman, an accountant, a store manager, or a businessman; and *blue-collar*, if the father was, for example, a foreman, a garagist, a mechanic, a baker, a railroad worker, or a farmer. These categories were distinct enough so that a panel of French and English Canadians acting as judges encountered very few disagreements in making unanimous classifications.

The results of this analysis indicate that there is a very strong relation between socioeconomic background, as measured here, and the forms of address used. The children from professional, white-collar and blue-collar backgrounds, respectively, used *tu* and *vous* with their parents in the following ratios: 13:2; 23:15; and 22:38; ($x^2 = 13.92$, $p < .001$). The contingency analysis indicates that it is the higher social class families that encourage the reciprocal use of *tu* between parents and children, and the lower class parents (actually, families where the father works mainly with his hands) that encourage the use of the nonreciprocal *vous* form when being addressed by their children. The pattern for the case where "mother" is addressed is nearly exactly the same as that for "parents" and is equally significant.

Further research on this problem is clearly called for. It is now necessary to determine how extensive this pattern is in French Canada (i.e., in other centers than Quebec City), at what age it starts, whether it is similar for girls and boys, whether some particular social class characteristics are typically associated with it, whether it was more pronounced with former generations in French Canada, and whether it is likely to hold up with the next generation. With these questions in mind, a more comprehensive study is now underway.

In addition to suggesting that significant social-class differences in social behavior can be studied through this aspect of speech, these findings also give us some insight into the linguistic demands made on children who have to learn to switch pronoun and verb forms from one social setting to another. Consider the case of the children from "working" class homes. They apparently face a difficult problem, relative to those from families of higher socioeconomic standing, since they are taught to use different pronoun and verb forms from those their parents use in what must appear to them as the same social setting. For example, it would be difficult for a child to comprehend why. when his mother asks, "Lequel veux-tu, mon garçon?" he, in reacting to the same social event, should have to use another form, for example, "Après vous, maman, lequel voulez-vous?" If started from infancy on, this discordance might make the task of language learning all that more exacting for those involved with nonreciprocal usage.

One can also examine the effects of this difference in linguistic demands on the way the child develops his generalizations about when to use one form or the other of address. For the French-Canadian boy, it appears that he can count on reciprocal tu usage with his peers, both boys and girls, if they are friends (see Table 1). He can also be fairly sure of reciprocal vous usage if the interlocutors are socially distant from him (e.g., teachers, priests, strangers). He can be certain of nonreciprocal usage with grandparents, it seems, and, if he is from the lower social classes, even with his parents. Thus, in learning the rules of usage, the lower-class boys in French Canada have a complicated set of rules to learn—that interaction with certain members of one's own family, parents as well as grandparents, calls for nonreciprocal usage. This rule is troublesome because it involves the parents, the very ones who are most instrumental in teaching him the language. The rules are apparently much more complicated for French Canadians than for the European French, who, if Brown's sample is representative, have a simpler task in regulating their forms of address with established degrees of familiarity. On the other hand, if by chance Brown's samples are not representative (Brown and Gilman, 1960, p. 270, suggest that their informants were from higher socioeconomic backgrounds), then it is possible that similar demands are made on certain subgroups in the European countries already studied.

NOTE

This research was supported by a grant from the Canadian Defence Research Board, Grant 9401-10. The writer is grateful to Michèle

Hendlisz, Sylvie Lambert, and Richard Tucker for help in collecting and analyzing the data.

REFERENCES

Brown, R. Social psychology. New York: The Free Press, 1965.

Brown, R., and Ford, M. Address in American English. J. abnorm. soc. Psychol., 1961, 62, 375-385.

Brown, R., and Gilman, A. The Pronouns of power and solidarity. In T. A. Sebeok (Ed.), Style in language. Cambridge, Mass.: M.I.T. Press, 1960.

15 A Psychological Investigation of French Speakers' Skill with Grammatical Gender

In Collaboration with G. R. Tucker,
A. Rigault, and N. Segalowitz

There are two major reasons why psychologists might become interested in grammatical gender. First, from a practical point of view, the mastery of gender is perhaps the most difficult and frustrating feature of the study of French as a second language, especially for those whose native language lacks gender distinctions. That is, the English speaker studying French must learn not only the French words for things, but also whether the new words are masculine or feminine. Since no rules for distinguishing gender classes are taught him, the whole process seems completely arbitrary. In contrast, French speakers, including very young children, seem to have no difficulty with gender, even with the gender of novel nouns.

This enviable skill which seemingly cannot be explained or transmitted can be regarded as a potentially interesting example of rule usage in language, analogous to the rule usage involved in syntax. However, it may prove easier to describe the influence of environmental influences on the development of skill with gender rules than has been possible with syntax rules so far (see, for example, Bever, Fodor and Weksel, 1965; McNeill, 1966). Thus, the study of gender may be a more explicable example of rule acquisition in language, serving both practical and theoretical ends.

One can regard the insufficient explanations usually offered by French speakers for their skill with gender assignments as examples of the linguistic myopia most native speakers have for the regularities existing in their own languages. According to one informant, the native French speaker associates _le_ or _la_ (or any other gender marker, such as _un_, _une_, _de la_ or _du_, all of which apparently function in distinctive co-ordinate systems) with each noun in the language, as a type of prefix. Thus, he simply learns the word lamain (as one word) for la main or lemari for le mari. On the other hand, there may well be some systematic pattern to gender distinctions in French; certain reliable clues may reside in the words themselves that assist native users in making gender assignments; French speakers may, at an early age, learn to make appropriate differentiations that enable them to abstract gender-determining regularities in their language.

Although most grammars indicate that the "endings" of French nouns may be related to gender distinction, still those who have systematically examined these relationships (e.g., Byrne and Churchill, 1950; Grevisse, 1964; and Sonet and Shortliffe, 1954) arrive at the rather discouraging conclusion that noun endings are of limited value and are generally unreliable indicators of gender.

With these thoughts in mind, a series of studies was conducted for the purpose of exploring French speakers' skill with grammatical gender.

The one suggestion we had from grammarians was the possibility that noun endings may actually help indicate gender to a French speaker. Our method of attack, therefore, was to develop lists of words with various endings, chosen on the basis of a preliminary analysis of all the nouns listed in Petit Larousse, which indicated that they were predominantly masculine, feminine, or ambiguous markers for the language as a whole. For example, -aison was found to occur in 64 feminine nouns and in 1 masculine noun. One purpose then was to check on the behavioral implications of these statistical facts about the corpus of French nouns.

Three pilot studies were conducted with 400 French-speaking boys and girls ranging in age from 8 to 16 years from Catholic public schools in Montreal and in Alma, Quebec. Results suggested that these native speakers made gender assignments which were influenced by the word endings and that the pattern of these assignments reflected the distribution of gender by ending in the corpus. These results suggested that we should enlarge our sample of word endings and use both real and invented words. The results also indicated that word "beginnings" might also have an influence on gender distinctions.

METHOD

Subjects. *S*s were 402 male and female grade 4, 5, 6, and 7 students from Catholic public schools in Montreal.

Design. Stimuli were 84 real and invented words selected with certain considerations in mind. Invented words are permissible French phonetic sequences which do not actually occur as words in the language (e.g., *florillon). Fourteen endings were studied: -aie, -ais, -é, -ée, -eur, -eure, -illon, -oi, -oie, -oir, -oire, -ssion, -stion, and -(a)tion. Six words were selected as exemplars of each of the 14 endings according to the following design: one exemplar was a frequently occurring word (from Français fondamental), two were rare words as judged by a French phonetician, one was an invented word which begins with the "ambiguous" initial syllable feuill- (six feminine, nine masculine in the Petit Larousse), one with the "feminine" initial syllable flor-, (seven feminine and three masculine in the Petit Larousse), and finally the sixth with the "masculine" initial syllable déb-(63 entries in the Petit Larousse are masculine, and 17 are feminine). Thus a 14 x 6 matrix was constructed with entries such as *floraie, *floralé, *florateur, monnaie, etc.

Procedure. A French phonetician recorded a randomized list of the 84 stimulus words. Each word was recorded twice in succession with a 3-sec pause between items. This tape-recorded list was presented to one-half of the *S*s by means of an "oral-graphic" procedure. The students followed, on their own questionnaires, the list of words as they were spoken on the tape. Un and une were printed to the left of each word. The other *S*s received an "oral" procedure. Only the articles un and une appeared on their questionnaires. In both cases, *S*s had only to indicate whether they thought the gender of each word was masculine or feminine by circling un or une. All *S*s were tested in their respective classes of 20-30 students.

Method of Data Analysis. Since *S* responded to each item with one of two alternatives (i.e., un or une), the data were considered to approximate a normal binomial distribution. Standard statistical procedures (Ferguson, 1966) were used to define confidence limits indicating whether words or groups of words were consistently or reliably chosen as masculine or feminine.

TABLE 1

Gender-Estimation Comparisons[a]

Ending	Proportion of masculine entries in *Petit Larousse*	Actual nouns: Frequent		Actual nouns: Rare (mean of two exemplars)		Invented nouns: Ambiguous initial syllable (feuill-)		Invented nouns: Masculine initial syllable (déb-)		Invented nouns: Feminine initial syllable (flor-)	
		0	0-G[b]	0	0-G	0	0-G	0	0-G	0	0-G
-aie	.00	.01**	.04**	.49	.21**	.91**	.67**	.72**	.36**	.68**	.20**
-ais	1.00	.99**	.99**	.82**	.86**	.70**	.70**	.82**	.90**	.69**	.82**
-é	.35	.01**	.02**	.47	.58*	.38**	.60**	.60**	.77**	.36**	.59**
-ée	.08	.01**	.01**	.31**	.14**	.41*	.09**	.45	.18**	.29**	.06**
-eur	.95	.21**	.21**	.86**	.95**	.97**	.96**	.92**	.96**	.95**	.96**
-eure	.56	.12**	.12**	.56	.35**	.87**	.61**	.96**	.65**	.53	.32**
-illon	.98	.99**	.99**	.84**	.84**	.91**	.91**	.99**	.96**	.82**	.87**
-oi	.94	.85**	.87**	.74**	.88**	.51	.71**	.83**	.93**	.65**	.79**
-oie	.76	.02**	.01**	.72**	.24**	.67**	.44	.65**	.82**	.47	.23**
-oir	1.00	.98**	.99**	.88**	.90**	.75**	.73**	.84**	.92**	.73**	.86**
-oire	.54	.22**	.18**	.66**	.56	.59*	.42**	.69**	.60**	.63**	.56
-ssion	.00	.02**	.01**	.11**	.21**	.17**	.26**	.11**	.17**	.21**	.17**
-stion	.13	.03**	.03**	.61**	.69**	.20**	.28**	.17**	.22**	.35**	.30**
-(a)tion	.00	.02**	.05**	.09**	.16**	.06**	.11**	.13**	.17**	.03**	.13**

[a] Entries in the table indicate the proportion of masculine choices prompted by each exemplar. To illustrate, when orally presented with the word *feuillation, 6% of the *S*s categorized it as masculine (and 94% as feminine), a result significant at the .01 level. When the word *débeur was presented by oral-graphic means, 96% of the *S*s chose this exemplar as masculine (and 4% as feminine), a result significant at the .01 level.

[b] Method of presentation: 0 = Oral, 0-G = Oral-graphic. $*p < .05$. $**p < .01$.

RESULTS

The results strongly suggest that endings reliably mark gender, in particular instances, and that the initial syllables also have an influence, although probably a less powerful one.

For all six types of exemplar, the following endings (with the results for all exemplars combined) were statistically reliable ($p < .01$) markers of masculinity: -ais, -eur, -illon, -oi, -oir. This was true for both oral and oral-graphic presentations, as can be seen in Table 1.

The following endings were statistically reliable feminine markers: -ssion, -stion, and -(a)tion. The ending -aie indicated masculinity when presented orally, but femininity with oral-graphic presentation.

We can compare these empirical findings with the statistical counts of endings suspected to be related to gender for all nouns listed in the *Petit Larousse*. These counts were undertaken in order to make just such comparisons with a very good approximation to the total corpus of French nouns. In order to facilitate the counting, all nouns listed in the *Petit Larousse* were put on I.B.M. data cards with a tag for their gender. These were then compiled as a type of inverse dictionary of nouns, with all noun endings with a particular syllable congregated in groups.[1] Using this approximation to the total corpus, we find the following number of masculine to feminine exemplars for each of the endings mentioned above: -illon, 64 M, 1 F; -ais, 70 M, 0 F; -oir, 220 M, 0 F; -eur, 1482 M, 78 F; -oi, 148 M, 10 F. Furthermore, the following number of feminine to masculine exemplars are found in the corpus for the endings our *S*s judged to be feminine: -(a)tion, 1159 F, 0 M; -(a, i, u)ssion, 33 F, 0 M; -aie, 58 F, 0 M. The difference found between -aie and -ais in gender assignment due to method of presentation may be explained by noting that the ending /ɛ/ of which -aie and -ais are allophones occurs predominantly in masculine nouns (564 M, 61 F). The ending spelled -aie, however, as we noted, is found exclusively in feminine nouns. Note how well these occurrences agree with the behavioral evidence reported, when these endings are placed in various novel word-like constructions. These endings then all represent stable, reliable markers of gender.

We noted some degree of confusion and ambiguity with the endings -é, -ée, -oire, -eure, and -oie. That is, exemplars of these endings are sometimes thought to be masculine and sometimes feminine. It is of interest that this ambiguity actually exists in the language. From the counts we note the following distribution: -oire, 44 F, 51 M; -eure, 6 F, 8 M; -oie, 5 M, 16 F; and /e/, covering the examples -é and -ée, 1398 M, 1393 F. It was noted that -ée always reliably indicates femininity with the oral-graphic form of presentation and we find in the corpus that there are, in fact, 357 F and 30 M nouns ending with -ée in the language. Some of the *S*s' confusion with é may be due to another aspect of the structure of French nouns: for all -é endings, there are 870 F and 478 M, whereas for -té endings there are 860 F and only 64 M, and for -ré endings there are 0 F and 62 M. Thus, the preceding phone appears to have a substantial influence and studies are now planned to work back systematically from the final phone for gender cues.

The effect of manipulating the initial syllable is evident in particular instances where the type of beginning strengthens or weakens the effects of a particular ending. The importance of beginnings also appears when one considers the exemplars with the ambiguous initial syllable as the base line for responding. If we compare the responses in the ambiguous case with those when masculine and feminine beginnings are used, it is seen that with oral presentation the exemplars with masculine roots become "more" masculine for 9 of the 14 endings, and the exemplars with feminine roots become "more" feminine for 9 of the 14 endings. With oral-graphic presentation 10 of the 14 endings beginning with the masculine root become more masculine and 7 of the 14 beginning with the feminine root become more feminine. Thus, it is clear that the initial syllable of the noun can also have an effect in marking gender, especially in cases where the ending provides an ambiguous clue.

DISCUSSION

These studies have shown that particular endings, at least those examined so far, reliably mark gender in French nouns and that the initial syllables apparently play a supporting role in the same regard. Furthermore, it would appear that all French nouns of more than one syllable lend themselves to an investigation of this sort; and since there was no systematic bias in the selection of endings to be examined in this study, one can anticipate that similar regularities will be uncovered as research progresses with other word endings and beginnings. The findings can be of relevance for those concerned with the acquisition of French, either as a first or later language. In the case of first-language learning, it seems apparent that the French child is able to distinguish and utilize, by induction, from the recurring regularities in the language, those patterns of cues that mark gender. He appears to be very skilled in generalizing from these patterns to novel occurrences. This line of reasoning is supported by the close correspondence found between the distribution of gender in the total corpus of French nouns and the behavioral evidence which has been reported. If one presents a French child with words he has never before encountered, he can consistently determine the appropriate gender form, and this is so for predominantly masculine, feminine, *and* ambiguous exemplars. It is obvious, therefore, that the French speaker is sensitive, although apparently at some level far below awareness, to these recurring patterns of regularities in his language. Much more research of a similar nature is needed to describe in detail the basic nature of these patterns.

As research progresses, it may turn out that certain important sound continua exist in French that provide higher-order cues to gender. Consider, for example, the results presented above for the ending -*on* /ɔ̃/. We have noted in our studies that -*illon*, -*on*, and -*çon* were reliably considered as masculine endings whereas -*aison*, -*ssion*, and -*(a)tion* were considered feminine endings. The ending -*xtion* was categorized ambiguously.[2] If one considers both the common final sounds and those immediately preceding, one can refer to a phonetic continuum composed of all endings whose final phone is /ɔ̃/. The extremes of this dimension indicate masculinity (e.g., -*illon*, -*on*), and femininity (e.g., -*tion*, -*ssion*) with a central region (e.g., -*xtion*) indicating ambiguity or ambivalence.

In the case of second-language learning, the results suggest that French grammarians have been hasty in their conclusion that there are no regularities or only minimal ones to gender determination. It should be possible to make the problem of gender acquisition a much easier one simply by structuring the manner of presenting vocabulary lists. For example, words with distinctive ending and beginning characteristics can be congregated so that the regularities will be highlighted. The language learner could then infer the underlying pattern of regularities for himself in a fashion analogous to the native speaker of the language. Of course, the gender cues can be explained to *S*s and, only later, the exception brought to their attention. Although one may be confident that the lists of exceptions can be reduced, we have already noted one of their characteristics: exceptions to the ending and beginning cues usually are frequently occurring monosyllabic nouns in the French language. Thus they can be relatively easily learned as separate items. Furthermore, vocabulary could be taught with somewhat more leniency; that is, students could be permitted to make "errors" on the far-out exceptions (such as bastion[3] actually being masculine) so that the basic regularities could be learned and the associated changes in sentences attendant on gender made and used with more confidence. The training procedures could be adapted, too, for young French speakers, permitting them to master more efficiently the basic rules for gender residing in their own language.

NOTES

This research was supported in part by a Canada Council grant to W. E. Lambert, and in part by a Canadian Defence Research Board Grant, number D77-94-01-10. We are particularly grateful to Mlle. Jenny Spire, now a graduate student at Yale University, for her assistance with the phonetic analyses involved in this investigation.

[1] This work was performed for us by Bernard Quemada at the Laboratoire d'Analyse Lexicologique of the Université de Besançon. We are very grateful to Dr. Quemada for the care and efficiency with which this work was done.

[2] The endings -on, -çon, -aison, and -xtion were examined separately in the pilot studies referred to. Furthermore, in those studies -ence was a reliable marker of femininity and -aix, -et and -ion were reliable markers of masculinity.

[3] The example of bastion is of interest. Its pronunciation is not typical of the feminine -tion ending and its historical roots are unique; it is a variant of bastillon (Dauzat et al., 1964), and we have found the -illon ending to be a reliable cue for masculinity.

REFERENCES

Bever, T., Fodor, J. A., and Weksel, W. On the acquisition of syntax. A critique of "contextual generalization." Psychol. Rev., 1965, 72, 467-482.

Byrne, L. S. R., and Churchill, E. L. A comprehensive French grammar with classified vocabularies. Oxford: Basil Blackwell, 1950.

Dauzat, A., Dubois, J., and Mitterand, H. Nouveau dictionnaire étymologique. Paris: Librairie Larousse, 1964.

Ferguson, G. A. Statistical analysis in psychology and education. (2nd ed.) New York: McGraw-Hill, 1966.

Français fondamental. Paris: L'institut Pédagogique National, 1954.

Grevisse, M. Le bon usage. Paris: Hatier, 1964.

McNeill, D. Developmental psycholinguistics. In F. Smith and G. A. Miller (Eds.) The genesis of language. Cambridge, Mass.: M.I.T. Press, 1966.

Petit Larousse. Augé, Gillon, Hollier-Larousse, Moreau et Cie. Paris: Librairie Larousse, 1959.

Sonet, E., and Shortliffe, G. Review of standard French. New York: Harcourt, Brace, 1954.

16 Bilingual Organization in Free Recall

In Collaboration with Maria Ignatow and Marcel Krauthamer

The investigation described below deals with (a) the organization of psychological processes, as inferred from *S*s' free recall of word lists, and (b) bilingualism. In studies of free recall, *S*s are typically asked to read through a list of 30 or 40 words and then to recall the words in any order. If there are organizational possibilities built into a list, *S*s very readily make use of them. For instance, if subsets of words that commonly associate with one another, or that belong to logical categories (e.g., types of trees or names of cities) are randomly distributed through a list, *S*s tend to group subsets in recall. When lists are constructed that do not have obvious organizational sets, *S*s characteristically create a personal system of organization that aids recall. Theories proposed to explain this tendency to group items on the basis of some aspect of similarity have led to the concept of "chunking" (Miller, 1963; Mandler, 1966). In the present study, interest centers on the role of chunking in free recall when two forms of organizational possibilities are available to bilingual *S*s—one, logical or semantic categories, the other, language. Although a recent study by Kolers (1965) demonstrated that language may in certain conditions be an important organizational schema for bilinguals, the present experiments were designed to test its importance when language is brought into competition with a possibly more powerful schema, namely semantic categories.

We are also interested here in examining the power of an associationistic principle for explaining clustering in free recall. Bousfield (1953) at first believed that clustering depended on the activation of some type of superordinate structure as specific instances of a category were encountered in the list. Jenkins and Russell (1952), however, questioned this interpretation since common associative links were apparent among clustered items. Thus a simpler interpretation was available, one based on associative strength or the likelihood of co-occurrence of particular pairs or sets of words in samples of the language, swaying Bousfield, among others (Cofer, 1965) to the associationistic view. Recent experiments, however, have reopened the issue and there is now a lively debate about the actual importance of associative strength in free-recall clustering (Cofer, 1965; Kendler, 1966; Shepard, 1966). The present study was planned as a contribution to the debate since the bilingual condition offers a unique opportunity to compare the associationistic and superordination interpretations.

There is a third purpose of the present study. Psychologists studying bilingualism are currently interested in the interdependencies of the bilingual's two languages. The aim of this type of study (e.g., Lambert, Havelka, and Crosby, 1958; Lambert and Fillenbaum, 1959; Jakobovits and Lambert, 1961; Kolers, 1965; Lambert and Preston, 1965; Preston and Lambert, 1967) is to understand how the bilingual's two language systems are stored in the brain, how they interact, and how they are usually kept functionally independent in usage. In the same spirit, the present experiments examine how bilinguals go about organizing materials presented to them in bilingual word lists where, in certain instances, either language or semantic category or both may be utilized as organizational schemas, while in other instances, the two possible schemas are placed in competition.

METHOD

Subjects. Parallel experiments were conducted, one using Russian-English bilinguals, the other, French-English bilinguals. The 24 French-English bilinguals, 12 male and 12 female, had all received schooling in both languages at elementary and high school, and all but two were presently post-graduate university students in French. The *S*s considered themselves, and were judged by others who knew them well, to be equally skilled in the use of both languages.

The 24 Russian-English bilinguals, 18 female and six male, were all of Russian origin. Seventeen were Russian-language majors at a university. Their education from primary school on was in English, although all had attended Russian parochial school 1 day a week through high school. They all considered themselves to be equally skilled in the audiolingual use of both languages, although they clearly had more experience in reading and writing English.

The Word Lists. The word lists were constructed from English, French, and Russian cultural norms of associations given to the names of 43 semantic categories, e.g., types of fish, men's first names, or types of disease. The (American) English norms of Cohen, Bousfield, and Whitmarsh (1957) were considered appropriate for use with Canadian *S*s, in light of the findings of Lambert and Moore (1966). New norms were developed, however, for French and Russian, with the procedure of Cohen et al. used as a model. In one case, 60 seniors in a French-Canadian high school were asked to give (in writing) the first four examples that came to mind on reading the superordinate names of the 43 categories, e.g., to list four types of fish. The norms place the examples in order from most to least popular. The Russian norms were compiled from the responses of 25 Russian adults (not those used as *S*s). The lists, then, contained popular associates to common category names, each associate having an obvious translation equivalent, with the exception of certain male first names. However, the Male First Names category was rotated systematically through all types of lists (see below). Since the *S*s were fully bilingual, they would certainly have had experience with the associates and their translations.

Experimental Design. Each *S* was presented 10 40-item lists, one list at a time, with instructions to remember as many items as possible and to be prepared to recall them with no restrictions as to order. Four of the 10 lists contained four different categories with 10 words to a category (e.g., 10 types of fish, 10 male first names, etc.); the other six lists did not include category subsets, i.e., the 40 items in each list comprised one item chosen from each of 40 different semantic categories as represented in the norms. These different list types will be referred to as Category lists and No-Category lists, the latter serving as comparison and control conditions. To counteract primacy and recency effects, three of the six No-Category lists came as the first three lists presented to each *S* and three as the last three in the series of 10. The general design and a typical sequence follows: (1) English, no category (NC); (2) French (or Russian) NC; (3) Mixed (English and French) NC; (4) English, category (C); (5) French, C; (6) Mixed, Concordant; (7) Mixed, Discordant; (8) English, NC; (9) French, NC; (10) Mixed, NC. Thus, Lists 1 and 8 in the design are both no-category lists of 40 English items; lists 2 and 9 are no-category in French (or Russian). Lists 3 and 10, to be referred to as mixed, each have 20 English and 20 French items with no built-in categorization possibilities. List 4 is an English list comprising four categories with 10 examples per category (e.g., 10 types of fish), and List 5 is an equivalent French list. Lists 6 and 7 are mixed-language lists with built-in categories; these are comparable in one respect to the category mixed list. The special feature of List 6 is that 20 items covering two distinct categories with 10 examples each are in English, and 20 items covering two additional distinctive categories are in French. In this list there is a concordance between languages and semantic categories. List 7, in contrast, has a discordance between language and semantic categories. Each of its four categories has equal numbers of English and French examples (e.g., five types of fish in French and five in English).

This design, then, permits one to (a) assess the importance of semantic categories in comparison with a no-category base line in terms of total items recalled and degree of clustering in recall (the pairs of no-category lists coming at the start and at the end of the experimental period are averaged); (b) to determine the influence of Mixed-Language lists by comparing them with unilingual lists in both No-Category and Category conditions; (c) to examine the combined and separate importance of the linguistic and semantic modes of categorizing in a condition where their concordance might be either facilitative or competitively disruptive, and in a condition where their discordance should be disruptive relative to the other category conditions but possibly facilitative relative to the No-Category conditions.

Each *S* was presented six standard No-Category lists, the first three and last three in the series of 10. Their order was randomized so that one *S* would receive the lists in the order of the example given above, another in the order 9, 8, 10, (5, 6, 7, 4), 1, 3, 2, etc. These lists were made comparable to all others in terms of each word's popularity in the category norms. All lists comprised items chosen from the 10 or 12 most popular category examples found in the norms. In the mixed list, no more than three words in the same language appeared consecutively.

The presentation order of the category lists followed a four-factorial plan, covering all possibilities with 24 *S*s. Furthermore, each *S* had a different combination of four categories in each of his category lists, although the same 16 semantic categories were used for all *S*s. Constraints in these lists were that (a) no more than three words in one language appeared consecutively (for the two mixed lists); (b) no two items from the same semantic category appeared consecutively after randomization of the list items; (c) for the Discordance list, no translations or synonyms between languages within a category were allowed, e.g., blouse and blouzka would not both appear as members of the "articles of clothing" category.

Testing Procedure. In order to create a bilingual atmosphere and to avoid a set in one language, *S*s were given instructions in one language, followed by a brief summary in the other, half of them receiving English first, half French (or Russian) first. They were told in advance that some lists would be unilingual, others mixed, and that after one run through a list, they would be given 2 min for recall of as many items as possible in any order. For the French study, the items were printed on 3 X 5 cards and were flipped at intervals of approximately 2 sec. The *S*s read the words aloud. Since the Russian *S*s were more experienced at reading English, their lists were read to them by a perfectly bilingual *E* at a 2-sec rate. The *S*s repeated the words after the *E*. Each *S*'s recall was tape recorded for 2 min; a 3-min rest was given after each recall period.

Response Measures. Measures were taken of (a) the total items correctly recalled, (b) the extent of category clustering, and (c) the extent of language clustering. (a) The total number of words correctly recalled excluded all types of errors and repetitions. Separate analyses will be mentioned where credit was given for translation errors, i.e., correct semantic choices given in the wrong language. (b) Clusters of items fitting the same semantic category were bracketed and counted. In devising a ratio score, we subtracted one from the total number of items congregated on the ground that the first item is really not part of the run. The ratio was the number of items in a category run over the total of all items recalled. Thus, if *S* recalled: FLOOR, CEILING, DOOR, HALL (r_1 = 3), followed by APPLE, LEMON, PEAR (r_2 = 2), followed by KNIFE, GUN (r_3 = 1), the ratio would be 6 (i.e., 3 + 2 + 1) over 9 or .67. (c) For the

Mixed-Language lists, a similar ratio was devised for clusters of same-language responses, and the sum of separate language clusters was divided by the total of items recalled. For example, the recall FOX, RABBIT, TURNIP, BEAR, MOUSE (r_1 = 4), followed by POMME, CITRON (r_2 = 1), would become 5 (i.e., 4 + 1) over 7 or .71. This ratio is independent of the amount recalled, and it gives more credit than usual clustering methods for longer runs even when the total of items clustered is the same. That is, the usual methods would give equal credit to four two-item clusters as to two four-item clusters, whereas this method highlights the longer runs, in this example six vs. four.

Error Analysis. Attention was given to two types of errors only: (a) category intrusions, items belonging to an appropriate category but not appearing in the actual word list, and (b) translation equivalents, semantically correct translations of actual list items. When either of these errors occurred in the flow of recall, it was decided that they would not break up (nor, of course, contribute to) the category or language run they would have contributed to if they had not been errors.

RESULTS AND DISCUSSION

Considering first Rows I and V in Table 1, it is evident that the greater possibilities for organization available in the Category lists, compared to the No-Category lists, have a general and marked facilitative effect on amount recalled. This is true for both the French and Russian experiments. There are however, important variations among subconditions within the category and no-category variants of the experiment.

With regard to the No-Category conditions, it is of interest that the mixed list was as well recalled as were the unilingual ones. This is clearly so for the Russian version and partly so for the French. (One discrepant result is examined separately below.) This finding confirms the results of Kolers' (1965) experiment, and extends the generality of the outcome to category lists (Kolers dealt only with No-Category lists). Kolers found that bilingual *S*s recalled mixed lists of English and French monosyllables as efficiently as they recalled

TABLE 1
List Comparisons and Group Means

		No-category lists[a]			Category lists			
	French study	English (a)	French (b)	Mixed (c)	English (d)	French (e)	Concordant (f)	Discordant (g)
I.	Total recall[b]	10.83	12.65	10.88	19.17	18.21	18.67	15.50
II.	Category clustering				.61	.62	.62	.52
III.	Language clustering			.49			.73	.47
IV.	Errors[c]							
	Categorical intrusions				6	12	6	20
	Translations			7			3	17
	Russian study	English (a)	Russian (b)	Mixed (c)	English (d)	Russian (e)	Concordant (f)	Discordant (g)
V.	Total recall	12.08	12.50	11.40	20.92	17.75	19.04	15.13
VI.	Category clustering				.62	.60	.59	.45
VII.	Language clustering			.42			.71	.45
VIII.	Errors							
	Categorical intrusions				6	7	13	10
	Translations			7			3	34

[a]Means based on two lists.

[b]The differences among means in Rows I–III and V–VII were tested with F and found to be significant at the .05 level or better. The following group comparisons were tested with the Newman-Keuls procedure: Row I: b > a at .06 level; b > c at .05 level; g < d, e and f at .01 level, but g > c at .01 level; Row II: g < d, e and f at .01 level; Row III: f > c and g at .01 level; Row V: d > e at .01 level; d > f at .05 level; g < d, e and f at .01 level, but g > c at .01 level; Row VI: g < d, e and f at .01 level; and Row VII: f > c and g at .01 level.

[c]Entries in Rows IV and VIII are group totals for each type list.

unilingual lists. Rather than being handicapped in storing and retrieving items presented bilingually, the experienced bilingual apparently encounters little or no difficulty. Perhaps the bilingual uses the language contrast as a distinguishing feature of words analogous to a monolingual distinguishing nouns from adjectives in a unilingual list, presumably without a decrement in recall. Generalizing a notion of Brown and McNeill (1966), it may be that a word is filed multiply in the bilingual's memory, once according to each of its distinctive properties, e.g., language, semantic content, and part of speech, suggesting a basic similarity of bilingual and mono-lingual modes of organizing verbal materials. It also may be that the bilingual uses language as a distinctive marker or "tag" (Yntema and Trask, 1963) that helps differentiate words within a list, thereby aiding recall. The fact that the mixed lists were no better recalled may be due to a memory limit reached in this study. Another design working below such a limit might reveal that mixed lists are even better recalled than unilingual ones.

The English-French bilinguals showed a stronger capacity to store and retrieve French, in contrast to English, list items (Row I, Table 1). One might view this difference as a clear indicant of the French dominance of these bilingual *S*s, but it may signify something more. First, Kolers (1965) noted that unilingual lists of French monosyllables were better recalled than comparable lists in English, even for *S*s whose language histories suggest an English dominance. Kolers argued that there may be more lexical and phonemic distinctiveness among French than English words. This or some alternative explanation becomes more interesting in the light of the present recurrence of this difference with real French words, especially since no difference of this sort is apparent in the Russian version of the experiment. However, note also that when the same *S*s turn to processing the category-list items there is then a clear equivalence of English and French capacity and a very pronounced English dominance for the Russian-English *S*s. Considering the No-Category results only, one would conclude that the English-French bilinguals are dominant in French and the English-Russian bilinguals are balanced in skills, whereas the category-list results suggest that the English and French skills are balanced and the other group's skill in Russian is inferior.

This pattern of results casts some doubt on the adequacy of Kolers' explanation since lexical and phonemic distinctiveness should be as great in the category as in the No-Category case. However, we have no alternative explanation for the superior recall of the French No-Category list.

These results can be examined from another perspective. The demands made on a *S* in the category condition, where he must have the capacity in both of his languages to reshuffle mentally and organize list items according to semantic categories, are quite different from those made on him in the No-Category condition, where he must simply store and hold items in rote fashion, encountering difficulties when he tries, within the time limits of stimulus presentation, to organize along purely subjective lines. Assuming that the more demanding case provides the more revealing measure of dominance or balance, the results for the category lists are consistent with the linguistic experiences of both groups of *S*s. The English-French group is balanced in all aspects of language skill while the English-Russian is balanced only in the audiolingual aspects of their two languages, and otherwise dominant in English. Thus, a potentially important distinction can be drawn between the simple storage demands made on *S*s in the No-Category lists, and more complex demands for processing and organizing verbal materials in the category lists. This distinction is relevant to the measurement of bilingual balance.

The Discordant and Concordant lists affect recall in particular ways. In both the French and Russian versions of the study (Rows I and V, Table 1), the Discordant lists are the least well recalled of all category lists, even when, in a separate analysis, credit is given for translation errors. Yet they are still much more easily recalled than are any of the No-Category lists. Thus, placing language and semantic content in competition (the essential feature of the Discordant condition) depresses recall in one sense but in another does not depress it seriously.[1] The other rows in Table 1 provide three clues about the *S*s' approach to the Discordant list: (a) The *S*s are handicapped in their capacity to organize items according to their membership in particular semantic categories, i.e., the Discordant lists are always markedly lower than others in terms of category clustering (see Rows II and VI). (b) Yet they make as much use of language variations as an organizational schema as they do when recalling the Mixed No-Category lists (Rows II and VII). (c) At the same time, they make relatively more translation and intrusion errors (Rows IV and VIII). These findings suggest that the process of activating a superlinguistic, superordinate category [such as fruit (English)—FRUIT (français)] is not as easily accomplished through bilingual examples (e.g., apple, CITRON, orange, PAMPLEMOUSSE) as is the activation of a corresponding unilingual category. Although the linguistic mixture in the categories of the Discordant list does hamper the capacity to categorize, still the presence of categories is a major aid in organizing for recall as is evident when Discordant with Mixed No-Category lists are compared (Rows I and V, Table 1).

What is the nature of this advantage of categories? Because they are built up through bilingual examples, it is difficult to rely on an associationistic explanation of categorization in this instance. That is, one cannot argue that the clustered items are linked through common word-word associations encountered in the language since it is highly unlikely that the English "orange" is ever followed by the French "pamplemousse" in the written or verbal environments of bilinguals. Nor is it true that the *S*s' category-clustering scores are artifacts due to their using only one of their languages to make clusters, since approximately equal numbers of English and French, and English and Russian items were recalled for each category in the Discordant lists. Thus, the activation of some form of superlinguistic superordinate structures, rather than superordinates in either language or reliance on word-to-word associations, seems more appropriate as an explantion of clustering in this instance.

Although recall is decidedly better with the Concordant than the Discordant or any of the No-Category lists, for both French and Russian versions, still there is no advantage of Concordant over the unilingual category lists. (We will presume that the Russian group's superiority with English reflects language dominance.) Thus in the Concordant lists, where all examples of a particular category appeared in one language or the other, language could have been used as a separate and supportive coding schema that could be expected to aid recall.[2] This feature of the Concordant condition is of theoretical interest in view of Mandler's (1966, p. 47) recent suggestion that "parallel" or "separate, though overlapping organizational schemas" may markedly increase human memory. Certain clues as to why no actual facilitation occurred in this case are available in Table 1. One might conclude that the ability to categorize has not been affected since *S*s are able to categorize as well in the Concordant condition as in the unilingual category conditions (Rows II and VI) and there is no strong evidence that categorical intrusions are more numerous (Rows IV and VIII). However, there is a very large amount of language clustering in the Concordant condition which holds for both French and Russian versions (Rows III and VII). Thus *S*s in the Concordant condition apparently relied too much on language as an organizational schema. In this case language would lead them to congregate items for the two categories presented in each language, and prompt longer recall runs in each language while detracting from the semantic clarity of each category and thereby reducing recall from its potential level. Bilinguals, it appears, are vulnerable in the sense that they may be enticed to misuse language as an organizational schema which, to the extent that it detracts from the optimal use of available categories, adversely affects recall. These results, then, actually reflect on the limitations of the present design. The possibility of facilitation in the Concordant condition remains open. We may have, in one sense, reduced the number of categories in the Concordant condition from four clear categories with 10 examples each to two general language categories with 20 examples each. According to Bousfield and Cohen (1956a) this shift would reduce clustering and recall. A fairer test would require a design providing an equal number of categories and languages, i.e., either one category for each language, using bilingual *S*s, or one category for each of the several languages known by multilingual *S*s.

In summary, a good deal of evidence has emerged suggesting that, for bilinguals, language is an ancillary means of organizing information in memory. The semantic categories appear as the powerful organizational schemas. The role that language does play is seen mainly in the subtle differences that occur when the two schemas are brought into competition. This conclusion is supported, first, by the marked differences in recall between Category and No-Category conditions in contrast with the slight differences between unilingual and bilingual conditions. In fact, in the No-Category case, where the bilingual cannot do much more than merely store information in a routine fashion, recall is not affected by the bilingual nature of the input. This suggests that in such situations bilinguals regard code variations as simple distinctive features of the elements to be stored and are not hampered in any way by their presence. However, when more complex demands are made on his language skill, as in the category condition, recall can be disrupted when code variations conflict with the process of establishing categories, or it can be enhanced if code variations occur so as to highlight the distinctiveness of the categories. Even when the two coding systems are in a discordant relation and information is presented bilingually, the ability to chunk information, as an aid in recall, is not seriously reduced. In this case, for example, bilinguals are more likely to confuse the code variations, as reflected in the relatively large number of translation errors made. This fact indicates, however, that they are focusing on categories and are able to do so effectively even with the distraction of language switches. Because they can effectively utilize bilingual information to establish categories, it is suggested that chunking is not based solely on word-to-word associations but also on the activation of some type of superordinate structure that works across languages.

It was also shown that a bilingual's capacity to use each of his two languages expresses itself differently according to the task requirements. If, as in the No-Category case, he must merely store information first in one of his languages and later in the other, with little opportunity to reorganize, his relative skills in the two languages can be quite different from the case where he can effectively reorganize information, as in the Category lists. The suggestion was made that bilingual balance or dominance can be more faithfully assessed through the more demanding task.

NOTES

This research was supported by grants to W. E. Lambert from The Canada Council and from the Defence Research Board of Canada, grant Number 9401-10. The authors are very grateful to Richard Tucker and Norva Hepler of McGill for advice and valuable suggestions.

[1]In two early studies, Bousfield and Cohen (1956a, 1956b) found that clustering was more pronounced in the recall of 40-item lists comprised of eight categories with five examples each than of lists of four categories with 10 examples each, and in "dual-level" lists where a major category (e.g., animals) was subdivided (e.g.,

canine vs. feline examples). Further research is needed to determine whether bilingual *S*s react to the Discordant List as analogous to an 8 x 5 (eight subcategories with five unilingual examples each) or as a dual-level list.

[2]This condition is analogous in certain respects to the "facilitation" condition of Gonzalez and Cofer, 1959 (see Cofer, 1965, p. 263), where item pairs made up of an appropriate modifier and a noun (e.g., POWERFUL LION or BLUE DRESS) were much better recalled and categorized than were comparable lists of unmodified nouns.

REFERENCES

Bousfield, W. A. The occurrence of clustering in the recall of randomly arranged associates. J. gen. Psychol., 1953, 49, 229-240.

Bousfield, W. A., and Cohen, B. H. Clustering in recall as a function of number of word categories in stimulus-word lists. J. gen. Psychol., 1956a, 54-55, 95-106.

Bousfield, W. A., and Cohen, B. H. The effect of a dual-level stimulus-word list on the occurrence of clustering in recall. J. gen. Psychol., 1956b, 55, 51-58.

Brown, R., and McNeill, D. The "Tip of the Tongue" phenomenon. J. verb. Learn. verb. Behav., 1966, 5, 325-337.

Cofer, C. N. On some factors in the organizational characteristics of free recall. Amer. Psychologist, 1965, 20, 261-272.

Cohen, B. H., Bousfield, W. A., and Whitmarsh, G. A. Cultural norms for verbal items in 43 categories. Technical Report No. 22, 1957, Univ. of Connecticut, Contract Nonr 631, Office of Naval Research.

Gonzalez, R. C. and Cofer, C. N. Exploratory studies of verbal context by means of clustering in free recall. J. genet. Psychol., 1959, 95, 293-320.

Jokobovitz, L. A., and Lambert, W. E. Semantic satiation among bilinguals, J. exp. Psychol., 1961, 62, 576-582.

Jenkins, J. J., and Russell, W. A. Associative clustering during recall. J. abnorm. soc. Psychol., 1952, 47, 818-821.

Kendler, H. H. Coding: Associationistic or organizational? J. verb. Learn. verb. Behav., 1966, 5, 99-106.

Kolers, P. A. Bilingualism and bicodalism. Lang. and Speech, 1965, 8, 122-126.

Lambert, W. E., Havelka, J., and Crosby, C. The influence of language acquisition contexts on bilingualism. J. abnorm. soc. Psychol., 1958, 56, 239-244.

Lambert, W. E., and Fillenbaum, S. A pilot study of aphasia among bilinguals. Canad. J. Psychol., 1959, 13, 28-34.

Lambert, W. E., and Moore, N. Word association responses: Comparisons of American and French monolinguals with Canadian monolinguals and bilinguals. J. Pers. soc. Psychol., 1966, 3, 313-320.

Lambert, W. E., and Preston, M. The interdependencies of the bilingual's two languages. Paper presented at The Verbal Behavior Conference, September 1965, New York City.

Mandler, G. Organization and memory. In K. W. Spence and Janet T. Spence (Eds.), The psychology of learning and motivation: advances in research and theory. New York: Academic Press, 1966.

Miller, G. A. The magical number seven, plus or minus two: Some limits on our capacity for processing information. Psychol. Rev., 1956, 63, 81-97.

Preston, M. S., and Lambert, W. E. Interlingual interference in a bilingual version of the Stroop color-word task. McGill Univ., mimeographed, 1966.

Shepard, R. N. Learning and recall as organization and search. J. verb. Learn. verb. Behav., 1966, 5, 201-204.

Yntema, D. B., and Trask, F. P. Recall as a search process. J. verb. Learn. verb. Behav., 1963, 2, 65-74.

17 Ethnic Identification and Personality Adjustments of Canadian Adolescents of Mixed English-French Parentage

In Collaboration with Carol Aellen

The social environments of most cosmopolitan cities afford young men and women of various ethnic origins many opportunities to develop friendships, fall in love, and marry. Often the relationships formed in these settings involve religious and linguistic as well as ethnic differences, Montreal being a particularly interesting example in North America. With so little information about the consequences of intermarriage, one may exaggerate by over- or under-emphasizing the adjustments required of those who form such unions, just as one cannot be certain which generation group, the offspring of mixed marriages or their parents, encounters the greater conflicts. The major purpose of the present study is to provide information by focusing on the adjustments made by adolescent children of English-French mixed marriages in the Montreal setting, examining the degree and direction of the offspring's ethnic identifications as well as a selected set of their attitudes, values, and personality characteristics.

The children of these mixed marriages come in contact with and are usually expected to learn the distinctive social and behavioral characteristics of the two cultures represented in their families. The question is (a) whether the demands made on them necessarily generate conflicts, (b) whether the experience with two cultures possibly broadens and liberalizes the child, or (c) whether some combination of both outcomes is typical. In addition to the cultural demands made on them, the children of mixed ethnic marriages may face other difficulties to the extent that their parents, as suggested by Gordon (1966) and Saucier (1965), may have married outside their ethnic group because of personal instability and immaturity. Much of the previous research suggests that persons who intermarry often have relatively strong feelings of alienation, self-hatred, and worthlessness, and are disorganized and demoralized. Mixed ethnic children might well find it difficult to identify with their parents if these characteristics are typical or representative. On the other hand, people may intermarry in many instances because they have developed essentially healthy attitudes and orientations that are still inappropriate within their own ethnic group, making intermarriage with a sympathetic outsider particularly attractive. They may have become, like Park's marginal man, "the individual with the wider horizon, the keener intelligence, the more detached and rational viewpoint. . . always relatively the more civilized human being" (Park, 1964, p. 376). The purpose of this investigation was to examine both these possibilities as objectively as possible. Although the main emphasis of the study is on the consequences of mixed ethnic marriages, it deals more generally with a special type of intergroup relations taking place in a bicultural community and with the adjustments that ethnic groups make to maintain their identities. In this sense, it is an extension of the recent research on intercultural contacts conducted at McGill (see the review of Lambert, 1967).

PROCEDURE

Subjects

Since no record of the ethnic origin of students is kept in Canadian schools, *S*s of mixed French-English background were located by the principals of those schools that the school superintendents thought would have a good share of students with mixed ethnic parentage. The teachers of particular classes simply asked students to indicate whether they had one parent who was of French origin and the other who was of English descent. A questionnaire was then administered to groups of students who likely had mixed ethnic backgrounds and detailed answers permitted us to select those who actually did. In the same schools, comparable groups of students with "homogeneous" parents (both French or both English) were collected in the same manner. Of the 310 questionnaires that were completed, 191 were used for the study. Nine did not clearly state their ethnic origin, 37 were of European origin (other than British) or of Acadian,

Indian, or Franco-American origin, one (only) mixed ethnic subject was excluded because his parents were separated; although 36 altogether were eliminated because they came from homes in which one or both parents were missing, 36 more were omitted because they were too old or too young for our purposes. This left four groups aged 14 to 17, inclusive, with the required ethnic composition, two groups attending English-language and two French-language, publicly financed, Catholic, parochial schools. Thus, religious variation was eliminated by having all *S*s Catholic. One group from the English-language schools had parents of English-Canadian or British background (EC homog, n = 51), and a second had mixed French-English background (EC mixed, n = 41). Similarly, one group from the French-language schools had parents of French-Canadian background (FC homog, n = 60), and a second had mixed French-English background (FC mixed, n = 39). The classification of *S*s into homogeneous and mixed groups followed the scheme proposed by Wessel (1931).

The groups were compared for variations in age, socioeconomic class, number of siblings, and intelligence (as measured by tests standarized for each language group) and there were no significant differences among them. All groups reported similar numbers of relatives living in Montreal, with the exception of the FC mixed group; fewer members of the FC mixed group reported that they had 25 or more relatives in the city.[1]

None of the EC homog or FC homog *S*s reported that a second language was used in the home although many of the parents were said to be skilled in both languages. As expected, the mixed groups were significantly more likely than the homogeneous groups to describe themselves *and* their parents as having better skills in the second language.

Measuring instruments

Our major interest was in the effects a bicultural background might have on *S*s, whether it would promote feelings of anomie, alienation, inferiority or, in contrast, a sense of well-being and a broader and more tolerant social outlook. With this end in mind the following scales and measuring instruments were either selected from previous studies or developed for our own purposes. All materials were presented in English for those attending English schools and in French for those in French schools.

Identification

1. Two forms of the semantic differential were used to measure identification: (a) Form I was the same as that used by Lazowick (1955), including adjectives with high loadings on the three standard semantic factors (evaluation, potency, and activity). (b) Form II comprised adjectives with heavy loadings on the evaluative factor only. *S*s rated the following concepts: Form I—me, my mother, and my father; Form II—me, the typical French Canadian, the typical English Canadian, and me as I would like to be. Each *S*'s score on a concept was his average rating on the 7-point scales separating the bipolar adjectives. As a measure of parental and ethnic identification, each *S*'s score for me was subtracted from his score for the appropriate contrasting concepts, and difference scores were used as an index of profile similarity.

2. Ethnic identification was also measured by a social distance scale which asked *S*s to indicate their reactions to such statements as "What is your general impression of those English Canadians you know as individuals?" Scores could range from minus eighteen (indicating strong identification with French Canadians and a rejection of English Canadians) through zero, reflecting no preference for one group or the other, to plus eighteen, indicating a pro-English bias.

Self-esteem and stability

1. If interethnic marriages have a harmful effect on the children of such families, one would expect the mixed ethnic *S*s to have relatively low self-esteem, stronger feelings of uncertainty about social interaction, and comparatively less confidence in the norms and goals of society. With this as a working hypothesis, the following measures were given to all groups of *S*s. Self-ratings on

(a) Form I and (b) Form II of the semantic differential for the concept me were taken as an estimate of how competent and valuable the *S* feels himself to be.

2. A measure of psychological maturity (see Katz and Zigler, 1967) was derived by calculating the profile differences between the *S*'s ratings of me and me as I would like to be.

3. The sensitivity to others scale, developed by Lambert and Gardner (1962), measures anxiety about social interactions and reveals abnormal sensitivity to other people's reactions to the *S*'s behaviour. The set of questions includes such items as: "I usually have a hard time anticipating how others will feel about what I am going to say." Seven-point response scales were provided.

4. Finally, as a measure of anomie, five items concerned with feelings of dissatisfaction with society, cynicism about the value of planning ahead, and disbelief in equality of opportunity were selected from the scales developed by Srole (1956), Roberts and Rokeach (1956), McCloskey and Schaar (1965), and Lambert and Gardner (1962). The items were also scored along a 7-point response scale, and two items were reversed to avoid response-set bias.

Perception of parents

If interethnic marriages affect family relationships through cultural conflicts or confusions of identity, such consequences should be apparent in the way children in such families view their parents. The following measures were used to assess these views.

1. The perception of parents inventory, developed by Schutz (1958), consists of pairs of contrasting statements about the degree to which parents satisfy their children's needs for inclusion, control, and affection. Schutz proposes that satisfactory interpersonal relations require a balance of these three component needs. Scores range from 1 to 5 and extreme scores on this measure are considered undesirable, e.g., a high score on inclusion would suggest that parents were oversolicitous while low scores would reflect indifference

or neglect. Mixed ethnic *S*s might have extremely low scores if their parents were so absorbed in their own difficulties that they neglected their children. High scores might be expected if the parents are oversensitive about the possible problems involved in raising children in a bicultural home.

2. It will be recalled that *S*s also rated each parent on Form I of the semantic differential scale, and these ratings were used as an index of the *S*s' perceptions of their parents. The complete list of bipolar adjectives used was: potency—strong-weak, rugged-delicate, heavy-light; activity—hot-cold, active-passive, fast-slow; and evaluative—happy-sad, fresh-stale, clean-dirty.

Peer relationships

We also wanted information about the types of relationships the different groups of boys developed with their peers in order to determine, for example, whether the mixed ethnic *S*s feel that they have been accepted socially and to what extent they have assimilated some of the values and goals of their peers, especially those with whom they associate at school. The following scales and procedures were used to help answer these questions.

1. The FIRO-B questionnaire developed by Schutz (1958) was designed to evaluate interpersonal relationships. Guttman-type items assess the type of behaviour wanted from others as well as the type of behavior typically expressed toward others with regard to inclusion, control, and affection. Scores range from 0 to 9 on each set of items and extreme scores are believed to indicate abnormal tendencies toward or demands for one or more of the component processes. Low mean scores on inclusion would suggest that the mixed ethnic boys respond to social rejection by withdrawal, while high scores would suggest strong tendencies to overcome social barriers. Similarly, extreme scores on the affection scale should reflect any tendency among the mixed ethnic *S*s for feelings of rejection which might be revealed in low scores on affection wanted and affection expressed. Furthermore, if their bicultural background has affected them, then the mixed ethnic *S*s might show some pattern of extreme scores on the scales of wanted and expressed control.

2. It is assumed that ease of interaction with peer groups depends on an ability to predict the other group's important values, and this ability was indirectly estimated by having *S*s list the three qualities they felt they should have in order to be accepted by their friends, and three qualities that would be most disliked, using questions adapted from those of Szabo, Goyer, and Gagné (1964). The common fraction of overlap between any two groups on each set of qualities serves as an index of the agreement between the two groups. The degree of congruence of valued traits between the mixed ethnic *S*s and both of the homogeneous groups was estimated by the extent of overlap of their trait nominations.[2]

3. The influence of a peer group may also be estimated, in the case of ethnic groups, by asking whether any preference for marrying a member of the reference group (represented by the ethnic make-up of the school attended) has developed. Since the mixed ethnics attending both English and French schools come from families in which the mother was either English or French Canadian in approximately equal numbers, any tendency for those attending English (or French) schools to prefer to marry an English (or French) Canadian would represent the influence of the peer group.

Attitudes

1. Recent studies (Lambert, 1967) have shown that both English- and French-Canadian college students evaluate English Canadians more favorably than French Canadians. The tendency for French Canadians to downgrade their own group was also noted (see Peal and Lambert, 1962) among ten-year-old French-Canadian bilinguals. To determine whether the mixed ethnic *S*s would develop a similar set of feelings, reflecting a view that the origin of one of their parents was inferior, their attitudes toward French and English Canadians were measured by Form II of the semantic differential scales.

2. Attitudes toward English and French Canadians were also determined by two scales of 28 items, adapted from the study of Jones and Lambert (1959). These items dealt with *S*s' acceptance or rejection of the goals, means, status relationships, and solidarity systems of English- and French-Canadian societies. For example,

one item dealing with family goal reads: "English (French) Canadians look on their children mainly as sources of income." The same items were worded once with English Canadians and once with French Canadians as a reference point.

3. Attitudes toward England and France were assessed by asking for comparative ratings of France and England in relation to Canada. A typical item was: "Compared to Canadians, the English are an unimaginative people." This scale permits one to examine various notions, for example, that homogeneous groups might identify more closely with their country of origin while mixed groups might have equally strong ties with both countries of origin, or a stronger identification with Canada.

4. The groups were also tested for anti-democratic leanings and ethnocentric attitudes, using the F and E scales of Adorno, Frenkel-Brunswick, Levinson, and Sanford (1964). Means for the F scale were based on five items selected from Form 60 and included two reversal items developed by Christie, Havel, and Seidenberg (1958), while the ethnocentrism scale consisted of six items, two of which were revised to read "foreigner" and "minorities" rather than "Jews," to avoid religious bias. With these we could determine whether the mixed ethnic *S*s, who come from families where there might be great cultural conflict, are more authoritarian as a result of family-generated anxiety or whether their bicultural background has had the effect of making them less ethnocentric than the homogeneous groups.

Values

1. English and French Canadians are believed to have quite different sets of values, English Canadians, for example, repeatedly being said to be more materialistic than French Canadians who supposedly place more value on spiritual matters and the family. To the extent that these stereotypes are valid, the mixed ethnic *S*s might well have difficulties incorporating and integrating two different sets of values passed on to them through their parents. In order to examine the similarities and differences of values, *S*s were asked to list (a) those qualities they feel their parents are trying to pass on to

TABLE I

Group comparisons of mean scores on the various measures

	a EC homog	b EC mixed	c FC mixed	d FC homog	F	df	Sheffé comparisons*
1. Identification with ECs	.21	.28	.25	.17	.70	3,174	—
2. Identification with FCs	.87	.63	.07	.06	8.92**	3,174	a>c, d; b>d
3. Social distance scores	6.94	3.58	-2.71	-7.50	59.64**	3,186	a>c, d; b>c, d; c>d
4. Self Ratings, SD scales:							
Evaluative	5.38	5.34	5.50	6.03	7.86**	3,182	d>a, b, c
Activity	4.80	4.90	5.33	5.11	2.76*	3,182	—
Potency	4.50	4.34	4.05	4.30	.39	3,182	—
5. Anomie	3.59	3.68	3.41	3.83	1.71	3,179	—
6. Perception of parents:							
Inclusion	3.56	4.00	4.02	3.21	3.96*	3,183	d<c,b;b+c>a+d
7. SD ratings of my mother	4.48	4.61	4.75	4.94	3.59*	3,185	a<d
8. FIRO-B subscores							
Inclusion: Expressed	5.26	4.97	5.56	5.20	.45	3,186	—
Wanted	4.32	4.26	4.51	4.21	.09	3,186	—
Control: Expressed	2.76	2.68	3.82	3.31	1.90	3,186	—
Wanted	4.02	3.75	3.07	3.88	1.72	3,186	—
Affection: Expressed	3.30	3.58	4.17	3.76	1.02	3,186	—
Wanted	2.72	3.36	4.97	4.29	6.20**	3,186	a<c, d

TABLE I (Continued)

Group comparisons of mean scores on the various measures

	a EC homog	b EC mixed	c FC mixed	d FC homog	F	df	Sheffé comparisons*
9. Marriage preferences:							
French-Canadian girls	6	6	20	40	$\chi^2 = 82.22$**	3	—
English-Canadian girls	37	26	5	1			
10. F scale scores	4.19	4.46	4.24	4.41	.93	3,176	—
11. E scale scores	4.35	4.44	4.38	4.65	1.21	3,179	—
12. Attitudes toward English-Canadians	5.36	5.41	4.95	4.53	12.00**	3,181	d<a, b
13. Evaluative ratings of French-Canadians	4.37	4.75	5.37	5.46	14.03**	3,175	a<c, d; b<c, d
14. Achievement value orientations	4.61	4.43	4.37	4.07	3.41*	3,183	a>d
16. Boys' occupational aspirations**	2.50	2.51	2.45	2.83	3.23*	3,158	d>a+b+c

*A positive difference shows that the group rates itself higher than the reference group. A negative difference indicates that the reference group is rated higher. Multiple group comparisons are made with Sheffé's procedure, as described in Ferguson (1966).

**Entries are group means of "filial aspirations indices" used by Lambert and Klineberg (1963). Individuals were assigned scores of 1, 2, or 3, depending on whether their aspiration was socio-economically lower than father's actual occupation (1), the same(2), or higher(3). Occupations were classified in accordance with the socio-economic scale developed by Blishen (1961).

them, and (b) those qualities they will want to pass on to their own children. The overlap coefficient (see note 2) was used as a measure of degree of intergroup similarity of qualities.

2. The comparative value placed on achievement was assessed with Rosen's (1959) achievement value orientation scale. Two questions were reversed by making minor changes in the wording. Rosen had found that variations in cultural background were more important than social class differences in determining achievement values. With this scale we could compare groups to test various hypotheses, e.g., that those parents who have married outside their ethnic group may have already assimilated the individualistic achievement values characteristic of English-speaking groups of North America, or that mixed ethnic families who send their children to English schools have adopted such values, while those who send their children to French schools have not.

3. Lambert and Klineberg (1963) found that French-Canadian youngsters have a higher mean occupational aspiration index (measured by comparing children's aspirations with their father's actual occupation) than do English-Canadian children. Yves de Jocas and Guy Rocher (1957) have pointed out that "the channels and barriers of mobility" for French and English Canadians are different and that French Canadians go up the scale step-by-step while English Canadians seem to move more rapidly to the top. In order to determine whether these barriers affect the aspirations of mixed ethnic *S*s, they were asked to give their occupational aspirations and these were compared with their fathers' actual occupations.

RESULTS AND DISCUSSION

Parental identification

Analysis of variance applied to the scores for parental identification showed no differences among groups, either for identification with mother or with father (for mother, $F = .74$, $df = 3,182$; for father, $F = .49$, $df = 3,181$). It was quite clear, however, that the subjects identify more closely with fathers than with mothers since correlated *t* tests for distance scores between the concepts *me* and mother were significant for all four groups, while none was significant for the me and father comparison, indicating greater profile similarity between sons and fathers. The important point is that the mixed ethnic groups were as able as the homogeneous ones to relate to their fathers. (The distance scores for the me-mother comparison were: EC homog, $t = 3.89$, $df = 47$, $p < .001$; EC mixed, $t = 3.97$, $df = 39$, $p < .001$; FC mixed, $t = 3.94$, $df = 37$, $p < .001$; FC homog, $t = 2.77$, $df = 59$, $p < .01$.)

The mixed ethnic groups showed the same pattern of identification with parents as did the homogeneous groups, developing particularly close associations with their fathers as would be expected for boys in their mid-teens. There is then no symptom of abnormality or within-family conflict over identification with parents for the adolescents from mixed ethnic backgrounds.

Ethnic identification

With regard to ethnic identification, measured by profile similarities, no differences among groups were found for identification with English Canadians (see Table I, row 1), and in only one case—that of the FC homog group—was there a reliable profile difference between means for the ratings of me and the typical English Canadian ($t = 2.24$, $df = 56$, $p < .05$). The positive scores indicate that subjects tend to rate themselves higher than the typical English Canadian.

In contrast, there were important group differences for identification with French Canadians, as summarized in Table I, row 2. In this case, there is a marked effect due to the school attended: the two groups attending French schools (the FC homog and the FC mixed) identify more closely with the typical French Canadian than do the two groups attending English schools. Furthermore, when the profile similarities for me and the typical French Canadian were compared, both the EC homog ($t = 5.38$, $df = 46$, $p < .001$) and the EC mixed ($t = 3.37$, $df = 37$, $p < .01$) had significantly discrepant profiles, suggesting again that they see themselves as different from French Canadians, and this is in contrast to the self-perceptions of the FC homog and FC mixed groups. Note again how the importance of the school group in shaping the identifications of the two mixed groups is suggested by the dual identification demonstrated by mixed ethnic subjects attending the French school. In contrast, the mixed ethnic subjects attending English schools are no different from the EC homog group in their tendencies to distinguish themselves from the French Canadians. It is possible that the contrast between the two ethnically mixed groups stems from a differential attractiveness of the two basic Canadian cultures and the relative dominance of the English Canadian cultural system, as has been discussed in other contexts (see Lambert, 1967).

When ethnic identification is measured by social distance scales, the mean difference obtained (see Table I, row 3) between the FC homog and FC mixed groups is due to the FC mixed group's tendencies to maintain closer friendships with English Canadians ($p < .05$) and to prefer to work with English Canadians ($p < .05$). While the means for the EC mixed and EC homog groups did not differ significantly either on total scores or on specific items, there is none the less a trend for the EC mixed group to welcome somewhat closer social contact with French Canadians. Thus, the mixed ethnic subjects, especially those in a French-Canadian academic environment, relate themselves to both aspects of their ethnic backgrounds.

Self-esteem and stability

Analysis of variance of the self-ratings on both forms of the semantic differential showed no significant mean differences among groups for over-all scores. However, for the evaluative subscores (on Form I) the FC homog subjects rate themselves significantly higher than do any of the other groups (see Table I, row 4) suggesting again that the FC mixed subjects may have tempered their self-concepts to bring them in line with those of the typical English Canadian. On the activity dimension the two groups in French schools rate themselves as more active than do the two attending English schools.

No differences were found among groups on the discrepancy between self and ideal-self ratings, the sensitivity to others measure, or on anomie. Thus there are again no symptoms of disturbance or anxiety among the mixed ethnic subjects on any of these indices. In fact, the means of all groups fall on the non-anomic side of the anomie scale, reflecting various degrees of social satisfaction rather than alienation or normlessness. The important point is that the mixed ethnic boys are not exceptions to this pattern.

Perception of parents

Comparisons among groups on the Schutz measure of perception of parents reveal no reliable differences for either control ($F = 1.12$, $df = 3,182$, ns) or affection ($F = 1.05$, $df = 3,183$, ns). There is, however, a significant difference between the mixed and homogeneous ethnic groups for inclusion (see Table I, row 6). The mixed groups (especially the FC mixed one) perceive their parents as taking a much greater interest in them and interacting more frequently with them than either of the homogeneous groups.

The fact that the parents of the mixed ethnic subjects were perceived as more inclusive did not, however, give rise to higher evaluative ratings of parents, since the evaluative subscores of the semantic differential ratings for parents showed no significant group differences either for _mother_ ($F = .54$, $df = 3,185$, ns) or for _father_ ($F = 1.41$, $df = 3,186$, ns). Thus, the attitudes of the mixed ethnic subjects toward their parents are essentially similar to those of the homogeneous groups. Furthermore, the groups did not differ from one another on the potency subscore ratings (for _mother_, $F = .92$, $df = 3,185$, ns; for _father_, $F = .58$, $df = 3,186$, ns). The significant differences which were found on the activity subscores for both _mother_ ($F = 13.77$, $df = 3,185$, $p < .01$) and _father_ ($F = 5.09$, $df = 3,186$, $p < .01$) appear to account for the higher ratings given to _mother_ on the total score for this measure (Table I, row 7). The total ratings for _father_, however, did not reach significance ($F = 1.72$, $df = 3,186$, ns). It should be noted that the group differences on the activity dimension do not account for the higher rating on inclusion noted for the mixed ethnic groups because for activity the major difference lies between the two homogeneous ethnic groups, while for inclusion the two mixed groups contrast with the two homogeneous groups.

Peer relationships

If mixed ethnic subjects have difficulty in being accepted by their peers it is not reflected in any consistent manner in the group comparisons of FIRO-B scores. There were no differences among the groups on any of the FIRO-B measures with the exception of wanted affection (Table I, row 8), and here the significant mean differences are between the EC homog subjects, who signify that they desire comparatively little affection from their peers, and the two groups attending the French-language schools who desire considerably more. Because the EC mixed group is intermediary (not reliably different from either the EC homog or the two FC groups), these findings appear to reflect both the influences of the peer culture of the school attended by the mixed ethnic subjects and their own strategies of coping with two sets of cultural norms. Thus, the EC mixed group is not as extreme as the EC homog group, suggesting that they are somewhat more "warm" and therefore more "French" in their desire for affection from friends. The tendency for both mixed ethnic groups to desire relatively more affection from friends is congruent with their perceptions of parents as being relatively more attentive and interested in them as family members.

TABLE II
Group comparisons of equivalent first-choice responses

	Qualities necessary for acceptance by friends	Qualities disliked in other persons
FC homog-FC mixed	.54	.60
EC homog-FC mixed	.49	.14
EC homog-FC homog	.47	.20
FC homog-EC mixed	.47	.21
EC mixed-FC mixed	.39	.12
EC homog-EC mixed	.34	.56

Note.—Entries are summed common fractions of overlap between paired groups using the method described by Rosenzweig (1964).

This general trend, for the mixed ethnic subjects to adopt the standards of their peer groups, is supported by the pattern of qualities they say they like and dislike in other persons (see Table II). That is, the greatest amount of overlap between groups for liked qualities is between the two French groups, and the least amount is between the two English groups, similar to the alignment of groups on wanted affection. Thus, the greater need for affection from peers expressed by the two FC groups may depend on their having a more standardized and clearer definition of what traits are required for comfortable peer interaction. For disliked qualities, however, there is a large response overlap between mixed and homogeneous groups attending the same language schools. For example, of the 99 responses obtained when the FC mixed and FC homog groups are combined, 48 gave "menteur" (liar) as the most disliked quality. The responses of the EC groups, although more diverse, still show high agreement (e.g., "bold" was given 24 out of 92 times, and "tough" was given 18 times). Thus, the academic environment overrides ethnic mixture as the important determiner of what traits are judged to be desirable or undesirable. In general, however, there are no distinctive characteristics of the mixed ethnic subjects that emerge with this measure.

The same factor determines the popularity of girlfriends. When the boys were asked whether they would prefer to marry a French-Canadian or an English-Canadian woman when they are older (see Table I, row 9), it was found that the choice depended on the language of the school attended: mixed ethnic subjects in English schools favouring English girls and those in French schools favouring French girls. At the same time, significantly greater numbers of FC homog boys compared to EC homog refused to express a preference ($\underline{X}^2 = 3.85$, $\underline{p} < .05$).

Attitudes

There were no significant differences among groups in authoritarianism or ethnocentrism as measured by the F and E scales (see Table I, rows 10 and 11). The mean scores for all groups fall slightly above the neutral point indicating a slight endorsement of authoritarian and ethnocentric ideologies.

Although there were no differences in these more general attitudinal dispositions, there were important differences among groups in attitudes toward specific groups, i.e., English and French Canadians. The mean scores for the 28 items measuring attitudes toward French Canadians showed no significant differences among groups; however, on the measure of attitudes toward English Canadians there was a reliable tendency for the FC homog group (in particular) to discriminate against English Canadians (see Table I, row 12). Further more, when each group's attitudes toward English Canadians and French Canadians are compared (with correlated $\underline{t}$ tests), the EC homog group had reliably more favourable attitudes towards ECs ($\underline{t}$ = 3.32, $\underline{df}$ = 48, $\underline{p} < .001$), as did the EC mixed group ($\underline{t}$ = 2.71, $\underline{df}$ = 37, $\underline{p} < .05$) while the FC homog group strongly favoured FCs ($\underline{t}$ = 6.52, $\underline{df}$ = 56, $\underline{p} < .001$). It is of interest that the EC mixed group showed no reliable preference one way or the other ($\underline{t}$ = 1.20, $\underline{df}$ = 35, ns).

The semantic differential ratings of attitudes gave complementary results. In this case there were no significant group differences for the evaluative measure of attitudes toward English Canadians, whereas the evaluative ratings given to French Canadians by both the EC homog and EC mixed groups were comparatively unfavourable (see Table I, row 13). Furthermore, the EC homog group significantly favoured the English Canadians over the French Canadians on this measure ($\underline{t}$ = 4.05, $\underline{df}$ = 47, $\underline{p} < .001$) and the FC homog group significantly favoured the French Canadians ($\underline{t}$ = 2.42, $\underline{df}$ = 56, $\underline{p} < .05$). It is noteworthy that in this instance neither the EC mixed nor the FC mixed group showed a reliable preference or bias.

Analysis of the preference for England or France over Canada indicated no differences among groups, although the EC homog group reliably favoured England over France ($\underline{t}$ = 2.60, $\underline{df}$ = 46, $\underline{p} < .02$); no other comparisons were significant.

In terms of authoritarian and ethnocentric attitudes, the mixed ethnic subjects are neither more broadminded nor more prejudiced than the homogeneous groups.[3] Although these basic attitudinal dispositions are alike for all groups, the groups do differ significantly when their attitudes toward the major Canadian reference groups are examined, and it is the FC mixed group who show no bias for one ethnic group or the other in contrast to both groups of homogeneous subjects who clearly favour their own ethnic groups over the other. In this case, too, the EC mixed group were less extreme than the EC homog group, although they were still generally more biased than the FC mixed one.

Values

Intergroup comparisons were made between those qualities or character traits the boys think their parents are trying to teach them as well as those qualities they would like to teach their own children (see Table III). The overlap of qualities among all groups is quite large, especially for values being stressed by parents. Still there is a slight trend for the ethnically mixed groups to receive value training which draws on both English-Canadian and French-Canadian reference groups as is evident when one contrasts their various overlap scores with those for the two homogeneous groups. A similar pattern is apparent in the qualities subjects want to pass on to their own children, and in this case there is a distinctively marked similarity between the FC mixed and FC homog groups as to how they plan to socialize their own children. This pattern is more pronounced for the French Canadians than for the English Canadians whose responses reveal greater diversity.

Parental values are exemplified by such qualities as ambition (14 of 92 choices for both EC groups and 18 of 99 choices for both FC groups), politeness (EC = 11; FC = 13), trustworthiness (EC = 7; FC = 10), and religiousness (EC = 8; FC = 5). Similarly, the qualities the boys would like to teach their own children are responsibleness (EC = 14; FC = 9), ambition (EC = 12; FC = 0), politeness (EC = 5; FC = 16), and frankness (EC = 0; FC = 15). Note that the qualities to be stressed with the next generation have more of a success character for the EC groups (responsibility and ambition) while those stressed by the FC groups are of a more interpersonal nature (politeness and frankness).

TABLE III
Group comparisons of equivalent first-choice responses

	Qualities parents are teaching *S*s	Qualities *S*s would teach their own children
EC mixed-EC homog	.61	.57
EC mixed-FC mixed	.60	.56
FC mixed-FC homog	.60	.77
EC mixed-FC homog	.56	.56
FC homog-EC homog	.50	.40
FC mixed-EC homog	.48	.40

Note.—Entries are summed common fractions of overlap between paired groups using the method described by Rosenzweig (1964).

These choices, in turn, are consistent with the findings for achievement value orientations in that the EC homog group scores signficantly higher than the FC homog group (see Table I, row 14); The ethnically mixed groups fall between these extremes. In this case, too, the mixed ethnic subjects have adjusted their values in accordance with both aspects of their ethnic backgrounds.

Comparing the occupational aspirations of the boys with the actual occupations of their fathers, however, we find that the group with the highest aspirations is the FC homog group (Table I, row 15). That is, a greater number of the FC homog subjects desire an occupation that is higher socio-economically than that of their fathers. Since the groups are similar with regard to socio-economic status, this fact cannot be attributed to lower status on the part of this group.

Finally, there is no distinctive pattern for the mixed ethnic subjects in their occupational aspirations. Rather it is the FC homog group who appear to want to outdo their fathers more than do any of the other three groups.

In conclusion, the profile of characteristics of the subjects with mixed ethnic parentage is a healthy one in every respect when comparisons are made with groups with homogeneous ethnic backgrounds: they identify with their parents, especially with their fathers, as well as the comparison groups do; they relate themselves to and identify with both ethnic reference groups, this being particularly so for those in a French academic environment; they show no signs of personality disturbances, social alienation, or anxiety, nor do their self-concepts deviate from those of the comparison subjects; they see their parents as giving them relatively more attention and personal interest, and their attitudes towards parents are as favorable as those of the comparison groups; they seek out distinctively affectionate relationships with peers; their general attitudinal orientations are similar to those of the comparison groups while their specific attitudes towards both English and French Canadians are relatively unbiased; the values they receive from their parents show the influence of both ethnic backgrounds as do their achievement orientations which are less extreme than those of the comparison groups. Rather than developing a divided allegiance or repressing one or both aspects of their backgrounds, as has been noted among the offspring of immigrants to America (Child, 1943), they apparently have developed a dual allegiance that permits them to identify with both their parents and to feel that they are wanted as family members. One of the mixed ethnic boys summed up this finding by saying: "I respect both my parents, and I respect their origins." One might argue that the concern of the parents of mixed ethnic adolescents to "include" their children is exaggerated, a symptom of tension and value conflict, but such an interpretation is negated by the apparent success these parents have had in passing on a sense of being wanted. There are, however, many features of this pattern of results that need further study.

The profile sketch given above is more pronounced for the mixed ethnic subjects who are part of the French-Canadian high school environment. These young people may be more susceptible to the English-Canadian culture than those attending English-Canadian schools would be to French-Canadian culture because of the Canadian cultural tug of war which seems, at least until recently, to be controlled by the more powerful and prestigious English-Canadian communities (see Lambert, 1967).

Two general modes of adjustment to their mixed ethnic backgrounds became apparent. In one case, these young men incorporate both ethnic streams of influence, which are either modified by the parents before they are passed on to their children, or are tempered by the adolescents themselves, so that they are less extreme than those represented by either of the major reference groups. This amalgamation or tempering possibility is inferred from the tendency for the two ethnically mixed groups to distinguish themselves from the two homogeneous groups in certain instances, e.g., their unbiased ethnic identifications, their perceptions of parents as being inclusive, their favorable attitudes towards both English and French Canadians, or their less extreme achievement values. In the other case, they show a tendency to adapt their views according to the predominant features of the academic-cultural environment they find themselves in; this form of adjustment is inferred from the tendency of the mixed ethnic groups to line up with the respective homogeneous groups that attend high school with them, e.g., their choices of the traits they plan to pass on to their own children, the personality traits they see as undesirable, and their judgments of the relative attractiveness of English-Canadian or French-Canadian girls. Further research is needed to explain why either academic environment or mixed ethnic background has the greater influence in certain comparisons and not in others. It now becomes important, too, to understand why some mixed ethnic families decide on French or English schooling since this factor does play so influential a role in the types of adjustments made.

NOTES

This research was supported by grants from the Canada Council to W. E. Lambert and from the Defence Research Board of Canada, Grant Number 9401-10.

[1] Still the pattern of family visiting for the FC mixed group was similar to that of the FC homog group. In fact, visiting patterns appear to be related to the language of the school attended because both subgroups of boys attending English-language schools significantly more often ($\chi^2 = 23.34$, $p < .001$) indicated that their parents spent more time visiting friends than relatives in contrast to both groups of boys attending the French-language schools who reported that their parents spent more time visiting relatives than friends.

[2] The group overlap coefficient is defined as follows: "For each response that is given by both groups, the fraction of *S*s in each

group who gave the response is found and the smaller of the two fractions is taken as the Common Fraction. The sum of the Common Fractions is the Group Overlap Coefficient" (Rosenzweig, 1964, p. 60).

[3] The fact that all four means fall slightly on the authoritarian and ethnocentric side of the neutral points may well be due to the religious background of the *S*s. It has been informally noted in previous research employing the F and E scales that Catholic high school and college students typically score comparatively high on these scales, Robert C. Gardner noting the fact with samples of students in western Canada and both Gardner and Lambert noting it with Quebec students. If valid, this factor would, perhaps as an artifact, raise all scores and reduce intergroup differences.

REFERENCES

Adorno, T. W., Frenkel-Brunswick, E., Levinson, D. J., and Sanford, R. N. The authoritarian personality, New York: John Wiley, 1964.

Blishen, B. R. The construction and use of an occupational scale, In B. R. Blishen, L. E. Jones, K. O. Naegele, J. Porter, eds., Canadian society, Toronto: Macmillan, 1961, pp. 477-85.

Child, I. L. Italian or American? The second generation in conflict, New Haven: Yale University Press, 1943.

Christie, R., Havel, J., and Seidenberg, B. Is the F scale irreversible? Journal of Abnormal and Social Psychology, 1958, 56, 142-59.

De Jocas, Y., and Rocher, G. Inter-generational mobility in the province of Quebec, In B. R. Blishen, L. E. Jones, K. O. Naegele, and J. Porter, eds., Canadian society, Toronto: Macmillan, 1961, pp. 466-77.

Ferguson, George A. Statistical analysis in psychology and education, New York: McGraw-Hill, 1966.

Gordon, A. I. Intermarriage, Boston: Beacon Press, 1966.

Jones, F. E., and Lambert, W. E. Attitudes toward immigrants in a Canadian community, Public Opinion Quarterly, 1959, 23, 537-46.

Katz, P., and Zigler, E. Self-image disparity: a developmental approach, Journal of Personality and Social Psychology, 1967, 5, 186-95.

Lambert, W. E. A social psychology of bilingualism, Journal of Social Issues, 1967, 22, 91-109.

Lambert, W. E., and Gardner, R. C. A study of the roles of attitudes and motivation in second language learning, United States Office of Education, 1962 (mimeo).

__________ Cultural comparisons of boys' occupational aspirations, British Journal of Social and Clinical Psychology, 1963, 2, 55-65.

Lambert, W. E., and Klineberg, O. Children's views of foreign peoples: a cross-national study, New York: Appleton, 1967.

Lambert, W. E., and Moore, Nancy. Word-association responses: comparisons of American and French monolinguals with Canadian monolinguals and bilinguals, Journal of Personality and Social Psychology, 1966, 3, 313-20. [In this volume, pp. 197-211.]

Lazowick, L. M. On the nature of identification, Journal of Abnormal and Social Psychology, 1955, 51, 175-83.

McCloskey, N., and Schaar, J. H. Psychological dimensions of anomy, American Sociological Review, 1965, 30, 14-40.

Park, R. E. Personality and cultural conflict, Publication of the American Sociological Society, 1931, 25, 95-110.

Peal, Elizabeth, and Lambert, W. E. The relation of bilingualism to intelligence, Psychological Monographs: General and Applied, No. 546, 1962. [In this volume, pp. 111-59.]

Roberts, A. H., and Rokeach, M. Anomie, authoritarianism, and prejudice: a replication, American Journal of Sociology, 1956, 61, 355-8.

Rosen, B. C. Race, ethnicity, and the achievement syndrome, American Sociological Review, 1959, 24, 47-60.

Rosenzweig, M. R. Word associations of French workmen: comparisons with associations of French students and American workers and students, Journal of Verbal Learning and Verbal Behavior, 1964, 3, 57-69.

Saucier, J. F. Psychiatric aspects of interethnic marriages, Montreal: McGill University, 1965 (mimeo).

Schutz, W. C. *FIRO: A three-dimensional theory of interpersonal behavior*, New York: Rinehart, 1958.

Srole, Leo. Social integration and certain corollaries: an explanatory study, *American Sociological Review*, 1956, 21, 709-16.

Szabo, D., Goyer, F., and Gagné, D. Valeurs morales et délinquance juvenile, *L'Annèe sociologique*, 1964, 75-100.

Wessel, B. B. *An ethnic survey of Woonsocket, Rhode Island*, Chicago: University of Chicago Press, 1931.

18 Psychological Aspects of Motivation in Language Learning

One can very profitably view the learning of a second language in much the same way that Mowrer views the child's learning of the first language.[1] Mowrer's fascinating "autistic" theory differs in an essential manner from Skinner's more mechanical approach to the problem.[2] For Mowrer, word learning for talking birds and for children takes place when the sounds of words have come to carry a reinforcement power in themselves so that the learner wants to produce words. The sounds become reinforcing agents themselves through the association the infant makes between the nice qualities of certain people and the words they use. First language learning is motivated by basic desires to communicate with, to become similar to, and to belong with valued people in one's environment, first family members and then others in the linguistic community. In other terms, the infant language learner has to identify with language users to the extent that he wants to be like them in many ways, and this includes learning their code and the distinctive ways they use their code. It is not a simple case of a child emitting words and immediately being reinforced, as Skinner seems to suggest. Instead, Mowrer argues that the word sounds used by valued people in the infant's life space take on a reinforcing quality of their own and this is sufficient to bring the words into existence and to serve as the base for the acquisition of the more complex features of the language.

In similar fashion, several of us who have considered the matter carefully have come to believe that the successful learner of a second language also has to identify with members of another linguistic-cultural group and be willing to take on very subtle aspects of their behavior, including their distinctive style of speech and their language. We also feel that there are various types of motivation which can underlie his willingness to be like another group's members. For example, the learner may find that in mastering certain features of another social group's language he has made the crucial step in becoming an acculturated part of a second linguistic-cultural community. Advancing toward bi-culturality in this sense may be viewed in some cases as a broadening experience. If pushed beyond a point, however, this progress in a second language could engender a feeling of not comfortably belonging in one social group or the other. With a different orientation, a language learner may look on his learning task as making him better educated or more cultured, or as equipping him with a useful skill for his future occupation, with little regard for the culture or the people represented by the other language. In other circumstances, one might consider learning another group's language as a means of getting on the "inside" of a cultural community in order to exploit, manipulate or control, with clearly personal ends in mind.

A series of studies carried out at McGill has been concerned with such topics, and various findings have increased our confidence in a social-psychological theory of language learning. This theory, in brief, holds that an individual successfully acquiring a second language gradually adopts various aspects of behavior which characterize members of another linguistic-cultural group. The learner's ethnocentric tendencies, his attitudes toward the other group, and his orientation toward language learning are believed to regulate or control his motivation to learn and ultimately his success or failure in mastering the new language. His orientation is thought of as being "instrumental" in form if the purposes of language study reflect the more utilitarian value of linguistic achievement, such as getting ahead in one's occupation if he masters the language, and "integrative" if the student is oriented to learn more about the other cultural community as if he desired to belong to or become a potential member of the other group. It is also argued that some may be anxious to learn another language as a means of being accepted in another cultural group because of dissatisfactions experienced in their own culture while others may be as interested in another culture as they are in their own. However, the more proficient one becomes in a second language, the more he may find that his place in his original membership group is modified at the same time as the other linguistic-cultural group becomes something more than a reference group for him.

It may, in fact, become a second and competing membership group for him. Depending upon the compatibility of the two cultures, he may experience feelings of chagrin or regret as he loses ties in one group, mixed with the fearful anticipation of entering a relatively new group. The concept "anomie" first proposed by Durkheim,[3] and more recently extended by Srole,[4] and Williams,[5] refers to the feelings of social uncertainty or dissatisfaction which we believe characterize serious students of a second language and those who become bilingual.

Perhaps the elements of this theory and their implications for language teachers will become more meaningful if we examine briefly the basic research studies that gave the theory its present form.

The first studies[6] were carried out in 1959 through 1961 with English-speaking Montreal high school students studying French. They were all carefully tested for their language learning aptitude and verbal intelligence as well as their attitudes toward French people and the French Canadian community, the intensity of their motivation to learn French, and their orientations toward learning the language. Our measure of motivational intensity is conceptually similar to Jones'[7] index of interest in learning a language that he found to be important for successful language learning among Welsh students. A factor analysis indicated that aptitude and intelligence formed one factor that was statistically independent of a second comprising indices of motivation, type of orientation toward language and social attitudes toward French-Canadians. Furthermore, the measure of achievement in French used (final overall grade) was reflected equally prominently in both factors. This means that achievement in French was dependent upon both aptitude and intelligence on the one hand, and a sympathetic orientation toward the other linguistic-cultural group on the other. The orientation apparently sustained a strong motivation to learn the other group's language and led to better performance in French at the end of the year. It was also made clear that students with an integrative orientation were the more successful in language learning when compared with those more instrumentally oriented. (We have not concentrated on the manipulative orientation mentioned earlier and we are aware that a certain degree of error in classifying students may occur until attention is given to this form of orientation).

In summary, this study indicated that two quite independent factors are important in learning a second language: a) a general language-learning aptitude, and b) a favorable attitude toward the other linguistic group, coupled with a sympathetic orientation toward learning that group's language. The fact that these determinants are independent means, first, that they do not correlate (thus, knowing a student's aptitude score does not help one predict his attitude or motivations), and second, that a person without aptitude can learn the language well if the attitude and motivation are strong, at the same time as a person with unfavorable attitudes and motivation can do well if his aptitude is strong. If follows, too, that a person with both aptitude and the proper orientation will be particularly likely to do well in the study of a second language.

Robert Gardner's 1960 study confirmed and extended these findings. Using a larger sample of English-Canadian high school students and incorporating various measures of French achievement, the same two independent factors were revealed, and again both were related to French achievement. But whereas aptitude and achievement were especially important for those French skills stressed in school training (e.g., grammar and vocabulary), the acquisition of audio-lingual skills was determined primarily by measures of the attitudes, motivation and orientations of the students. Further evidence indicated that the component elements that make up the integrative motive are very similar in nature to those that form the democratic or non-authoritarian ideological syndrome, and this finding opens up the possibility that basic personality dispositions may be involved in language learning efficiency.

In the 1960 study, information had also been gathered from parents about their orientation toward the French-Canadian community. These data suggested that the student's orientation toward the other group is developed within the family. That is, students with an integrative disposition to learn French had parents who also were integrative and sympathetic to the French community. The students' orientations, however, were not related to their parents' skill in French nor to the number of French acquaintances the parents had, indicating that the integrative motive is less likely due to having experience with the French language at home than to some favorable, family-wide attitudinal disposition toward French-Canadian people.

A study by Moshe Anisfeld and myself[8] extended the experimental procedure to samples of Jewish high school students studying Hebrew at parochial schools in Montreal. They were administered tests measuring their orientation toward learning Hebrew and their attitudes toward the Jewish culture and community, as well as tests of verbal intelligence and language aptitude. These tests were compared with measures of achievement in the Hebrew language at the end of the school year. The results support the generalization that both intellectual capacity and attitudinal orientation affect success in learning Hebrew. However, whereas intelligence and linguistic aptitude are relatively stable predictors of success, the attitudinal measures vary from one social-class district of the city to another. A measure of a Jewish student's desire to become more acculturated into the Jewish tradition did relate to achievement in Hebrew for children in a district of Montreal where Jewish parents were concerned with problems of keeping Jewish traditions while adjusting to their own middle-class community. In another district, made up of Jews more recently arrived in North America who were clearly of a lower socio-economic class level, the measure of desire for Jewish acculturation did not correlate with achievement in Hebrew whereas measures of pro-Semitic attitudes or pride in being Jewish did. Thus, the interplay of aptitude, attitudes and motivation was more complex but very similar when the other language being learned was Hebrew.

More recently, students undergoing an intensive course in French at McGill's French Summer School were examined for changes in attitude during the study period.[9] These were mainly American University students or secondary school language teachers who referred themselves more to the European-French than the American-French community in their orientations to language learning. In this study, we found that feelings of anomie increased markedly during the course of study. As students progressed to the point that they said they "thought" and even dreamed in French, their feelings of anomie, as measured by Srole's scale of anomie, also increased. At the same time, they began, for the first time, to use English in various situations even though they had pledged to use only French for the six-week period. The pattern suggests that these advanced students of French experienced feelings of social upset when they concentrated on and commenced to really master the second language and, as a consequence, we hypothesize they developed stratagems, such as reverting to English, to control or minimize such feelings.

In another study[10] we compared 10-year old monolingual and bilingual students on measures of intelligence. Of relevance here is the fact that bilingual children have markedly more favorable attitudes towards both language communities than do the monolingual children. Furthermore, the parents of bilingual children hold the same strongly sympathetic attitudes toward both groups in contrast to the parents of monolingual children, suggesting to us that the development of linguistic skills in a second language, extending to the point of bilingualism, are controlled or at least influenced by family-shared attitudes toward the other linguistic-cultural community.

The most recent investigation has been conducted this year (1968) outside of Quebec in a mainly English-Canadian Ontario community by H. J. Feenstra and R. C. Gardner.[11] Their results, based on tests of grade 9 high school students' performance in French, also reveal the importance of attitudes toward the other language group for the degree of achievement reached in learning that group's language. They also found a direct interplay between parents' attitudes towards French Canadians and their children's achievement in learning French.

These findings are consistent and reliable enough to be of more general interest. Because of the possible practical as well as theoretical significance of this approach, it seemed appropriate to test its applicability in a cultural setting other than the bi-cultural Quebec or Ontario. Accordingly, another investigation was conducted in various regional settings in the United States, two of them also bi-cultural and a third more representative of "typical" urban American cities.[12] The bi-cultural settings permitted us to examine the role of attitudes working two ways: attitudinal dispositions of American students toward linguistic minority groups in their immediate environment, and the attitudes of members of the cultural minority group toward the general American culture about them. In this study, we were interested in comparing the importance for second language learning of intellectual ability and language learning aptitude, on the one hand, and social attitudes toward the "other" language group and motivation to learn the language, on the other. Our attention was first directed to an examination of how these variables affect the language learning of American students who come from homes where only English is spoken. In order to compare the results of the U.S. investigation with earlier studies carried out with English-speaking students learning French in Montreal, we chose two samples of students from bicultural communities in Louisiana and Maine. A third sample of students was drawn from the public school system of Hartford, Connecticut. The Connecticut setting did not have a distinctive sub-community of Franco-Americans in its immediate environment comparable to those in the Louisiana and Maine districts studied. Thus, the Hartford students would not be expected to have a distinctive linguistic-cultural group in their immediate experience toward which favorable or unfavorable attitudes would have developed through direct contact.

As in our earlier work, a large battery of tests was administered to these students early in the year, and, near the end of the year, tests of achievement in French were given, and grades in French were obtained from teachers. The tests were intercorrelated and factor analyzed. The results were similar to those of the Montreal studies: in the American case, two independent factors also underlie the development of skill in learning a second language, an intellectual capacity and an appropriate attitudinal orientation toward the other language group coupled with a strong motivation to learn the language.

The second phase of the investigation was concerned with the roles of language-learning aptitude, motivation and attitudes in the linguistic development of potentially bilingual Franco-American students—those coming from homes in which French was the major language spoken. Two samples of Franco-American high school students were chosen from the Louisiana and Maine settings. The analysis indicated that the young person's attitudes toward his own linguistic group and the American culture around him influence his progress in mastering both English and French. If he faces and resolves his cultural conflict so that he can view himself as both American and French he will develop good skill in both languages. If he resolves the conflict by emphasizing either his French or American heritage he reflects this form of adjustment by developing a dominance in one language at the expense of the other. Incidentally, when the attitudes of the Franco-American students from Louisiana were compared with those from Maine, it became clear that the community studied in Maine enjoys a comparatively dynamic and distinctively French existence while the Louisiana group seemed to be more rapidly merging into the general American society. For example, the Maine Franco-Americans show a decided superiority over the American students in their French skills whereas the Louisiana Franco-Americans show little or no advantage in French over American students.

Furthermore, when we examined the stereotypes both American and Franco-American students hold of French people, we found that all groups except one have generally unfavorable stereotypes of French people. Again, the Franco-Americans from Maine were the exception, and they gave evidence of a basic pride in their French heritage. The consequences of holding negative stereotypes toward the very people whose language one is supposed to learn became apparent in this analysis.

We also looked into the various values American students bring to the language-learning process. The results indicated that achievement in foreign language training is not the central goal for most American students. Rather it is apparently incidental to the more challenging goal of trying to find and prepare one's way for the future. Intelligence coupled with a value placed on achievement are major determiners of success in most school work, including the study of language. This, I feel, represents an interesting challenge for language teachers because if they could get below the achievement motive or harness it to more appropriate motives, the whole business of teaching languages might take on a quite different complexion.

What might be the significance of these findings for teachers of second or foreign languages? As I see it, both the results and the structure of the investigations described should be instructive for many language teachers who, because of pressures on their time to teach large numbers of students the routine introduction to a foreign language, may lose sight of the fascinating events taking place within the minds and the emotions of their students. We social psychologists have already won over a small number of enthusiastic converts from the language teaching profession who saw some value and some enjoyment in taking part in research of the type outlined here. Because of their special skills and experience they contribute a great deal to what little progress has been so far made in attempts to unravel the processes of teaching and learning foreign languages. We are still proselytizing, mind you, because there is so much yet to be known. For those who have to stay at the front lines with students, perhaps they will see somewhat more clearly the significance of their role as interest stimulators, convincing students that foreign language is much more than maze learning, that it is the code of a different and interesting social group. The challenge is to go beyond the mere achievement motives of students and to link language teaching with more appropriate and more productive motives.

NOTES

Reprinted from the May 1969 Issue of the Bulletin of the Illinois Foreign Language Teachers Association. This is a somewhat shortened version of the paper presented by Professor Lambert at the Fourth Southern Conference on Language Teaching in New Orleans, Feb. 22-24, 1968.

[1]Mowrer, O. H. Learning theory and the symbolic processes. New York: Wiley, 1960.

[2]Skinner, B. F. Science and human behavior. New York: Macmillan, 1953.

[3]Durkheim, E. Le suicide. Paris: Alcan, 1897.

[4]Srole, L. Social dysfunction, personality and social distance attitudes. Paper given at the American Sociological Society, 1951, Chicago, Illinois.

[5]Williams, R. M. American Society. New York: Knopf, 1952.

[6]Gardner, R. C., and Lambert, W. E. Motivational variables in second-language acquisition. Canadian Journal of Psychology, 1959, 13, 266-272; Gardner, R. C. Motivational variables in second-language acquisition. Unpublished Ph.D. thesis, McGill University, Redpath Library, 1960.

[7]Jones, W. R. Attitude towards Welsh as a second language. A preliminary investigation. British Journal of Educational Psychology, 1949, 19, 44-52; Jones, W. R. Attitude towards Welsh as a

second language. A further investigation. British Journal of Educational Psychology, 1950, 20, 117-132.

[8] Anisfeld, M., and Lambert, W. E. Social and psychological variables in learning Hebrew. Journal of Abnormal and Social Psychology, 1961, 63, 524-529.

[9] Lambert, W. E., Gardner, R. C., Barik, H. C. and Tunstall, K. Attitudinal and cognitive aspects of intensive study of a second language. Journal of Abnormal and Social Psychology, 1963, 66, 358-368.

[10] Peal, Elizabeth, and Lambert, W. E. The relation of bilingualism to intelligence, Psychological Monographs, 1962, No. 546, 76, 27, 1-23.

[11] Feenstra, H. J. Aptitude and motivation in second-language acquisition, Unpublished Ph.D. dissertation. The University of Western Ontario, London, Ontario, 1967.

[12] Lambert, W. E., Gardner, R. C., Olton, R., and Tunstall, K. A study of the roles of attitudes and motivation in second-language learning. Mimeographed, McGill University, 1962.

19 Psychological Studies of the Interdependencies of the Bilingual's Two Languages

For some time now a rotating group of students and I have been interested in the bilingual person's capacity to use one or the other of his two languages efficiently, that is, with surprisingly little interference from the other. When one thinks for a moment about the psychology and neurophysiology of this capacity, its complexity and its intrigue become clear. How is it that the bilingual is able to "gate out" or, in some fashion, set aside a whole integrated linguistic system while functioning with a second one, and a moment later, if the situation calls for it, switch the process, activating the previously inactive system and setting aside the previously active one? Both linguists and psychologists have been attracted to this phenomenon because an understanding of it would likely shed light on various aspects of bilingual behavior, linguistic, psychological, and neurological. In fact, Uriel Weinreich[1] suggests that any comprehensive or useful theory of bilingualism must account for this "effectively separated use of the two languages," as well as for the interferences that take place between the two languages. We have attempted to contribute to the psychology of such a theory by analyzing different features of the bilingual person's skills. My plan for this paper is to review and discuss these research efforts, giving more attention to ongoing studies than to earlier ones, and yet making it evident that the earlier ones gave us the experience needed to make what we feel is some progress in this field.

In 1954, Susan Ervin and Charles Osgood[2] developed several notions about bilingualism which suggested to us that language-acquisition contexts may contribute importantly to the interdependencies of the bilingual's two languages. Ervin and Osgood believed that a bilingual could develop either a "compound" or a "coordinate" relation between his two languages, depending on how he acquired the two. The compound relation would apparently be engendered through experiences in mixed acquisition contexts, for instance in settings where the same interlocutors used two languages interchangeably to refer to the same environmental events. A coordinate relation would be developed through experience in two distinctive linguistic settings where interlocutors rarely switched languages. They suggested that translation equivalents would have a more similar meaning and would likely have a more common neurological representation for compound bilinguals than they would for coordinate bilinguals who, presumably because of the distinctiveness of their language-acquisition contexts, would be more likely to develop two functionally separated systems of meanings, one attached to each of their languages.

We have considered the differences between compound and coordinate bilingualism more as an interesting contrast than as a rigid typology. Certainly a typical sample of the bilinguals we have worked with would distribute themselves along a continuum of compoundness-coordinateness, and one should only expect to find differences of a comparative sort in the behavior of selected groups of compound and coordinate bilinguals. It is also probable that any particular bilingual will develop a compound relation between his languages for certain of his experiences and a coordinate relation for other experiences. Nevertheless, if the underlying theory is correct, there are many interesting comparisons that should emerge when groups selected to represent the extremes of the continuum are contrasted. Furthermore, those comparisons should satisfy the psychologist's interest in learning as well as his curiosity about the neurophysiology of mediating processes.

THE EARLIER STUDIES

In our first studies[3] we argued that if there was anything to these notions about compound and coordinate bilinguals, then extended experience in separated language-acquisition contexts should enhance the functional separation of the bilingual's two languages, while experience in mixed contexts should reduce the functional separation of the two language systems. More specifically, we sought out groups of bilinguals with different acquisition histories and tested them, anticipating that those with experience in separated contexts would give evidence of (1) comparatively greater semantic distinctiveness between a word in one language and its translation equivalent in the other, (2) more associative independence of translation equivalents in their two languages, and (3) relatively less facility in translating.

In general the results confirmed the first two predictions. It was found that semantic differences of translation equivalents, measured with semantic rating scales, were greater for coordinate than for compound bilinguals. Then, in recalling a list of words, compound bilinguals profited more from rehearsing in advance with the translation equivalents of these words, indicating dependencies across languages which did not appear with coordinate bilinguals. In the third instance, there was no difference between the groups in speed of translation. The pattern of results suggested that both groups could move from one language to the other equally well when directed to, but that compound bilinguals had a stronger proclivity to do so in situations where it was not required, possibly because, for them, there was greater semantic similarity for words in the two languages.

These findings prompted a further question. We had been reading about aphasia among bilinguals, some of whom would apparently lose the functioning of only one of their languages following a cerebral "insult" or accident of one sort or another, while others would lose complete or partial facility with both languages. Since coordinate bilinguals were presumed to have more functionally separated neural structures underlying their two languages than compound bilinguals do, we should expect that brain damage leading to aphasia would be more likely to affect both languages of the compound bilingual and produce a more selective disturbance in one or the other of the languages of the coordinate. We[4] made contact with a number of bilingual aphasics in the Montreal area and compared their postaphasic linguistic abilities and handicaps with those described in the published medical reports of bilingual aphasics from other parts of the world.

The results of this exploratory study were very encouraging in that they supported the theoretical contrast between compound and coordinate forms of bilingualism, although it became very apparent that much more research on the topic is called for before alternate interpretations can be discarded. It was found that patients whose histories suggested that their languages were essentially in a compound relationship showed a generalized aphasic disorder in the sense that both languages were affected by the neurological disturbance. In contrast, patients whose histories fit the coordinate pattern typically showed a more specific language disorder following injury, one language more affected than the other. The trouble here is that we did not have sufficient information about such factors as the extent of brain damage involved, the type of language retraining given during the recovery period, whether it favored one language only, or, in most published cases, the details of actual language loss suffered at the time of the aphasia.

At about the same time, we were investigating the interesting phenomenon of verbal or semantic "satiation," the effects of continuous repetition of a word on its meaning. We had developed a means of measuring these effects based on the rating scales of the "semantic differential,"[5] and had found that the continuous repetition of a word, such as house, would lead to a reliable decrease in the intensity of its connotative meaning. What would happen if a bilingual were given this treatment, and we examined the repetitions's effect on the translation equivalent, say maison, for a French-English bilingual? And, more particularly, would there be more cross-language satiation for compounds than for coordinates, as one would expect? The results[6] were in the predicted direction, in fact a little too much so: the compound bilinguals showed cross-language satiation in meaning, as expected, while the coordinates went to an unanticipated extreme in that the other language equivalents showed a slight generation of meaning. Thus, the groups differed, but certain questions about the coordinates are still unanswered.

While the satiation study increased our confidence in the differences between compounds and coordinates, another investigation conducted about the same time tempered our enthusiasm and made us realize that the matter may be quite complex. In this instance,[7] compound and coordinate bilinguals were asked to read through a mixed series of English and French words and to remember which words functioned as a signal that an electric shock—a jolting one administered to a finger—was to follow. Subjects rapidly learned that the words _verte_ or _boy_, for example, were the critical ones, and when they appeared on a screen, would promptly press a key that, if activated soon enough, would cancel the shock. After these associations were well established, we presented each subject with a new mixed list of words, some of which were the translations of the original "shock" words (e.g., "green" and "garçon"). We expected compounds to be more prompt than coordinates in pressing the shock-release key when these translation equivalents appeared, since cross-language associations (e.g., _green_ and shock) would be more automatically built up from the original association (i.e., _verte_ and shock) for compound bilinguals; however, we found no differences between compounds and coordinates in this instance, which was surprising since most of these subjects were the same as those used in the semantic satiation study where clear differences had been revealed.

We were equally surprised with the outcome of a second study conducted with the same subjects. In this study, each bilingual was asked to memorize a mixed list of English and French words, and, after a waiting period, to read through a longer mixed list made up of some of the original words, some "new" ones, and some _translations_ of the originals. For example, _glove_ and _printemps_ were in the list learned originally, while their translations ("_gant_" and "_springtime_") were on the composite list. Thus, subjects were required to switch languages rapidly in memorizing the list, and they had to remember which words appeared in which language. We expected that compounds would make more "translation" errors in the later recognition tests, confusing, for example, _glove_ with "_gant_," than the coordinates; however, no reliable differences turned up! These studies need to be repeated and carefully reexamined, but until that time we offer the following explanation for our failure to elicit group differences. Both of these procedures required that "errors" be made in storing the originally memorized words, that is, "generalizations" across languages had to occur. We thoroughly believed that such generalization errors would be numerous, that bilinguals, especially compounds, would have difficulty remembering both the words _and_ the languages they represented. Actually there were surprisingly few errors of this sort made in either of these studies. Apparently both types of bilinguals can "tag" a lexical item as belonging to one language or the other with little or no additional mental effort. This fact has recently been made clear in the current studies of bilingual organization in free recall, to be discussed below. These investigations show that bilinguals can store and remember as many items from mixed-language lists as they can from monolingual lists, and translation-type errors are really uncommon. Thus, bilinguals, even compounds, may have no trouble remembering that boy, and not "garçon," was the critical word in the conditioning experiment where vigilance was demanded, even though, judging from the satiation study, cross-linguistic interactions can take place in other situations. The task still before us, of course, is to delineate which situations do encourage, and which do not encourage, such interactions.

CURRENT STUDIES: THE STROOP PROCEDURE

Recently we have tried different approaches to examine the bilingual's capacity to keep his two languages functionally distinct. The difference is that we are now asking general questions about all bilinguals, and the compound-coordinate continuum is examined only as a second step. The question of central interest is: Does the activation of processes in one language system make the other language system inoperative? Penfield and Roberts[8] suggest that there is some type of switching mechanism in the brain which shuts off one linguistic system while the other is in function. Hebb[9] and Milner[10] have also described possible neurological mechanisms that could explain, at one level of generalization, this capacity to "gate out" potentially antagonistic or competing systems. However, before one can neurophysiologize fruitfully about such mechanisms, it is necessary to demonstrate that a real phenomenon exists and to describe its behavioral and psychological characteristics.

To explain this problem, we searched for a procedure that would present the bilingual with a conflict wherein both of his languages would be simultaneously brought into play. We fortunately hit upon the possibility of adapting a procedure, the Stroop Test,[11] which has had a long and interesting history in experimental psychology. This test consists of several large cards on one of which are one hundred small patches made of colored inks or crayons arranged in ten rows with ten patches to a row. A subject is timed while naming the colors as rapidly as possible. A second card includes one hundred common words (such as APPLE, MAN, HOUSE, etc.), each of which is printed in one of several colors, and again the task requirement is to name the crayon colors as fast as possible. On a third card, there are one hundred color words (such as RED, BLUE, ORANGE, etc.) printed with red, blue, brown, and yellow crayons. On this card, a subject would encounter a sequence such as: RED printed in orange ink, followed by BLUE in brown ink, ORANGE in red, BROWN in blue, etc., and he would be asked to name the crayon colors (orange, brown, red and blue) as rapidly as possible. The problem lies in keeping the color words from impinging on the requirement of naming the crayon colors, a very difficult task because the word reading tendency is highly automatized for literate people, and the procedure very compellingly calls into play a decoding process that interferes with the required encoding process. The time taken to work through the interference card is decidedly longest.

We adapted this procedure for use with bilinguals, constructing different sets of three cards for various groups of bilinguals (a French, Hungarian, and German set, for instance), so that the second card would contain common noncolor words (e.g., in French MAISON, GARÇON, PRINTEMPS, etc.), and the third card would contain color words (e.g., in French ROUGE, JAUNE, BLEU, etc.). Subjects were given a battery of ten test cards: the color-patch card was used once for measuring speed of color naming in English and once for measuring speed of color naming in French; the English noncolor-word and color-word cards were used twice, once when the subject named the crayon colors in English and once when he named the colors in French; and the two French cards were used in a similar fashion. The general scheme for English-French bilinguals is outlined in Table I.

Now we can assess the interference caused by simultaneously activating the decoding and encoding processes of the same language or the decoding process in one language and the encoding process of the other language. For example, we would expect more interference in cells 1 and 4, where the encoding and decoding processes of the same language are simultaneously activated (the subject in cell 1 has to say "red," for example, to name the crayon color in which the color word BLUE is printed) than in cells 2 and 3

TABLE 1
The Stroop Paradigm

Response language	Stimulus material				
	English color words	French color words	English noncolor words	French noncolor words	Color patches
English	1	2	5	6	9
French	3	4	7	8	10

where the simultaneously activated decoding and encoding processes involve different languages (in cell 2, for example, the subject must say "red" to name the crayon color in which the color word JAUNE is printed). It is assumed that it is easier to gate out a distractor from the other language than it is to gate one out from the same language, since encoding and decoding processes within a language are likely to be mutually facilitative, thereby providing many opportunities for interference with the Stroop procedure. Furthermore, we would expect the distractors in cells 5 through 8 to be more easily set aside. They could even be processed simultaneously with comparatively less interference. Cells 9 and 10 provide an index of encoding balance, and subjects are chosen who are essentially balanced in speed of color naming in their two languages. These cells also serve as a comparison point, since no verbal materials occur as distractors.

Our first investigations were pilot studies conducted with small samples of balanced bilinguals.[12] The results indicated that bilinguals are unable to shut out the other language. If they are naming colors in French, the English noncolor and color words impinge as much as French ones do, and the interference is clearly evident in the extra time taken for color naming on cards with verbal materials compared to the time taken for control cards of color patches. There is, however, a stepwise progression of interference, clearly occurring more when color words are used as background distractors than when noncolor words are used. Furthermore, subjects revealed that the background language was fully active when working through the color-word cards. Suppose a subject encountered the sequence: ROUGE in yellow, VERT in red, and BLEU in brown, and was required to respond in English with "yellow, red, brown," etc. One of the most common errors in these cross-language tests was to translate the stimulus word from French to English and respond with "yellow, *green, brown," for example. This type of error reveals that the encoding system is dominant at the moment, as though the switch was clearly thrown open for English, but that the other language impinged to the extent of winning out in the choice of the appropriate color name. In other terms, the French decoding process became fused with the English encoding process.

We would have expected, nevertheless, that bilinguals would be better able to shut out distractions from the other language than those from the same language, that is, that cells 2 and 3 in Table 1 would have faster color naming scores than cells 1 and 4. In the preliminary studies, there was no indication that this was so; however, when special conditions were established, the expected interaction between cells 1, 2, 3, and 4 came to light. For these conditions, two groups of German-English bilinguals were used. One group worked with color-word cards on which English and German translation equivalents had very similar phonemic beginnings, such as ROT <u>and</u> RED, or GRÜN and Green. The other group was presented cards with translation equivalents having very dissimilar phonemic beginnings, for example, SCHWARTZ and BLACK, or GELB and YELLOW. It was found that bilinguals can gate out the other language distractors better than same language distractors when the color words (and color names) of the two languages are phonemically dissimilar. Thus, bilinguals apparently need a built-in linguistic mode of demarcation to reduce somewhat the interplay of his two language systems.

We are currently repeating these studies with larger samples of English-French bilinguals, and the results so far available already require some important modifications of the generalizations just made. For this investigation[13] we selected twenty compound and twenty-one coordinate bilinguals who were very evenly balanced in their French and English skills. Our definitions of compound and coordinate were simplified: compound bilinguals were defined as those brought up in a thoroughly bilingual home environment from infancy on, while coordinates were those who had learned their second language at some time after infancy, usually after ten years of age and usually in a setting other than the family.[14]

The results are summarized in Table 2. Note first the marked increase in interference, reflected in increased time scores, from the color-patch to the noncolor-word, to the color-word conditions. Second, note that there is a noticeable difference between compounds and coordinates in the color-word condition. The pattern for the compounds is very similar to that noted in the pilot studies where there is no essential difference between same-language and other-language distractions (cells 2 and 3 are essentially the same as 1 and 4). When tested for significance, the interaction between cells is not significant (testing the difference between differences, $(d_1 - d_2) - (d_3 - d_4)$, $t = 0.70$). On the other hand, the interaction among cells is highly significant for the coordinate bilinguals, the difference between differences produces a $t = 2.88$, significant beyond the 0.01 level. Although these results are exactly in accord with the expectation that coordinates would be better able to gate out the other language than would compounds because of the greater functional segregation of the coordinate's two languages, these findings are not strong enough to give us full confidence on this issue, since an analysis of variance indicates that there is not a statistically significant difference between cell interactions for compound and coordinate groups, even though the interaction in one instance is, by itself, highly significant, and the other, by itself, is clearly not significant. The difference, nevertheless, is very encouraging, suggesting that the coordinate relation between languages, developed through acquisition contexts, permits these bilinguals to encode more easily in one language and set aside the potential distraction that would derive from decoding in the other language, even in this condition where the two processes are so forcibly brought simultaneously into play.

In the third place, the overall analysis indicated that when the results for the compounds and coordinates are combined, the interaction between cells 1, 2, 3, and 4 is highly significant ($p < 0.001$), indicating that bilinguals, particularly the coordinates, are less distracted by the other language decoding process than by same-language decoding. The major trend, however, is still evident: there is an increasing amount of interference from the other language

TABLE 2
Compound-Coordinated Comparisons on the Stroop Test*

Bilingual type	Number of subjects	Response language	Distracting Stimulus				
			English color words	French color words	English noncolor words	French noncolor words	Color patches
Compounds	20	English	1 54.41	2 53.67	5 42.26	6 43.27	9 38.09
		French	3 51.58	4 54.31	7 40.40	8 41.88	10 37.36
Coordinates	21	English	50.95	44.40	38.53	37.17	35.11
		French	48.31	49.16	38.69	38.27	35.08

*Entries are the average times, in seconds, required by subjects to name the colors of a fifty-item Stroop-type card. The number of items was reduced from one hundred to fifty because, in the pilot studies, we noted marked improvement in color naming with practice and we wanted to examine reactions before practice had a leveling effect.

as the distractors change from patches to noncolor words to color words. Thus, it appears that the other language "seeps in," even though it seems to do so less for the coordinate bilinguals. There are, however, many aspects of this question still to be explored.

CURRENT STUDIES: BILINGUAL ORGANIZATION IN FREE RECALL

The investigations[15] I want to discuss now deal with two matters of current psychological interest: the organization of psychological processes, as inferred from subjects' free recall of word lists, and bilingualism. The purpose of the study is to cast light on theoretical concerns in these two research areas by extending the standard ways of studying both the structure of memory and bilingualism.

Research on free recall, in its basic form, requires subjects to read through a list of, for example, thirty or forty words, and to recall its contents in any order. If there are organizational possibilities built into a list, subjects very readily make use of them. For instance, if subsets of words that commonly associate with one another, or that belong to logical categories (e.g., types of trees or names of cities), are randomly distributed through a list, subjects typically congregate these subsets in recall. Even when lists without obvious organizational sets are used, subjects characteristically create a personal system of organization that aids recall. This tendency to congregate items on the basis of some general form of similarity is reminiscent of an associative theme that has run through the whole history of philosophy and psychology. A modern version of this theme has been brought to bear on the strategies people use in tasks requiring memory, and has led to the valuable concept of "chunking."[16] One of the present concerns is the role of chunking in free recall when two forms of organizational possibilities are available to bilingual subjects, one, logical categories, the other, language. The recent research of Kolers [17] suggests that language may be an important organizational schema for bilingual subjects.

We are also interested here in the comparative importance of the associational principle as a means of explaining congregation in free recall. Three research groups are important in this regard: Bousfield,[18] Jenkins and Russell,[19] and Cofer.[20] Bousfield, the pioneer in this research domain, at first believed that the category clustering observed in free recall was likely to be the result of activation of some type of superordinate structure that encompassed the specific instances brought to attention at different points in the list. Jenkins and Russell, however, demonstrated that the associative links among verbal items were sufficient as an explanation of free recall congregations. This simpler interpretation, based on associative strength, or the likelihood of co-occurrence of particular pairs or sets of words in samples of the language, swayed Bousfield and his co-workers, as well as Cofer, to the associationistic view. Recent experiments have reopened the issue, and there is now a lively debate about the importance of associative strength in free recall clustering.[21]

Also of interest are the interdependencies of the bilingual's two languages. The present experiments examine how bilingual subjects go about organizing materials presented to them in bilingual word lists, where, in certain instances, either language or content category, or both, may be utilized as organizational schemas, while in other instances, the two possible schemas are placed in competition. Although the use of bilingual lists is unnatural for bilingual subjects whose linguistic environments are usually systematically unilingual from setting to setting, still the procedure, like the Stroop Test, of bringing the two into play is extremely valuable as a means of examining how both languages affect psychological processes. Parallel experiments were conducted, one using Russian-English bilinguals, the other, French-English bilinguals, in order to have, for purposes of reliability, evidence from more than one pair of languages.

METHOD

Subjects. — The twenty-four French-English bilinguals, twelve male and twelve female, were young adults, all having received schooling in both languages at the elementary and high school levels, and all but two were presently postgraduate students in French. The subjects considered themselves, and were judged by others who knew them well, to be equally skilled in the use of both of their languages.

The twenty-four Russian-English bilinguals, eighteen female and six male, were also young adults, all of Russian origin. Their education from primary school on was in English, although all had attended Russian parochial school one day a week. Seventeen of the twenty-four were Russian language majors at the university level. They all considered themselves to be equally skilled in the audio-lingual use of both languages, although they clearly had much more experience in reading and writing English.

The word lists. —The word lists were constructed on the basis of English, French, and Russian norms of culturally distinctive examples of semantic categories, such as types of fish, men's first names, or types of disease. The (American) English norms of Cohen, Bousfield, and Whitmarsh[22] were considered appropriate for use with Canadian subjects in light of the findings of Lambert and

Moore.[23] New norms were developed, however, for French and Russian, using the procedure of Cohen _et al._ as a model. In one instance, sixty seniors in a French-Canadian high school were asked to write the first four examples that came to mind when the superordinate names for forty-three categories were given them, for example, to list four types of fish. The norms place the examples in order from most to least popular. In the other instance, the responses of twenty-five Russian adults (not those used as subjects) were used to compile the Russian norms.

Experimental design. — Each subject was presented ten forty-item lists, one list at a time, with instructions to remember as many items as possible and to be prepared to recall them with no restrictions as to order. Four of the ten lists contained four different categories with ten words to a category (e.g., ten types of fish, ten male first names, etc.); the other six lists did not include category subsets, that is, each list consisted of forty items, one chosen from each of forty different semantic categories as represented in the norms. These different list types will be referred to as "category lists" and "no-category lists," the latter serving as comparison and control conditions. To counteract primacy and recency effects, three of the six no-category lists came as the first three lists presented to each subject, and three as the last three in the series of ten. The general schema for the design is given in Table 3. Thus, lists 1 and 8 in the design are both no-category lists of forty English items; lists 2 and 9 are similar lists in French. Lists 3 and 10, to be referred to as "mixed," each have twenty English and twenty French items with no built-in categorization possibilities. List 4 is an English list comprising four categories with ten exemplars per category (e.g., ten types of fish) and list 5 is an equivalent French list. Lists 6 and 7 are mixed-language lists, with built-in categories; these are comparable in one respect to the no-category mixed list. The special feature of list 6 is that the twenty items covering two distinct categories with ten examples each are in English, and twenty items covering two additional distinctive categories are in French. In this list there is a _concordance_ between languages and semantic categories in the sense that particular categories are reliably marked or set off by one language or the other. List 7, in contrast, has a _discordance_ between language and semantic categories; each of its four categories has equal numbers of English and French examples (e.g., five types of fish in French and five in English).

TABLE 3
General Experimental Design, French Version*

	No-category lists			Category lists			No-Category lists			
Order	1	2	3	4	5	6	7	8	9	10
Type	English	French	Mixed	English	French	Mixed concordant	Mixed discordant	English	French	Mixed
Total items	40	40	40	40	40	40	40	40	40	40

*Exactly the same design was used for the Russian version.

This design, then, permits one to (1) assess the importance of semantic categories in comparison with a no-category base line in terms of total items recalled and degree of clustering in recall (the pairs of no-category lists coming at the start and at the end of the experimental period are averaged); (2) to determine the influence of mixed language lists by comparing them with unilingual lists in both no-category and category conditions; (3) to examine the combined and separate importance of the linguistic and semantic modes of categorizing in a condition where their concordance might be either facilitative or competitively disruptive, and in a condition where their discordance should be disruptive relative to the other category conditions but possibly facilitative relative to the no-category conditions.

For the no-category lists, each subject was presented six standard lists but the order of presentation was randomized, that is, one subject would receive the lists in the order shown in Table 1, another in the order 9, 8, 10, (5, 6, 7, 4) 1, 3, 2. These lists were made comparable to all others in terms of the popularity frequencies of category examples taken from the category norms. One constraint in the mixed list was that no more than three words in the same language appeared consecutively.

The presentation order of the category lists follows a 4 factorial plan, all possibilities covered with twenty-four subjects. Furthermore, each subject had a different combination of four categories in his lists, out of sixteen categories chosen for our purposes. Constraints in these lists were that (1) no more than three words in one language appeared consecutively (for the two mixed lists); (2) no two items from the same semantic category appeared consecutively after randomization of the list items; (3) for the discordance list, no translations or synonyms between languages within a category were allowed, for example, BLOUSE and BLOUZKA would not both appear as members of the "articles of clothing" category.

Testing procedure. — In order to create a bilingual atmosphere and to avoid a set in one language, subjects were given instructions in one language with a summary review in the other, half of them receiving English first, half French (or Russian) first. They were told in advance that some lists would be unilingual, others mixed, and that after one run through a list, they would be given two minutes for recall of as many items as possible in any order. For the French study, the items were printed on 3 x 5 cards and flipped at intervals of approximately two seconds. Subjects read the words out loud. For the Russian subjects, who were more experienced at reading English, the words were read to them by a perfectly bilingual experimenter at a two-second rate. Subjects repeated the words after the experimenter. Each subject's recall was recorded on tape for two minutes; a three-minute rest followed each recall period.

Response measures. — Measures were taken of (1) the total items correctly recalled, (2) the extent of category clustering, and (3) the extent of language clustering. The total number of words correctly recalled excluded all types of errors and repetitions. Clusters of items fitting the same semantic category were bracketed and counted. In devising a ratio score, we subtracted one from the total number of items congregated, arguing that the first item is really not part of the run. The ratio was the number of items in a category run over the total of all items recalled. Thus, if the subject recalled *floor*, *ceiling*, *door*, *hall* ($r_1 = 3$), followed by *apple*, *lemon*, *pear* ($r_2 = 2$), followed by *knife*, *gun* ($r_3 = 1$), the ratio would be 6 (i.e., 3 + 2 + 1) over 9 or 0.67. For the mixed language lists, a similar ratio was devised for clusters of same language responses, and the sum of separate language clusters was divided by the total of items recall. For example, the recall *fox*, *rabbit*, *turnip*, *bear*, *mouse* ($r_1 = 4$), followed by *pomme*, *citron* ($r_2 = 1$), would become 5 (i.e., 4 + 1) over 7 or 0.71. This ratio is independent of the amount recalled, and it gives more credit than usual clustering methods for longer runs even when the total number of items clustered is the same, that is, the usual methods would give equal credit to four two-item clusters as to two four-item clusters, whereas this method highlights the longer runs, in this example 6 versus 4.

Error Analysis. — Attention was given to two types of errors only: (1) *category intrusions*, items belonging to an appropriate category but not appearing in the actual word list, and (2) *translation* equivalents, semantically correct translations of actual list items. When both these errors occurred in the flow of recall, it was decided that they would not break up (nor, of course, contribute to) the category or language run in which they might be embedded.

Group Mean Comparisons, Total Items Recalled

French Study (Overall F test, 36.86; $p < 0.001$)

	No-category lists[a]			Category lists			
	English	French	Mixed	English	French	Concordant	Discordant
Mean Number Items Recalled (from 40)	10.83	12.65	10.88	19.17	18.21	18.67	15.50

Comparisons: English (no-category) vs. French (no-category)[b]; French (no-category) vs. Mixed[c]; English (category) vs. Discordant[d]; French (category) vs. Discordant[d]; Concordant vs. Discordant[d]; Mixed vs. Discordant[d].

Russian Study (Overall F test, 41.22; $p < 0.001$)

	No-category lists[a]			Category lists			
	English	Russian	Mixed	English	Russian	Concordant	Discordant
Mean Number	12.08	12.50	11.40	20.92	17.75	19.04	15.13

Comparisons: English (category) vs. Russian (category)[d]; English (category) vs. Concordant[c]; English (category) vs. Discordant[d]; Russian (category) vs. Discordant[d]; Concordant vs. Discordant[d]; Mixed vs. Discordant[d].

[a] Based on two lists.
[b] This comparison just misses significance at the 0.05 level.
[c] Significant at the 0.05 level; Newman-Keuls test of multiple-group comparisons (B. Winer, *Statistical Principles in Experimental Design* [New York, 1962]).
[d] Significant at the 0.01 level.

TABLE 5

Group Mean Comparisons, Category Clustering

French Study (Overall $\underline{F}$ test, 3.1999; $\underline{p} < 0.05$)

	Category lists			
	English	French	Concordant	Discordant
Mean category clustering ratio	0.61	0.62	0.62	0.52
	/			/*
		/		/*
			/	/*

Russian Study (Overall $\underline{F}$ test, 8.65; $\underline{p} < 0.01$)

	Category lists			
	English	Russian	Concordant	Discordant
Mean category clustering ratio	0.62	0.60	0.59	0.45
	/			/*
		/		/*
			/	/*

*Significant at the 0.01 level; Newman-Keuls test of multiple-group comparisons.

RESULTS AND DISCUSSION

The major findings are summarized in Tables 4 through 7. Considering first Table 4, it is evident that the greater possibilities for organization available in the category lists, compared to the no-category lists, have a general and marked facilitative effect on recall, and this fact is true of both the French and Russian versions of the experiment, with their procedural idiosyncrasies. This outcome was certainly expected in light of a large accumulation of research on categorization and is to be viewed as strong supportive evidence. Nevertheless, there are important variations among conditions in the

TABLE 6
Group Mean Comparisons, Language Clustering

French Study (Overall F test, 43.03; $p < 0.001$)

	No category, Mixed	Concordant	Discordant
Mean language clustering ratio	0.49	0.73	0.47
	/________	________/*	
		/________	________/*

Russian Study (Overall F test, 33.45; $p < 0.001$)

	No category, Mixed	Concordant	Discordant
Mean language clustering ratio	0.42	0.71	0.45
	/________	________/*	
		/________	________/*

*Significant at the 0.01 level; Newman-Keuls test of multiple-group comparisons.

two major variants of the experiment, that is, the category and no-category comparison.

With regard to the no-category conditions, it is of interest that the mixed list was as well recalled as the unilingual ones for the Russian version and partly so for the French. (One discrepant result is examined separately below.) This finding confirms the results of Kolers' experiment, one that was analogous to the no-category division of the present study. Kolers also found that bilingual subjects recalled mixed lists of English and French monosyllables as well as they recalled unilingual lists. From the perspective of the person who is clumsy in his command of a foreign language, this facility of bilinguals with mixed lists is surprising. It appears, however, that the experienced bilingual makes use of the difference in languages as just some distinctive feature of words and is not hindered in any way by storing and retrieving words according to the appropriate language,

TABLE 7
Group Totals, Selected Error Types*

	French Study				
	No-category lists		Category lists		
	Mixed	English	French	Concordant	Discordant
Categorical intrusions	. . . .	6	12	6	20
Translation equivalents	7	. . . .	. . . .	3	17
	Russian Study				
	No-category lists		Category lists		
	Mixed	English	Russian	Concordant	Discordant
Categorical intrusions	. . . .	6	7	13	10
Translation equivalents	7	. . . .	. . . .	3	34

*Entries are total occurrences for each group of twenty-four subjects.

much as a monolingual would distinguish nouns from adjectives in a list without disturbing recall.[24] Furthermore, the bilingual may find that the language variations act as distinctive markers or "tags"[25] that help differentiate list items, thereby aiding recall. The fact that the mixed lists were no better recalled may be due to a memory limit reached in this study; with another research design, working below such a limit, one might find that the mixed lists would then be better recalled than unilingual ones.

We set aside for separate comment the finding that the English-French bilinguals showed a stronger capacity to store and retrive French, in contrast to English, list items. One might view this difference merely as an indicant of the French dominance of these bilingual subjects, but it actually signifies something more.

First, Kolers also noted that unilingual lists of French monosyllables were better recalled than comparable lists in English, even for subjects whose language histories suggest an English dominance. Kolers argued that there might be more lexical and phonemic distinctiveness among French than English words and that this phenomenon might account for the difference. This, or some alternative explanation, becomes more interesting in the light of the present reoccurrence of this difference, this time with real French words, especially since no difference of this sort is apparent in the Russian version of the experiment. However, note also in Table 4 that when the same subjects turn to processing the category list items there is then a clear equivalance of English and French capacity and a very pronounced English dominance for the Russian-English subjects. The matter of assessing bilingual balance or dominance is of considerable current interest.[26] In this instance, one would conclude from the no-category conditions that the English-French bilinguals are dominant in French and the English-Russian are balanced in skills, while from the category list evidence he would conclude that the English and French skills are balanced and the other group's skill in Russian is inferior. Since lexical and phonemic distinctiveness should be as great in the category conditions as in the no-category case, these data, taken as a pattern, cast some doubt on the adequacy of Kolers' explanation. One can, however, view this pattern from another perspective. The demands made on a subject in the category condition, where he must have the capacity in both of his languages to mentally reshuffle and organize list items according to semantic categories, are quite different from those made on him in the no-category condition: there he must simply store and hold items in rote fashion, encountering difficulties when he tries, within the time limits of stimulus presentation, to organize along purely subjective lines. Assuming that the more demanding case provides the more revealing measure of dominance or balance, the results for the category condition are then seen as fully consistent with the linguistic experiences of both groups of subjects, the French group being balanced in all aspects of language skill, and the Russian being balanced only in the audio-lingual aspects of their two languages. Thus, if consideration is given to the pattern of results, we encounter a potentially important distinction between the simple storage demands made on subjects in one instance, and the more complex demands for processing and organizing verbal materials made in the other. This distinction has relevance for the measurement of bilingual balance. Still, further research is needed to explain why French lists are particularly easily recalled. It may turn out that some factor like phonemic distinctiveness has its main effect in instances where less demands of a cognitive nature are made, but is overshadowed by the organizational requirements of complex cases; it is very likely, though, that this puzzle will turn out to be more complex than that.

If we now examine the concordant and discordant lists, we realize that different types of mixed lists affect the bilingual's recall in particular ways. Turning again to Table 4, it is very evident, in both the French and Russian versions of the study, that the discordant lists are the least well recalled of all category lists, even when credit is given for translation errors, but that they are still much more easily recalled than are any of the no-category lists. The intermediary position of these lists indicates that placing language and semantic content in competition, as is done in discordant lists, depresses recall in one sense, but, in another sense, does not depress it seriously. Tables 5, 6, and 7 provide three clues about the subjects' approach to the discordant list: (1) The subjects are handicapped in their capacity to organize items according to their membership in particular semantic categories, that is, the discordant lists are always markedly lower than others in terms of category clustering (see Table 5); (2) yet they make as much use of language variations as an organizational schema as they do when recalling the mixed no-category lists (Table 6); (3) at the same time, they make many translation and intrusion errors (Table 7). These findings suggest that the process of activating a superordinate category (e.g., fruit) is not as easily accomplished when bilingual examples (e.g., APPLE, CITRON, ORANGE, PAMPLEMOUSSE) are used to prime it as when unilingual examples are available for this purpose.

Although handicapped, relatively, subjects can still organize to their advantage, even when forced to use bilingual examples, as is evident when one compares their recall in the discordant and no-category conditions. Thus, although the linguistic mixture in the categories of the discordant list has affected the capacity to categorize, still the presence of categories is a major aid in organizing for recall (compare discordant with mixed no-category lists, Table 4.)

What is the nature of this advantage of categories? Because they are built up through bilingual examples, it is difficult to rely on an associationistic explanation of categorization in this instance, that is, one cannot argue that the clustered items are linked through common word-word associations encountered in the language, since it is highly unlikely that the English "orange" is ever followed by the French "pamplemousse" in the written or verbal environments of bilinguals. Nor is it true, in this instance, that the subjects' category clustering scores are artifactually the result of their using only one of their languages to make clusters, since approximately equal numbers of English and French, and English and Russian items were recalled for each category in the discordant lists. Thus, the activation of superordinate structures, rather than word-to-word associations, seems more appropriate as an explanation of clustering in this instance.

These results do not indicate that associations across languages do not take place within the heads of bilinguals. Their capacity to use bilingual examples to advantage indicates that this type of association certainly occurs. Recently it has been found that the separate associational networks of English-French bilinguals are quite distinct,[27] and this fact may mean that the lack of associational overlap between English and French contributed in part to the presumed difficulty in priming a superordinate category with bilingual examples. The possibility also exists that compound bilinguals would experience less of a handicap than coordinate bilinguals in the discordant condition.

Turning again to Table 4, there is no advantage in recall for the concordant condition, comparing it with the unilingual category conditions for both versions of the study. (We will presume that the Russian group's superiority with English reflects a language dominance.) The concordant[28] condition is, however, decidedly better than the discordant, or any of the no-category conditions, for both French and Russian versions. Thus in the concordant lists, where all examples of a particular category appeared in one language or the other, language could have been used as a separate and supportive coding schema that could be expected to aid recall. This feature of the concordant condition is of theoretical interest in view of Mandler's[29] recent suggestion that "parallel" or "separate, though overlapping organizational schemas" may markedly increase human memory. Certain clues as to why no facilitation actually occurred in this instance are available in Tables 5, 6, 7. Judging from the results in Table 5, one might conclude that the ability to categorize has not been affected since the subjects are able to categorize as well in the concordant condition as in the unilingual category conditions, and there is no strong evidence that categorical intrusions are more numerous (Table 7); however, there is a very large amount of language clustering in the concordant condition (Table 6) which holds for both French and Russian versions. These findings suggest that the subjects relied too much on language as an organizational schema which led them to congregate the pairs of categories common to each language, keeping in mind that the examples of two categories were given in one language, and the examples of two other categories were given in the other language. This form of organization would prompt longer recall runs in each language but would adversely detract from the semantic clarity of each category and thereby reduce recall from its potential level. Thus, it appears that bilinguals are vulnerable in the sense that they may be enticed to misuse language as an organizational schema which, to the extent that it detracts from the optimal use of available categories, adversely affects recall. These results, then, actually reflect on the limitations of the present design, and the possibility of facilitation in the concordant condition remains open. For example, a fairer test would require a design providing an equal number of categories and languages, that is, either one category for each language, using bilingual subjects, or one category for each of the several languages known by multilingual subjects.

In summary, a good deal of evidence has emerged suggesting that, for bilinguals, language is a quite ancillary means of organizing information in memory when compared with semantic categories, which appear as powerful organizational schemas. The role that language does play is seen mainly in the subtle differences that occur when the two schemas are brought into play. This conclusion is supported, first, by the marked differences in recall between category and no-category conditions, in contrast with the lack of differences, or the relatively minor ones, attributable to comparisons of unilingual and bilingual conditions. In fact, in the no-category case, where the bilingual cannot do much more than merely store information in a routine fashion, recall is not affected by the bilingual nature of the input, suggesting that in such situations bilinguals regard code variations as simple distinctive features of the elements to be stored and are not hampered in any way by their presence.

When more complex demands are made on his language skill, however, as in the category condition where important aids in organization are available, recall can be disrupted when code variations conflict with the process of establishing categories, or it can very likely be enhanced if code variations occur so as to highlight the distinctiveness of the categories. Nevertheless, even when the two coding systems are in a discordant relation and information is presented bilingually, the ability to chunk information, as an aid to recall, is clearly reduced but not seriously so. In this instance, for example, bilinguals are more likely to confuse the code variations, as reflected in the relatively large number of translation errors made, but this fact indicates that they are focusing on categories and are able to do so effectively even with the distraction of language switches. Because they can effectively utilize bilingual information to establish categories, it is suggested that chunking is not based solely on word-to-word associations, but rather, in certain instances at least, on the activation of some type of superordinate structure that works across languages.

It was also shown that a bilingual's capacity to use each of his two languages expresses itself differently according to the task requirements. If, as in the no-category case, he must merely store information first in one of his languages and later in the other, with little opportunity to reorganize, his relative skills in the two languages can be quite different than when, as for the category lists, he can effectively reorganize information. The suggestion was made that bilingual balance or dominance can be more faithfully assessed through the more demanding task.

The final matter I want to discuss has to do with compound-coordinate differences in bilingual organization of list materials.[30] Attention was given only to the concordant and discordant conditions, for which we expected specific outcomes: coordinates should profit more from the language differences that highlight the content categories in the concordant list than should compounds, whereas coordinates should be more distracted by the bilingual buildup of categories in the discordant list, that is, where French and English examples (such as APPLE, PAMPLEMOUSSE, PEAR, CITRON) are mingled to determine each of the four content categories. Thus, the expectation is that the two groups will differ in particular ways in

TABLE 8
Compound-Coordinate Comparisons in Free Recall*

Bilingual type	Number of subjects	Concordant list	Discordant list
Compounds	20	15.55	14.75
Coordinates	23	16.87	13.87

*Entries are the average number of items recalled out of the 40 possible for each list.

their performance on the two types of list, the coordinates being better able than compounds to recall items in the concordant list but poorer than compounds in recalling items in the discordant list.

With this purpose in mind, two sizable samples of bilinguals were tested, one of coordinate bilinguals and the other, compounds. Actually these same subjects participated in the Stroop testing, discussed above. The results are presented in Table 8.

An analysis of variance and a group comparison of the differences between recall of the two lists reveal ($F = 3.25$, df 1, 41; $t = 1.80$, df 41, $p < 0.03$, with one-tailed tests) that, as expected, the coordinates show more functional segregation of their two languages than do the compounds. Although these results contribute to a very consistent pattern of differences between bilinguals who develop coordinate or compound relations between their two languages, still there is *much* more to be learned about this and similar contrasts that only more and better research will reveal.

As a final note, I would like to explain, to an audience of linguists, the rationale for conducting a continuous series of investigations around one major theme. This persistence should not be viewed as a dogged attempt to prove a point. Proving a point, expecially a complex one, with scientific methods requires a patient, almost endless search. There is no one study or set of studies that ever proves the point, and we certainly make no such claims in this instance. What we psychologists characteristically do in out investigations is to settle on some theoretical notion that is of interest, such as the compound-coordinate idea, usually because of its potential generality, and to regard it as an "hypothetical construct" to be described in every detail imaginable, tested for its validity, and ultimately related to and distinguished from other, better established constructs. This is what we meant by "looking into" or "finding more out" about a particular notion. For most complex constructs there are no reliable criteria for testing validity, and the researcher must attempt to establish what has been referred to as "construct validity."[31] Time-consuming as this process is, still it is the stimulating feature of research where a whole set of one's own hypotheses, derived from personal speculations about the basic nature of the construct, are put to test, and a whole network of empirical relations is gradually built up. One can never prove the validity of the construct, nor be certain of its status, because at any point a more incisive research study can cast doubt on the already accumulated evidence, causing at least some major revision of thought about the construct, if not its rejection from serious consideration. At best one can only increase confidence in the existence of the construct and its implications; and, when this confidence is healthy enough, the construct becomes of interest and use to others. Our own confidence in the compound-coordinate matter is still only luke-warm; but, regardless of its fate, the important point is that in our attempts to validate this construct we are "finding out a good deal more about" bilingualism and bilinguals.

NOTES

The research reported herein has been supported by research grants from the Canadian Defense Research Board and from the Canada Council.

[1]U. Weinreich, Languages in Contact (New York, 1953).

[2]S. M. Ervin and C. E. Osgood, "Second Language Learning and Bilingualism," Journal of Abnormal and Social Psychology 49: 139-146 (1954).

[3]W. E. Lambert, J. Havelka, and Cynthia Crosby, "The Influence of Language-Acquisition Contexts on Bilingualism," Journal of Abnormal and Social Psychology 56: 239-244 (1958).

[4]W. E. Lambert and S. Fillenbaum, "A Pilot Study of Aphasia among Bilinguals," Canadian Journal of Psychology 13:28-34 (1959). [In this volume, pp. 72-79.]

[5]W. E. Lambert and L. Jakobovits, "Verbal Satiation and Changes in the Intensity of Meaning," Journal of Experimental Psychology 60:376-383 (1960).

[6]L. A. Jakobovits and W. E. Lambert, "Semantic Satiation among Bilinguals," Journal of Experimental Psychology 62:576-582 (1961).

[7]R. M. Olton, "Semantic Generalization between Languages" (unpublished master's thesis, McGill University, 1960).

[8]W. Penfield and L. Roberts, Speech and Brain Mechanisms (Princeton, 1959).

[9]D. O. Hebb, A Textbook of Psychology (Philadelphia, 1958).

[10]P. M. Milner, "The Cell Assembly: Mark II," Psychological Review 64:242-252 (1957).

[11]J. R. Stroop, "Studies of Interference in Serial Verbal Reactions," Journal of Experimental Psychology 18:643-661 (1935). M. S. Preston is the coinvestigator for this project.

[12]M. S. Preston, "Inter-lingual Interference in a Bilingual Version of the Stroop Color-Word Task" (unpublished Ph.D. dissertation, McGill University, 1965).

[13]Maria Ignatow was the co-worker on this research.

[14]This change simplifies and clarifies the contrast intended. For example, in our earlier work (see Olton, op. cit.), we confused the compound category by including those who learned a second language through the intermediary of the first, i.e., by supposedly indirect methods. We also had stressed current language usage, letting it have as much or more weight in the decisions of classification as the manner in which the two languages were originally learned. Clearly, much more research is needed on all of these assumptions.

[15]The coworkers on this research were Maria Ignatow and Marcel Krauthammer, an undergraduate Honours student at McGill.

[16]G. A. Miller, "The Magical Number Seven, Plus or Minus Two: Some Limits on Our Capacity for Processing Information," Psychological Review 63: 81-97 (1956); G. Mandler, "Organization and Memory," in K. W. Spence and Janet T. Spence, eds., The Psychology of Learning and Motivation: Advances in Research and Theory (New York, 1966).

[17] P. A. Kolers, "Bilingualism and Bicodalism," Language and Speech 8:122-126 (1965).

[18] W. A. Bousfield, "The Occurrence of Clustering in the Recall of Randomly Arranged Associates," Journal of General Psychology 49:229-240 (1953).

[19] J. J. Jenkins and W. A. Russell, "Associative Clustering during Recall," Journal of Abnormal and Social Psychology 47:818-821 (1952).

[20] C. N. Cofer, "On Some Factors in the Organizational Characteristics of Free Recall," American Psychologist 20:261-272 (1965).

[21] H. H. Kendler, "Coding: Associationistic or Organizational?" Journal of Verbal Learning and Verbal Behavior 5:99-106 (1966); R. N. Shepard, "Learning and Recall as Organization and Search," ibid. 5:201-205 (1966).

[22] B. H. Cohen, W. A. Bousfield, and G. A. Whitmarsh, "Cultural Norms for Verbal Items in 43 Categories" (Technical Report no. 22, 1957, University of Connecticut, Contract NONR 631 [00], Office of Naval Research).

[23] W. E. Lambert and Nancy Moore, "Word Association Responses: Comparisons of American and French Monolinguals with Canadian Monolinguals and Bilinguals," Journal of Personality and Social Psychology 3:313-320 (1966).

[24] This interpretation is not incompatible with Kolers'; he argued that "the system properties of the two languages enabled the fluent bilingual to accommodate their respective elements with no loss in efficiency of recall" (p. 126).

[25] D. B. Yntema and F. P. Trask, "Recall as a Search Process," Journal of Verbal Learning and Verbal Behavior 2:65-74 (1963).

[26] Weinreich, op. cit.; W. E. Lambert, "Measurement of the Linguistic Dominance of Bilinguals," Journal of Abnormal and Social Psychology 50:197-200 (1955); W. E. Lambert, J. Havelka, and R. C. Gardner, "Linguistic Manifestations of Bilingualism," American Journal of Psychology 72:77-82 (1959); W. F. Mackey, "The Measurement of Bilingual Behavior," The Canadian Psychologist 7:75-92 (1966).

[27] Lambert and Moore, op. cit.

[28] This condition is analogous in certain respects to the "facilitation" condition of Gonzalez and Cofer, 1959 (see Cofer,

op. cit., p. 263), where item pairs made up of an appropriate modifier and a noun (e.g., *powerful lion* or *blue dress*) were much better recalled and categorized than were comparable lists of unmodified nouns.

[29] Mandler, *op. cit.*, p. 47.

[30] This research is being conducted by Maria Ignatow and myself. We are extremely grateful to Dr. John Macnamara for his discussions of the work and his suggestions for interpretation of the results.

[31] For an extremely instructive article describing this whole process, see L. J. Cronbach and P. E. Meehl, "Construct Validity in Psychological Tests," *Psychological Bulletin* 52: 281-302 (1955).

20 Measuring the Cognitive Consequences of Attending Elementary School in a Second Language

This paper reports on a longitudinal, community-based study of two groups of English-Canadian children (a Pilot and a Follow-up class) who undertook their elementary schooling exclusively in French for Kindergarten and Grade I, and then, from Grades II through V mainly in French except for two half-hour daily periods of English Language Arts. This report focuses on the working hypotheses that guided the evaluation and on the measurement techniques used to assess the program's impact on the cognitive development of the children. This educational experiment has universal relevance since it touches on an educational matter faced also by minority groups in all countries and by most citizens in developing nations.

The parents of the children were concerned about the ineffectiveness of current methods of teaching foreign languages, and were impressed with recent accomplishments in teaching science and mathematics in the early elementary grades. They also realized that, as residents of a bicultural and bilingual society, they and their children are part of a much larger experiment in democratic co-existence that requires people of different cultures and languages to develop mutual understanding and respect. An essential first step for them was learning the other group's language thoroughly. The program worked out may well serve as a model because the overall scheme (referred to as a home-school language switch) is simple enough to be tried out in other bi- or multicultural communities around the world, or, and perhaps of more importance, in essentially unicultural settings where a serious desire exists to develop second or foreign language proficiency. In any case, a basic educational issue is involved here: rather than estimating how many years of schooling should be provided in order to develop an undefined level of ability in a foreign language, the educator in this case asks how one goes about developing complete bilingual balance in the home and school languages (see Lambert and Tucker, 1971).

The hypotheses that guided us are given below along with a resumé of the types of measures used and the overall results obtained. We have compared the linguistic, cognitive and attitudinal development of the Pilot and Follow-up experimental groups with control children carefully matched on non-verbal I. Q. and social class background, who followed normal English-Canadian and French-Canadian academic programs. The Experimental and English Control classes were also comparable as to parental attitudes toward French people, and culture, and motivation to learn the other language; in fact if given the opportunity, the large majority of the control parents would have placed their children in experimental classes.

(1) What effect does such an educational program have on the the Experimental children's progress in home language skills compared with the English Controls? The overall answer is that they are doing just as well as the Controls, showing no symptoms of retardation or negative transfer. On tests of English word knowledge, discrimination and language usage, the Experimental Pilot Class falls above the 80th percentile on national norms as do the Controls, indicating that those in the experimental program do as well as the Controls and still perform at a very high level in terms of national norms. Their reading ability in English, their listening comprehension and their knowledge of concepts in English (Peabody Picture Vocabulary) are all at the same level as those of the English Controls.

All signs are favorable also as to their progress in English expressive skills. When asked to retell or invent short stories in English they do so with as much comprehension and with as good or better command of rhythm, intonation, enunciation and overall expression. Their spontaneous productions are as long and complex and their vocabulary as rich and diverse.

Their facility at decoding and utilizing descriptive English speech produced by children or adults is also at the same level as that of the Controls, and their word associations in English show as much maturity and appropriateness. Since they were at the same time reliably _faster_ in making associations in English than the Controls, their speed of processing English may be advanced over that of the Controls.

(2) _How well do children progress in developing foreign language skills under such a scheme when compared with children from French-speaking homes who follow a normal all-French program of study?_ The answer is that they fare extremely well. Their French listening comprehension score was comparable to that of the Controls from Grade II on, and their knowledge of complex French concepts, measured with a French version of the Peabody Picture Vocabulary Test, is remarkably advanced. In fact, at the Grade IV level, they score at the same level as the French controls. From Grade I on, they have developed native-like control over the smaller units of French, but when asked to retell and invent short French stories, the linguists rating their oral proficiency find that their rhythm and intonation and their overall expression in French are noticeably inferior to that of the French Controls, even at Grade IV. Still, they have much better overall expression, enunciation, and rhythm and intonation when inventing stories of their own rather than simply _retelling_ stories, suggesting that they are particularly motivated and clever when permitted to express _their own_ flow of ideas with their own choice of expressions. The verbal content of their productions in French is as long and complex as that of the Controls and shows a similar degree of comprehension and vocabulary diversity. They make more errors in their French productions, especially errors of gender and contraction, but after Grade II, they do not make more syntax-type mistakes. Their free associations in French are as rapid, mature and appropriate as those of the Controls. They also show as much aptitude as the Controls in decoding spontaneous descriptions given by French adults or children their own age. By Grade IV, however, they are no longer as able as native speakers to decode the descriptions of children even though they are still as proficient as the Controls when decoding adult descriptions. Amazing as the progress is when one considers their concurrent standing in English competence, there is room for improvement in the expressive skills in French, assuming that it is desirable to become native-like in the spoken aspects of the language. Imaginative changes could be introduced into the program as it now stands so as to assure the high level attained in the more passive skills while increasing expressive

capacities as could easily be done by teaching physical education, music and arts (subjects that lend themselves naturally to social communication) in French. Teachers, new at this type of program as they all were, have perhaps overlooked the need to compensate for the lack of occasions outside school for improving skill in French expression. We believe now that attention can be directed to the content and fluency of the child's speech without sacrificing appropriate form, structure and style. Interaction with French children (up to now practically non-existent) would also improve the decoding abilities.

(3) How well do children following this program perform in comparison with Controls on tests of a non-language subject matter such as mathematics? The answer is that they perform at the same high level (both groups scoring beyond the 80th percentile) in both computational and problem-solving arithmetic tests. One can be confident that these children have been as able as the French control groups to grasp, assimilate and utilize mathematical principles through French, and that they are able to transfer this knowledge, acquired exclusively through French, to English when tested in arithmetic skills through English. The teachers in the Experimental program are not better trained in mathematics than those in the Control classes nor is more time devoted to mathematics; their texts are French versions of those used in the English Control classes.

(4) What effect does a bilingual program such as this, extended through Grade IV, have on the measured intelligence of the children involved? There is no sign at the end of Grade IV of any intellectual deficit or retardation attributable to the bilingual experience judging from yearly retesting with Raven's Progressive Matrices and Lorge-Thorndike tests of intelligence. On the standard measures of creativity there is evidence that the Experimental children are also at the same level and slightly advanced in generating imaginative and unusual uses for everyday objects. This mental alertness is consonant with their generally faster rate of making free associations in English, noted earlier.

(5) What effect does the home-school language switch have on the children's self concepts and their attitudes towards French people in general? At the Grade II and III levels their attitudes were much more fair and charitable than those of the English and French

Control children. They were less ethnocentric and less biased towards their own ethnic group, and they had healthy views of themselves as being particularly friendly, nice, tall and big but not extreme in smartness, or goodness, suggesting that suspicion and distrust between groups may be effectively reduced by means of this particular academic experience.

However, in the Spring 1970 testing, we found both the Grade IV and III level groups essentially similar to the English Controls in their attitudes: neutral to slightly favorable toward European French, more hostile towards French-Canadians and clearly favorable to their own group. We are not certain what caused this shift, e.g., the French-Canadian demands for separatism that were intense at this time; a realization that the few French-Canadians they meet at school happen to be from a lower social-class background and are academically poorer; or just wanting to be like others in their peer group as they grow older, i.e., not wanting to appear too French.

It was important therefore to test the children again in 1971 after the social nightmare of the 1970 kidnappings and the menacing demands for secession were quelled, at least temporarily. Thus in the Spring of 1971 when the Pilot Classes were in Grade V and the Follow-ups in Grade IV, the children were asked, through a more informal interview-type questionnaire, for their attitudes toward French Canadians and toward the European French. By this time, we find that the Experimental children have unmistakably more favorable attitudes toward French Canadians and French French people than do the English Controls; the Experimentals also give various signs that they are much more clearly identified with French people and their way of life. After five years in the program, then, we were delighted to see that the children had broadened and liberalized their perceptions of the other ethnic group to the point that they, relative to the English Controls, thought of themselves as being *both* English and French Canadian in outlook. We consider this outcome to be at least as important as the mastery of the other group's language.

There was no evidence at any point that the children's self concepts were confused or different, relative to the Controls: at all grade levels the Experimental children described themselves in optimistic and healthy terms.

In Perspective

Although the procedure seems remarkably effective in this Canadian setting, permitting us to challenge various claims made about the harmful effects of early bilingual education, still the scheme is not proposed as a universal solution for those nations planning programs of bilingual education. Instead a more general guiding principle is offered: in any social system where there is a serious widespread desire or need for a bilingual or multilingual citizenry, then priority for early schooling should be given to the language or languages least likely to be otherwise developed or most likely to be neglected. In the bilingual case, this will often call for the establishment of two elementary school streams: one conducted in language A and one in language B, with teachers who either are or who function as though they were monolingual. If A were the more prestigious language, then native speakers of A would start their schooling in B, and after functional bilingualism is attained, use both languages for their schooling. Depending on the socio-cultural setting, various options are open to the linguistic minority group: pre-kindergarten or very early schooling, with half day in B, half in A; concentration on B until reading and writing skills are certified, with switching delayed; or a completely bilingual program based on two monolingually organized streams, etc. Rather than teaching languages A and B as languages, emphasis in all cases would be shifted from a linguistic focus to using the languages as vehicles for academic content.

The Province of Quebec provides a convenient illustrative example. Here the French-Canadians—a national minority group but a clear majority in the Province—have a fairly powerful political movement underway based on French as the "working language" and a desire to separate politically from the rest of Canada. For English-speaking Canadians who see the value and importance of having two national languages, the home-school language switch as described here is an appropriate policy since French for them would otherwise be bypassed except in typical second-language training programs that have not produced the required proficiency and since it is certain that the use of English will be supported because of the English nature of the rest of Canada and the proximity to the U.S.A. French-Canadians, however, have reason to fear a loss of their language faced as they are with the universal importance of English and the relatively low status attached to minority languages in North America. French-Canadians also may denigrate their dialect of French, since it is at variance with that version given such high status in France. The home-school switch would worry them, as it would any North American minority group, because they believe that English would easily swamp out French, and that their home language is not standard enough, making training in "school" French a requisite. In such circumstances, a valuable alternative would be to start a pre-kindergarten program at age 4 with half day in French and half day in English taught by two different teachers presenting themselves as monolinguals, continuing through kindergarten. Starting at Grade I, two separate academic offerings could be instituted, one fully French and the other fully English, with options for each student to move from one to the other for one or several courses until the two languages are brought to equivalent and high-level strengths. Such a program could, of course, integrate French- and English-Canadian children who so far have remained essentially strangers to one another because of separate schools based on religion and language.

In the Canadian setting, however, political decisions could have important counteracting consequences. For instance, a widespread movement for unilingualism and separatism could postpone the thorough mastery of English beyond the receptive early years and all the advantages of being bilingual could easily pass from the minority group to the powerful English-speaking majority whose children now have the opportunity to become fully proficient in French _and_ English.

NOTE

A paper delivered at the conference on "Cultural Factors in Mental Test Development, Application and Interpretation" in Istanbul, Turkey, July, 1971.

REFERENCE

Lambert, W. E. and Tucker, G. R. _The bilingual education of children._ Rowley, Massachusetts: Newbury House, in press.

21 The Effects of Speech Style and Other Attributes on Teachers' Attitudes Toward Pupils

In Collaboration with C. R. Seligman and G. R. Tucker

Perhaps too many educators believe that our schools are places where capable students can succeed regardless of their physical appearance, racial origins or social class. From personal experiences of various sorts, this belief may be questionable. At the research level, it has been shown (Beez, 1968; Meichenbaum, Bower and Ross, 1969; Rosenthal and Jacobson, 1968) that a teacher's expectations for her pupils may actually affect the latter's performance. If a teacher's attitudes or expectations can play such a crucial role in the determination of pupils' academic success, it would seem valuable to examine some of the factors which contribute to the formation of these expectations.

Certain behavioral features appear to elicit evaluative reactions clearly and consistently. Spoken language, for example, has been found to exert a major influence on a listener's impression of a speaker's personality (Brown, 1969; Labov, 1966; Lambert, 1967; Tucker and Lambert, 1969). In these studies, speech appeared to act as a conspicuous indicator of a speaker's ethnic, cultural or social class group; and it apparently evoked those stereotypes which the listener felt were appropriate to the group so represented.

Williams (1970) has recently elaborated on these ideas with regard to the kinds of judgments teachers make about tape-recorded speech samples of male and female, white and black, lower and upper class children. He demonstrated that teachers, rather than evaluating the children in terms of many varied details, use two gross judgmental dimensions: Confidence . . . Eagerness and Ethnicity . . . Nonstandardness. Furthermore, he showed that teachers' responses are elicited by certain salient linguistic cues such as the number of unfilled pauses and the pronunciation of sounds like th. The subjective status ratings of the children made by the teachers corresponded with the objective speech analyses made by linguists.

In another recent study, Frender, Brown and Lambert (1970) investigated the relationship between speech characteristics and scholastic success. They found that lower class pupils who received better grades had a distinctly different speech style than others with poorer grades, controlled for age, verbal and nonverbal intelligence. The better students used intonation more appropriately and spoke in softer voices. Furthermore, the tone of their voices was not so low pitched as that of the poorer students. The authors concluded that "how a child presents himself through his speech . . . may very well influence teachers' opinions and evaluations of him." Their study, however, was correlational and can only suggest the importance of speech style as a possible determinant of teachers' attitudes.

The present study was designed to explore the influence of speech style in relation to other personal stimulus cues on the formation of teachers' expectations of pupil behavior. Compositions, drawings, photographs and speech samples were obtained from Grade III boys. These materials were then evaluated separately by several groups of experienced student-teachers. Later, a new group of student-teachers was presented with all possible combinations of these cues and asked to form a composite subjective impression of each child, using 7-point rating scales. We predicted that the powerful effect of speech style, reported in earlier studies, would again affect the teacher's overall evaluation of each child, even when she had other attributes to consider during her assessment.

METHOD

Preparation and Pretesting of Stimulus Materials

Information was collected about 36 Grade III English speaking boys enrolled in two elementary schools in Montreal. One school was chosen from a working class district and the other from an upper class area.

For each boy, samples of his speech, art work, and writing were obtained as well as his photograph and non-verbal intelligence score. The boys were asked by their home-room teachers to write a composition and to make a drawing on the topic "Voyage to the Bottom of the Sea." This was performed as a regular classroom activity.

Several weeks later, samples of the boys' speech were recorded. Each boy read aloud the same passage from a standard Grade III reader. His voice was recorded after two practice trials. The length of the voice sample varied from half a minute to one minute.

In addition, color photographs were taken showing the full face and upper chest of each boy against a solid background. Finally, each boy was given a non-verbal intelligence test (Raven, 1956).

Compositions. Mimeographed copies were made of the children's compositions, with spelling errors corrected but grammar and punctuation errors left unchanged. Sixteen female student-teacher judges read the compositions and evaluated them on ten characteristics using 7-point rating scales (e.g., Plot: simple . . . complex; Structure: organized . . . disorganized). Eight judges evaluated 18 of the compositions (half from each school); and the other eight, the remainder.

Drawings. Nine female student-teachers evaluated each of the 36 original drawings. Their instructions were similar to those given for the evaluation of compositions, but with a different set of eight characteristics applicable to drawings (e.g., Proportion of Figures: good . . . bad; Use of color: appropriate . . . inappropriate). Half of the drawings were rated on one day; the other half, the next.

Photographs. Eleven female student-teachers were asked to try to form a subjective impression of the child in each picture, and then to evaluate him on twelve characteristics using scales such as friendly . . . unfriendly; uncooperative . . . cooperative. All photographs were evaluated during one session.

Voices. Eleven female student-teachers were asked to listen to each voice, and to form a subjective impression of the child. Then they were asked to evaluate his speech on the following eleven characteristics, Pronunciation: inarticulate . . . articulate, inaccurate . . .

accurate; Speed of speech: quick . . . slow; Intonation: much . . . little, appropriate . . . inappropriate; Pitch: high . . . low; Quality: smooth . . . hoarse; Individual characteristics: nervous . . . confident, fluent . . . stumbles, sounds privileged . . . sounds disadvantaged, sounds unintelligent . . . sounds intelligent. Half of the voices were rated in a morning period; and the remainder in the afternoon.

Final Selection and Pairing of Stimulus Materials. The stimulus materials from all 36 children were evaluated during this initial screening. Then eight of each kind of stimulus material (compositions, drawings, photographs and voices) were chosen. Compositions and drawings were selected with regard to the judges' evaluations on the characteristic Overall Evaluation of Composition (or Drawing): poor . . . excellent. Photographs and voices were selected with regard to the judges' evaluations on the characteristic Looks (Sounds): unintelligent . . . intelligent. Although judges had evaluated each behavior sample using various characteristics, only those specifically mentioned above were used for the final selection of the stimulus materials. In the case of compositions, for example, the average of all the judges' ratings was calculated for each composition for the characteristic Overall Evaluation of Composition: poor . . . excellent. In terms of these averages, four very "poor" compositions and four very "good" compositions were chosen, such that the Raven scores of the children who wrote these compositions were matched. Thus, no difference in measured non-verbal intelligence existed between the poor and the good groups. In the same way, four good and four poor drawings, photographs, and voices were selected. That is, the judges' ratings for each behavior sample on the characteristic in question were averaged, and then four good and four poor exemplars were chosen so that the children in the good and the poor groups did not differ in measured non-verbal intelligence.

Then, all combinations of poor and good voices, photographs, etc., were made, with one restriction: a good drawing was always paired with a good composition, and a poor drawing with a poor composition. Therefore, drawings and compositions comprised one unit of information. Each combination of good or poor voices (V), photographs (P) or drawings-compositions (DC) can be taken to represent a hypothetical child. For example, one hypothetical child, defined by three separate behavior samples, may sound intelligent, look unintelligent and show skill in composition and drawing.

Subjects

The subjects (*S*s) for the main experiment consisted of 19 upper year, female, education students completing their work at a teachers college in Montreal. All *S*s had previous experience as student-teachers, and intended to enter the teaching profession after graduation.

Procedure

Each *S*, tested individually, was told that she was taking part in an experiment to determine the bases by which pupil-to-pupil comparisons are made. As a preliminary step, she was to become familiar with a small sample of children. To that end, she was to receive information about eight Grade III boys. She was asked to try to form a subjective impression of each child based on certain types of information. First, she was shown a photograph. When she had examined it to her satisfaction, the tape-recorded voice was played. Then she was given the drawing to inspect, and finally the composition to read. All stimulus materials, except the tape-recorded speech sample, remained in full view for as long as *S* wished. The *S* was then asked to integrate all the information as well as possible so as to form a composite evaluation of the child. At that point, *S* was directed to evaluate the child on a list of characteristics, using 7-point rating scales (e.g., unintelligent . . . intelligent). The same procedure was repeated for the other seven hypothetical children.

For the *S*s, there was no question of hypothetical children; the reality of each child was readily accepted. The order of presentation of materials was constant throughout. It was chosen because it seemed to most closely approximate the real life school situation, i.e., it is more typical for a teacher to see a child before reading one of his compositions. Four orders were used, however, to present the eight children to the judges.

Method of Analysis

The data was analyzed using six separate three-way analyses of variance, with repeated measures. The independent variables were voice (good and poor), photograph (good and poor), and drawing and composition, considered together (good and poor). Scores on the various rating scales were the dependent measures. Each rating scale was analyzed separately.

RESULTS

The results, summarized in Table 1, reveal that the boys with good voices were always evaluated significantly more favorably than those with poor voices. Not only were they judged to be more intelligent, more privileged, and better students, but they were also seen as being more enthusiastic, self-confident and gentle. Furthermore, the boys who looked intelligent (i.e., those with "good" photographs) were considered to be significantly better students, more privileged and more self-confident than the boys who looked unintelligent. Those boys who had written a good composition and made a good drawing were perceived to be significantly more intelligent, better students and more enthusiastic than those whose drawings and compositions were poor. The results of Williams (1970) and Frender *et al.* (1970) suggest that special attention should be given to the rating of pupils' intelligence, scholastic potential and status and the reader is directed to examine Table 1 in this regard.

Significant interactions were found among various factors on two traits: self-confidence and gentleness. Consider first the judges' ratings on the scale: Not self-confident . . . self-confident since Williams has suggested that this trait is particularly important in teachers' subjective evaluations. The significant interaction between photograph and drawing plus composition ($F = 7.50$, 1/18 *df*, $p < .05$) is shown in Figure 1. It seems apparent that the type of photograph affects the judges' ratings relatively little when they are also presented with a good drawing plus composition. However, when the teachers were presented with a poor drawing plus composition, their overall evaluations were markedly influenced by the type of photograph.

The interaction between voice and photograph was also significant for this trait ($F = 4.68$, 1/18 *df*, $p < .05$) and is shown in Figure 2. When the voice was good, the pupil was viewed as possessing self-confidence whether his photograph was good or poor. When the voice was poor, however, he was perceived as having relatively less self-

TABLE 1

Summary of Analyses for each Rating Scale

		Intelligent	Good Student	Privileged	Enthusiastic	Self-Confident	Gentle
Voice (*V*)							
good $\overline{x}$		5.55	5.17	4.77	5.26	4.93	4.63
poor $\overline{x}$		4.56	3.89	4.37	4.14	3.67	3.85
F (1/18 *df*)		35.53**	25.63**	4.41*	15.46**	26.38**	8.25*
Photograph (*P*)							
good $\overline{x}$		5.21	4.76	5.18	4.77	4.60	4.21
poor $\overline{x}$		4.92	4.30	3.96	4.63	4.00	4.27
F (1/18 *df*)		2.24	11.78**	19.43**	0.52	10.63**	0.07
Drawing and Composition (*DC*)							
good $\overline{x}$		5.51	4.97	4.75	5.10	4.35	4.31
poor $\overline{x}$		4.62	4.09	4.39	4.30	4.25	4.17
F (1/18 *df*)		27.61**	19.80**	2.23	7.36*	0.22	0.55
V × *P*	*F* =	1.58	0.11	2.65	0.68	4.68*	11.39**
V × *DC*	*F* =	2.54	0.01	2.01	4.27	1.25	20.82**
DC × *P*	*F* =	0.36	2.52	0.28	1.71	7.50*	2.94
V × *P* × *DC*	*F* =	0.21	0.51	3.55	1.22	0.36	37.82**

*indicates $p < .05$

**indicates $p < .01$

confidence with a good photograph and extremely little with a poor photograph.

With regard to the trait: Tough . . . gentle, voice has its greatest influence on the *S*s' evaluation of gentleness with both good DC (see Figure 3) and good P. The effect of voice was minor with poor DC or poor P.

Likewise the importance of the voice cue is revealed by the significant three-way interaction for this same trait (Figure 4). The change from poor V to good V greatly increased *S*s' judgment of gentleness with poor P and good DC; with good P and poor DC; and with good P and good DC. However, there was a huge decrease in *S*s' evaluation of gentleness when poor V was changed to good V with poor P and poor DC. This latter finding was particularly interesting. It suggests that the judges' reactions may have been motivated by a belief that anyone who can write like that (i.e., well) could "talk better" if he wanted to.

DISCUSSION

Clearly, speech style was an important cue to the teachers in their evaluations of students. Even when combined with other cues, its effect did not diminish. However, teachers' perceptions were not determined in a simple or categorical manner since cues other than speech showed their effects.

Interesting comparisons can be made between Williams' Confidence . . . eagerness dimension and our *S*s' responses to the characteristics enthusiasm and self-confidence. Williams (1970) found that this dimension accounted for many of the teachers' attitudes toward pupils. In the present study, it was shown that other factors beside speech could influence this dimension. For example, children who had written a good composition and made a good drawing were felt to be more enthusiastic than those children who did not. Students who looked intelligent were perceived as more self-confident than those who looked unintelligent. In addition, significant interactions were found on the self-confidence trait between voices and photographs, and photographs and drawings plus compositions (Figures 1 and 2).

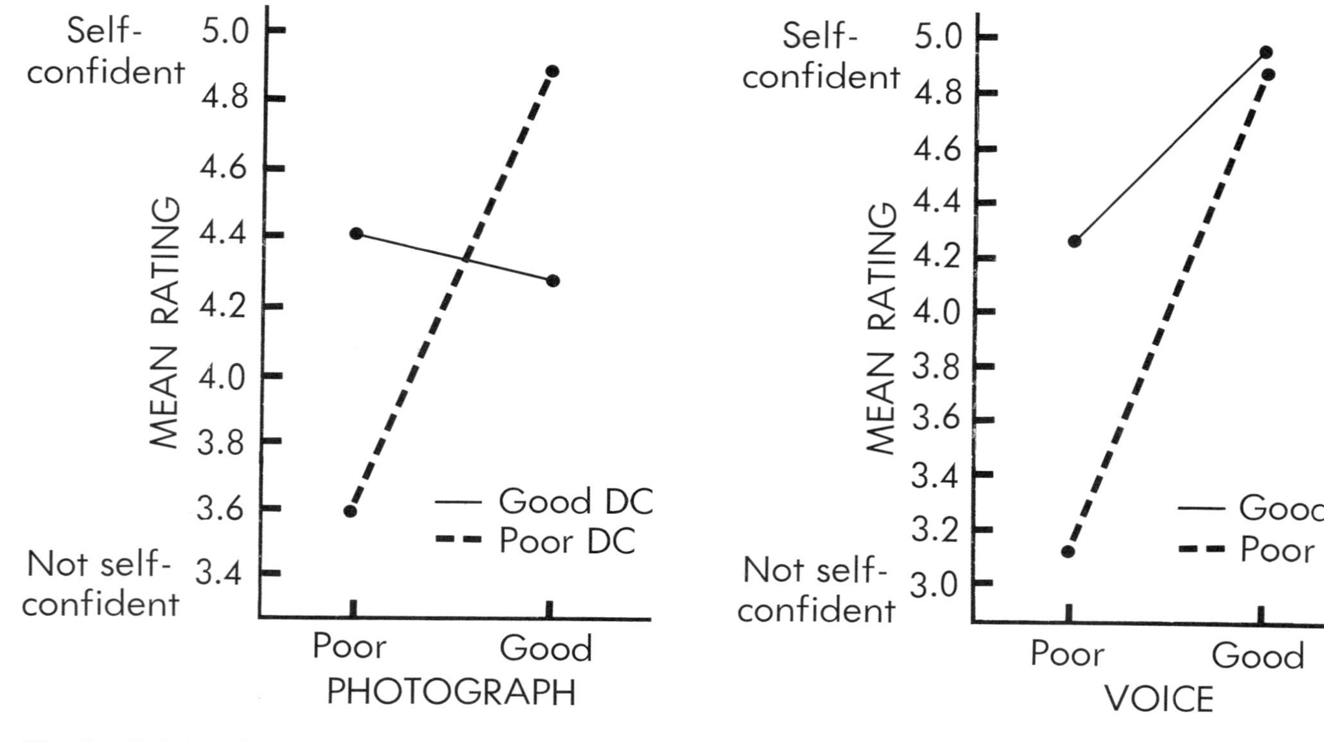

Fig. 1. Relationship between ratings of photograph and drawing plus composition for the confidence dimension.

Fig. 2. Relationship between ratings of voice and photograph for the confidence dimension.

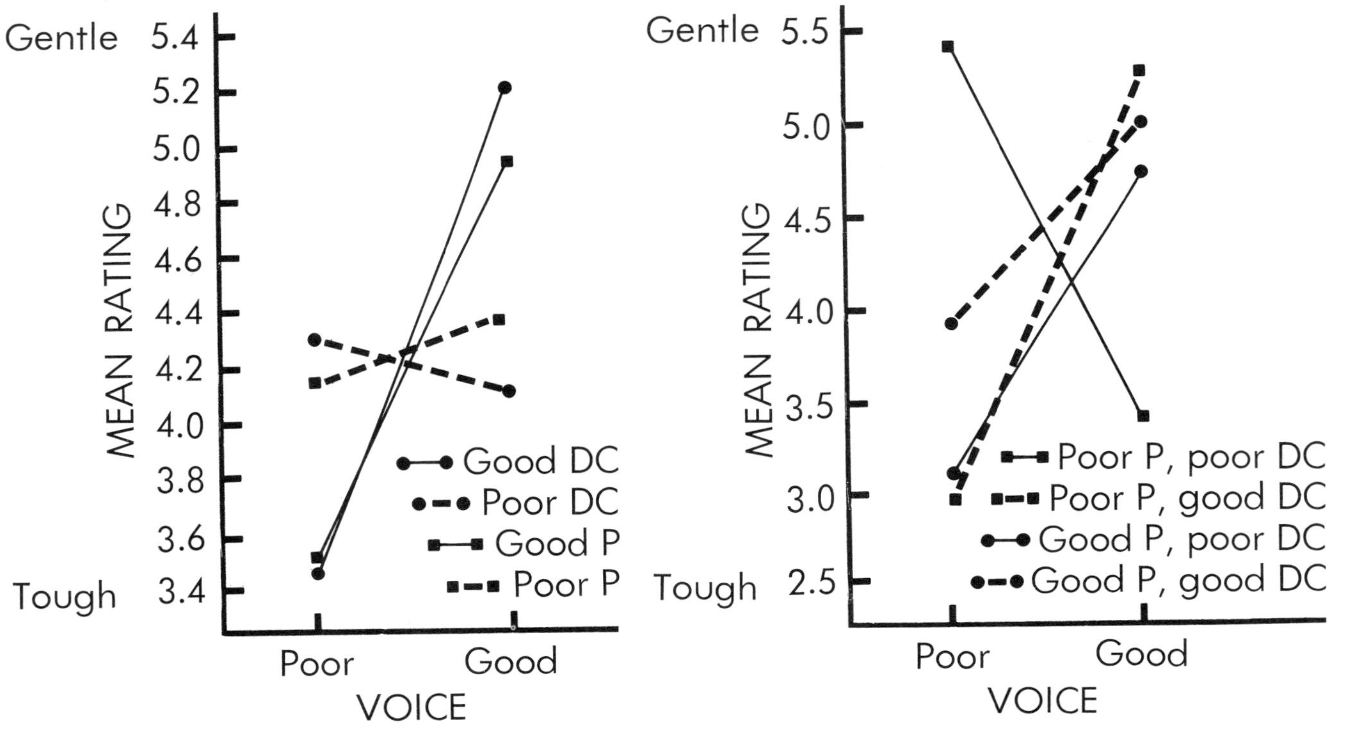

Fig. 3. Relationship between ratings of voice and photograph; and ratings of voice and drawing plus composition for the gentleness dimension.

Fig. 4. Relationship among ratings of voice, photograph, and drawing plus composition for the gentleness dimension.

The study by Frender *et al.* (1970) suggested that a lower class child's speech style may mark or caricature him and thus hinder his advancement in school. In our study it was demonstrated that while speech is certainly critical other variables may also be important. Unintelligent looking pupils were seen as being more disadvantaged than more intelligent looking ones. And, if the perception of status is a vital determinant of the way a teacher will act toward a student, then more attention must be given to physical appearance. It would be intriguing to redo the study by Frender *et al.* with a multidimensional approach using, for example, video-taped stimulus materials including physical appearance as well as speech style as crucial variables.

One would have hoped that teachers, when evaluating a child's intelligence or academic potential, would have relied only on relevant information. Surely, drawings and compositions reveal more about a student's creativity and capacity for self-expression than a photograph or speech sample. Yet, the results showed that *S*s considered voice when judging intelligence, and both voice and physical appearance when rating student capability.

The fact that *S*s made serious systematic judgments about students' abilities based on possibly irrelevant information, such as voice and physical appearance, is of great social importance. We wonder just how many boys who look and sound "unintelligent" were discouraged from continuing their education because they did not receive the appropriate feedback from their teachers.

The underlying assumption of this study is that teachers should not hold biased stereotypes and attitudes toward their students. It is not clear, however, how teachers' attitudes affect students' performance. Is it simply that teachers purposefully or unintentionally downgrade the marks of those students they dislike or have low expectations for? Or, does a pupil who feels his teacher does not respect him develop too much anxiety to cope adequately with that teacher's course material?

We suggest that teachers must be made more aware of the processes by which they evaluate their students. It is the responsibility of the teaching colleges to impress on aspiring teachers that their decisions about students must be made cautiously, and always with regard to their educational implications.

The results of the present study, however, have only begun to illuminate the dynamics of the student-teacher interaction. The direction for future research is evident. In addition to taking into account the intrinsically active nature of interpersonal relationships by varying the stimulus modality and using video-taped stimulus materials, other studies should be conducted systematically varying the social class, ethnic background, role, sex and age of both speakers and judges. These investigations must examine the importance of speech characteristics relative to other personal attributes while at the same time investigating the relative importance or contribution of various speech characteristics to the complex task of person perception.

NOTE

This research was supported, in part, by grants from the Canada Council and Defence Research Board to W.E. Lambert and G.R. Tucker. We wish to thank the officials of the Protestant School Board of Greater Montreal for their cooperation, and also Miss A. Creaghan of St. Joseph's Teachers College for her assistance during the final phase of the study. We are grateful to Professors Dell Hymes and William Labov for their critical reading of an earlier version of this paper.

REFERENCES

Beez, W.V. Influence of biased psychological reports on teacher behavior and pupil performance. Proceedings of the American Psychological Association's 76th Annual Convention, 1968, 605-606.

Brown, B. The social psychology of variations in French Canadian speech styles. Unpublished Ph.D. dissertation, McGill University, Montreal, 1969.

Frender, R., Brown, B. and Lambert, W.E. The role of speech characteristics in scholastic success. Canadian Journal of Behavioral Science, 1970, 2, 299-306.

Labov, W. The social stratification of English in New York City. Washington, D.C.: Center for Applied Linguistics, 1966.

Lambert, W.E. A social psychology of bilingualism. Journal of Social Issues, 1967, 23, 91-109. [In this volume, pp. 212-35.]

Meichenbaum, D.H., Bower, K.S. and Ross, R.R. A behavioral analysis of teacher expectancy effect. Journal of Personality and Social Psychology, 1969, 13, 306-316.

Raven, J.C. Colored Progressive Matrices: Sets A, Ab, B. London: Lewis, 1956.

Rosenthal, R. and Jacobson, Lenore. Pygmalion in the Classroom. New York: Holt, Rinehart and Winston, 1968.

Tucker, G.R. and Lambert, W.E. White and Negro listeners' reactions to various American-English dialects. Social Forces, 1969, 47, 463-468.

Williams, F. Psychological correlates of speech characteristics: On sounding "disadvantaged." Journal of Speech and Hearing Research, 1970, 13, 3, 472-488.

Author's Postscript

When Anwar Dil invited me to present a selection of what he referred to as my "writings" for the series on Language Science and National Development, I had mixed emotions. Although deeply complimented by the invitation, I nevertheless wondered whether it was wise for a psychologist to talk about language in the company of linguists, especially a psychologist who has never really tried to be all that scientific in his approach to psychology. What bothered me even more, though, was the feeling I had in looking back that I hadn't done all that much writing. It seemed instead to be one long series of experiments with matters of significance tests, sampling of subjects and scanning empirical data as major preoccupations. On rereading, however, there is a story that is told, and for me it has been fun to go back. Hopefully it will be useful to have the parts of the story brought together, even though, unfortunately, some parts appear more than once.

One thing that becomes evident in these articles is that I have never taken steps to become a linguist in any sense of the word, not even to learn the jargon. This stubbornness which undoubtedly limits the value of my work calls for some type of explanation. Einar Haugen has argued in his contribution to this series that "without a solid background in linguistic analysis and observation there can be no good sociolinguistics," and he may be right for psycholinguistics as well. The trouble with Einar's idea is that one can just as truthfully say that without a solid background in psychology or in sociology, there also can be no good psycholinguistics or sociolinguistics. As I have come to see it, there is a value in having people from different disciplines and academic backgrounds examine the same common set of phenomena but analyze and interpret them from their very own perspectives, even if the interpretation is naive from some other point of view. In other words, I see it as a good development that we have two or more varieties of psycholinguistics and sociolinguistics, one with the linguist's frame of reference, the other with the psychologist's or the sociologist's. In much the same way, psychologists and sociologists approach the content matters of social psychology with their own distinctive styles, and the field, I believe, becomes stronger as a consequence.

However, to argue for independence of approaches and stubbornness in not attempting to integrate disciplines does not mean keeping one's distance from neighboring disciplines. Quite to the contrary, I feel that my own psychological point of view has been liberalized and enriched enormously through discussions and collaboration with linguists. Rereading the selections presented here shows me how much I am indebted to friends like Weinreich, Ferguson, Greenberg, Fishman, Haugen and Labov, even though my major reference group comprised psychologists like McCurdy, Klineberg, Osgood, my brother William W. Lambert, Hebb, Pfaffman and Mowrer whose influences are equally apparent. But what characterizes my work most is the collaboration I have enjoyed with a wonderful and talented group of undergraduate and graduate students from psychology and linguistics who have kept me honest (or nearly so), hard working, and continually interested in new ideas. Their influence is seen in the multiple authorship of most of these papers.

I see myself then as a psychologist who happens to be interested in language. Language became a research interest ever since my two children began to talk, for they almost naturally, it seemed, used English with me and French with my wife. At the same time, my wife was teaching me about culture through the contrasts and comparisons we were forced to make between North America and her native land, France, as we began to bring up our children. In the process I learned from my wife that culture really is a paper-thin wrapping for people who are pretty much people wherever you find them. From my children I learned that two languages and two cultures come naturally and easily if given half a chance, and that more than one of either makes life so much more interesting. In reality then this selection of works is a running account of my attempts to understand the psychology of language and culture through family experiences.

The account starts with an early paper on attempts to measure degrees of bilingual competence, written at about the time my children were showing flawless control of two languages. That early study got me off on a second research direction because of some peculiar cases of bilingual adults who were dominant in their second, recently-acquired language. Attempts to solve these riddles led to the motivations of language learners, and started a whole set of studies conducted in collaboration with several graduate students at McGill. Bilingualism and second-language learning have provided one challenge after another mainly because the bilingual condition seems to provide a clearer look at the processes of language. Experimenting with bilinguals permits one to slow these processes down somewhat so that one can start to think of the neurophysiology of language, the relationship of thought and language, and the role learning plays in language development. These more psychological aspects of language are represented in one subset of papers reproduced here.

Another subset deals with the social-psychology of language and bilingualism which, in my mind, is a separate but equally fascinating topic. The alternation between the psychology and the social-psychology of language reflects my own intellectual zig-zagging of interest, from the inner workings of language, to the outside influences on language, to the inside and outside effects of language. The last article in the series brings things up-to-date with an ongoing study of the importance of children's style of language on teachers' evaluations of them as pupils.

The topics treated here are not in my estimation limited in their meaning to any particular socio-cultural context, and thus they may be of value to scholars and educational planners in developing nations who realize the importance of pushing our understanding of language and bilingualism much further. It is for this reason in particular that I want to thank Anwar Dil for permitting me to present my views on language.

Montreal
November 1971

Bibliography of Wallace E. Lambert's Works

Compiled by Anwar S. Dil

List of Abbreviations:

Acta Psychol	Acta Psychologica
Am J Psychol	American Journal of Psychology
Brit J Psychol	British Journal of Psychology
Brit J Soc	British Journal of Sociology
Brit J soc clin Psychol	British Journal of Social and Clinical Psychology
Can J Behav Sci	Canadian Journal of Behavioural Science
Can J Psychol	Canadian Journal of Psychology
IRAL	International Review of Applied Linguistics
J abn soc Psychol	Journal of Abnormal and Social Psychology
JC	Journal of Communication
J educ Psychol	Journal of Educational Psychology
J exp Psychol	Journal of Experimental Psychology
J Pers	Journal of Personality
J pers soc Psychol	Journal of Personality and Social Psychology
J Soc Iss	Journal of Social Issues
J soc Psychol	Journal of Social Psychology
JVLVB	Journal of Verbal Learning and Verbal Behavior
Mod lang J	Modern Language Journal
MSLL	Georgetown University Monograph Series on Languages and Linguistics
Psych Monogr	Psychological Monographs
Publ Op Q	Public Opinion Quarterly
Soc Forc	Social Forces

1952 a. Comparison of French and American modes of response to the Bogardus social distance scale. Soc Forc 31.155-60.

b. (With H. G. McCurdy). The efficiency of small human groups in the solution of problems requiring genuine co-operation. J Pers 20.478-94.

1955 a. Measurement of the linguistic dominance of bilinguals. J abn soc Psychol 50.197-200.

b. Associational fluency as a function of stimulus abstractness. Can J Psychol 9.103-6.

1956 a. Developmental aspects of second-language acquisition. Parts I, II, III. J soc Psychol 43.83-104.

b. (With A. Paivio). The influence of noun-adjective order on learning. Can J Psychol 10.9-12.

c. (With Y. Taguchi). Ethnic cleavage among young children. J abn soc Psychol 53.380-82.

d. The use of Pareto's residue-derivation classification as a method of content analysis. Contributions à l'Etude des Sciences de l'Homme 3.183-91.

1957 (With F. H. Lowy). Effects of the presence and discussion of others on expressed attitudes. Can J Psychol 11.151-56.

1958 (With J. Havelka and C. Crosby). The influence of language-acquisition contexts on bilingualism. J abn soc Psychol 56.239-44.

1959 a. (With J. Havelka and R. C. Gardner). Linguistic manifestations of bilingualism. Am J Psychol 72.77-82.

b. (With C. C. Wimer). The differential effects of word and object stimuli on the learning of paired associates. J exp Psychol 57.31-36.

c. (With R. C. Gardner). Motivational variables in second-language acquisition. *Can J Psychol* 13.266-72.

d. (With S. Fillenbaum). A pilot study of aphasia among bilinguals. *Can J Psychol* 13.28-34.

e. (With A. Paivio). Measures and correlates of audience anxiety ("stage fright"). *J Pers* 27.1-17.

f. (With F. E. Jones). Attitudes toward immigrants in a Canadian community. *Pub Op Q* 23.537-46.

1960 a. (With R. C. Hodgson, R. C. Gardner, and S. Fillenbaum). Evaluational reactions to spoken languages. *J abn soc Psychol* 60.44-51.

b. (With H. C. Barik). Conditioning of complex verbal sequences. *Can J Psychol* 14.87-95.

c. (With L. A. Jakobovits). Verbal satiation and changes in the intensity of meaning. *J exp Psychol* 60.376-83.

d. (With E. Libman and E. G. Poser). The effect of increased salience of a membership group on pain tolerance. *J Pers* 28.350-57.

1961 a. (With M. Anisfeld). Social and psychological variables in learning Hebrew. *J abn soc Psychol* 63.524-29.

b. A cross-national comparison of ethnocentrism, perception of similars, and affection vis-a-vis other peoples. *Acta Psychol* 19.1-8.

c. (With R. C. Gardner *et al.*). A study of the roles of attitudes and motivation in second language learning. Montreal, Canada: McGill University. 185 p. (Mimeographed)

d. Aspects psychologiques de l'étude d'une deuzième langue. Brunswick, Maine: The Franco-American Institute.

e. (With L. A. Jakobovits). Semantic satiation among bilinguals. J exp Psychol 62.576-82.

1962 a. (With E. Peal). The relation of bilingualism to intelligence. Psych Monogr 76:27. Whole No. 546.

b. (With L. A. Jakobovits). Semantic satiation in an addition task. Can J Psychol 16.112-19.

c. (With L. A. Jakobovits). Mediated satiation in verbal transfer. J exp Psychol 64.346-51.

d. (With M. Anisfeld and N. Bogo). Evaluational reactions to accented English speech. J abn soc Psychol 65.223-31.

e. (With R. N. Kanungo and S. M. Mauer). Semantic satiation and paired-associate learning. J exp Psychol 64.600-607.

1963 a. Behavioral evidence for contrasting forms of bilingualism. MSLL 14.73-80.

b. (With R. Kanungo). Semantic satiation and meaningfulness. Am J Psychol 76.421-28

c. (With R. Kanungo). Paired-associate learning as a function of stimulus and response satiation. Brit J Psychol 54.135-44.

d. (With O. Klineberg). Cultural comparisons of boys' occupational aspirations. Brit J soc clin Psychol 2.56-65.

e. Psychological approaches to the study of language. Parts I, II. Mod lang J 47.51-62, 114-21.

f. (With M. Anisfeld and S. R. Munoz). The structure and dynamics of the ethnic attitudes of Jewish adolescents. J abn soc Psychol 66.31-36.

g. (With R. C. Gardner, H. C. Barik, and K. Tunstall). Attitudinal and cognitive aspects of intensive study of a second language. J abn soc Psychol 66.358-68.

63 h. Psychological approaches to second-language learning and bilingualism. *Curricular Change in the Foreign Languages* (Princeton, New Jersey: College Entrance Examination Board), 23-31.

i. Reading for meaning. *Northeast Conference on the Teaching of Foreign Languages*, ed. by W. F. Bottiglia (Menasha, Wisconsin: George Banta Company), 23-60.

1964 a. (With L. A. Jakobovits). Stimulus-characteristics as determinants of semantic changes with repeated presentation. *Am J Psychol* 77.84-92.

b. (With S. Messer, L. A. Jakobovits, and R. Kanungo). Semantic satiation of words and numbers. *Brit J Psychol* 55.155-63.

c. (With E. Anisfeld). Evaluational reactions of bilingual and monolingual children to spoken languages. *J abn soc Psychol* 69.89-97.

d. (With R. Kanungo). Effects of variations in amount of verbal repetition on meaning and paired-associate learning. *JVLVB* 3.358-61.

e. (With W. W. Lambert). *Social psychology*. Englewood Cliffs, New Jersey: Prentice Hall. viii, 120 p.

1965 a. (With M. Anisfeld and G. Yeni-Komshian). Evaluational reactions of Jewish and Arab adolescents to dialect and language variations. *J per soc Psychol* 2.84-90.

b. (With F. E. Jones). Occupational rank and attitudes toward immigrants. *Pub Op Q* 29.137-44.

1966 a. (With M. Anisfeld). When are pleasant words learned faster than unpleasant words? *JVLVB* 5.132-41.

b. (With N. Moore). Word-association responses: comparisons of American and French monolinguals with Canadian monolinguals and bilinguals. *J per soc Psychol* 3.313-20.

c. (With H. Frankel and G. R. Tucker). Judging personality through speech: a French-Canadian example. *JC* 16. 305-21.

1967 a. (With O. Klineberg). *Children's views of foreign peoples: a cross-national study*. New York: Appleton-Century-Crofts. ix, 319 p.

b. (With S. P. Cohen and G. R. Tucker). The comparative skills of monolinguals and bilinguals in perceiving phoneme sequences. *Language and Speech* 10.159-68.

c. (With A. S. Hayes and G. R. Tucker). Evaluation of foreign language teaching. *Foreign Language Annals* 1. 22-44.

d. (With L. A. Jakobovits). A note on the measurement of semantic satiation. *JVLVB* 6.954-57.

e. A social psychology of bilingualism. *J Soc Iss* 23.91-109.

f. The study of verbal or semantic satiation. *Research in Verbal Behavior and Some Neurophysiological Implications*, ed. by K. Salzinger and S. Salzinger (New York: Academic Press), 151-54.

g. (With F. E. Jones). Some situational influences on attitudes toward immigrants. *Brit J Soc* 18.408-24.

h. The use of *tu* and *vous* as forms of address in French Canada: a pilot study. *JVLVB* 6.614-17.

i. (With M. S. Preston). The interdependence of the bilingual's two languages. *Research in Verbal Behavior and Some Neurophysiological Implications*, ed. by K. Salzinger and S. Salzinger (New York: Academic Press), 115-21

1968 a. (With G. R. Tucker, A. Rigault, and N. Segalowitz). A psychological investigation of French speakers' skill with grammatical gender. *JVLVB* 7.312-16.

b. (With A. E. Ellison). Reduction of response interference through verbal repetition. Brit J Psychol 59. 147-55.

c. (With M. Ignatow and M. Krauthamer). Bilingual organization in free recall. JVLVB 7. 204-14.

d. (With C. R. Nott). Free recall of bilinguals. JVLVB 7. 1065-71

e. (With A. S. Tarampi and G. R. Tucker). Audience sensitivity and oral skill in a second language. Philippine Journal for Language Teaching 6:1-2. 27-33.

1969 a. (With O. Klineberg). The development of children's views of foreign peoples. Childhood Education 45. 247-53.

b. (With G. H. Yeni-Komshian). Concurrent and consecutive modes of learning two vocabularies. J educ Psychol 60. 204-15.

c. (With J. MacNamara). Some cognitive consequences of following a first-grade curriculum in a foreign language. J educ Psychol 60. 86-96.

d. (With M. S. Preston). Interlingual interference in a bilingual version of the Stroop color-word task. JVLVB 8. 295-301.

e. (With C. Aellen). Ethnic identification and personality adjustments of Canadian adolescents of mixed English-French parentage. Can J Behav Sci 1. 69-86.

f. (With E. Anisfeld). A note on the relationship of bilingualism and intelligence. Can J Behav Sci 1. 123-28.

g. (With G. R. Tucker and A. Rigault). Students' acquisition of French gender distinctions: a pilot investigation. IRAL 7. 51-55.

h. (With G. R. Tucker). White and Negro listerners' reactions to various American-English dialects. *Soc Forc* 47. 463-68.

i. (With M. Samuels and A. Reynolds). Communicational efficiency of children schooled in a foreign language. *J educ Psychol* 60.389-93.

j. Psychological aspects of motivation in language learning. *The Bulletin of the Illinois Foreign Language Teachers Association*, May 1969, 5-11. [Reprinted in *The Florida FL Reporter*, Spring/Summer 1969, 95-97, 169.]

k. (With N. Segalowitz). Semantic generalization in bilinguals. *JVLVB* 8.559-66.

l. (With C. Rawlings). Bilingual processing of mixed-language associative networks. *JVLVB* 8.604-9.

m. Some current psycholinguistic research: the *tu-vous* and *le-la* studies. *Substance and Structure of Language*, ed. by J. Puhvel (Berkeley and Los Angeles: University of California Press), 83-98.

n. Psychological studies of the interdependencies of the bilingual's two languages. *Substance and Structure of Language*, ed. by J. Puhvel (Berkeley and Los Angeles: University of California Press), 99-126.

1970 a. (With M. Just and N. Segalowitz). Some cognitive consequences of following the curricula of the early school grades in a foreign language. *MSLL* 23.229-79.

b. (With G. R. Tucker and D. M. Taylor). Some thoughts concerning work in developing countries. *Canadian Psychologist* 11.392-96.

c. (With G. R. Tucker). The effect on foreign language teachers of leadership training in a foreign setting. *Foreign Language Annals* 4:1.68-83.

1971 a. (With M. Davine and G. R. Tucker). The perception of phoneme sequences by monolingual and bilingual elementary school children. Can J Behav Sci 3.72-76.

b. (With A. Yackley). Inter-ethnic group competition and levels of aspiration. Can J Behav Sci 3.135-47.

c. (With A. Yackley and R. N. Hein). Child training values of English Canadian and French Canadian parents. Can J Behav Sci 3.217-36.

d. (With D. O. Hebb and G. R. Tucker). Language, thought and experience. Mod lang J 55.212-22.

e. Measuring the cognitive consequences of attending elementary school in a second language. Paper presented at the conference on "Cultural Factors in Mental Test Development, Application and Interpretation" in Istanbul, Turkey, July 1971. In this volume, pp. 322-28.

f. (With C. R. Seligman and G. R. Tucker). The effects of speech style and other attributes on teachers' attitudes toward pupils. In this volume, pp. 329-41.

g. (With R. C. Gardner). Attitudes and motivation in second-language learning. Rowley, Massachusetts: Newbury House, in press.

h. (With G. R. Tucker). The bilingual education of children. Rowley, Massachusetts: Newbury House, in press.

Lambert, Wallace E. 1922-

Language, Psychology, and Culture: essays by Wallace E. Lambert. Selected and Introduced by Anwar S. Dil. Stanford, California: Stanford University Press [1972]

xvi, 362 p. 24cm.

(Language science and national development series, Linguistic Research Group of Pakistan)

Includes bibliography.

I. Dil, Anwar S., 1928- ed.

II. (Series) III. Linguistic Research Group of Pakistan